THE LOCATION OF RELIGION

The Location of Religion
A Spatial Analysis

Kim Knott

Routledge
Taylor & Francis Group

LONDON AND NEW YORK

First published 2005 by Equinox Publishing Ltd, an imprint of Acumen

Published 2014 by Routledge
2 Park Square, Milton Park, Abingdon, Oxon OX14 4RN
711 Third Avenue, New York, NY 10017, USA

Routledge is an imprint of the Taylor & Francis Group, an informa business

Notices
Practitioners and researchers must always rely on their own experience and knowledge
in evaluating and using any information, methods, compounds, or experiments
described herein. In using such information or methods they should be mindful of
their own safety and the safety of others, including parties for whom they have a
professional responsibility.

To the fullest extent of the law, neither the Publisher nor the authors, contributors, or
editors, assume any liability for any injury and/or damage to persons or property as a
matter of products liability, negligence or otherwise, or from any use or operation of
any methods, products, instructions, or ideas contained in the material herein.

ISBN 13: 978-1-90476-874-6 (hbk)   ISBN 13: 978-1-84465-749-0 (pbk)

British Library Cataloguing-in-Publication Data
A catalogue record for this book is available from the British Library.

Jack Anderson's 'Toward the Liberation of the Left Hand' (from *Towards
the Liberation of the Left Hand,* 1977), quoted in Chapter 6, is reprinted by
permission of the University of Pittsburgh Press.

Typeset by Forthcoming Publications Ltd.

Contents

Acknowledgments

Although this book began formally to take shape during a period of study leave in 2001–2002, its general themes no doubt have earlier roots in the period of my scholarly formation as a student at the University of Leeds. In this context I should like to thank Ursula King, Michael Pye, and Bob Towler. Without the disciplinary guidance they provided I would not have developed an interest in the methodology of religious studies, nor would I have learnt the research and writing skills that I have attempted to display here, and that I now try to model to my own students as they did to me. I hope in the matter of scholarly lineage I am not a disappointment to them. I must also mention Haddon Willmer who, despite being their contemporary at Leeds, outstayed them. I knew him better as a colleague than a student, a colleague from 'the other side', from theology rather than religious studies. As well as collegial reciprocity and management wisdom—for he preceded me as Head of Department and taught me a great deal about surviving the role—I learnt from him, as I did from Michael, about thinking locally. We worked together on religion and locality, jointly directing a project and running a conference in the late 1990s. It was in this work that the seeds of this book were sown.

The real research and writing were completed between November 2001 and July 2004. For the first ten months I was on study leave—for which I must thank the Department of Theology and Religious Studies and the Faculty of Arts at the University of Leeds. This came in the wake of a period as Head of Department and Head of the School of Humanities, and as a panellist in the Research Assessment Exercise. Not only was I tired, I was thoroughly demoralised, as my colleagues and friends will know. I lacked confidence as a researcher, and it took that study leave and the early chapters of this book to restore it. My departmental colleagues shared my despondency, but we did our best to support one another. Beyond the Department I must thank Brian Bocking—for an understanding post-RAE phone conversation—and Marion Bowman and Helen Waterhouse, for their comforting words and good cheer. A trip to the University of Stirling in that year was also important in confirming that the research was taking shape and was of interest to other people.

The second half of the book was written once I was back at work. By then I was thinking about the case study. My university colleagues proved invaluable. The idea of the left hand came from Philip Mellor who had run a seminar on Robert Hertz's essay on 'The Pre-Eminence of the Right Hand' in his Sociology of Religion module. Elizabeth Sirriyeh talked to me about Islamic traditions on the hands (and found the fascinating Iranian revolutionary poster referred to in Chapter 3); Kevin Ward introduced me to 'The Broad Way and the Narrow Way' and Dorothy Leek provided me with my first image of it; Hugh Pyper and David Levene talked to me about Hebrew, Christian, and Roman conceptions of the hands; Denis Flannery and David Lindley lent me books; Al McFadyen listened. I offer my thanks to each of you, and all my other departmental colleagues for constant encouragement and support.

Our postgraduates must also be mentioned, in particular Louise Child, whose PhD thesis first gave me the idea to work on the non-Western case of the Tantric left hand; Alison Yeung, for bravely bringing together two other epistemological fields in her work on Tillich and the Tao; Andrew Kennedy, for early discussions on the philosophy of place; and Martin Hobson, whose open approach to the sharing of ideas and ability to connect unlikely disciplines and contexts has led to refreshing conversations. I am sorry that I can't mention all my undergraduate and postgraduate students individually. Most of you kept me cheerful!

Mel Prideaux, Mat Francis, and Myfanwy Franks, along with my colleague Sean McLoughlin, have worked with me on research projects during the last two years, and have shared the burden as well as the pleasures of the research process. Myfanwy — with whom I continue to work on our Arts and Humanities Research Board project, 'Locating Religion in the Fabric of the Secular' — shares in the task of taking forward some of the ideas expressed in this book in new case studies. Having inspiring people to work with has been very important.

For support beyond the Department, I wish to thank colleagues in the British Association for the Study of Religions, the BSA Sociology of Religion Study Group, and the European Association for the Study of Religions for helpful responses to my papers at congenial conferences in 2003, associates of the Oxford Centre for Hindu Studies for assistance with references to Tantra, and, most recently, students and staff of comparative religion at Åbo Akademi and the University of Turku for a warm welcome and a real willingness to discuss research issues (in English!). I enjoyed Socrates Exchange visits with Tim Jensen, and an invitation from Martin Baumann to participate in the deliberations of the Swiss Society for the Science of Religion. In addition to enjoyable and helpful exchanges with Liv Ingeborg Lied, Erica Meyer-Dietrich, Oliver Davies, and Nick Allen, I want also to thank Chris McManus. We have never met, but my case study of the left hand is indebted to his prize-winning book and website. I hope he enjoys my contribution to this fascinating subject.

For reading parts of the manuscript and for kind and constructive comments (which where possible I took on board), sincere thanks to Philip Mellor, Martin Hobson, Grace Davie, and Jeremy Carrette (and to Grace, Jeremy, and Jim Beckford for references which helped me to obtain funding to take this work further). I also owe an immense debt of gratitude to Veikko Anttonen of the University of Turku who shares this interest in religion, space, and the body, and who has been kind enough to maintain a correspondence with me, to provide copies of his papers, and to respond to my questions with ideas and references. *Kiitoksia paljon!*

Strangely, perhaps, I wish to thank all those at Leeds City Council who have contributed to maintaining the green spaces, footpaths, bridleways, and public parks of this fine city. These have been my walking and thinking spaces over many years. I am also indebted to my many teachers at Adel Equestrian Centre—equine and human alike—for another kind of spatial practice.

Finally, to all my family and friends, especially John, Anita, Frances, Maizy, and Bertie for conversations round the dinner table, I send my love and thanks for your enthusiasm, enquiries, patience, and support. All my creative efforts are for Anita, who in every sense 'keeps me in my place'.

Introduction

The aim of this book is to develop a spatial methodology in order to examine religion in Western modernity. I hope that this will offer a new perspective on the relationship between religion and the physical, social, and cultural arenas in which it is situated, and thus on the nature and presence of that which we in the West call 'religion'. This is a study then in *locating* religion. For some the focus on location may signal a consideration of geographical places, material objects, the built environment, perhaps social institutions; for others it may be read metaphorically to imply 'imaginary sites', 'cultural spaces', and 'ideological positions'.[1] Both are intended. From a broad understanding of space and place that is both dynamic and relational, I proceed to develop the terms of a spatial analysis which I then use, in the second half of the book, to examine the place of religion in the taken-for-granted body-space of the left hand.

Several questions need addressing at the outset. Why a spatial analysis? What is this likely to contribute to our understanding of contemporary religion and its study? And, given that religions are commonly seen as institutions and communities which cohere around traditions of belief and practice and are sustained by 'chains of memory',[2] what is the value of an approach which seems to prioritise the spatial over the temporal, the synchronic over the diachronic?

Why a spatial analysis of religion? First, because it is timely. Space has been considered seriously in Western social and cultural theory, and human geography since the mid-1980s,[3] following a spatial turn observed

---

1.   It is in this latter sense that Homi Bhabha refers to 'the location of culture' in his book of the same name, *The Location of Culture* (London and New York: Routledge, 1994). His interest lies in charting the place of postmodern culture in the realm of 'the beyond', at the margins and in the in-between spaces which allow for the self-conscious, often political expression of the self.

2.   See Danièle Hervieu-Léger, *Religion as a Chain of Memory* (Cambridge: Polity, 2000), p. 107, and Chapter 7.

3.   A formative interdisciplinary volume was *Social Relations and Spatial Structures* (Basingstoke: Macmillan, 1985), edited by a geographer, Derek Gregory, and a sociologist, John Urry.

in the writings of influential continental intellectuals such as Benjamin, Foucault, Bourdieu, Lefebvre, and de Certeau.[4] Ideas about space underpin discussions on urbanisation, globalisation, identity, diaspora, commodification and consumption, and the nature of modernism and postmodernism—all of which are important in debating contemporary religion. Secondly, a spatial analysis is methodologically novel in the study of religions, and with such novelty comes the hope for new insights. Although the field of religious studies has produced many serious studies of sacred space, in some of which models and typologies have been formulated, this is rather different from what I have in mind. The aim here is not to focus explicitly and exclusively on sites which proclaim themselves to be religious (though these will at times be considered), nor to establish what is sacred or holy about such places. Such approaches will be reviewed in Chapter 4 in the context of examining what previous studies of religion have to offer a spatial analysis. My intention is rather to look closely at contemporary everyday spaces in order to discern the location of religion within them,[5] by considering its dynamic relations with the other features of those spaces (social, cultural, physical, political, economic), the place of religion in their structure, its active and passive modes, and its possibilities for dominance, resistance, and liberation. By so doing, I think we shall see that there are no data that are irrelevant for the study of religion, and that there are no places in which religion may not, in some sense or other, be found.

Thirdly, such an analysis emerges, both substantively and methodologically, from my previous work. In projects with students engaged in the religious mapping of Leeds,[6] colleagues and I have stressed the importance of discerning that which is 'locally particular'—that peculiar concatenation and interaction of factors, of which religious organisations and individuals are a part, which produce local knowledge and make a neighbourhood what it is (hence different from other neighbourhoods).[7] As students' analytical gaze zooms in from the relational nature of the neighbourhood to the particular place of religious groups within it, we ask them to consider how local forms of Christianity or Islam differ both

4.   For an introduction to the work of these and other key theorists on space, see Mike Crang and Nigel Thrift (eds.), *Thinking Space* (London and New York: Routledge, 2000).

5.   How 'religion' is conceived for this project is discussed in Chapter 3.

6.   Leeds is the city in northern England in which I live and work. For details of this student research and its pedagogical value, see Kim Knott, 'Issues in the Study of Religions and Locality', *Method and Theory in the Study of Religion* 10 (1998), pp. 279-90.

7.   I have borrowed the phrase 'local particularity' from Timothy Jenkins, *Religion in English Everyday Life: An Ethnographic Approach* (New York and Oxford: Berghahn Books, 1999), pp. 77-84.

from those generic forms they have met in textbooks and from other local forms, whether in Britain, in Africa, or in Asia. Such investigations require methodological dexterity as they involve a variety of practical methods and benefit from an engagement with several disciplines, including geography, sociology, anthropology, history, and cultural studies.[8]

The development and application of a spatial analysis for religion has evolved, falteringly rather than smoothly, from within this local research methodology. It does not represent a desire on my part to move from ethnography to social and cultural theory or from the particular to the general. I continue to press for religion to be studied in localities and particular places for reasons related to both research and pedagogy. How then do I explain the move from 'locality' to 'space' and from 'local religions' to religion on a broader canvas? First, as we shall see in Chapter 1, we need no longer think in terms of the Cartesian conception of abstract space. Secondly, I do not recommend a change in scale so much as a consideration of a range of scales, from small to large, from local to global, applying the same approach (a spatial analysis) to them all. This is necessary because, in late-modernity, these very scales are interconnected. If we want to learn more about religion at the global level, we need to consider it locally, and vice versa.

My aims in terms of the theory of space, place, and location are three-fold: to reflect upon space as a medium in which religion is situated; to develop a spatial strategy for examining the relationship between religion and its apparently secular context; and to consider the spaces produced by religions, religious groups, and individuals in contemporary Western societies. For this study then space is seen as a *medium*, a *methodology*, and an *outcome*.[9] Rather than starting with hypotheses about the relation between religion and space or the interaction of religion with the other social and cultural dimensions of space, I begin with two open questions: What is the location of religion in the secular West? What do we learn about the nature and place of religion from investigating its location?

Why a spatial analysis — one that looks first and foremost at the social and cultural place of religion synchronically — when religions are so obviously diachronic constructions, repeatedly construed by adherents from traditions of belief, practice, organisation, and experience? In his

8.   I discuss these methodological concerns in 'Community and Locality in the Study of Religions', in Tim Jensen and Mikael Rothstein (eds.), *Secular Theories on Religion: Current Perspectives* (Copenhagen: Museum Tusculanum Press, 2000), pp. 87-105.

9.   Following Lefebvre, 'Is space indeed a medium? A milieu? An intermediary? It is doubtless all of these, but its role is less and less neutral, more and more active, both as instrument and as goal, as means and as end' (*The Production of Space* [Oxford and Cambridge, MA: Basil Blackwell, 1991 (French edn 1974)], p. 411).

investigation of the idea of religion in *Beyond Phenomenology*, Gavin Flood stresses its temporal character:

> A picture emerges of traditions defining themselves against each other through time and developing terminologies which articulate their self-understanding. These terms imply tradition-specific narratives of origin and purpose along with practices and observances which constrain an individual's life from birth to death.[10]

Time and tradition are of the essence it seems, both for religions and for the religious individual. It is perhaps not surprising then that, when Flood calls later for a new research agenda for religious studies,[11] he stresses that 'inquiry into religions should be historicist'.[12] How then can a spatial analysis, which is not first and foremost historicist, be justified?

Several theorists who first pressed the case for the foregrounding of space in an account of modernity—Foucault, Jameson, and Lefebvre, noted the relationship of space to time and history. Foucault, who saw space as the domain of the relations between knowledge and power, referred to modernity as the epoch of space not time.[13] He was critical of the privileging in social thought of historicality over spatiality.[14] Jameson noted the change from a diachronic to a synchronic experience, with the shift from modernism to postmodernism, 'I think that it is at least empirically arguable that our daily life, our psychic experience, our cultural languages, are today dominated by categories of space rather than by categories of time'.[15]

10. Gavin Flood, *Beyond Phenomenology: Rethinking the Study of Religion* (London and New York: Cassell, 1999), p. 46.

11. I have used the term 'religious studies' to denote the discipline conducted in departments of the same name in Britain and North America (also known as *Religionswissenschaft* and the science of religion). I have used the phrase 'study of religion/s' where my intention has been to include the broader span of studies of religion/s, irrespective of the discipline in which the study is located.

12. Flood, *Beyond Phenomenology*, p. 235.

13. Michel Foucault, 'Of Other Spaces (Des espaces autres)', *Diacritics* 16.1 (1986), pp. 22-27 (22). This essay was first written in 1967, but not published until after Foucault's death. Foucault's failure to take the dialectic of space and time seriously has been criticised by C.C. Lemert and G. Gillan in *Michel Foucault: Social Theory as Transgression* (New York: Columbia University Press, 1982). They suggest that, for Foucault, 'history does not run through time but emerges from the relations of a time that is spatialised' (Chris Philo, 'Foucault', in Crang and Thrift [eds.], *Thinking Space*, pp. 205-38 [226]).

14. This came across, and was criticised, in his interview with the editors of a journal of radical geography: 'Questions on Geography: Interview with the Editors of *Hérodote*', in C. Gordon (ed.), *Power/Knowledge: Selected Interviews and Other Writings, 1972-77, by Michel Foucault* (Hemel Hempstead: Harvester Press, 1980), pp. 63-77.

15. Frederic Jameson, *Postmodernism, Or the Cultural Logic of Late Capitalism* (London: Verso, 1991), p. 16.

Lefebvre, who focused more explicitly on defining and accounting for space than either Foucault or Jameson, proposed that the time was right to progress from an inventory of things in space to a knowledge of the production of space[16] which, whilst giving credence to time, subsumed the experience of it within space:

> Let everyone look at the space around them. What do they see? Do they see *time*? They live time, after all; they are *in* time. Yet all anyone sees is movements. In nature, time is apprehended within space — in the very heart of space.[17]

Yet it would have been folly for these theorists to have ignored time and history altogether. Foucault used a spatial awareness to critique the 'project of total history' and to bring in an alternative 'general history' or genealogy.[18] Lefebvre's project, the focus of which was the *production* of space, was as he saw it necessarily historical.[19] His work has been seen variously as an attempt to historicise space and to spatialise history.[20]

A project which foregrounds space or uses a spatial analysis need not neglect time, and need not be a-historical or anti-historicist. I shall say more about the relations between these and their relevance for a spatial analysis in Chapter 1, but I must stress that an attempt to examine religion spatially should not be thought to ignore time and history even if it does not deal directly with them. To assume this is to fall back on the dualistic notion that there are two inseparable dimensions of time and space, and that to focus on one means to neglect the other. The 'binding of time and space'[21] and time-space compression,[22] witnessed by recent theorists in their examination of globalisation, suggest that it is difficult to consider one without the other in researching late-modern social processes and issues.

Having said this, I do not wish to claim more for this project than is appropriate. The methodological focus is not on time, nor is the approach predominantly historical. My concern is rather to see what happens when we look at institutions and processes that are commonly defined in terms

16. Lefebvre, *The Production of Space*, pp. 7, 91.

17. Lefebvre, *The Production of Space*, p. 95. See Tim Unwin, 'A Waste of Space? Towards a Critique of the Social Production of Space', *Transactions of the Institute of British Geographers* 25.10 (2000), pp. 11-29 (21-22), for a critique of Lefebvre's position on time.

18. See Philo, 'Foucault', pp. 209-13, on *The Archaeology of Knowledge*.

19. Lefebvre, *The Production of Space*, p. 46.

20. Stuart Elden, 'Politics, Philosophy, Geography: Henri Lefebvre in Recent Anglo-American Scholarship', *Antipode* 33.5 (2001), pp. 809-25 (817).

21. Anthony Giddens, *The Constitution of Society* (Cambridge: Polity, 1984), and *The Consequences of Modernity* (Cambridge: Polity, 1990).

22. David Harvey, *The Condition of Postmodernity* (Oxford: Basil Blackwell, 1990).

of traditions of belief and practice from an unusual perspective, in terms of their spatial character and location. At the end of the experiment we may be forced to conclude that such a perspective is flawed or inappropriate, but we must pursue the experiment in order to find out. As the discussion in Part I will show, however, we may expect a spatial analysis of religion to yield a greater knowledge of some or all of the following issues:

- the everyday spatial practices of religious people;
- the infusion of spaces by religion and discourse about religion;
- the religious production of places and spaces;
- the competing ideological positions within and between contemporary religions;
- the presence (survival?) of 'religion' in a 'secular' context;
- religious (and secular) power relations, including relations of gender, sexuality, class, and race;
- the politics of religious identities and the contestation of spaces;
- the utilisation by religions of capital and their transmission with the flow of capital.

In his discussion of alternative geographies of modernity Rob Shields makes his focus 'the logic of common spatial perceptions accepted in a culture'.[23] He reminds us that 'social divisions and cultural classifications are often spatialised, that is expressed using spatial metaphors or descriptive spatial divisions'.[24] Examples in British society and culture include references to class (*upper, middle, lower*), to social place and ideological position, to *high* and *low* culture, to *insiders* and *outsiders*, to those at the *centre* of power or on the *margins* of society. Spatial awareness and spatial thinking are so taken-for-granted that we frequently forget their importance.[25] However, in recent years spatial metaphors have reached new heights of popularity, especially in social and cultural theory.[26] They have been used, in particular, to demarcate the dimensions and politics of identity, and the possibilities of resistance to oppression. Examples of terms used in this way have included 'position, location, situation,

23. Rob Shields, *Places on the Margin: Alternative Geographies of Modernity* (London and New York: Routledge, 1991), p. 29.

24. Shields, *Places on the Margin*, p. 29.

25. The pervasiveness of spatial metaphor and its wide range of uses are discussed by George Lakoff and Mark Johnson, particularly in *Metaphors We Live By* (Chicago and London: University of Chicago Press, 1980), and *Philosophy in the Flesh: The Embodied Mind and its Challenge to Western Thought* (New York: Basic Books, 1999).

26. For example, Adrienne Rich ('a politics of location'), bell hooks ('radical standpoint', 'politics of location', 'choosing the margin'), Homi Bhabha ('third space', 'the location of culture'), Paul Gilroy ('the Black Atlantic'), Gillian Rose ('the politics of paradoxical space'), Michael Featherstone ('third culture').

mapping; geometrics of domination, centre–margin, open–closed, inside–outside, global–local; liminal space, third space, not-space, impossible space; the city'.[27] However, whilst there is much evidence of their use, there is less evidence of a full engagement with their complex meanings. Casual users have largely ignored debates about the nature of space and place, the relation between real and imagined, material and metaphorical uses of these terms, their history and its relation to ideological and disciplinary standpoints, and the matrix of the spatial and temporal. Not surprisingly, critical geographers have deplored the shallowness and lack of roots of much spatial imagery in contemporary writing, in particular the failure to acknowledge the dynamism of space itself, and the tendency to treat it as a passive container for social processes and events.[28] I have tried to confront potential criticisms of this kind by engaging as fully as possible with these issues in Chapter 1 in the process of formulating appropriate terms for a spatial analysis of religion.

Catherine Bell, in unravelling and re-appraising ritual theory and practice, suggests a 'three stage method of critical-historical analysis'.[29] She suggests that, before proposing an interpretive framework (stage 2) and then applying it to case studies (stage 3), an analysis of historical definitions of the problem or issue should be undertaken (stage 1). Following her approach, I look in Part I at the ways in which 'space' and 'religion' have been discussed in recent studies, and at how scholars of religion have attended to space as both a context and an issue for religion. In order to avoid using space as no more than a backdrop against which to position religion, I discuss its contours in some detail in Chapters 1 and 2. I make particular reference to the influential work of Henri Lefebvre, notably his book *The Production of Space*,[30] and to those who have subsequently engaged with his ideas. This discussion is followed, in Chapter 3, by a consideration of what is meant by 'religion' in this study, and of how I intend to treat it given the problematization of the category in recent years. A field of religious/secular relations is introduced and explained.

27. Michael Keith and Steve Pile (eds.), *Place and the Politics of Identity* (London: Routledge, 1993), p. 1.

28. Keith and Pile (eds.), *Place and the Politics of Identity*, p. 2; Lefebvre, *The Production of Space*, p. 3; Neil Smith and Cindi Katz, 'Grounding Metaphor: Towards a Spatialized Politics', pp. 67-83 (68-69), and Doreen Massey, 'Politics and Space/Time', pp. 141-61 (141-42), in Keith and Pile (eds.), *Place and the Politics of Identity*.

29. Catherine Bell, 'Pragmatic Theory', in Jensen and Rothstein (eds.), *Secular Theories on Religion*, pp. 9-20 (9). See also Catherine Bell, *Ritual Theory, Ritual Practice* (New York and Oxford: Oxford University Press, 1992), p. 5.

30. Henri Lefebvre, *La production de l'espace*, first published in 1974. It was considered disappointing by many of his Marxist peers, but interest in it was roused following its translation into English by Donald Nicholson-Smith in 1991.

In Chapter 4, I then review studies of sacred space, geography of religion, and religion, globalisation, and locality before setting out the terms of a spatial approach in Chapter 5. In Part II, I apply this methodological approach to a single case study, of the left hand, through its various contemporary Western representations. In conclusion, I review the research process and evaluate the spatial approach for locating religion within the everyday, ostensibly secular spaces of Western modernity.

Part I

The Development of a Spatial Approach for the Study of Religion

Chapter 1

Opening Up Space for the Study of Religion

Like 'religion', 'space', 'place' and 'location' are concepts that have helped people to think about their social, cultural, and physical experience, their relationships to other people, things, and the cosmos. There is a history of thinking about space, place, and location, and there continues to be a lively debate about their meaning. It would be inappropriate to go into these in any detail here, but this dynamic interpretative process does suggest the need for me to clarify my use of these terms. As I hope to show in the discussion that follows, the framework for my analysis emerges from late-twentieth-century conceptions of space, articulated principally by Henri Lefebvre and a group of radical social geographers, that are self-consciously geared to contemporary global circumstances and their interpretation.

My perspective takes its inspiration and much of its method from the project of Henri Lefebvre in *The Production of Space*.[1] I cannot claim to share his personal and intellectual engagement with Marxism,[2] but I am inspired by his enthusiasm for a spatial analysis and his hope that it offers a transdisciplinary and timely approach to the understanding of social and political relations, as well as the possibility of uniting previously separated fields of enquiry.[3] Within the study of religions there has

---

1.   I have focused on this book in particular, with reference to several others, but have not made a complete study of Lefebvre's works, written over a lifetime spanning the twentieth century (1901–91). I have used English translations of his works.

2.   Lefebvre, *The Production of Space*, pp. 419-21; Rob Shields, *Lefebvre, Love and Struggle: Spatial Dialectics* (London and New York: Routledge, 1999); Elden, 'Politics, Philosophy, Geography'; Andy Merrifield, 'Henri Lefebvre: A Socialist in Space', in Crang and Thrift (eds.), *Thinking Space*, pp. 167-82; Neil Brenner and Stuart Elden, 'Henri Lefebvre in Contexts: An Introduction', *Antipode* 33.5 (2001), pp. 763-68; Stuart Elden, *Understanding Henri Lefebvre: Theory and the Possible* (London and New York: Continuum, 2004).

3.   On 'unitary theory' and transdisciplinarity, see Lefebvre, *The Production of Space*, pp. 11, 413.

long been recognition of the value of a polymethodic approach, irrespective of the underlying conceptualisation of 'religion' itself. What Lefebvre offers is more than a conjoining of methods from different disciplines, however. He proposes a theoretical reunification of the physical, mental, and social dimensions of our lived experience.[4] The scholar of religions is thus offered a potentially useful analytical approach to material, ideological, and social forms of religion and their embeddedness in a broader network of social and cultural relations.

The discussion that follows, whilst being derived initially from Lefebvre's commentary upon social space and its production, is informed also by a wider, but not exhaustive, reading in social geography and social and cultural theory. This reading no doubt reflects my own interests, the availability of resources and my idiosyncratic route through them.[5] The purpose of the discussion in this chapter is to explain what I understand by space and to identify the general terms of a spatial approach to religion by briefly reviewing a number of issues, particularly the material and metaphorical uses of spatial terminology, the body, the social nature of space, the relations between space and time, and space and power, and key terms such as place and location, and their relationship to space.

Material and Metaphorical Space

In the majority of polite enquiries about this project it has been important to signal at an early stage the significance of both material and metaphorical understandings of space. Once it is clear that I do not mean *outer space*, the listener often settles for an image of *abstract space*. Yet even that proves difficult to imagine into a meaningful relationship with religion. Abstract space—with its roots in the geometrical space of Euclid and, later, Descartes—conveys a sense of emptiness, of being a passive container for bodies and objects, of being homogeneous. Such a space may contain religion or even be a *tabula rasa* or backdrop against which it is enacted, but how can it illuminate religion, let alone provide the terms for a spatial analysis?[6]

---

4.   Lefebvre, *The Production of Space*, p. 11: 'The aim is to discover or construct a theoretical unity between "fields" which are apprehended separately...the fields we are concerned with are, first, the *physical*—nature, the cosmos; secondly, the *mental*, including logical and formal abstractions; and, thirdly, the *social*'.

5.   I shall return to the issue of my own standpoint in Chapter 3.

6.   This view is supported by Edward S. Casey who writes that 'space on the modernist conception ends by failing to locate things or events in any sense other than that of pinpointing positions on a planiform geometric or cartographic grid' (*The Fate of Place: A Philosophical Enquiry* [Berkeley: University of California Press, 1997], p. 201). See also Lefebvre, *The Production of Space*, Chapters 4 and 5.

In an effort to unseat this image, which is very far from what I intend in a spatial analysis, my next move is to introduce the idea that space or rather spaces are both material and metaphorical, physical and imagined. A powerful religious example of this comes from the Hindu religious tradition of Vaishnavism in the form of Braja, the land of the young Hindu god Krishna.[7] Braja is an actual geographical region in north India, noted for its forests, holy rivers, and town of Vrindavan. It is associated with the childhood mythology of Krishna, being the place where he sported with his cowherder friends and wooed Radha. It is the site where, in the sixteenth century, Rupa and Sanatana Goswami, two Vaishnava theologians, theorised about love of God. But Braja has other dimensions too. It is an imagined space, alive in the minds and hearts of devotees, poets, artists, and theologians alike, in which Krishna sports eternally with his followers.[8]

Vrindavan, at the spiritual heart of Braja, is — for servants of Krishna — the place where liberation may be achieved. It is the place to leave the body, to die. It is also the place to live in mind and spirit for, as devotees are fond of saying, 'Wherever you are is Vrindavan!'. The devotee's body, ritually marked with sandalwood paste, becomes the temple of the Lord; Krishna dances on the tongue of the chanting devotee. The pastimes of Krishna in Vrindavan are thus extended beyond its physical boundaries by those who worship him and spread the teachings associated with him elsewhere in India or beyond.[9] Both material and metaphorical Vrindavans are the spaces of Vaishnava devotional practice. It would be a mistake, however, to dissociate this poetics of Vrindavan from the politics of the town and the religious ideology associated with it, an ideology that may discipline and oppress as often as it liberates.[10]

7.   Vaishnavism is the name given to the religion of those who worship Vishnu or one of his incarnations, usually Krishna or Rama. For more on Braja and the worship of Krishna, see David L. Haberman, *Journey Through the Twelve Forests: An Encounter with Krishna* (New York and Oxford: Oxford University Press, 1994), and David R. Kinsley, *The Sword and the Flute* (Berkeley: University of California Press, 1975).

8.   Michel de Certeau in *The Practice of Everyday Life* (Berkeley: University of California Press, 1984), reflecting upon Western cities, writes of 'a strange toponymy that is detached from actual places and flies high over the city like a foggy geography of "meanings"…a second poetic geography on top of the geography of the literal, forbidden or permitted meaning' (pp. 104-105).

9.   Related issues on the embodiment and transplantation of Krishna beyond Vrindavan and India are dealt with by Nye in his discussion of the placing of Krishna in rural Hertfordshire, England: Malory Nye, *Multiculturalism and Minority Religions in Britain: Krishna Consciousness, Religious Freedom, and the Politics of Location* (Richmond: Curzon, 2001), pp. 51-66.

10.   The poetics and politics of sacred space are discussed by David Chidester and Edward T. Linenthal in their introduction to *American Sacred Space* (Bloomington and Indianapolis: Indiana University Press, 1995). See Chapter 4.

In the case of references to Braja, material and metaphorical spaces are irrevocably linked together by the mythic narrative of Krishna's youth and his pastimes. In other cases, however, a reference to an imagined or cultural space in an intellectual context may bear no obvious relation to a material base. Spatial metaphors may seem to float freely from what were once their moorings, and this may create confusion about what is meant by the spaces to which they refer. In the opening pages of *The Production of Space*, Lefebvre chastises Foucault:

> [He] never explains what space it is that he is referring to, nor how it bridges the gap between the theoretical (epistemological) realm and the practical one, between mental and social, between the space of the philoso- phers and the space of the people who deal with material things.[11]

This matters for two reasons. First, the failure to interrogate the material roots of theoretical spaces may result in the production of knowledge which itself seems to be extra-ideological.[12] Secondly, a lack of clarity on the relationship between mental and material spaces leads to an inade- quate account of the nature of space itself, especially the place of the body in understanding it.[13] In recent years, some scholars have called for the re- materialisation of social and cultural geography.[14]

Others who, like Lefebvre, have pursued a spatial politics or investi- gated social spatiality have also expressed anxiety about the widespread and often uninformed use of spatial metaphors by social and cultural theorists. Doreen Massey insists that the meaning of spatial terminology remains contested and should not be used naively on the assumption that its meaning is clear.[15] She is joined by other social geographers in her condemnation of the problematic de-politicisation of the spatial brought about by an uncritical used of spatial terminology.[16] Space is often cast in

11. Lefebvre, *The Production of Space*, p. 4. For Foucault on his use of spatial metaphors in *The Order of Things*, see Michel Foucault, 'Space, Knowledge and Power', in Paul Rabinow (ed.), *The Foucault Reader: An Introduction to Foucault's Thought* (London: Penguin, 1991), pp. 239-56 (254), and for references to Foucault's spatial ter- minology in *The Archaeology of Knowledge*, see Jeremy R. Carrette, *Foucault and Religion: Spiritual Corporality and Political Spirituality* (London and New York: Routledge, 2000), pp. 105, 173-75.

12. Lefebvre, *The Production of Space*, p. 6.

13. See discussion of the work of George Lakoff and Mark Johnson below.

14. In particular, see Peter Jackson, 'Rematerializing Social and Cultural Geogra- phy', *Social and Cultural Geography* 1.1 (2000), pp. 9-14, and for a critique, Matthew B. Kearnes, 'Geographies that Matter—The Rhetorical Deployment of Physicality', *Social and Cultural Geography* 4.2 (2003), pp. 139-52.

15. Massey, 'Politics and Space/Time', p. 141.

16. Massey, 'Politics and Space/Time', p. 142; Keith and Pile (eds.), *Place and the Politics of Identity*, p. 1; Smith and Katz, 'Grounding Metaphor', p. 68.

the role of an abstract arena or passive container. As Neil Smith and Cindi Katz write, 'the spaces and spatial practices that serve current metaphors in social, cultural and political theory are neither so fixed nor so unproblematic as their employment as metaphor would suggest'.[17] Clarity of meaning and use, awareness of their contested nature, acknowledgment when using them of the active role of space and its relationship to power and ideology, an understanding of the conditions of material as well as mental and metaphorical spaces, and an ability to connect the two realms through the body all emerge as important considerations for the employment of spatial terminology and for a spatial analysis.

Whilst it has been radical geographers who have argued the politics of metaphor and material spaces, it has been the cognitive philosophers, George Lakoff and Mark Johnson, who have most successfully established the link between matter (body) and metaphor, through the mind. In their 1980 work, *Metaphors We Live By*, they stressed the pervasiveness of metaphor in our everyday experience and thought processes, and — of orientational metaphors — wrote, 'these spatial orientations arise from the fact that we have bodies of the sort we have and that they function as they do in their physical environment'.[18] In their more recent work, *Philosophy in the Flesh*, they have argued that it is no longer possible, given developments within cognitive science, to accept a Cartesian view of disembodied reason, and a separation of mind and world.[19] The nature of the physical body, its verticality and sidedness, its neural structures, its cognitive unconscious, all contribute to the shaping of reason, the concepts we use — which are inherently metaphorical — and our understanding of the world around us and our place within it.[20]

The Body

Although it was severed from the mind by Descartes, the body has been central to Western thinking about space and place since the time of Aristotle. Seen from a contemporary perspective, however, it was the young Kant who mused most fruitfully on their relationship in a short essay

---

17. Smith and Katz, 'Grounding Metaphor', p. 71. Smith and Katz challenge Foucault for 'occlud[ing] the actual spatial source of such metaphors as domain, field, region' (p. 73), and praise Adrienne Rich for her acknowledgment of the spatial as well as social relationality of the term 'location' in her 'politics of location' (pp. 76-77).

18. Lakoff and Johnson, *Metaphors We Live By*, pp. 3 and 14. See also Donald G. Macrae, 'The Body and Social Metaphor', in Jonathan Benthall and Ted Polhemus (eds.), *The Body as a Medium of Expression* (London: Allen Lane, 1975), pp. 59-73 (63-64).

19. Lakoff and Johnson, *Philosophy in the Flesh*, pp. 5 and 408-409.

20. This view of embodied reason has implications for the study of religion, see Veikko Anttonen on the notion of the 'sacred', discussed in Chapters 3 and 4 below.

written in 1768, 'Concerning the Ultimate Foundation of the Differentiation of Regions in Space'.[21] Kant concluded his essay by advocating the
approach of the 'geometers', their idea of absolute space, and the dichotomous nature of the body and the mind, all of which, as will become
apparent, are unattractive to our current sensibilities. However, he did so
by reasoning about space and its regions *through the body*.[22] Kant's own
purpose, which was to see if he could prove 'that absolute space has its
own reality independently of the existence of all matter and that it is itself
the ultimate foundation of the possibility of its composition', need not
concern us here.[23] Two of his observations are significant, however. First,
he noted the way in which the intersection of the surfaces associated with
the three spatial dimensions and their relation to the body generated 'the
concept of regions in space', notably of 'above and below', 'right and left'
and 'front and back'.[24] In this sense, the extremities of the body become
central to organising positions in the different regions of space. Kant's
second observation — to which I shall return in Part II — was of the 'incongruent counterpart'.[25] Working with scientific findings from his time,
Kant perceived an organic and sensory difference between the two sides
of the human body, left and right. Whilst being 'ordered symmetrically
with respect to the vertical surface', when the two hands are taken as an
example, it is clear that 'the surface that includes the one could not possibly include the other' (as can be seen when we place the left hand over
the right hand within the same plane, that is without turning one hand
over).[26] What can be taken from these observations for understanding the

21.   In G.B. Kerferd and D.E. Walford (translation and introduction), *Kant: Selected
Pre-Critical Writings and Correspondence with Beck* (Manchester: Manchester University
Press; New York: Barnes & Noble, 1968), pp. 36-43.

22.   It is Kant's Cartesian conclusion regarding imagination, reason and the body
that Mark Johnson sought to overturn in his study *The Body in the Mind: The Bodily
Basis of Meaning, Imagination and Reason* (Chicago and London: Chicago University
Press, 1987), pp. xxvi-xxix. The problem with Kant's position was noted by Edward S.
Casey in 'How to Get from Space to Place in a Fairly Short Stretch of Time: Phenome-
nological Prolegomena', in Steven Feld and Keith H. Basso (eds.), *Senses of Place* (Santa
Fe: School of American Research Press, 1996), pp. 13-52 (21), and Jonathan Z. Smith in
To Take Place: Toward a Theory of Ritual (Chicago and London: University of Chicago
Press, 1987), p. 27 and footnote. Bennett, however, pointed out that, as his later work
showed in the 1770s and 1780s, Kant himself was ambiguous about the conclusions
that could be drawn from his ideas about the body and space (especially on the
asymmetry of right and left). Jonathan Bennett, 'The Difference between Right and
Left', *American Philosophical Quarterly* 7 (1970), pp. 175-91 (176).

23.   Kerferd and Walford, *Kant*, p. 37.

24.   Kerferd and Walford, *Kant*, p. 38.

25.   Kerferd and Walford, *Kant*, p. 41.

26.   Kerferd and Walford, *Kant*, p. 42.

physical, mental, and social nature of space?[27] First, the different positions, parts, regions of space are understood relationally by way of our bodies. And, secondly, the way we orient places physically and mentally derives from our asymmetrical bilaterality. In short, our bodies allow us to experience and conceptualise the relationships between things, places, persons (as well as regions), and to identify differences, for 'in the constitution of bodies differences, and real differences at that, can be found'.[28]

Kant's chief claim, then, was that, without the body, things would be unoriented; it is the body that gives us directions.[29] This in itself is of considerable significance for understanding the spatial nature of religion, whether in sacred places, ritual practice, or value systems.[30] In so claiming, however, he made a further observation about differences in the body that has become significant for conceptualising space as relational. This idea, further developed by Merleau-Ponty, later emerges particularly strongly in the work of feminist theorists for whom it is not just the universal body but the *sexed* body that organises concepts of space, location, form, size, direction etc.[31] Differentiation is experienced by the child in relation to the mother's body.[32] Furthermore, the maternal body itself becomes seen as a place of pleasure for others — man and child — whilst the woman has no place of her own.[33] Thus, from the sexed body emerges the perception of difference, and also of relations of power. These are significant for space, in the ways it is conceived (in language), represented (e.g. in the built environment), and ultimately reproduced for human identity and becoming.[34] To turn to a religious example, this is

27. For a more in depth examination of this issue, see Casey, *The Fate of Place*, Chapter 10, 'By Way of the Body'.

28. Kerferd and Walford, *Kant*, p. 43. See Lakoff and Johnson, *Philosophy in the Flesh*, pp. 35-36; J.Z. Smith, *To Take Place*, p. 28.

29. Casey, *The Fate of Place*, pp. 205-206.

30. J.Z. Smith, *To Take Place*, Chapter 2, 'Father Place'; Veikko Anttonen, 'Rethinking the Sacred: The Notions of "Human Body" and "Territory" in Conceptualizing Religion', in Thomas A. Idinopulos and Edward A. Yonan (eds.), *The Sacred and its Scholars: Comparative Methodologies for the Study of Primary Religious Data* (Leiden: E.J. Brill, 1996), pp. 36-64.

31. For examples, see Adrienne Rich, 'Notes Towards a Politics of Location', in *idem, Blood, Bread and Poetry: Selected Prose 1979–85* (London: Virago Press, 1986), pp. 210-31; Luce Irigaray, *An Ethics of Sexual Difference* (Ithaca, NY: Cornell University Press, 1993); Elizabeth Grosz, *Space, Time, and Perversion* (New York and London: Routledge, 1995), Chapter 5.

32. De Certeau, *The Practice of Everyday Life*, pp. 109-10.

33. Luce Irigaray, whose work on place is discussed by Casey in *The Fate of Place*, pp. 327-28.

34. Lefebvre (*The Production of Space*, pp. 243-44) was aware of the role of the sexed body for space (the paternal and maternal bodies). He discussed, in particular, the phallic formant of abstract space (pp. 286-87). However, as Virginia Blum and Heidi

made explicit by Grace Jantzen, who—drawing on the work of Hannah Arendt—looks forward to a new feminist, pantheist symbolic grounded in 'natality' rather than death.

> Human beings are not gods who can create *ex nihilo*. The new things that we can begin are begun out of our bodily and material existence; and the capacity for such new possibilities is because we come into the world through birth, that we are 'natals'… There could be no truck with the 'view from nowhere' (Nagel 1986) of disembodied and unsituated minds denying their foundation: it is only from within our gendered embodiment that the source and criteria of religious imagination can be drawn.[35]

Jantzen, with Luce Irigaray and Julia Kristeva, makes clear the link between the sexed body, relations of power, the emergence of a religious symbolic, and the space for women—as well as men, who already have a 'divine horizon'—to flourish and realise their possibilities.[36]

Whilst the focus here has been on the body as the basis for understanding space in its conceptual and symbolic sense, it is important also to recognise the link between the body and social space, both for small scale, micro relations and for the global and societal.[37] In the conclusion to *The Production of Space*, Lefebvre reminds us that,

> The whole of (social) space proceeds from the body, even though it so metamorphoses the body that is may forget it altogether—even though it may separate itself so radically from the body as to kill it. The genesis of a far-away order can be accounted for only on the basis of the order that is nearest to us—namely the order of the body. Within the body itself, spatially considered, the successive levels constituted by the senses…prefigure the layers of social space and their interconnections.[38]

It was the failure of Western thought to remain true to this fact, and instead to sever body from mind, subject from object, and mental from social, that led to 'the body's metamorphosis into abstractions, into signs

Nast have shown, he did not pursue its consequences and failed to discuss the counter-strategies and power associated with non-masculinist sites and activities. Virginia Blum and Heidi Nast, 'Where's the Difference? The Heterosexualization of Alterity in Henri Lefebvre and Jacques Lacan', *Environment and Planning D: Society and Space* 14 (1996), pp. 559-80.

35. Grace Jantzen, *Becoming Divine: Towards a Feminist Philosophy of Religion* (Manchester: Manchester University Press, 1998), pp. 45-46.

36. Jantzen, *Becoming Divine*, pp. 45-46 See particularly Luce Irigaray, 'Divine Women', in Morny Joy, Kathleen O'Grady and Judith L. Poxon (eds.), *French Feminists on Religion: A Reader* (London and New York: Routledge, 2002), pp. 40-48, and Julia Kristeva, 'Stabat Mater' in the same volume, pp. 114-38. The concept of a gendered 'divine horizon' comes from Irigaray, 'Divine Women', p. 41.

37. The relation of the human and social body has been pursued by sociologists and anthropologists alike, notably Robert Hertz, Marcel Mauss, Mary Douglas, and, more recently, Chris Shilling and Bryan Turner.

38. Lefebvre, *The Production of Space*, p. 405, and Chapter 3, 'Spatial Architectonics'.

of non-body'.[39] This process continues to work its way out, even at a time when the body is reasserting itself in both philosophical and sociological theory.

Bryan Turner, in arguing against the consequences of a contemporary deconstructionist view of the body — that 'the lived body drops from view as the text becomes the all-pervasive topic of research'[40] — reminds us of those very biological and physiological foundations which Kant far-sightedly noted, but failed to capitalise upon, in 1768:

> One can adopt a foundationalist approach to the human body which avoids simplistic materialism and also allows us to understand how culture and social practices elaborate and construct the human body through endless relations based on social reciprocity.[41]

For understanding social as well as conceptual space then we must *both* start with the body (its material properties and social formation and location), *and* follow the body's course through its many representations.[42] This dual strategy has been pursued for forms of religious life in the West by Philip Mellor and Chris Shilling in *Re-Forming the Body*.[43] Starting with the sensory body — and argued from a Durkheimian perspective — they focus on the three re-formations, of the Catholic 'mediaeval body', the 'Protestant modern body', and what they call the 'baroque modern body', that contemporary Janus-faced form of embodiment which holds together aspects of the Protestant modern body and a new sensuality.[44] In thinking about the latter, especially the tension within the contemporary moral order between indifference and violence, they wonder whether modern Western societies are witnessing 'the human body's resilience to cognitive control and [with it] the enduring significance of sacred forms of sociality'.[45]

In this study, the body will be understood to be formative for conceptual development, social relations, and the imagination of both in relation to space: '[it] determines the conditions for the possibility of experience,

---

39. Lefebvre, *The Production of Space*, p. 407. See also Lakoff and Johnson, *Philosophy in the Flesh*, whose work seeks to overturn this failure and to posit a new philosophy on the basis of embodied realism.

40. Bryan S. Turner, *The Body and Society: Explorations in Social Theory* (London, Thousand Oaks, New Delhi: Sage Publications, 2nd edn, 1996), p. 28. He has in mind here the work of feminist deconstructionists such as Judith Butler.

41. B.S. Turner, *The Body and Society*, p. 26.

42. Lefebvre, *The Production of Space*, p. 194: 'The body serves as point of departure and as destination'.

43. Philip A. Mellor and Chris Shilling, *Re-Forming the Body: Religion, Community and Modernity* (London, Thousand Oaks, New Delhi: Sage, 1997).

44. Mellor and Shilling, *Re-Forming the Body*, pp. 8-13.

45. Mellor and Shilling, *Re-Forming the Body*, p. 201.

which prefigures the structures of knowledge. The body is not clay to be molded, but instead is effecting the molding'.[46] It will be seen to be repeatedly reproduced in the sinister examples to be discussed in Part II. Furthermore, it will be vital for making sense of the way in which religion is located in those examples, because the body is not only fundamental to our understanding of space but also to the way in which we account for and theorise religion and the sacred.[47]

The Relational and Dynamic Nature of Space

In a now well-known essay on space and politics, Doreen Massey outlined the chief properties of a contemporary spatiality. As these have proved to be central for my development of a framework for the spatial analysis of religion, I quote them at length here and discuss them below:

> The spatial is socially constituted. 'Space' is created out of the vast intricacies, the incredible complexities, of the interlocking and the non-interlocking, and the network of relations at every scale from local to global. What makes a particular view of these social relations specifically spatial is their simultaneity. It is a simultaneity, also, which has extension and configuration. But simultaneity is absolutely not stasis. Seeing space as a moment in the intersection of configured social relations (rather than an absolute dimension) means that it cannot be seen as static. There is no choice between flow (time) and a flat surface of instantaneous relations (space). Space is not a 'flat' surface in that sense because the social relations which create it are themselves dynamic by their very nature… It is not the 'slice through time' which should be the dominant thought but the simultaneous coexistence of social relations that cannot be conceptualized as other than dynamic. Moreover, and again as a result of the fact that it is conceptualized as created out of social relations, space is by its very nature full of power and symbolism, a complex web of relations of domination and subordination, of solidarity and co-operation.[48]

When Henri Lefebvre wrote about 'space' he meant, first and foremost, *social space* rather than geographical space or geometrical space.[49] He envisaged those spaces that were the production of human action and interaction. Furthermore, a central question for his project was, 'What is the mode of existence of social relations?'.[50] He answered this by saying that,

46. Mary Keller (on the work of Lakoff) in *The Hammer and the Flute: Women, Power, and Spirit Possession* (Baltimore and London: The Johns Hopkins University Press, 2002), p. 67.

47. J.Z. Smith, *To Take Place*; Anttonen, 'Rethinking the Sacred'; see Chapters 4 and 9 for further discussion.

48. Massey, 'Politics and Space/Time', pp. 155-56.

49. Lefebvre, *The Production of Space*, p. 26.

50. Lefebvre, *The Production of Space*, p. 129, reiterated on p. 401 and p. 404.

social relations, which are concrete abstractions, have no real existence save in and through space. Their underpinning is spatial. In each particular case, the connection between this underpinning and the relations it supports calls for analysis.[51]

For Lefebvre, then, this is the starting point for his enquiry — the need to analyse the connections between particular sets of social relations and their spatial embodiment. In taking forward this idea, by social relations I mean actual relations between people, but also between people and things, people and places, people and symbols, and the imagined relations between these.

If we place Lefebvre's question alongside the first point in Massey's quotation, we see the two sides of the connection between the social and the spatial. Social relations exist in and through space, *and* 'the spatial is socially constituted'. Religion, then, which is inherently social, must also exist and express itself in and through space, and must play its part in the constitution of spaces. The spatial underpinning of religion is witnessed at all levels, from the expression of hierarchical relations (divine, clerical, lay) in the physical enactment of the Eucharist in Christianity, to the local, national and global extension of religious structures and institutions by their repeated reproduction in new settings through mission or migration. That spaces themselves may be constituted by socio-religious relations is illustrated not only in the development of places of worship and other sacralised sites, but also by such things as ritual transformations of the human body and the religious production of distinctive narrative and doctrinal spaces (capable of winning the support of individuals and communities and thus engaging in ideological struggles in the public arena).

In the quotation with which I began this section, Doreen Massey went on to make a series of related points about the complexity and dynamism of space and its relation to time that are pertinent to a spatial analysis of religion. They may be summarised as the spatial properties of configuration, simultaneity, extension, and power, properties that were earlier identified, though not discussed at length, by Foucault in his 1967 lecture 'Des espaces autres'.[52]

---

51. Lefebvre, *The Production of Space*, p. 404. We may find a broadly similar view in Shields, *Places on the Margin*, p. 7: Shields writes, 'social spatialisation will be used to designate this social construction of the spatial which is a formation of both discursive and non-discursive elements, practices, and processes'. See also Keith and Pile, *Place and the Politics of Identity*, p. 6; Edward W. Soja, *Thirdspace: Journeys to Los Angeles and Other Real-and-Imagined Places* (Cambridge, MA: Basil Blackwell, 1996), p. 46.

52. Foucault, 'Of Other Spaces', p. 22 ('configuration'), p. 22 ('simultaneity'), p. 23 ('extension'). Foucault refers obliquely to power in space throughout the lecture. Massey does not refer to this earlier discussion by Foucault.

Understanding more about the configuration of religious relations in space is at the heart of this study. Religions—their groups, adherents, practices, beliefs, texts, and artefacts—do not exist independently of their non-religious counterparts. They are particular forms of cultural expression, are fully social, and are as subject to political and economic forces (both within and without) as are other institutions and ideological systems. But what is their place in the configuration of these features of human life? Do they have an identifiable place? And how might these questions be answered from the perspective of a spatial analysis?

According to Lefebvre,

> Space does not eliminate the other materials or resources that play a part in the socio-political arena, be they raw materials or the most finished of products, be they businesses or 'culture'. Rather, it brings them all together and then in a sense substitutes itself for each factor separately by enveloping it.[53]

It is in and through space that these very dimensions are brought together.[54] They become more amenable to analysis by being spatially enveloped, at least, that is a presupposition of this study.[55] Lefebvre commends his spatiology for enabling disciplines to be united in their examination of this configuration, a view reiterated by Shields: 'social spatialisation is thus a rubric under which currently separated objects of investigation will be brought together to demonstrate their interconnectedness and co-ordinated nature'.[56] Shields then applies this rubric to a variety of marginal places. Another analyst whose approach revolves around the idea of configuration is Robert Sack. In his geographical study of consumption, he seeks to demonstrate the mutually constitutive character of places, forces, and perspectives.[57] By way of a useful illustration, he looks at the space of a commodity, stating that,

53. Lefebvre, *The Production of Space*, pp. 410-11. The danger here is that seeing human life as enveloped by space, and thus through a spatial lens, may obliterate other ways of perceiving it. This is a necessary risk for this project.

54. It was Martin Heidegger who suggested that places hold or gather things together (*versammlung*) in his 'Building, Dwelling, Thinking', in David Farrell Krell (ed.), *Martin Heidegger: Basic Writings* (London: Routledge, rev. edn, 1993), pp. 343-63 (355); see also Casey, *The Fate of Place*, Chapter 11.

55. This spatial envelopment acts as a form of closure which then facilitates understanding (by making material and its complex interrelations amenable to definition, categorisation, comparison and other kinds of analysis). Such 'linguistic closures' have a drawback, however, because they close 'material' in one particular way at the expense of other possible closures. Such closures (or envelopes) then become accepted ideas that are rarely questioned or challenged. See Hilary Lawson's detailed analysis of closure in *Closure: A Story of Everything* (New York and London: Routledge, 2001).

56. Shields, *Places on the Margin*, p. 31.

57. Robert David Sack, *Place, Modernity, and the Consumer's World: A Relational Framework for Geographical Analysis* (Baltimore: The Johns Hopkins University Press, 1992), p. 2.

…whether a dress or an automobile, [it] embodies social relations. It is produced and consumed under specific labor conditions and social contexts…
A commodity contains elements of the natural world, because it is drawn
from raw materials and becomes situated in physical space…[it] also
contains elements from the realm of meaning, because cultures attach value
or meaning to the objects they use or consume.[58]

This brings us on to simultaneity, which, according to Massey, is what
makes social relations spatial, space being 'a moment in the intersection
of configured social relations'.[59] This is further elaborated with reference
to the idea of the co-existence of relations (in space) and of the *presence* of
such relations, of which Lefebvre says, 'this space is always, now and
formerly, a *present* space, given as an immediate whole, complete with its
associations and connections in their actuality'.[60] What is the value of a
synchronic examination of religion? There is none if we understand by
this *only* the simultaneous occurrence of events. The value of such an
examination is only realised through an awareness of the *interconnectedness* of events and *relational nature* of the persons, objects, and places
that constitute space. The spaces of religion are synchronically dynamic
because at any time they are overlapping, co-existent, in parallel with
other spaces, and because they are internally in tension, being made up
of multiple, contested, real, and imagined sites and relations.[61] The complexity of this dynamic will become evident in the second part of this
study when simultaneity is considered in relation to the space of the left
hand.

Synchronous spaces contain the past within them. An English cathe-
dral may, for example, be situated on an early pre-Christian or Christian
site, and may contain within its fabric many phases of building. Its texts,
whether monumental, memorial, or manuscript, may add other historical
traces, as do its ritual and spatial traditions. Both de Certeau and Lefebvre
remark on this, the former writing of 'stratified places', the latter of an
'etymology of locations':

> The revolutions of history, economic mutations, demographic mixtures lie
> in layers within it, and remain there, hidden in customs, rites, and spatial
> practices. The legible discourses that formerly articulated them have
> disappeared, or left only fragments in language. This place, on its surface,
> seems to be a collage. In reality, in its depth, it is ubiquitous. A piling up of

58. Sack, *Place, Modernity, and the Consumer's World*, p. 105.
59. Massey, 'Politics and Space/Time', p. 155.
60. Lefebvre, *The Production of Space*, p. 37. For a discussion of 'presence' in the
work of Lefebvre, see Shields, *Lefebvre, Love and Struggle*, pp. 60-62.
61. Lefebvre, *The Production of Space*, pp. 86-87; see also Foucault on relations
among sites, 'Of Other Spaces', p. 23. See the discussions of globalisation in Chapter 4
and postcolonialism in Chapter 8.

> heterogeneous places. Each one, like a deteriorating page of a book, refers to a different mode of territorial unity, of socio-economic distribution, of political conflicts, and of identifying symbolism…[62]

> The historical and its consequences, the 'diachronic', the 'etymology' of locations in the sense of what happened at a particular spot or place and thereby changed it — all of this becomes inscribed in space. The past leaves its traces; time has its own script.[63]

The inscriptions of the past may be there to be identified and decoded, but it is the *present* space that shows its face and offers itself for observation. De Certeau writes of place as 'a palimpsest', of which science is only able to know fully the most recent text.[64] Foucault's example of museums and libraries, 'heterotopias in which time never stops building up and topping its own summit', adds a further interesting dimension to this.[65] They are modern sites driven by the desire to accumulate and represent everything, 'to enclose in one place all times, all epochs, all forms, all tastes'.[66]

But the dynamism of space is not restricted to the shimmering simultaneity of the relations that constitute it. It is also, as Massey suggests above, borne out of the movement or flow of people, things, ideas *through* spaces:

> Instead of being aware of a point as an infinitely small part of a straight line, we are now too well aware of it as an infinitely small part of an infinite number of lines, as the centre of a star of lines. Such awareness is the result of our constantly having to take into account the simultaneity *and extension* of events and possibilities.[67]

All intersections and configurations are the fluid outworkings of earlier occurrences or causes. They extend from those, in the past, to other events and consequences in the future. Thus, as Lefebvre suggests, 'production process and product present themselves as two inseparable aspects'.[68] Space and time cannot be teased apart. As the centre in a star of lines or 'the articulated moment in networks of social relations' what is needed is a sense of space 'which is extra-verted, which includes a consciousness of its links with the wider world, which integrates in a positive way the global and the local'.[69] But the sense of extension expressed here primar-

62. De Certeau, *The Practice of Everyday Life*, p. 201.
63. Lefebvre, *The Production of Space*, p. 37.
64. De Certeau, *The Practice of Everyday Life*, p. 201.
65. Foucault, 'Of Other Spaces', p. 26.
66. Foucault, 'Of Other Spaces', p. 26.
67. John Berger, from a 1971 essay on portrait painting, cited in Gregory and Urry, *Social Relations and Spatial Structures*, pp. 29-30 (my italics).
68. Lefebvre, *The Production of Space*, p. 37.
69. Doreen Massey, 'Power-Geometry and a Progressive Sense of Place', in Jon Bird, Barry Curtis, Tim Putnam, George Robertson and Lisa Tickner (eds.), *Mapping*

ily as spatial is also temporal. In their early writings on globalisation, Giddens referred to *distanciation*, the 'conditions under which time and space are organised so as to connect presence and absence',[70] and Harvey to *time-space compression*, the alteration to our conceptions of space and time that results from our experience of the speeding up of time and collapsing of spatial barriers.[71] Related to these ideas are those of the stretching out of social relations (across space and time), the crossing of spatial and temporal boundaries, and the acceleration of movements and communications. These phenomena have come about as a consequence of the new global order, particularly the opening up of world markets and the rise of the electronic economy. Religions, as embodiments and expressions of social relations and cultural forms, are affected by these processes of compression and stretching.[72]

That the social consequences of globalisation, especially the process of time–space compression, are uneven is a point made by several later critics, including Stuart Hall, from the perspective of cultural identity, and Doreen Massey from the politics of mobility and access.[73] Massey calls for a *power-geometry* of time–space compression in which its implications for various individuals and groups are given serious consideration. It is not capital alone, she suggests, that determines our experience of space/time, but other factors such as gender and ethnicity.[74]

But what is the relationship between space and power? How is power caught up in the spaces occupied and produced by religion? On the one hand, it is the social constitution of space that opens it up to the pursuit and exercise of power; on the other, it is the capacity of space to be shot through with ideology that makes it power-full. 'All spatialities are

the Futures: Local Cultures, Global Change (Futures, New Perspectives for Cultural Analysis; London and New York: Routledge, 1993), pp. 59-69 (66).

70. Giddens, *The Consequences of Modernity*, p. 14.

71. Harvey, *The Condition of Postmodernity*, p. 240 and following, though Lefebvre suggests that, in modernity, time is often concealed within space (Lefebvre, *The Production of Space*, pp. 95-96).

72. Issues of time and space, however, have been largely neglected by the principal writers on religion and globalisation such as Roland Robertson (*Globalization: Social Theory and Global Culture* [London, Thousand Oaks, New Delhi: Sage, 1992], and 'Globalization, Politics, and Religion', in R. Beckford and Thomas Luckmann [eds.], *The Changing Face of Religion* [Beverly Hills: Sage, 1989], pp. 10-23), and Peter Beyer (*Religion and Globalization* [London, Thousand Oaks, New Delhi: Sage, 1994]). See Chapter 4 for further discussion of religion and globalisation.

73. Stuart Hall, 'The Question of Cultural Identity', in S. Hall, D. Held and A. McGrew (eds.), *Modernity and Its Futures* (Cambridge: Polity; Milton Keynes: Open University Press, 1992), pp. 300-11; Massey, 'Power-Geometry'.

74. Massey, 'Power-Geometry', p. 66. See also Gillian Rose, *Feminism and Geography: The Limits of Geographical Knowledge* (Cambridge: Polity, 1993); Gill Valentine, *Social Geographies: Space and Society* (Harlow: Prentice–Hall [Pearson Education], 2001).

political because they are the (covert) medium and (disguised) expression
of asymmetrical relations of power'.[75]

The idea of space as full of power was central to the spatial conceptu-
alisations of both Foucault and Lefebvre. Foucault expressed the need for
a history of spaces that would 'at the same time be a history of powers...
from the great strategies of geopolitics to the little tactics of the habitat'.[76]
He explored the relationship of space, power, and knowledge in his
studies of the asylum, clinic, and panopticon. Lefebvre signalled the
spatial penetration of power in his 1973 book, *The Survival of Capitalism*:

> Power is everywhere; it is omnipresent, assigned to Being. It is everywhere
> *in space*. It is in everyday discourse and commonplace notions, as well as in
> police batons and armoured cars. It is in *objets d'art*, as well as in missiles...[77]

He too made the connection between knowledge and power in relation to
space, in his discussion of hegemony, the exercise of power over both
institutions and ideas. There is a form of knowledge that serves power
and one that resists it, he asserts.[78] But how does this affect space? He
asks whether it is conceivable that the influence of hegemony might leave
space untouched, but answers clearly in the negative.[79] Space is utilised,
often ingeniously, by dominant groups in the exercise of power.[80] It is
used to contain, even to obliterate others.[81] Spaces, through the construction and manipulation of boundaries, are used to include and exclude.[82]

75. Michael Keith and Steve Pile, 'Introduction, Part 2: The Place of Politics', in *idem*
(eds.), *Place and the Politics of Identity*, pp. 22-40 (38).

76. Michael Foucault, 'The Eye of Power: Conversation with J.-P. Barou and
M. Perrot', in Gordon (ed.), *Power/Knowledge*, pp. 146-65 (149).

77. Henri Lefebvre, *The Survival of Capitalism* (London: Allison & Busby, 1976
[French edn 1973]), pp. 86-87.

78. Lefebvre, *The Production of Space*, p. 10. Lefebvre has been justifiably criticised
for his tendency to equate power with dominance, thus with the capitalist order, and
his failure to site power in non-capitalist and non-masculinist activities and initiatives.
Blum and Nast suggest that he saw 'all struggles to date as consequently subordinated
to an overarching telos; ignored are the power of noncapitalist cultural projects,
struggles, and differences as well as the activities of those who have no representative
status in the capitalist system' (Blum and Nast, 'Where's the Difference?', p. 577).

79. Lefebvre, *The Production of Space*, p. 11.

80. Lefebvre's detailed account of the hegemonic nature of 'abstract space' demonstrates how a dominant space can appear to be one thing—neutral, homogeneous, and
passive—whilst being quite the opposite—masculine, phallocentric, actively authoritarian, and fragmented (*The Production of Space*, pp. 285-87, 308-11).

81. For example, *women*, see Rose, *Feminism and Geography*, and Grosz, *Space, Time
and Perversion*; and the *disabled*, see R. Butler and H. Parr (eds.), *Mind and Body Spaces:
Geographies of Illness, Impairment and Disability* (London: Routledge, 1999), and Valentine, *Social Geographies*.

82. See David Sibley, *Geographies of Exclusion: Society and Difference in the West*
(London and New York: Routledge, 1995).

Sometimes a group manipulates its space in order to serve the dominant order, at other times it does so in order to resist it, whilst individuals — according to de Certeau — continually subvert the imposed order by their everyday practices which produce cracks in the system and make spaces suitable for habitation.[83]

Religions are central to the operations of knowledge and power, having historically been both institutionally and ideologically dominant. Even though this dominance has been challenged more recently in many societies, religions remain key players in contemporary ethical, political, and ideological struggles for space, often in supporting roles. Lefebvre uses religion to illustrate the relation between ideology and space:

> What is an ideology without a space to which it refers, a space which it describes, whose vocabulary and links it makes use of, and whose code it embodies? What would remain of a religious ideology — the Judaeo-Christian one, say — if it were not based on places and their names: church, confessional, altar, sanctuary, tabernacle? What would remain of the Church if there were no churches? The Christian ideology, carrier of a recognisable if disregarded Judaism…, has created the spaces which guarantee that it endures.[84]

With this last point David Harvey is in agreement. He suggests that the preservation of the Church, its presence in postmodern society, 'has been won in part through the successful creation, protection and nurturing of symbolic places'.[85] But, in addition to the retention of once dominant forms of religion in the spaces they have carved out for themselves, there are cases of the invocation of religion in the creation of new subversive spaces. I shall illustrate this in the next chapter.

Knowledge, and the wielding of it for reasons of power, is increasingly on the agenda of the study of religions, for example, in studies of religious identity, religious nationalism, and gender and religion. Those who have discussed the nature of religion, however, often in an effort to avoid reductionism, have often failed to give full weight to its social and political dimensions. In order that social difference, gender issues, and political oppression and marginalisation are fully exposed to scrutiny in the

83. De Certeau, *The Practice of Everyday Life*, p. 106, and further, 'The surface of this [imposed] order is everywhere punched and torn open by ellipses, drifts, and leaks of meaning: it is a sieve-order' (p. 107). See also Blum and Nast, 'Where's the Difference?', p. 579.

84. Lefebvre, *The Production of Space*, p. 44. See the end of Chapter 3 for a discussion of Lefebvre's position in the field of religious/secular relations.

85. David Harvey, 'From Space to Place and Back Again: Reflections on the Condition of Postmodernity', in Jon Bird, Barry Curtis, Tim Putnam, George Robertson and Lisa Tickner (eds.), *Mapping the Futures: Local Cultures, Global Change* (London and New York: Routledge, 1993), pp. 3-29 (23).

investigation of religion, power needs to be reconceptualised as integral to it.[86] As power struggles of all kinds are played out in space—whether social, mental or physical space—a spatial analysis of religion cannot avoid confronting them, both directly and through their representations. The spaces that religion occupies and participates in are spaces of power —the challenge will be to discover the relationship between religion and power in any given space. This will require a close examination of the complexity of the social relations which constitute that space and the cultural symbols that represent it.

Another under-investigated aspect of power in the study of religions has been the role of capital,[87] and, again, I suggest that a spatial analysis can contribute to uncovering this. In late-modernity, under conditions of globalisation, how are religious institutions, communities, ideas, and practices shaped by the flow and accumulation of financial, human, and knowledge capital? What can we learn about religions from the ways in which they attract money and disperse it, and consume, produce and exchange goods? These processes can be witnessed in space. According to Andy Merrifield,

> Space, in the apt words of David Harvey, is an 'active moment' in expansion and reproduction of capitalism. It is a phenomenon which is colonized and commodified, bought and sold, created and torn down, used and abused, speculated on and fought over. It all comes together in space: space *internalizes* the contradictions of modern capitalism...[88]

Harvey himself makes it very clear that this material process has other dimensions too—cultural, affective, and social. In his illustration of the production and cultural reproduction of Times Square, he shows how, '[though] produced and dominated in the mode of political economy, it

---

86. See the plea by Rosalind Shaw, 'Feminist Anthropology and the Gendering of Religious Studies', in Ursula King (ed.), *Religion and Gender* (Oxford: Basil Blackwell, 1995), pp. 65-76 (73). See also Carrette on the place of power in the post-Foucauldian analysis of religion (*Foucault and Religion*, pp. 147-49), and Talal Asad, on the problematic separation of religion from power in post-Reformation Western thought, in *Genealogies of Religion: Disciplines and Reasons of Power in Christianity and Islam* (Baltimore and London: The Johns Hopkins University Press, 1993), pp. 28-29.

87. Exceptions to this include, of course, Marx, Engels, and Weber in the late nineteenth and early twentieth century, and, latterly, Bryan Turner whose work on religion, society, and the body has been strongly materialist in orientation. Peter Berger in the late 1960s and, more recently, rational choice theorists in the sociology of religion have adopted a market model for their investigation of the currency of religion in late-modernity. For discussions of the contemporary relationships between religion and capitalism, see Richard H. Roberts (ed.), *Religion and the Transformations of Capitalism: Comparative Approaches* (London: Routledge, 1995), and forthcoming work by Jeremy Carrette.

88. Merrifield, 'Henri Lefebvre: A Socialist in Space', p. 173.

was appropriated by the populace in an entirely different fashion' as a symbolic place of social and cultural plurality.[89] Conversely, reflecting on the cultic creation of Rajneeshpuram in Oregon, he notes that the search for authentic community was subsequently co-opted in the pursuit of financial gain.[90]

Harvey's understanding of the dynamic production and reproduction of these places and their complexity—as material, discursive, and symbolic—is enriched by the conceptual triad proposed by Lefebvre in *The Production of Space*.[91] Having discussed the properties of space—with reference to social relations, configuration, simultaneity, extension, and power—and the relevance of these aspects for the study of religion, it is to this triad that I shall turn in the next chapter in order to illustrate one of the ways in which spatial theory can be used to illuminate religion and its social and geographical location. Before that, however, I must complete my examination of the spatial terms to be invoked in this study: place and location.

Place and the Spatial Location of Religion

In so far as it is the long-term intention of this project to employ a spatial analysis to investigate the location of religion in the places of the body, artefacts, events, communities, localities and institutions, it is important that I say what I mean by both 'place' and 'location'. Of necessity, this must be a relatively short account, which therefore cannot do justice to their many meanings and uses, or the range of debates surrounding them.[92]

Let me say at the outset that I see places as parts of dynamic and relational space, and locations as situated positions vis-à-vis others.[93] Both place and location are conceived in social, mental, and physical terms, and, as concepts, are used to identify hierarchical and political positions

89.   Harvey, 'From Space to Place and Back Again', pp. 17-19.

90.   Harvey, 'From Space to Place and Back Again', pp. 19-21.

91.   Harvey discusses what he calls 'the Lefebvrian matrix' in *The Conditions of Postmodernity*, pp. 220-21, and in 'From Space to Place and Back Again', p. 17.

92.   For a different purpose, I have provided another account of place and location (and locality) in 'Religion and Locality: Issues and Methods', in Kim Knott, Kevin Ward, Alistair Mason and Haddon Willmer (eds.), *Religion and Locality* (Leeds: Community Religions Project, University of Leeds, forthcoming). See also Chapter 4, below, on religion and locality.

93.   Properly speaking, 'location' in geometric terms may refer simply to either a 'zero-dimensional space' or a point fixed by two or more lines, see Smith and Katz, 'Grounding Metaphor', p. 1. I am imbuing it with a relational sense, given that in cultural theory since the 1980s it has been a keyword for situating social and political positions and identities.

and stances.[94] As such, they correspond not only to the view of space that I outlined above, but to my intended purpose, to use a spatial analysis to look closely at certain domains (places) in order to see more clearly what religion is and how it relates to other aspects of the physical world, society, and culture (that is, *to locate religion*).[95]

The terms 'place' and 'location', along with 'community', 'locality', and the 'local' itself, were variously in or out of favour in the last century among sociologists and anthropologists. They were used from the 1930s to the 1960s in studies of small-scale societies, generally far away, but increasingly near to home, often rural, but increasingly urban, working class. As such, they became associated with a static, bounded, settled view of encapsulated geographical areas, social organisation and identity, and an insular view of culture as place- and group-bound. Such conceptions were strongly criticised from the late-1960s onwards.[96] But there was still life to be found in the old terms. 'Place' was revisited by humanistic geographers and philosophers influenced by the phenomenological school, in particular by the work of Heidegger and Merleau-Ponty;[97] and the 'local' and its semantic derivatives (along with 'place') were revitalised more recently by social geographers, sociologists, and anthropologists working on globalisation,[98] and by feminist and other cultural

94. See J.Z. Smith, *To Take Place*, on place as a social position within a hierarchical system, p. 45.

95. Hastrup and Fog Olwig discuss a similar process in the introduction to *Siting Culture* in which they seek to examine 'the role of place in the conceptualisation and practice of culture'. Karen Fog Olwig and Kirsten Hastrup (eds.), *Siting Culture: The Shifting Anthropological Object* (London and New York: Routledge, 1997), p. 2.

96. See, for example, Colin Bell and Howard Newby, *Community Studies* (London: George Allen & Unwin, 1971); Massey, 'The Political Place of Locality Studies'; Doreen Massey and Pat Jess (eds.), *A Place in the World? Places, Cultures and Globalization* (London: Oxford University Press and The Open University, 1995); Kim Knott, 'The Sense and Nonsense of Community', in Steven Sutcliffe (ed.), *Religion: Empirical Studies* (Aldershot and Burlington, VT: Ashgate, 2004), pp. 67-90.

97. For example, E.C. Relph, *Place and Placelessness* (London: Pion, 1976); Yi-Fu Tuan, *Space and Place: The Perspective of Experience* (Minneapolis: University of Minnesota Press, 1977); Christopher Tilley, *The Phenomenology of Landscape* (London: Berg, 1994); Casey, 'How to Get from Space to Place'.

98. For example, Massey, 'Power-Geometry and a Progressive Sense of Place', and Harvey, 'From Space to Place and Back Again'; Massey and Jess (eds.), *A Place in the World?*; Michael Featherstone, *Undoing Culture: Globalization, Postmodernism, and Identity* (London, Thousand Oaks, New Delhi: Sage, 1995); Arjun Appadurai, *Modernity at Large: Cultural Dimensions of Globalization* (Minneapolis: University of Minnesota Press, 1996); John Eade (ed.), *Living the Global City: Globalization as a Local Process* (London and New York: Routledge, 1997); Marc Augé, *Non-Places: Introduction to an Anthropology of Supermodernity* (London and New York: Verso, 1995 [French edn 1992]); see Chapter 4.

theorists eager to formulate a new terminology for the politics of location.[99]

'Place' has been reconceptualised as 'progressive' by Doreen Massey,[100]
and brought out of hiding by Edward Casey as an open event rather than
an entity.[101] Though working from different assumptions, these two
scholars, in particular, have been responsible for ensuring that it has been
'the fate of place' to be revived and renewed rather than overlooked or
left to become irrelevant. In the most complete enquiry yet, Casey enables
place to fight back from beneath the overwhelming abstraction and universalisation of space in a critical, historical examination from Aristotle to
Irigaray. After charting its disappearance and disempowerment (its over-
determination as a mere position on geometrical axes), he rediscovers the
virtues of place from Kant's work on the body (to exist as a sensible body
is to have a place), through the phenomenologists Husserl and Merleau-
Ponty (on the primacy of place), Heidegger (the gathered place as the
scene of the disclosure of Being), and the late-modern theorists, Bachelard, Foucault, Guattari and Deleuze, and Derrida, to Irigaray and Nancy
(on the divine as being-in-place). He concludes by surmising that,

> If 'it is granted to us to see the limitless openness of that space', we shall see
> it most surely in the undelimited localities of our concrete bodily move-
> ments, that is to say, in our most engaged experiences of being-in-place—in
> many different ways and in many different places.[102]

Although Casey and Massey might well argue over the issue of the
primacy of place,[103] they would agree that places are both open and
dynamic.[104] Massey's famous example of this is of the Kilburn High Road
in north-west London.[105] Before opening her accounts of Kilburn, she
takes the reader out to an imaginary satellite beyond existing satellites

99. For example, Rich, *Blood, Bread, and Poetry*; Rose, *Feminism and Geography*;
Bhabha, *The Location of Culture*; Heidi J. Nast and Steve Pile (eds.), *Places Through the
Body* (London and New York: Routledge, 1998).

100. Massey, 'Power-Geometry', pp. 66-68.

101. Casey, *The Fate of Place*, p. 339.

102. Casey, *The Fate of Place*, p. 342.

103. Casey offers 'a polyvalent primacy', denying that this could form the basis of
a new foundationalism (*The Fate of Place*, p. 337). Massey argues that her progressive
view of place runs counter to a Heideggerian view of embounded and singular, essen-
tialised places ('Power-Geometry', p. 64). Kennedy sees this (and Harvey's critique in
the same volume) as a misreading of Heidegger (Andrew Kennedy, 'Place and Space
in an Age of Immanence', in Knott, Ward, Mason and Willmer [eds.], *Religion and
Locality*, n.p. [forthcoming]).

104. Casey, *The Fate of Place*, pp. 339 and 342; Massey, 'Power-Geometry', pp. 66-68;
see also Massey and Jess, *A Place in the World?*, pp. 59-61.

105. Massey, 'Power-Geometry', pp. 64-66, and *Space, Place and Gender* (Cambridge: Polity, 1994), pp. 152-54.

and asks her to look back at the earth at various scales, from the 'move-ment and tune' of communications to a woman in sub-Saharan Africa. It is in the context of this journey that the reader is introduced to Kilburn as an example of a real place. Not only is it a multi-ethnic, multi-cultural place in itself, but it is also connected outwards to other parts of Britain and beyond,[106] 'while Kilburn may have a character of its own, it is abso-lutely not a seamless, coherent identity, a single sense of place which everyone shares'.[107] It is only when one sees Kilburn vis-à-vis other places, and acknowledges all of them to be socially constituted, full of power, and interconnected from the local to the global that its real char-acter begins to be understood: 'In this interpretation, what gives a place its specificity is not some long internalized history but the fact that it is constructed out of a particular constellation of relations, articulated together at a particular locus'.[108]

   In their book on place, culture, and globalisation, Massey and Jess make it clear that such places are set within the context of a wider space of stretched-out social relations. In this sense, they are 'meeting places', in social space, 'of connections and interrelations, of influences and move-ments'.[109] Another theorist who investigates this interrelationship of place and space, and in doing so returns us to Lefebvre, is Andrew Merrifield.[110] He sees Lefebvre's triad—which I shall discuss in detail in the next chapter—as offering a dialectical method for 'reconciling the way in which experience is lived and acted out in place, and how this relates to, and is embedded in, political and economic practices that are operative over broader spatial scales'.[111] It is thus a means of overcoming the dualistic Cartesian thinking that dominates geographical accounts of place. In this view, place is the nexus where Lefebvre's three spatial moments—conceived, lived, and perceived—meet, and where they attain 'a structured coherence'.[112] If space, according to Merrifield, is set to a particular dominant *conceived* representation, then place is oriented more

---

   106.   See also Massey and Jess, 'The Global in the Local', in their *A Place in the World?*, pp. 53-59.

   107.   Massey, 'Power-Geometry', p. 65.

   108.   Massey, 'Power-Geometry', p. 66. There is a debate about the uniqueness of places. Massey seems to be ambiguous about this, first affirming their uniqueness in 'Power-Geometry' (p. 65), then seeming to deny it (p. 66). She and Jess clearly affirm it in *A Place in the World?* (pp. 221-24). In Chapter 2 of *To Take Place*, Jonathan Z. Smith, using Durkheim, Dumezil, and Lévi-Strauss, builds an argument *against* the unique-ness of places to counter that generally put forward by geographers.

   109.   Massey and Jess, *A Place in the World?*, pp. 59 and 218.

   110.   Merrifield, 'Place and Space'.

   111.   Merrifield, 'Place and Space', p. 517.

   112.   Merrifield, 'Place and Space', p. 525. See Lefebvre, *The Production of Space* (Chapter 1, 'The Plan of the Present Work'), and my Chapter 2, below.

to the *lived* moment, being the arena where daily life practices are embedded, and from which challenges to the dominant order arise.[113] Spatial practices, which constitute *perceived* space, 'are dialectically implicated in both conceived space and lived space', and thus have a mediating role between place and space.[114] For Merrifield, as for Massey, place and space are 'different aspects of a unity'.[115]

Between them, Casey, Massey, and Merrifield identify those characteristics of place most relevant to this study, and describe the relationship of place to space. Later, I will be focusing on the place of the left hand and its representations in search of religion. Speaking generally, all places — including a body part such as the left hand — are gathered, produced and reproduced by spatial practice, configured and also openly extended by social relations, constrained by the dominant order, but the living expression of everyday practices and dynamic local interpretations (local knowledge) of that place. They are repeatedly bounded and settled in common discourse only to be punched through and unsettled by alternative accounts. The particularity of a place arises from the complexity of its social relations and the sum of the stories told about it. Being a progressive part of space, or a moment in space, it is open to a spatial analysis.

In Part II, in which my attention turns to the place of the left hand, the work will involve *locating* religion within the dimensions of space, which, following Lefebvre, we conveniently label physical, mental, and social, and in relation to those properties and aspects I discuss in Part I. After looking in more detail at the theoretical implications of Lefebvre's triad for religion in the next chapter, in Chapter 3 I shall turn to 'religion' itself and the difficulties of establishing, defining, isolating, or identifying that very entity that, later in the book, I will be seeking to locate. Even at this point, however, I can say with some certainty that the process of operationalising 'religion' is unlikely to produce a category suitable for precise location on a geometric grid. Were that the only meaning that could be given to the term 'location', then I would have to confess my use of it to be purely metaphorical. Taking my lead from scholars of identity politics, I adopt a more dynamic view that sees location as the outworking — but not the end-point — of a process of considering things, people, and events in relation to one another, both geographically and socially.[116] This does

113.   Merrifield, 'Place and Space', p. 525.

114.   Merrifield, 'Place and Space', p. 525.

115.   Merrifield, 'Place and Space', p. 525.

116.   See Gupta and Ferguson's 'ongoing project' of location, in 'Discipline and Practice: "The Field" as Site, Method, and Location in Anthropology', in Akhil Gupta and James Ferguson (eds.), *Anthropological Locations: Boundaries and Grounds of a Field Science* (Berkeley: University of California Press, 1997), pp. 1-40 (37).

not so much fix things—'religion' in my case—as situate them vis-à-vis others. In Chapter 3, the interconnections between the 'religious' and the 'secular', and their mutual constitution in a field of force relations will be discussed. Situating them in this way requires, as we saw earlier in the discussion on space and power, discerning the *uneven relations between them* as well as the *difference in their positions.*

In this chapter I have sought to identify the centrality of the body for space and the dimensions and properties of physical, mental, and social space in order to be able to undertake a spatial analysis of religion. The terms of this analysis will be finalised towards the end of Part I. Using the work of Lefebvre and of other social and geographical theorists, I have provided a dynamic perspective on space which I see as appropriate for locating religion in everyday, non-religious places as well as ostensibly religious ones. As a final word, we should remind ourselves that space is more than some mere container or backdrop for the antics of religions and religious people. It is the means and the outcome as well as the medium of social and cultural activity. Furthermore, in this account, it provides the method for illuminating religion and people's experience of it.

Chapter 2

Religion and Lefebvre's Spatial Triad

In the quotation by Doreen Massey of which I made use in the previous chapter, Massey described the characteristics of what she went on to refer to as a progressive sense of space, conveying not so much the idea of evolution as of repeated spatial reproduction. This active sense is important if we are to get away from the notion of abstract, passive space, and it is for this reason that Lefebvre made it clear that his project concerned not the *science of space*, but a deepening *knowledge of the production of space*.

As part of the process of opening up social space and its relations of production and reproduction to our understanding, Lefebvre proposed an analytical triad — not a typology of space/s, but three dialectically interconnected aspects of social space.[1] Their relationship was deemed by Lefebvre to be unstable, with one or another coming to the fore in different historical periods and societies, and all, to a greater or lesser extent, co-existing at any time.[2] His intention in identifying the triad was not theoretical or abstract, but concrete, and he sought to articulate it variously in relation to particular places or times, such as the spaces of the body, the Middle Ages, and modernity (abstract space).[3] Other scholars have gone on to apply it to different cases: Shields to Edmonton Mall, Harvey to Times Square, and Soja to Los Angeles, for example.[4]

What are Lefebvre's aspects, and how can they help in the process of opening up to scrutiny the spaces occupied and employed by religion?

1.   Lefebvre, *The Production of Space*, pp. 33, 38-40. It should be said that he also played around with the idea of 'a code' of space. His approach was to try out various analytical strategies in order to develop a working understanding of the nature of social space and its relations of production and reproduction rather than to produce a highly systematic model for their analysis.

2.   Lefebvre, *The Production of Space*, p. 46.

3.   Lefebvre, *The Production of Space*, see pp. 40, 45, 310-11. See Shields, *Lefebvre, Love and Struggle*, pp. 171-78, for a discussion of Lefebvre's use of historical periods.

4.   Shields, *Places on the Margin*, pp. 55-56; Harvey, 'From Space to Place and Back Again', pp. 17-19; Soja, *Thirdspace*, Part II.

Before addressing the second question, I shall introduce the triad, following the ordering adopted by a commentator on Lefebvre's work, Andrew
Merrifield.[5] These aspects do not refer first and foremost to physical
space, but rather to the way in which space — physical, mental, and social
— is experienced by people. It is sensed, thought, and practised.

Lefebvre's Three Aspects of Social Space

The first of these is *representations of space*, which Lefebvre also referred to
as 'conceived space' or 'conceptualised space'.[6] It comprises those dominant, theoretical, often technical, representations of lived space that are
conceived and constructed by planners, architects, engineers, and scientists of all kinds. It is the space of capital, its objective examples being
factories, monuments, towers and office blocks.[7] Always embedded in
such representations are ideology, knowledge, and power. This conceived space is at one remove from that which is lived, but is nevertheless
public, influential, authoritarian, and invasive in its mastery over the
body and everyday spaces.[8]

  Lefebvre's principal study of such representations is undertaken in
relation to 'abstract space' and its later contradictory developments. He
suggested, in fact, that, although space was traditionally lived before
being conceptualised, in the modern period 'representation precedes, and

  5.   Lefebvre's own order, first laid out on p. 33 of *The Production of Space* and
repeated elsewhere, is (a) spatial practice, (b) representations of space, (c) representational space (which I have referred to as 'spaces of representation'). Merrifield does
not state why he switches the order, placing 'spatial practice' at the end of the list.
However, in doing so, he introduces us to the aspect which assaults us most com-
monly and which is perhaps easiest for us to understand: representations of space; see
Andrew Merrifield, 'Place and Space: A Lefebvrian Reconciliation', *Transactions of the
British Institute of Geographers* NS 18 (1993), pp. 516-31 (522-27), and 'Henri Lefebvre: A
Socialist in Space', pp. 174-75. Other helpful accounts of the triad include Shields,
Places on the Margin, pp. 52-54, and *Lefebvre, Love and Struggle*, pp. 160-70, as well as
Lynn Stewart, 'Bodies, Visions, and Spatial Politics: A Review Essay on Henri
Lefebvre's *The Production of Space*', *Environment and Planning D: Society and Space* 13
(1995), pp. 609-18 (610-11). Edward Soja discusses the triad (or 'trialectics of spatiality'
as he prefers to call it) extensively in *Thirdspace*, but in my opinion he tends both to
misrepresent it (by identifying each of the moments with either mental, social, or
physical space when each has the potential to be all of these) and over-interpret it (as a
tool of postmodern criticism).
  6.   Lefebvre, *The Production of Space*, p. 38.
  7.   Lefebvre, *The Production of Space*, p. 49.
  8.   It is this conceptualised aspect that is pursued so effectively by Foucault in his
work on modern discipline, its processes, institutions, and architecture. For example,
Michel Foucault, *Discipline and Punish: The Birth of the Prison* (trans. Alan Sheridan;
London: Penguin, 1977).

is distinguishable from practice to such an extent that it has become possible to define a world of representations', the chief characteristics of which are the geometric, the visual, and the phallic.[9] However, Lefebvre also recognised the historical role of religious institutions and theologians in the conception of space, referring, for example, to Thomas Aquinas in his account of representations of space in the Middle Ages.[10]

Of the second aspect, *spaces of representation*,[11] Lefebvre wrote that it is,

> Space as directly *lived* through its associated images and symbols, and hence the space of 'inhabitants' and 'users', but also of some artists…, writers and philosophers, who *describe* and aspire to do no more than describe. This is the dominated — and hence passively experienced — space which the imagination seeks to change and appropriate. It overlays physical space, making symbolic use of its objects.[12]

What makes this *lived* space different to *perceived space* (see below) is the intervention of culture,[13] not as ideology (as in *conceived space*), but through the imagination as tradition and symbol. In his example of mediaeval life, he identified such spaces as the village church, graveyard, and belfry — all of which were, to a greater or lesser degree, interpretations or symbols of cosmological representations.[14] Such *lived* spaces, imbued with distinctively local knowledge, often run counter to spaces generated by formal, technical knowledge. They may be experienced as '"moments" of presence', glimpses of totality in the banality of everyday life when alienation is transcended.[15]

The hope Lefebvre invested in these 'moments' for the disruption of the dominant order, through their association with the clandestine and

9.   Stewart, 'Bodies, Visions, and Spatial Politics', p. 610. Lefebvre believed the idea of 'represention' to be more suitable than ideology in accounting for spatial conceptions and symbols (*The Production of Space*, p. 45). He discussed the three 'formants' or characteristics of abstract representations of space on pp. 285-87.

10.   Lefebvre, *The Production of Space*, p. 45.

11.   Stewart ('Bodies, Visions, and Spatial Politics', p. 610), Soja (*Thirdspace*, p. 10), and Shields (*Lefebvre, Love and Struggle*, pp. 161, 165) prefer 'spaces of representation' to Nicholson-Smith's translation, 'representational space', as more suggestive and closer to the original French.

12.   Lefebvre, *The Production of Space*, p. 39.

13.   Lefebvre, *The Production of Space*, p. 40. See also Soja on 'Thirdspace as both real and imagined' (*Thirdspace*, pp. 56-57).

14.   Lefebvre, *The Production of Space*, p. 45.

15.   For Lefebvre on 'The theory of moments', see Henri Lefebvre, *Critique of Everyday Life: Foundations for a Sociology of the Everyday* (London and New York: Verso, 2002 [French edn 1961]), pp. 340-58. See also Elden, *Understanding Henri Lefebvre*, pp. 170-73. Shields discusses the influences of both Dada and the mysticism of Joachim de Flore on Lefebvre's choice and use of the word 'moment' (Shields, *Lefebvre, Love and Struggle*, pp. 57-59): 'moments are revelatory of the totality of possibilities contained in daily existence' (p. 58).

underground side of social life,[16] has been taken up by later radical geographers, most notably Ed Soja in his articulation of a 'Thirdspace' of social and cultural resistance. (Soja equated Firstspace with spatial practices, see below, and Secondspace with representations of space, above.) Soja associated spaces of representation with the marginal, critical spaces identified by feminist and postcolonial cultural theorists such as Adrienne Rich, Gillian Rose, bell hooks, and Homi Bhabha.[17] His ideas have proved fruitful for the analysis of Biblical texts which use geographical and topographical references.[18] The potential of *religion* as a contemporary space of representation or third space, however, is arguably best explored by Christine Chivallon. Caribbean religious experience offers a space, she suggests, for the creation of a diasporic identity. 'The religious space', she says, 'is, above all, a space which serves to deconstruct the racial order inscribed in the British spaces and to replace them with representations, more mental than material, which are free from this categorisation', simultaneously criticising the imposed order and providing an alternative vision of the self.[19] Lived space, for all these theorists, is the vital arena of struggle towards individual and communal realisation.[20]

16. Lefebvre, *The Production of Space*, p. 33. A poignant example, of the disruption of the imposed order by a young girl (Anne Frank) through her diary, is given by Karen Bermann, 'The House Behind', in Nast and Pile (eds.), *Places through the Body*, pp. 165-80.

17. Soja, *Thirdspace*, Chapter 3 ('Exploring the Spaces that Difference Makes'), and Chapter 4 ('Increasing the Openness of Thirdspace'). See also bell hooks, *Yearning: Race, Gender, and Cultural Politics* (Boston: Southend Press, 1990); Adrienne Rich, *Blood, Bread, and Poetry: Selected Prose 1979–85* (London: Norton & Co., 1986); Rose, *Feminism and Geography*; Bhabha, *The Location of Culture*. Academic feminists have themselves taken up this terminology in the naming of an international interdisciplinary journal: _thirdspace_ (see <www.thirdspace.ca>).

18. I am grateful to Liv Ingeborg Lied for this information. See Lied, 'Approaching Heavenly Promised Lands: Jewish Eschatological Geography from Edward W. Soja's Thirdspace Perspective' (paper presented at the European Association for the Study of Religion Conference on Localisation and Globalisation, Bergen, May 2003). See other relevant papers in the Constructions of Ancient Space Seminar at <http://www.cwru. edu/affil/GAIR/Constructions/Constructions.html>, in particular papers by Jon L. Berquist, 'Theories of Space and Construction of the Ancient World' (paper delivered at the AAR/SBL Annual Meeting, 1999) and 'Critical Spatiality and the Uses of Theory' (paper delivered at the AAR/SBL Annual Meeting, 2002), both at <http:// www.cwru.edu/affil/GAIR/papers/>.

19. Christine Chivallon, 'Religion as Space for the Expression of Caribbean Identity in the United Kingdom', *Environment and Planning D: Society and Space* 19 (2001), pp. 461-83 (477).

20. Shields, *Lefebvre, Love and Struggle*, p. 164. In particular, he gives the example of squatters, illegal aliens, and third world slum dwellers as those who fashion counter-spaces on the social margins.

The third aspect, *spatial practice*, 'denotes the ways people generate, use, and *perceive* space'.[21] It structures all aspects of daily life and urban living, from minute, repeated gestures to the rehearsed journeys from home to work and to play.[22] It is experienced through practical perception, through commonsense, and is taken for granted.[23] Such practice embraces the activities of production and reproduction, and generates spatial competence and performance.[24] As Shields says, over time it may even be 'concretised in the built environment and sedimented in the landscape'.[25]

This aspect of everyday experience has been closely observed and analysed by Michel de Certeau, and it is from him that we get the sense of the 'strangeness' of the spatiality composed from these ordinary practices.[26] The paths which emerge from them 'give shape to spaces', which nevertheless remain 'a blind spot in a scientific and political technology'.[27] People's spatial practices then encounter and have at times to acknowledge the *conceived* order, but they form their own stories that are inaccessible to planners and scientists. Similarly, such practices connect with the *lived* order, the spaces of representation. They provide a degree of cohesion in interacting with both spaces, as we saw in Merrifield's account of place at the end of Chapter 1.

There is nothing intrinsically religious or secular about spatial practice. Religious meaning or purpose may be attributed to it; it may acquire a sense of sacrality from being enacted in a religiously meaningful space, or may be transformed by ritual process. However, a gesture or walking practice, even as genuflection or pilgrimage, is not *essentially* religious, for the same actions, directions, and co-ordinates might equally be denoted as having some other meaning — with reference to social rather than religious hierarchy, to tourism rather than a spiritual journey.

What is the significance of discussing these aspects of space for religion and its study? This question is partly one about *relevance* — the relevance of each aspect to the illumination of the category 'religion' — but also about *value*, their value in the process of studying religion.[28] Note that in

21. Stewart, 'Bodies, Visions, and Spatial Politics', p. 610.

22. Such everyday spatial practice was seen by Pierre Bourdieu as generated by *habitus*, in *The Logic of Practice* (Cambridge: Polity, 1990), p. 53.

23. Shields, *Lefebvre, Love and Struggle*, pp. 162-63.

24. Lefebvre, *The Production of Space*, p. 33. On competence and performance, see also Chapter 5 on 'Spatial Ability, Knowledge, and Place', in Tuan, *Space and Place*.

25. Shields, *Places on the Margin*, p. 53.

26. De Certeau, *The Practice of Everyday Life*, p. 93.

27. De Certeau, *The Practice of Everyday Life*, p. 97.

28. These aspects have also been discussed in a theological context by Tim Gorringe, in his *A Theology of the Built Environment: Justice, Empowerment, Redemption*

the discussion that follows I have returned to Lefebvre's own order—now we have some understanding of what he intended by each of the three aspects—and considered first spatial practice, followed by representational space, then the spaces of representation.

Religion and Spatial Practice

Spatial practices constitute the articulation of social spatiality. In discussing them, de Certeau refers to 'pedestrian speech acts' and 'walking rhetorics', and suggests that walking is to the urban system what a speech utterance is to a language.[29] If scrutinising spatial practice is a means to uncovering the spatial system which it expresses, it follows that a similar examination of habitual practices associated with religion must do likewise. As we shall see, however, reading spatial practice is not always as straightforward as it seems at first sight because of the way in which, as readers or 'hearers' (of spatial speech utterances), we ourselves are infected by the representations of the dominant spatial order. Lefebvre too notes this difficulty:

> [S]ocial space can in no way be compared to a blank page upon which a specific message has been inscribed... Both natural and urban spaces are, if anything, 'over-inscribed': everything therein resembles a rough draft, jumbled and self-contradictory. Rather than signs, what one encounters here are directions—multifarious and over-lapping instructions.[30]

First, imagine the everyday movements of self-identified religious people. In some ways these may be similar to the movements of those who do not see themselves as religious—they may take the same route to work, may walk along the same corridors, enter the same shops, and trace out similar paths between common activities at the health club. When, if ever, is it appropriate to refer to these practices as having a religious meaning? Furthermore, such religious people may add to their repository of practices other routine gestures and movements that arise as a result of their religious *disposition*. As Bourdieu suggested in his account of *habitus*, like other everyday practices these may be unselfconsciously and regularly performed.[31] They may include gestures such as the sign of the cross, routine phrases such as 'Jay shri Krishna' or 'inshallah',[32] and regular

(Cambridge: Cambridge University Press, 2002), pp. 33-34. He presents a 'trinitarian mapping of spatiality' (pp. 48-49) which responds to the revolutionary agenda of Lefebvre and Soja.

29. De Certeau, *The Practice of Everyday Life*, pp. 98-101.

30. Lefebvre, *The Production of Space*, pp. 142-43.

31. Bourdieu, *The Logic of Practice*, p. 53.

32. For Hindus, 'Jay shri Krishna' means 'hail Lord Krishna' or 'victory to Sri Krishna'; to Muslims, 'inshallah' means 'if Allah wills it'.

activities such as daily prayer or chanting, and the saying of a blessing or grace at mealtimes. They may even include movements that are not formally associated with religion, but which may be glossed as such by others.

Two Asian men walk together down a street in London or Toronto. One is wearing a turban; the other is not. A third man observes them and perceives the identity — and thus the spatial practice — of the former, but not the latter, to be religious, to be 'Sikh'. The 'Sikh' man wears a turban — an outward expression of cultural difference associated in the West with 'Sikh' religious identity.[33] Had his Asian companion — who is in fact a 'Christian' — sported facial hair and a turban, and the 'Sikh' been clean-shaven and bare-headed, the companion would no doubt have been taken for the Sikh and his going about (his spatial practice) seen as an outworking of a Punjabi Sikh *habitus*.[34]

In addition to the potential problem of the over-identification of symbols in the public domain as religious, and hence the possible reification of religion as a sign of difference,[35] this example raises an issue for understanding the relationship between spatial practice and religion. As I suggested earlier, spatial practice is lent meaning by social and cultural context. In the case of religion, it is actors and observers themselves who attribute religious meaning to it. What does this mean then for *interpreting* the spatial practice of apparently religious bodies, that is, those marked by visible religious symbols, such as the *hijab*, the turban, or *khanda*, the cross or fish, the star of David, or the *tilaka*?[36] It is premature to offer an answer to this question, though a degree of caution is required if we are both to avoid inscribing explicitly religious meanings where none are

33. In India a turban need not signal a religious identity. It is as likely to signal a caste or regional ethnic *habitus* as a religious one. For a discussion of the meaning of the turban in the West, see M. Walton-Roberts, 'Three Readings of the Turban: Sikh Identity in Greater Vancouver', *Urban Geography* 19.4 (1998), pp. 311-31.

34. Designation of the 'other' and the bodily performance of identity were perhaps given their fullest treatment by Judith Butler in her work on gender. How, on the one hand, we read and then judge another's body, and, on the other, subversively perform a chosen identity through the body were first discussed by her in *Gender Trouble: Feminism and the Subversion of Identity* (New York and London: Routledge, 1990). A recent summary of related work is provided and discussed by Gill Valentine in *Social Geographies*, Chapter 2, 'The Body'.

35. Gerd Baumann warns against this and offers a formulation for multi-relational thinking in *The Multicultural Riddle: Rethinking National, Ethnic, and Religious Identities* (Cambridge: Cambridge University Press, 1999), pp. 140-41.

36. *Hijab*, headscarf worn by some Muslim women; *khanda*, emblem of crossed swords signifying Sikh identity; the cross and fish, Christian symbols; the star of David, a symbol of Jewish identity (used and abused in the history of the Jewish diaspora); *tilaka*, sandalwood markings on the forehead which identify one as a Vaishnava or follower of Vishnu, Krishna or Rama.

intended, and to avoid seeing some kinds of spatial practice as *inherently* religious. However, some of the difficulties arising here may be mitigated if we recall that spatial practice at times connects with and plays out aspects of the other moments of Lefebvre's triad, of the conceived order (representations of space), and the lived order (the spaces of representation). Thus, the Asian man who chooses to wear a turban in a Western city will surely encounter the conceived multiculturalist order which measures religions against one another as parallel sets of identifiable symbols, irrespective of whether or not he intends to send a religious signal to those around him.[37] Privately, and with his spiritual peers, however, he may understand the turban (its colour, shape, and manner of tying) to be a liberating space of representation, to use Lefebvre's words, a symbol through which he lives out his relationship with the one Guru and transforms his everyday behaviour into actions of service. In this mode, as he understands it, his spatial practice may have a deeply religious meaning and intention, whether walking to school to collect his children or walking the same street in procession to honour the Guru at the time of *Vaisakhi*,[38] through which he opposes the normal secular interpretation of everyday behaviour.

There are other ways too in which spatial practice is significant for religion and its study. Places — and even 'non-places'[39] — emerge as a result of spatial practice. They are generated by it, become the focus of journeys to and fro, and are reproduced by repeated practice. As Merrifield puts it, 'place is a practised space'.[40] Places of worship are such places, and may include not only those with a substantial history and community presence, but also those that are formed by repeated informal ritual acts, like wayside shrines and domestic shrines, and those established for transi-

37.   Discussions of multiculturalism as a dominant discourse of difference in the West can be found in G. Baumann, *The Multicultural Riddle*, and Bhikhu Parekh, *Rethinking Multiculturalism: Cultural Diversity and Political Theory* (London: Macmillan, 2000).

38.   *Vaisakhi*, a Sikh spring festival celebrating the birth of the *khalsa* or Sikh community. What this last part of the story shows is that the turban is not merely a symbol of otherness in the West, it is also a self-conscious symbol of identity and community. What I haven't discussed here is the extent to which it is currently a signifier *within* Sikh circles of a dominant form of religiosity to the extent that clean-shaven Sikhs may be denied roles or status and seen as unorthodox. See Harjot S. Oberoi, *The Construction of Religious Boundaries: Culture, Identity and Diversity in the Sikh Tradition* (Delhi: Oxford University Press, 1994), for a discussion of the history of Sikh identity politics.

39.   'The traveller's space may…be the archetype of non-place', according to Augé, *Non-Places*, p. 86. Non-places include airport lounges, motorways and their service stations, transit camps.

40.   Thus reversing de Certeau's formulation that space is a practised place (*The Practice of Everyday Life*, p. 118). Like Merrifield, I prefer the reversal; see Merrifield, 'Place and Space', pp. 522 and n. 8, 528.

tory, individual acts of worship, prayer, and meditation, like airport chapels. The spatial practices that sustain these include not only the ritual activities which take place therein, but also the entrances and exits, the routes to and fro (whether local or global), and — in the case of those sites that attract pilgrims — the mental and virtual as well as physical excursions to them.[41]

Ritual practice itself is interesting when seen from the perspective of spatial practice as it is none other than spatial practice transformed by religious meaning,[42] and often — though not always — performed in the context of a space set apart as sacred and by an appropriate ritual practitioner.[43] The same general repertoire of gestures, actions, and movements is available for ritual transformation as it is for transformation in competitive sports or the practice of social graces.[44] In ritual, the chosen practices are repeatedly performed, often memorised to near perfection. In some ritual traditions, mastery and exactitude are essential for the ritual to be efficacious, and their achievement creates 'expert' practitioners. The cultural meaning of the ritual needs a space to be played out, whether a social space between ritual subjects, between subject and object, whether a sacrificial space, a space of liberation, of ritual conferment or of service. Sacred space is not the stimulus for ritual; ritual, as sacred-making behaviour, brings about 'sacred' space.[45] Ritual *takes place*, and *makes place* in this sense.[46]

Spatial practice, according to Lefebvre, 'denotes the ways people generate, use and perceive space'.[47] Religion, in its physical presence, social orderings, and cultural forms, is a consequence of spatial practice, though it is the attribution of meaning that gives such practice its character as 'religious'. But how does religion find significance in the other aspects of Lefebvre's triad, first in representations of space?

41.   For a new approach to pilgrimage focused upon spatial practice — movement and mobility — see Simon Coleman and John Eade (ed.), *Reframing Pilgrimage: Cultures in Motion* (London and New York: Routledge, 2004).

42.   Jonathan Z. Smith (*To Take Place*, pp. 103-14) provides an interesting discussing of this, in which he engages with Freud and Lévi-Strauss.

43.   Ritual practice might more properly be considered under the category of spaces of representation, but I treat it here because it certainly constitutes a transformation of spatial practice. It may act as a point of connection between these two aspects.

44.   See also Catherine Bell's discussion of ritual as social activity in *Ritual Theory, Ritual Practice*.

45.   On spatial and ritual practice as sacred-making behaviour, see Chapters 4 and 9.

46.   'What if place were an active product of intellection rather than its passive receptacle?', ruminates J.Z. Smith in his study of the place of ritual (*To Take Place*, p. 26).

47.   Stewart, 'Bodies, Visions, and Spatial Politics', p. 610.

Religion and Representations of Space

For Lefebvre, the contradictory space of late-modernity, a development of 'abstract space', is outwardly homogeneous (yet fragmented), universal (yet phallocentric), neutral (yet power-full and interested), and passive (yet, like all space, active and dynamic).[48] This is undoubtedly also an outwardly tolerant, but decidedly *secular* space, as Shields says, 'commodified as lots and private property, quantified by surveyors, and stripped of the old local gods and spirits of place'.[49] In twentieth-century Europe, space continued to be assigned to religion, but, generally, religion was confined to its allotted (often historical) spaces. In the public sphere in many European countries, the discourse was of religious decline — secularisation — not only the movement of lands from religious to non-religious use, but also the retreat of religion from dominant social and political space.[50] Certainly the conceived spatial order, of planners, policy makers, technocrats, architects, and scientists, was secular, if not actually anti-religious.

In the European Middle Ages, Roman Catholicism dominated popular mental space.[51] Religious conceptions of space had authority. The physical vestiges of that conceived order remain with us in the form of mediaeval cathedrals and church buildings. In addition, aspects of this order have infiltrated the current one in various ways.[52] This is apparent in both the continuation of once dominant themes, though now stripped of their religious meaning, and the marked absence of others. For example, the height, scale and grandeur of mediaeval church buildings and their style and decoration were mimicked in Britain in the nineteenth century in industrial, commercial, and public buildings. One repercussion of the capital creation associated with the success of manufacturing in this

48. See Chapter 5 in *The Production of Space*. The signs that this dominant space is breaking up may be seen in postmodernism. See the discussion below.

49. Shields, *Lefebvre, Love and Struggle*, p. 147.

50. Principal early participants in the scholarly debate about secularisation were Bryan Wilson, David Martin, and Peter Berger; see Bryan Wilson, *Contemporary Transformations in Religion* (London: Oxford University Press, 1976), and *Religion in Sociological Perspective* (London: Oxford University Press, 1982); David Martin, 'Some Utopian Aspects of the Concept of Secularisation', *International Yearbook for the Sociology of Religion* 2 (1966), pp. 86-96, and *A General Theory of Secularization* (Oxford: Basil Blackwell, 1978); Peter Berger, *The Sacred Canopy: Elements of a Sociological Theory of Religion* (New York: Anchor Books, 1990 [1967]). See Chapter 3 for further discussion.

51. Lefebvre refers to the religious spatial conception of this period as 'absolute space'; see Lefebvre, *The Production of Space*, p. 163, and Blum and Nast, 'Where's the Difference?', p. 565.

52. See Chapter 8 on religion and magic in mediaeval and early modern Europe, and their relevance for contemporary representations of the left hand.

period was the competitive denominational investment in urban church planting.[53] Similar neo-Gothic design features, building materials, and decorative motifs adorned all these monuments to capitalist enterprise, irrespective of their purpose.[54] The same patrons, often men successful in manufacturing, were behind the construction of both secular and religious edifices. The same architects were responsible for designing them. George Gilbert Scott, for example, who commended the Gothic style to fellow architects because of its principle of decoration,[55] designed in like manner churches, hospitals, and railway stations.[56]

Twentieth-century architects, engineers, and planners eschewed the conservative style of neo-Gothic in an attempt to represent the abstract, secular, and functional space of modernity, and to look forward rather than back.[57] The absence of the signs associated with an earlier Christian worldview was noteworthy. Nikolaus Pevsner notes of the work of Walter Gropius in the second decade of the twentieth century,

> Yet the character of the new buildings is entirely un-Gothic, anti-Gothic. While in the thirteenth century all lines, functional though they were, served the one artistic purpose of pointing heavenwards to a goal beyond this world, and walls were made translucent to carry the transcendental magic of saintly figures rendered in coloured glass, the glass walls are now clear and without mystery, the steel frame is hard, and its expression discourages all other-worldly speculation. It is the creative energy of this world in which we live and work and which we want to master, a world of science and technology, of speed and danger, of hard struggles and no personal security, that is glorified in Gropius's architecture.[58]

53. This speight of religious building in the nineteenth century should not be taken to signal the dominance or rise of a religious worldview, however.

54. Peter Ackroyd, for example, notes the Gothic *genius loci* of London and comments on the infusion of the spirit of neo-Gothic in that city in the nineteenth century; see Peter Ackroyd, *London: The Biography* (London: Vintage, 2001), pp. 580-81.

55. Nikolaus Pevsner, *Pioneers of Modern Design: From William Morris to Walter Gropius* (Harmondsworth: Penguin, rev. edn, 1960 [1936]), p. 19. George Gilbert Scott, in the opening address to the Architectural and Archaeological Society for the County of Buckinghamshire, called for the restoration of historic churches, commenting also on the revival of Gothic architecture, in *A Plea for the Faithful Restoration of Our Ancient Churches* (London: John Henry Parker, 1850).

56. In my own city of Leeds, in the mid-nineteenth century, George Gilbert Scott designed the churches of St John the Evangelist, Holbeck, and All Souls, Blackman Lane, as well as the Leeds Infirmary.

57. Jacobus illustrates the speed with which new ideas and motifs were taken up with reference to the skyscraper designs of Raymond Hood, who moved from a neo-Gothic conception in his Chicago Tribune Building (in 1923) to a simplified abstract one in his New York Daily News Buildings in 1930; see John M. Jacobus, Jr, 'USA', in *Encyclopedia of Modern Architecture* (London: Thames & Hudson, 1963), pp. 301-10 (305).

58. Pevsner, *Pioneers of Modern Design*, pp. 216-17.

The spatial conception which these modernist architects and planners held and to which they responded was assuredly secular. However, they could not remove the traces of the earlier Christian order from the landscape entirely; rather, they built around and between its remains, vying with them for size, height, impact, and authority. In common, as Lefebvre noted, was their testimony to the phallus in their verticality, their representation of power and violence, their masculinity.[59] This was still in evidence in the late 1960s, when, in London alone, some four hundred tower blocks were erected.[60]

Views differ on the extent to which modernism has been socially, eco-nomically, and culturally transformed in the last thirty years. Is the current order postmodern, radically modern, or merely late-modern?[61] However this is argued theoretically, it is important to note those shifts in the conception of space that have occurred as modernism has developed. The abstract and often contradictory space of modernism, as Lefebvre depicted it, though still strongly implicated in the public order, has been challenged by a discourse of heterogeneity, difference, and *bricolage* (though some might see this as seeded within modernism rather than running counter to it).[62] The changing condition of Western societies, whether conceived as late-modern or postmodern, and the representa-tions of space associated with it are of potential importance for religion in so far as they may signal a destabilisation of the secular mood and the possibility of a re-entry of religion into the public sphere under the banner of difference. Harvey notes, for example, how, in 1987, the Vatican saw fit

59. See Lefebvre, *The Production of Space*, pp. 261-62, 286-87. Lefebvre's recognition of the phallocentric and masculine nature of conceived space has been discussed as positive, but limited and unreflexive by Shields, *Lefebvre, Love and Struggle*, and Blum and Nast, 'Where's the Difference?'. The modernist conception and construction of a masculine cultural environment and the erasure of women, femininity, and the maternal is discussed by Elizabeth Grosz, 'Women, *chora*, Dwelling', in Sophie Watson and Katherine Gibson (eds.), *Postmodern Cities and Spaces* (Cambridge, MA, and Oxford: Basil Blackwell, 1995), pp. 47-58. Examples of modern verticality can be found in the skyscrapers designed for American cities by Ludwig Mies van der Rohe in the 1950s (William H. Jordy, 'Mies van der Rohe', in *Encyclopedia of Modern Architecture*, pp. 198-99).

60. Ackroyd, *London*, p. 759; see also Gorringe, *A Theology of the Built Environment* (p. 99), on the expression of an authoritarian and classist ideology in the building of tower blocks in 1950s and 1960s Britain.

61. For some of the many discussions of this, see J.F. Lyotard, *The Postmodern Condition* (Manchester: Manchester University Press, 1984); Harvey, *The Condition of Postmodernity*; Giddens, *The Consequences of Modernity*, and *Modernity and Self-Identity* (Cambridge: Polity, 1991); Zygmunt Bauman, *Intimations of Postmodernity* (London: Routledge, 1992).

62. Lefebvre's own hope for a differential space emerges in Chapter 6 of *The Production of Space*.

'to [enter] the fray on the side of the postmodern', seeing Marxism and liberal secularism as philosophies whose time had passed.[63] Philosophical trends are only a very partial guide to the social and political order inscribed in contemporary institutions, laws, policies, and the built environment, however. The latter run behind the former. In Europe and America, liberal secularism will be with us for a long time yet, played out through its lasting spatial representations.[64]

Ironically, the representatives of the modern order, for all their espousal of a secular worldview, often protected religious spaces through the planning process.[65] In Britain, for example, the listing and grading of buildings of historical significance has continued to favour the survival of the public face of historic Christianity (thus shackling local church communities with expensive programs of conservation and sometimes curbing innovative spatial renewal). The importance of such buildings to the landscape of the British imagination has led to their retention and recycling, sometimes as non-Christian or new Christian places of worship, more often as offices, warehouses, or homes.[66] (It is also worth noting that, where new church buildings *were* erected in the mid-twentieth century, they often resembled offices and warehouses, being essentially functional, geometric in design, and constructed of modern building materials.[67]) Additionally, one response to the modernist abstraction of the mid-twentieth century has been to adopt a conservative approach to new building programmes, with the result that the design features of

63. Harvey, *The Condition of Postmodernity*, p. 41.

64. Of most lasting significance are the representations embedded in constitutions and laws.

65. For discussions of religion and planning law, for Britain, see Richard Gale and Simon Naylor, 'Religion, Planning and the City: The Spatial Politics of Ethnic Minority Expression in British Cities and Towns', *Ethnicities* 2 (2002), pp. 387-409, and Nye, *Multiculturalism and Minority Religions in Britain*; for the United States, see Shelley Saxer, 'Sacred Spaces and Planning Law: Property Rights and the Regulation of Religious Activities in the United States', in Peter W. Edge and Graham Harvey (eds.), *Law and Religion in Contemporary Society: Communities, Individualism and the State* (Aldershot: Ashgate, 2000), pp. 115-27.

66. Park notes a similar process in the United States, citing the studies of Foster on the recycling of church buildings in Minnesota and Manitoba, where they were even used as chicken coops, hog barns, and granaries; see Chris Park, *Sacred Worlds: An Introduction to Geography and Religion* (London and New York: Routledge, 1994), p. 211.

67. Berdichevsky in Park, *Sacred Worlds*, p. 210. For an interesting local case, see the Anglican parish church of Belle Isle, Leeds, erected as part of a new council housing estate in 1939 under the direction of the socialist vicar and labour councillor, Charles Jenkinson. The church was built in a modernist, functional style in the same materials as neighbouring houses. See Alistair Mason, 'Jenkinson and Southcott', in *idem* (ed.), *Religion in Leeds* (Stroud: Alan Sutton, 1994), pp. 141-60 (146).

earlier periods (including those commonly associated with church architecture) have proliferated. In both these cases — of conservation and architectural conservatism — the façade has rarely mirrored the function of the
building, yet some purpose has no doubt been served through this
association with the religious representations of an earlier period. The
other response, which has been to develop a critique of modernism and a
postmodern architectural form, has made space for the renewed possibility of sacred buildings. Gulzar Haider, an architect of Pakistani heritage
and designer of mosques, has suggested that,

> ...the academic inquisition against modernism has provided numerous
> opportunities. As the design canons of modernist minimality and pure
> composition have come under attack, there has been a new air of respect-
> ability for the study of ornament, craft, tradition, form, symbol, text,
> inscriptions, and, above all, the philosophical underpinnings of archi-
> tectural intentions.[68]

The rise of social and cultural pluralism in Europe and North America
has led to the utilisation of existing planning legislation by groups for
which it was never intended. The registration of previously non-religious
buildings (houses, schools, factories) for religious uses, and the planning
of new places of worship has been undertaken by Jewish, Muslim, Hindu,
and Sikh groups with varying degrees of success in different Western
countries and states, and the cities within them.[69] Such legislation has
been used at times to stifle the opportunity for such groups to establish
and reproduce themselves physically, and at others to extend that opportunity. A drive round a British, Canadian, or North American city would
raise again the question of the significance of religion in the public
domain. Do these new places of worship suggest the re-insertion of
religion, in all its multicultural glory, into the dominant order and its

68. Gulzar Haider, 'Muslim Space and the Practice of Architecture: A Personal
Odyssey', in Barbara Daly Metcalf (ed.), *Making Muslim Space in North America and
Europe* (Berkeley and London: University of California Press, 1996), pp. 31-45 (41).

69. For Britain, see publications arising from 'Ethnicity and Cultural Landscapes', a
Leverhulme project, 1998–2001, University of Oxford (directed by Ceri Peach): Simon
Naylor and James Ryan, 'The Mosque in the Suburbs: Negotiating Religion and
Ethnicity in South London', *Social and Cultural Geography* 3 (2002), pp. 39-59, and
'Tracing the Geographies of Religious Minorities in the UK: Using Surveys and Case-
Studies', in Knott, Ward, Mason and Willmer (eds.), *Religion and Locality*, n.p. (forth-
coming); Gale and Naylor, 'Religion, Planning and the City'. For the United States, see
publications associated with The Pluralism Project at the University of Harvard
(directed by Diana Eck) at <http://www.pluralism.org>: Diana L. Eck, *A New Reli-
gious America: How a 'Christian Country' has Become the World's Most Religiously Diverse
Nation* (San Francisco: HarperSanFrancisco, 2001). See also H. Coward, J. Hinnells and
R.B. Williams (eds.), *The South Asian Diaspora in Great Britain, Canada, and the United
States* (Albany: State University of New York Press, 2000).

conceived space?[70] What do these monuments to religious communal achievement express about the nature of that order, and the place of religion and religious communities within it?[71] These things cannot be taken as read, but must be unpicked with care, taking into consideration not only the surface spaces, but also the spatial struggles occurring beneath them.

Moving briefly from the physical and social spaces of religious buildings to the civic, constitutional, and legal territory that is at the heart of the modern state, we see again that religion (Christianity in its various forms) retains an historical place which may provide a space of opportunity to new religious groupings in the West. In Britain, changes to the composition and form of state and civic ceremonies may reflect the way secularism and religion are viewed and situated publicly, and the extent to which there is a preparedness to extend such ceremonial spaces to include faith traditions other than Christianity.[72] In the West as a whole we may look to human rights discourse and legislation, and their national embodiments, for an initial sense of the mental and social space currently attributed to religion.[73] With their origins in secular Enlightenment thinking, such rights preserve a segmented space for religion alongside rights relating to race, gender, disability, and sexuality. Being afforded the right, and having it protected under the law, to freedom of thought, conscience, and religion, and having the right to uphold it in public or private,

70. Do they challenge the idea of secularisation, or suggest we are moving from what has been a secularised society to one in which religion is again socially significant? See my 'Britain's Changing Religious Landscape: Drowning or Waving?', *Berichte zur deutschen Landeskunde* 78.2 (2004), pp. 213-29. For a discussion of the theoretical options concerning 'resacralisation' and secularisation, see Mellor and Shilling, *Re-Forming the Body*, pp. 164-65, 188-89.

71. See, for example, discussions about the formation of new Islamic and Hindu public spaces in Daly Metcalf (ed.), *Making Muslim Space in North America and Europe*, and Naylor and Ryan, 'The Mosque in the Suburbs', and 'Tracing the Geographies'.

72. See Grace Davie, *Religion in Britain Since 1945: Believing Without Belonging* (Oxford: Basil Blackwell, 1994), and Sophie Gilliat-Ray, 'Civic Religion in England: Traditions and Transformations', *Journal of Contemporary Religion* 14.2 (1999), pp. 233-44.

73. Beyond the West, whilst the United Nations and NGOs carry and reproduce this discourse, there continues to be a debate about the extent to which it represents a new wave of Western domination and colonial intention. For discussions of the relationship between religions and human rights, see Malcom D. Evans, 'Religion, Law and Human Rights: Locating the Debate', in Peter W. Edge and Graham Harvey (eds.), *Law and Religion in Contemporary Society: Communities, Individualism and the State* (Aldershot: Ashgate, 2000), pp. 177-97; Irene Bloom, J. Paul Martin and Wayne L. Proudfoot (eds.), *Religious Diversity and Human Rights* (New York: Columbia University Press, 1996); Nye, *Multiculturalism and Minority Religions in Britain* (Chapter 8, 'The ECHR, HRA, and "Freedom of Religion" in Britain').

through acts of worship, teaching, practice, and observance is no guaran-
tee that it will be respected, however. We have here yet another example
of the difficulty of reading social space (in this case in its legal form).
Following Lefebvre, we must not settle for the obvious in analysing such
spaces. With reference to the reading of edifices, but equally applicable to
other cases, he stated,

> Monumentality, for instance, always embodies and imposes a clearly intel-
> ligible message. It says what it wishes to say—yet it hides a good deal
> more: being political, military, and ultimately fascist in character, monu-
> mental buildings mask the will to power and the arbitrariness of power
> beneath signs and surfaces which claim to express collective will and
> collective thought. In the process, such signs and surfaces also manage to
> conjure away both possibility and time.[74]

The social and mental space of political and legal discourse is also
inscribed with power and the will to control and define, as well as the
apparently more noble desire to embody emerging notions of equality
and difference.

I have mentioned briefly some of the ways in which Lefebvre's
'conceptualised space', the dominant space of those who theorise and
represent it publicly, is relevant in relation to contemporary religion and
its study. What this discussion has not yet covered—and Lefebvre does
not consider—is the extent to which, *within* the domain or cultural field of
a religion, the status quo is also maintained through the embeddedness of
a theological, doctrinal, philosophical, or cosmological order (which
extends itself beyond the mental space of ideology to social and gender
hierarchy, ritual practice, ethics, and lifestyle). *Within* a religion, denomination, or community, the maintenance of this dominant order, its expression in space, and articulation in spatial practice has a high priority.
Nevertheless, spatial struggles are ongoing, struggles between dominant
and demotic discourses, between authorised and unauthorised representatives, orthodox and heterodox positions.

A major case of such a struggle, witnessed in many religious institutions during the last century, has been that of women in their quest to
find acceptable spaces to inhabit within religions.[75] In varying ways, with
differing degrees of success, sometimes by means of negotiation or
reform, and sometimes by more radical measures, women have inserted
themselves into traditionally male spaces to such an extent that those
spaces—whether physical, mental or social—have at times changed quite

74. Lefebvre, *The Production of Space*, p. 143.
75. See Ursula King, *Women and Spirituality* (London, Macmillan, 2nd edn, 1993),
and *idem* (ed.), *Religion and Gender* (Oxford: Basil Blackwell, 1995).

substantially. The physical spaces of worship, liturgy, and ritual have been altered to accommodate women as participants, even as specialists. Linguistic and narrative spaces, in some religious groups, have been opened up to include references to women and the feminine, including the feminine aspect of the divine. And in many religious bodies, women have moved into new roles, embodying spaces new to them, even becoming representations in their own right of a changing order.[76] The questions on the lips of feminists are: 'What is the extent and depth of this spatial transformation?', and 'Is it sufficiently embedded to enable women to retain the ground they have gained?'. Those of a reformist persuasion may be hopeful regarding the future; those whose diagnosis of the state of traditional religions is that they are inherently and irredeemably patriarchal may be less so. Feminist philosophers and post-Religion feminists are more inclined to take the struggle beyond existing religious institutions and the process of reform and transformation, to the fields of language and the self, poetry, and psychoanalysis in search of a divine relevant to women and their accomplishment *as women*.[77]

Whether it is new and different spaces that are sought or a stake in existing spaces, the struggle for space goes on. In his conclusion to *The Production of Space*, Lefebvre states with conviction that 'no one can avoid trial by space'.[78] He goes on,

> Moreover — and more importantly — groups, classes or fractions of classes cannot constitute themselves, or recognize one another, as 'subjects' unless they generate (or produce) a space. Ideas, representations or values which do not succeed in making their mark on space, and thus generating (or producing) an appropriate morphology, will lose all pith and become mere signs, resolve themselves into abstract descriptions, or mutate into fantasies.[79]

He lays bare the territorial drive that lies at the heart of both representations of space and spaces of representation.

---

76. Examples in British popular culture include the *Vicar of Dibley* (BBC 1, played by Dawn French), and 'Janet', one-time vicar of Ambridge, in the radio soap-opera *The Archers* (BBC Radio 4).

77. See contributions by Mary Daly, *Beyond God the Father* (London: The Women's Press, 1986 [first published 1973]); Julia Kristeva, *In the Beginning was Love: Psychoanalysis and Faith* (New York: Columbia University Press, 1987 [French edn 1985]); Luce Irigaray, *Sexes and Genealogies* (New York: Columbia University Press, 1993 [French edn 1987]); Naomi Goldenberg, *Resurrecting the Body: Feminism, Religion and Psychoanalysis* (New York: Crossroad, 1990); and Jantzen, *Becoming Divine*. For Kristeva and Irigaray, see also Joy, O'Grady and Poxon (eds.), *French Feminists on Religion*.

78. Lefebvre, *The Production of Space*, p. 416.

79. Lefebvre, *The Production of Space*, pp. 416-17.

Religion and Spaces of Representation

We have seen how Lefebvre's aspect of spatial practice engages with religion, and how representations of space, the conceived order, have used and been infiltrated by religious ideas, and at times, expunged of them. In the last example, we saw how dominant representations began to be broken open by religious women eager to gain a space within traditional religious institutions (either a space to share with men—equality—or a separate and different, but nonetheless valued space). Some, eschewing the idea of a space being made for women by men within essentially patriarchal institutions, began to explore the possibility of women finding a spiritual arena outside them.[80] In highlighting these developments, we have already trespassed on Lefebvre's third aspect, his *lived* order or 'spaces of representation'. We saw earlier that this was different from the spatial practice of directly perceived space because of the intervention of culture.

If at times in the past this lived space was the defining public moment, it is now, according to Lefebvre, subsumed beneath the weight of the conceptualised spatial order of modernity. Nevertheless, it has the capacity to be repeatedly revived by individuals and groups seeking to live symbolically in opposition to that which is normative and dominant. In 1968, the same year that Lefebvre himself was involved in the lived moment of student unrest in Paris, Mary Daly published *The Church and the Second Sex* and took her first steps outside the Church in pursuit of a claimed space for women:

> Women's space: Space created by women who choose to separate our Selves from the State of Servitude: FREE SPACE; Space in which women actualize Archimagical Powers, releasing the flow of Gynergy; Space in which women Spin and Weave, creating cosmic tapestries; Space in which women find Rooms, Looms, Brooms of our Own.[81]

This chosen space of alterity, which was variously experienced by Daly and other feminists as either a real or an imagined one, is a clear case of

80. See the spiritual feminist accounts of, among others, Starhawk, *The Spiral Dance: A Rebirth of the Ancient Religion of the Great Goddess* (San Francisco: HarperSanFrancisco, tenth anniversary edn, 1989 [1979]); Susan Starr Sered, *Priestess, Mother, Sacred Sister: Religions Dominated by Women* (New York: Oxford University Press, 1994); Carol Christ, *Rebirth of the Goddess: Finding Meaning in Feminist Spirituality* (Reading, MA: Addison Wesley, 1997); Melissa Raphael, *Thealogy and Embodiment: The Post-Patriarchal Reconstruction of Female Sacrality* (Sheffield: Sheffield Academic Press, 2001). See also post-Christian positions, Mary Daly, *Beyond God the Father; Outercourse: The Dedazzling Voyage* (London: The Women's Press, 1992); Daphne Hampson, *After Christianity* (London: SCM Press, 1996).

81. Mary Daly with Jane Caputi, *Websters' First New Intergalactic Wickedary of the English Language* (London: The Women's Press, 1987), p. 101.

an attempt to create a space of representation through which to live imaginatively in opposition to the normal order.[82] A further example is the one drawn in detail by Christine Chivallon, and referred to earlier, of the space of resistance afforded to some African-Caribbeans in Britain by the Christian life.[83] Her spatial analysis of interviews conducted with black church members in the south of England demonstrates how a mental space is invoked which liberates the speakers from the crushing discourse of racial difference and racism, and offers the possibility of transcendence and connection with others, both black and white. Chivallon builds critically on the work, not only of Lefebvre, but also of Hall, Gilroy, and Bhabha on the meaning and position of hybridity as diasporic resistance, which the latter speaks of as a third space of enunciation.[84] In her analysis Chivallon is able to meet the powerful criticism made by Gillian Rose, that Bhabha's third space remains theoretical and cannot be lived,[85] with an example that reframes hybridity as,

> … a socially constructed form which simply expresses how the members of a group find, daily, the ways and means of making permeable, and thus less violent and constraining, the boundaries that necessarily give meaning to the world and to its social relationships.[86]

Religion in this context becomes a living response to the racial contours and boundaries of British society.

Many people strive to live in a way that runs counter to the norm, though more may live in thrall to it. Even the former are at times compromised by the ideological power of the imposed order, witnessed in the contemporary spaces of advertising, the retail mall, the media (from news print to movies), and the spatial expression of public policy (through posters, billboards, pamphlets, party political broadcasts, and ministerial statements). Oppositional spaces are far from always religious in

82. See Raphael, *Thealogy and Embodiment*, pp. 241-45, for a discussion of the postmodern margin of feminist spirituality.

83. Chivallon, 'Religion as Space for the Expression of Caribbean Identity'. For a further case, see Glenn Bowman's examination of two in-between spaces opened up by beleaguered Palestinians, in 'Nationalising the Sacred: Shrines and Shifting Identities in the Israeli-Occupied Territories', *Man* 28 (1993), pp. 431-60.

84. Bhabha, *The Location of Culture*, pp. 36-39. Soja identifies the third space of Bhabha with Lefebvre's 'spaces of representation' or lived space (*Thirdspace*, pp. 139-44).

85. Gillian Rose, 'The Interstitial Perspective: A Review Essay on Homi Bhabha's *The Location of Culture*', *Environment and Planning D: Society and Space* 13 (1995), pp. 365-73 (372). See also Katharyne Mitchell's critique of Bhabha's discussion of the third space of hybridity (as 'disarticulated from history and political economy') in 'Different Diasporas and the Hype of Hybridity', *Environment and Planning D: Society and Space* 15 (1997), pp. 533-53.

86. Chivallon, 'Religion as Space for the Expression of Caribbean Identity', p. 480.

character, but religion, spirituality, and the sacred have certainly
provided the meaning and symbolic expression for many moments of
disruption or resistance.[87] When we look at recent Western examples
which seem to buck the trend of modernist secularity — the emergence of
communities of road protesters and new age travellers (the new tribal-
ism), the welling-up of popular mourning (after football tragedies, or the
death of Diana, Princess of Wales), or the rise in interest in spiritual
objects (crystals, Buddhas, incense), spiritual exercises (tai chi, yoga), and
spiritual processes (feng shui, divination) — we are hard pressed to evaluate the extent to which they reside as mock counter-spaces within the
dominant order, and hence as a veiled expression of its interests, or constitute genuine spaces of resistance.[88] The question also remains, 'Are
they or are they not religious?', an issue to which we shall turn in the next
chapter.

If new eruptions of religious or spiritual interest constitute a possible,
though not necessarily lived space which might counter the dominant
order, what of the old religions? To what extent can they renew or rein-
vent themselves such that they offer a similar opportunity? They certainly
have the potential to transform themselves because they are dynamic,
being made up of changing constituencies of people who adhere to them.
As social bodies that either adapt to their contexts or die, they are engaged
in a continual process of renewal, of conserving yet innovating. But does
this process necessarily fit them for resistance to the dominant order or
liberation from it, or does it bring them ever closer to its norms and
values? At least in their original conceptions, religions offered spaces of
representation, of vision and promise. Those people who now come new
to those religions or revert enthusiastically to them must hope that they
can continue to do so, perhaps by 'sing[ing] the Lord's song in a strange
land', in a new language, or to a new tune.[89] We shall briefly consider
these possibilities in turn.

---

87. 'Religion', 'spirituality', and the 'sacred' will be discussed in Chapters 3, 4,
and 9.

88.   Lefebvre is suspicious of late-modern leisure spatialisation as an expression of
the conceived capitalist order (rather than as counter to it), but also recognises the
possibility of genuine resistance and revolt through carnivalesque inversions (*The
Production of Space*, pp. 58-59). This issue is also discussed by Chris Rojek in *Ways of
Escape: Modern Transformations in Leisure and Travel* (Lanham, MD: Rowman & Littlefield, 1994), and Kevin Hetherington, *Expressions of Identity: Space, Performance, Politics*
(London, Thousand Oaks, New Delhi: Sage, 1998). See also my discussion of contemporary 'spiritual' spaces in my 'Britain's Changing Religious Landscape'.

89.   I have borrowed a phrase from Ps. 137.4 (well known from the popular
spiritual, 'From the Waters of Babylon').

Since the Second World War, in particular, countries in the West have experienced a period of cultural diversification.[90] Migration, from South and East Asia, the Middle East, Africa, Latin America and the Caribbean, and Eastern Europe, has led to an increase in religious plurality, and, for the migrants themselves, has inevitably brought about religious as well as social change. The new countries may have been rather unsympathetic environments for incoming religions, but they have nevertheless provided a space of opportunity — whether to reproduce familiar institutions and practices which barely engage with the new setting at all, or to create living spaces of representation from the resources of both the old and new. If Chivallon's Caribbean example illustrates the latter, Parekh's stinging rebuke of the failure of migrant Hindus to make the most of their diasporic experience is strongly suggestive of the former:

> It is striking that overseas Hindus have remained religiously parasitic on India, importing its movements and cults but neither transforming them in the light of their needs, nor throwing up a new movement fashioned in the crucible of the diasporic experience, nor even adding new gods and goddesses to their pantheon. They have not thrown up a single religious leader of stature, nor provided a coherent critique of traditional beliefs and practices, nor offered a novel interpretation of these on the basis of the problems they faced... Diasporic Hindus have produced no yogi, saint or acharya, and made little contribution to the spiritual deepening of their religion. In this sense there is no diasporic Hinduism, a distinct form of Hinduism created by overseas Hindus in the light of their unique experience and needs.[91]

How migrants adapt their religious meanings, symbols, and practices is only one area to look in considering the capacity of old religions for renewal. A further one, singing the familiar song in a new language, might best be illustrated by the process of transplantation and mission, the movement not only of a religion to a new place, but also to a new constituency. Buddhism, to take one multi-faceted example, has undoubtedly been renewed through its journey to the West, and has provided symbolic spaces for many people for whom Judeo-Christianity has been

90. While this is generally true, it is also the case that the mid-late twentieth century was a time when dominant powers sought, all too successfully, to eradicate particular socio-cultural groups from their midst. The holocaust of the 1940s and the more recent massacre of Srebrenica (July 1995) are horrific examples of the determination to cleanse a nation by means of the erasure of particular ethno-religious communities (the Jews and Gypsies of western and central Europe, and the Bosnian Muslims).

91. Bhikhu Parekh, 'Some Reflections', *New Community* 20.4 (1994), pp. 603-20 (612). Parekh's view has been discussed and tempered by Martin Baumann in 'Sustaining Little Indias: Hindu Diasporas in Europe', in Gerrie ter Haar (ed.), *Strangers and Sojourners: Religious Communities in the Diaspora* (Leuven: Peeters, 1998), pp. 95-132.

found wanting.[92] Whilst some Buddhist communities in the West have sought legitimacy by reproducing textual, institutional, or practical norms associated with the region of origin,[93] others have been more outwardly context-sensitive, a case in point being Friends of the Western Buddhist Order (FWBO), a 'consciously "western" Buddhist group'.[94] However, in an article in which he poses the question of a 'Protestant Buddhism', Philip Mellor makes it clear that,

> the adoption of Buddhist religious forms by English people does not entail such a radical break with western structures and influences as has often been envisaged. Individuals may take personal decisions to become Buddhists, but Christian discourses and forms of life continue to have an observable influence on English Buddhism.[95]

He suggests, then, that the process of translation of Buddhism to a new geographical location is not merely a matter of the decision on the part of a movement to adapt itself, to a greater or lesser extent, to the new context, but also of its members carrying their context—of liberal Protestant culture—into the movement with them, like mud on their boots. Mellor infers that Buddhist groups in England provide a space of opportunity, not because 'they divert western culture into new religious channels, but because they explore the existing religious channels in new ways'.[96] In this sense, Buddhism in the West opens up a space for the renewal of *Western religiosity* rather than Buddhism per se.[97]

Singing a familiar song to a new tune is yet another means of religious renewal which may offer a space for resistance or liberation. What I have in mind here are those traditional symbols that are taken up afresh and invested with novel meaning in new circumstances, be these of place or

92. I do not mean to suggest that Buddhism does not have the capacity to be renewed within its traditional homelands, merely to add that exposure to a different constituency may bring new challenges. To take one example, its capacity to be renewed by feminism, and to offer spiritual practices to women turned off by traditional Western religious fare is discussed by Rita M. Gross, *Buddhism After Patriarchy: A Feminist History, Analysis, and Reconstruction of Buddhism* (Albany: State University of New York Press, 1993).

93. For a discussion of the issue of legitimacy in British Buddhism, see Philip A. Mellor, 'Protestant Buddhism? The Cultural Translation of Buddhism in England', *Religion* 21 (1991), pp. 73-92; and Helen Waterhouse, *Buddhism in Bath: Authority and Adaptation* (Leeds: Community Religions Project, University of Leeds, 1997).

94. Mellor, 'Protestant Buddhism?', p. 73.

95. Mellor, 'Protestant Buddhism?', p. 73.

96. Mellor, 'Protestant Buddhism?', p. 90.

97. See also Simon G. Smith, 'Buddhism and the Postmodern: The Nature of Identity and Tradition in Contemporary Society' (PhD thesis, University of Leeds, 1997), on the FWBO as a contemporary de-universalised religious movement, and the coming together of Western and Buddhist philosophies.

time. The *hijab*, the headcovering worn by some Muslim women, is a pertinent example having become a focus in recent times for political struggle in various countries. It has been at the centre of debates in Europe, Turkey, Egypt, Iran, Algeria, and Afghanistan about religious identity, gender politics, religious and racial discrimination, Westernisation, and social and educational exclusion. It is a multivalent symbol, and this above all has enabled it to transcend its historical associations and to be ascribed new meanings in different contexts by a range of constituencies and interest groups.[98] Variously, it may be read as a sign of wealth, protection, oppression, modesty, exclusion, community, defiance, power, or rejection of Westernisation. Of most interest here is its capacity in non-Islamic states to stand as a sign of difference, anti-Western but in the West, and, for those who choose to wear it (white Muslim as well as Asian and Middle Eastern Muslim women), a positive Islamic symbol that transforms seclusion into sisterhood.[99] *Hijab* is a religious space that simultaneously confines yet liberates the female body.[100] It forms a boundary that both excludes others, on grounds of both gender and religion, and expresses a shared identity. It may signal Islamic ideas not only on modesty, but also on the gift of the body by a woman to her husband. It may be read as a critical discourse on both the sexually inscribed dress of Western women and on male transgression of a woman's private space. For many Muslim women in the West it has become a site of experimentation in religious identity.

98.   For recent discussions, see F. El Guindi, *Veil: Modesty, Privacy, and Resistance* (Oxford: Berg, 1999), and Myfanwy Franks, *Women and Revivalism in the West: Choosing 'Fundamentalism' in a Liberal Democracy* (Basingstoke and New York: Palgrave, 2001).

99.   On seclusion and *hijab*, see Fatima Mernissi, *Women and Islam: An Historical and Theological Enquiry* (trans. Mary Jo Lakeland; Oxford: Basil Blackwell, 1991), and *The Veil and the Male Elite* (New York: Addison-Wesley, 1991). On white Muslim women and the *hijab*, see Myfanwy Franks, 'Crossing the Borders of Whiteness? White Muslim Women Who Wear the *Hijab* in Britain Today', *Ethnic and Racial Studies* 23.5 (2000), pp. 917-29. Also on *hijab* and difference in Europe, see Claire Dwyer, 'Veiled Meanings: Young British Muslim Women and the Negotiation of Differences', *Gender, Place and Culture* 6.1 (1999), pp. 5-26; Rachel Bloul, 'Engendering Muslim Identities: Deterritorialization and the Ethnicization Process in France', in Metcalf (ed.), *Making Muslim Space*, pp. 234-50; Joseph H. Carens and Melissa S. Williams, 'Muslim Minorities in Liberal Democracies: The Politics of Misrecognition', in Rajeev Bhargava (ed.), *Secularism and Its Critics* (Oxford: Oxford University Press, 1998), pp. 137-76.

100.   For some Muslim women, the *hijab* and the body within it are one. Removing the *hijab* is tantamount to peeling off the skin: 'Her body is not simply the inside of the veil: it is of it…' (Meyda Yeğenoğlu, 'Sartorial Fabric-ations: Enlightenment and Western Feminism', in Laura E. Donaldson and Kwok Pui-lan [eds.], *Postcolonialism, Feminism, and Religious Discourse* [New York and London: Routledge, 2002], pp. 82-99 [96]).

It has been my intention in this chapter to explore in brief the explanatory possibilities for contemporary religion arising from the application of Lefebvre's spatial triad. I have not discussed the triad critically, leaving that task to those more competent in social geography,[101] but have chosen instead to look at the relevance of each of Lefebvre's three aspects for religion and its study.[102] At this stage, the result has been a superficial engagement of each aspect with a range of examples, but later in the book I shall utilise the triad, along with the spatial dimensions and properties identified in the previous chapter, to analyse religion in the case of the left hand. As such, the aspects of the triad become a vital part of the terms of a spatial analysis for the study of religion. I shall return to them briefly at the end of Part I when they will be brought together with other features of space in a provisional framework.

101.   See my comments in Chapter 9. Critics include Blum and Nast, 'Where's the Difference?', and Unwin, 'A Waste of Space?'.
102.   I pursue this further in Chapter 4 when I draw a parallel between J.Z. Smith's analysis of spatial maps and Lefebvre's dialectical triad, and in Chapter 9.

Chapter 3

Opening Up Religion for a Spatial Analysis

If the primary focus of the previous chapters was space, with religion taking a secondary position for the purpose of providing illustrations and cases, in this and the following chapters the principal focus is religion, with space entering the frame first as medium (the context in which religion is to be analysed) and later as method (providing the analytical terms). Several questions will be addressed in the following discussion. In this chapter, I shall ask how 'religion' might be formulated, given our time and place — the late-modern West — for a spatial study of this kind? In Chapter 4, I shall consider what the academic study of religion brings to this project in terms of the analysis of religion and space, and in Chapter 5, the issues raised in Part I will be brought together and the spatial approach summarised.

By way of introduction, I shall bridge the gap between the focus on space in the previous chapters and on religion in this one by thinking aloud about the spaces occupied by 'conventional religion'[1] — by which I mean religious institutions, their traditions, beliefs, and practices, and those who to a greater or lesser extent adhere to them. This is what most people in the West generally mean by 'religion'.[2] Such a process has the benefit of both demonstrating the remarkable variety of places available for a spatial analysis of religion (even in its most common-sense form), and, more importantly, of contributing to the problematisation of the category 'religion' for an analysis of contemporary space.

1.   'Conventional religion' was used by Robert Towler in juxtaposition to his term 'common religion'. He defined it thus: 'Alternatively called official religion and church religion, conventional religion includes the principal religions of the world and their long-established sub-divisions' (*The Need for Certainty: A Sociological Study of Conventional Religion* [London and Boston: Routledge & Kegan Paul, 1984], p. 4).

2.   This is the *emic* usage. I take this as my starting point, but not my final destination in the chapter.

As we saw earlier, Lefebvre undertook an investigation of the dynamism of space in all its social, physical, and mental manifestations. Given such an understanding, what examples of conventional religious places come to mind? Perhaps the most obvious are those that impinge on our visual experience of public space, namely places of worship—churches, synagogues, mosques, gurdwaras, mandirs and so on. If we enter one of these, our other senses are often brought into play. We may think of such places, first and foremost, as examples of physical space, but if we spend time in them we see that they are resolutely social in so far as they include and exclude, incorporate, consecrate, bring together, release, and confer status on persons. What is more, in being theological representations in their own right, and in being repeatedly imagined as community centre, sanctuary, classroom, and venue for jumble sales, youth clubs, mother and toddler groups, or legal advice sessions, they are mental spaces.[3] Each place of worship, furthermore, is a cluster of smaller places, inanimate and animate, including the objects encountered there (from icons and symbols to flowers and ephemera), the practising and believing bodies that congregate and pass through, and the interactions and moments—ritual and ordinary—that occur therein. Some of these objects, bodies (their postures and practices), and events are specific to buildings dedicated to worship, whilst others may find expression in other sacralised sites and settings or, indeed, in apparently profane ones.[4] Natural sites associated with pilgrimage, or temporary sacred spaces transformed by religious processions, the enactment of ritual practices, and mass prayer, chanting or singing are examples of the spilling out of conventional religion—via bodies, events and objects—into public spaces beyond the temple. And what of private spaces? Religious individuals and families often sacralise spaces within their homes through the construction of shrines, altars, prayer or meditation rooms. They may invite fellow adherents to participate in study circles or ritual occasions, whether regular or in celebration of the events of the life-cycle or festive calendar. Religious icons, images, symbols, pictures, and ritual implements may be either part of the furniture or displayed during acts of worship. The body, furthermore, may be transformed according to the conventions and requirements of the religious community, either in terms of dress (e.g. by donning a cross, turban, *hijab*, or sandalwood neckbeads), in conformity

---

3.   This is a clear example of what the philosopher Hilary Lawson means by 'alternative closures'. He gives the example of a car (at once a vehicle, a machine, an object of desire, a shiny surface, a tradeable object etc.). The possible alternative closures of 'a place of worship' are numerous (*Closure*, p. 11).

4.   For a discussion of 'sacred', 'profane', and the process of 'sacralisation', see Chapters 4 and 9.

with a religious regime (e.g. Islamic *salat* or prayer, Hindu *puja* or worship), or at times of fasting and feasting.

The insertion of conventional religions into apparently profane spaces may be witnessed through missionary activities, such as the mailing of religious leaflets through doors, the displaying of posters on billboards, advertising in shops, broadcasting of views, and launching of Internet sites. Further examples might include the presence of religious representatives in non-religious institutions or at secular events, such as London's Millennium Dome or the millennium celebrations held in other Western cities, or at civic occasions. Such representatives may be branded according to their tradition, through their dress, symbols of the faith, insistence on religious requirements, enactment of ritual, or distribution of literature, food, candles etc. Conventional religions may also be apparent in the wider society through cultural and educational representations. They are often depicted in literature, film, and on television, not always respectfully. They make an appearance in pedagogical materials used in the teaching of religion, ethics, development, cultural and political history. These media are mental spaces in and of themselves, but the places — physical and social — where they are consumed, such as schools and libraries, are also worthy of investigation in terms of the outreach and presentation of conventional religions.

I hope it is obvious from this short account that religions in their conventional forms are active in a variety of places, sacred and profane, public and private. They inhabit spaces, but also transform and create them. This is something to which I shall return later in the book. This variety has the potential to stimulate a great many fascinating spatial investigations. It has already led to several significant studies to which I shall refer in the next chapter. Before that, however, I wish to return to my common-sense starting point — of conventional religion — and raise some questions about its definitional adequacy for a study of this kind.

A Game of Two Halves? Evaluating the Shifting Fortunes of the 'Religious' and the 'Secular'

In the Introduction, I referred to my interest in investigating apparently non-religious places as well as ostensibly religious ones, and everyday spaces as well as spaces set apart or special. I have shown above — albeit briefly — how such places can sometimes be inhabited by conventional religions, even transformed or sacralised by them. However, such apparently 'non-religious' and everyday spaces are also claimed as 'secular', as the domain of 'culture' or 'science' as opposed to religion. In fact, that is the way in which they are almost invariably represented in the West. It is commonly thought that if spaces are not formally religious, they must be secular. Take, for example, the nation state. Irrespective of the historical role, or even established role (in the case of Britain) of religion in the state, or the place of religion in its constitution or laws, it is generally seen as secular. This is true also for the public arenas of education and health, despite any foundational roles played by religious institutions, or current interventions.[5] According to the commonly aired view of secularisation, then, religious and secular roles and institutions are differentiated:

> [R]ationalization has cost religion its claims to govern society as a whole, and it finds itself forced back into a specialized social sphere, with the task of producing and treating symbolic assets, appropriate to religious institutions, which are designated for the purpose. In this specially appointed sphere, religion wears a compact, organized, formalized appearance.[6]

Another way in which religion is commonly differentiated from other domains is in being separated from the political sphere and confined to the private. As Richard King has suggested, 'privatized religion becomes both clearly defined and securely contained by excluding it from the public realm of politics'.[7] As a researcher of religion who is interested in looking at the operation of 'religion' in space, how am I to respond to this? Should I concede the retreat of 'religion' and settle for examining it spatially within private lives and ostensibly religious organisations?

In order to raise the possibilities open to me in formulating 'religion' for this study, I must first examine the position of the 'religious' and the 'secular' in late-modernity, how current ideas about them arose, and how they are located ideologically within the study of religions and beyond.

5.   See the forthcoming publications by Kim Knott and Myfanwy Franks from the research project 'Locating Religion in the Fabric of the Secular: An Experiment in Two Public Sector Organisations (a School and Health Centre)', May 2004–April 2005, supported by an Innovation Award from the Arts and Humanities Research Board. We may note that, within higher education, there have been moves not only to secularise institutions but also disciplines, including the study of religions itself, first by distinguishing the 'science of religion' from 'theology'—now expressed in the institutional structures of higher education in the United States and many European countries—and latterly by dissolving discourse about 'religion' into discourse about 'culture' or 'social science'. For a discussion of the early history of this process, see Eric Sharpe, *Comparative Religion: A History* (London: Gerald Duckworth, 1975); for an account of contemporary debates, see Russell T. McCutcheon, *Manufacturing Religion: The Discourse on Sui Generis Religion and the Politics of Nostalgia* (New York and Oxford: Oxford University Press, 1997), and *The Discipline of Religion: Structure, Meaning, Rhetoric* (London and New York: Routledge, 2003), and Timothy Fitzgerald, *The Ideology of Religious Studies* (New York and Oxford: Oxford University Press, 2000).

6.   Hervieu-Léger, *Religion as a Chain of Memory*, pp. 108-109.

7.   Richard King, *Orientalism and Religion: Postcolonial Theory, India and 'The Mystic East'* (London and New York: Routledge, 1999), p. 11.

As a complex modern power relationship, the 'religious' and the 'secular' together constitute what Foucault has called,

> ...*in potentia*, a strategy of struggle, in which the two forces are not super-imposed, do not lose their specific nature, or do not finally become confused. Each constitutes for the other a kind of permanent limit, a point of possible reversal.[8]

It is crucial then to acknowledge the force relations at work both in the engagement between the 'religious' and the 'secular' in the socio-political domain, and within any intellectual account of it.[9] Writing of Foucault on religion, Jeremy Carrette has made the importance of this very clear:

> Religion for Foucault was always part of a set of force relations and discursive practices which order human life...a reading that does not position religion in some separate realm but inside a political struggle of knowledge-power. In this way Foucault provides a radical framework to question the politics of all religious and theological thinking. He brings religion back into history and back into the immanent struggle of identity and subjectivity.[10]

It follows that religious (and secular) discourse and practice, and discourse *about* 'religion' (and the 'secular') is similarly implicated in this struggle. Impassioned debates within the academy, whether about secu-larisation or regarding the meaning of 'religion' or the 'sacred' and methodologies for their study, are clear evidence that a 'political struggle of knowledge-power' is in process.[11] The presence of such force relations should be borne in mind in what follows.

Scholars who have written about the emerging relationship between the 'religious' and 'secular' have dealt generally with historical conditions or with discourse about the two.[12] Those who have looked back in order

8.   Michel Foucault, 'The Subject and Power', in Hubert L. Dreyfus and Paul Rabinow (eds.), *Michel Foucault: Beyond Structuralism and Hermeneutics* (Chicago: University of Chicago Press, 2nd edn, 1983), pp. 208-26 (225) (cited in Bell, *Ritual Theory, Ritual Practice*, p. 201.)

9.   The reader will perhaps be better placed than I to sense any unacknowledged ideological tendencies on my own part (either through bias, oversight, or negligence). My own stance will be discussed later in the chapter.

10.   Jeremy R. Carrette (ed.), *Religion and Culture: Michel Foucault* (New York: Rout-ledge, 1999), p. 32.

11.   See R. King, *Orientalism and Religion*, pp. 40-53, for a consideration of related issues.

12.   It is noteworthy that most of these scholars focus on explaining the changing nature of 'religion' and the process of 'secularisation' rather than on defining the 'secu-lar'. As a reader one is left to assume the meaning of the 'secular' from accounts about industrialisation, cultural change in modernity, social differentiation, and privatisa-tion. The exception, whose approach to the secular will be discussed below, is the philosopher Charles Taylor.

to gain a perspective on the salience of religion (secularisation debaters) have asked how religious people were in the past and have sought answers in historical evidence such as church rolls and legal documents. Those who have either focused on 'religion' as an object of study, or on theorising it as a concept, have looked back to earlier attempts to objectify it, to distinguish it from other domains (such as 'society' and the 'sacred') and other related concepts (such as 'faith'), and to differentiate its forms (e.g. 'world religions', 'traditional religions', 'new religions'). It is the second of these tasks — that of theorising religion — that is relevant here. It is not necessary for me to undertake the archaeological work required to historicise the relationship between the religious and secular, as that has been done by other scholars. I shall allude to their work rather than reproducing it in detail, as my aim here is to examine the current problem and the force relations within it, rather than to describe the historical situation in full.

The terms 'religious' and 'secular' have been intertwined in Western thought. According to King, in a 'pagan' Roman context, *religio* bore a relation to *traditio*, to the teachings and rituals associated with one's ancestors.[13] Early Christians, however, sought to distinguish the two, and to identify *religio* with 'the worship of the true' as opposed to the false,[14] with theistic belief and an exclusive path, and with 'a fundamental dualism between the human world and the transcendent world of the divine'.[15] In the mediaeval period, the related English term 'religious' came to refer to those who pursued a monastic life, with 'secular' (from the Latin *saeculum*) referring to those working within the world, to ordinary parish clergy and those in higher eccesiastical positions.[16] It was also used to refer to ordinary or profane time, as opposed to God's time or spiritual time.[17] Commenting on the difference inherent in these meanings, Taylor suggests,

> The existence of these oppositions reflected something fundamental about Christendom, a requirement of distance, of non-coincidence between the Church and the world. ...but more fundamentally, the need for distance, for a less than full embedding in the secular, was understood as essential to the vocation of the Church.[18]

13. R. King, *Orientalism and Religion*, pp. 35-36.
14. R. King, *Orientalism and Religion*, p. 36 (quoting Lactantius).
15. R. King, *Orientalism and Religion*, p. 37.
16. Asad, *Genealogies of Religion*, p. 39; Charles Taylor, 'Modes of Secularism', in Rajeev Bhargava (ed.), *Secularism and Its Critics* (New Delhi: Oxford University Press, 1998), pp. 31-53 (32).
17. Taylor, 'Modes of Secularism', p. 32; Ruth Abbey, *Charles Taylor* (Teddington: Acumen, 2000), pp. 204-205.
18. Taylor, 'Modes of Secularism', p. 32. Also Asad, *Genealogies of Religion*, p. 39.

This distance, however, did not constitute a formal separation in the modern sense, ' "religion"…as some *separate* sphere, apart from the "secular" order, did not exist'.[19]

It is in this need to distinguish otherworldly affairs from those of the worldly order that the relationship between the 'religious' and the 'secular' arises, bringing with it the possibility of disagreement, tension, and — later — opposition regarding the boundary between the two.[20] A further differentiation, this time of relevance to the ideological dichotomy, 'religion' and 'secularism', came about during the Western Enlightenment.

The historical emergence of the concept 'religion', meaning a system of belief and practice comparable to other such systems, has been charted by several scholars, including Wilfred Cantwell Smith, Peter Harrison, and John Bossy.[21] They show the way in which the term *religio* was used during the Reformation by Zwingli and Calvin to distinguish true piety from false superstition, thus to signal a plurality of religious responses.[22] This separation led, in the work of Bodin, Bacon, Cherbury, Grotius, Browne, and Hobbes, to the term being used to signal a plurality of different religions, of which the former wrote, 'all are refuted by all'.[23] This notion was central to the rise of Western secularisms as it led to the perceived need of nation states to manage religious differences, whether

19. John D. Caputo, *On Religion* (London and New York: Routledge, 2001), p. 43. See also Jorge Arditi, *A Geneaology of Manners: Transformations of Social Relations in France and England from the Fourteenth to the Eighteenth Century* (Chicago and London: University of Chicago Press, 1998): 'the lines separating religion from many spheres of practice whose boundaries today we take for granted did not exist, and therefore the fusion between the religious and those other spheres was complete' (p. 29).

20. See Alan Gilbert, *The Making of Post-Christian Britain* (London and New York: Longman, 1980), Chapter 2, 'Secularization and Western Culture'. It should be noted, however, that the differentiation of the two into separate spheres was no doubt exacerbated by a growing atheistic tendency in the West. See Rodney Stark, 'Atheism, Faith, and the Social Scientific Study of Religion', *Journal of Contemporary Religion* 14.1 (1999), pp. 41-62.

21. Wilfred Cantwell Smith, *The Meaning and End of Religion* (London: SPCK, 1978); Peter Harrison, *'Religion' and the Religions in the English Enlightenment* (Cambridge: Cambridge University Press, 1990); John Bossy, 'Some Elementary Forms of Durkheim', *Past and Present* 95 (1982), pp. 3-18; see also Robert Jackson, *Religious Education: An Interpretive Approach* (London: Hodder & Stoughton, 1997), Chapter 3, 'The Representation of Religions', for a summary of W.C. Smith's account.

22. This distinction and resultant plurality built on the early Roman uses of the term *religio*, as discussed by R. King, *Orientalism and Religion*, pp. 35-37.

23. Stark, 'Atheism, Faith, and the Social Scientific Study of Religion', p. 44. See also W.C. Smith, *The Meaning and End of Religion*, pp. 37-40, and Bossy, 'Some Elementary Forms', pp. 6-7.

intra-religious (different branches of Christianity) or inter-religious.[24] Taylor suggests that, in the seventeenth century, the two most favoured understandings of secularism could be described as 'the common ground strategy' and the 'independent political ethic'.[25] The first aimed 'to establish a certain ethic of peaceful co-existence and political order...which, while still theistic, even Christian, was based on those doctrines which were common to all Christian sects, or even to all theists'.[26] The second, associated with Grotius, 'allows us to abstract from our religious beliefs altogether' and to deduce 'certain exceptionless norms' on the basis of an examination of the human condition.[27] The first presupposed the possibility of convergence between a plurality of different religious or moral positions; the second developed a humanist response predicated upon the idea that an independent source of values could be identified. The response to intra- and inter-religious differences in the sixteenth and seventeenth centuries required scholars to consider the implications for political morality and church–state relations. It was Hobbes in *Leviathan* who developed the most outspoken early modern example of the independent ethic,[28] in which religion in general, and 'Christian religion' in particular, was located in the private sphere, the realm of conscience, apart from the public sphere of the state.

Both Taylor and Gilbert examine the intellectual changes occurring in Europe and America which led to the emergence of a predominantly secular society and culture.[29] Although each considers the matter from an historical perspective, their purposes differ. Taylor is concerned with the nature of secularity and Gilbert with the secularisation of society. The former examines the adequacy of explanations concerning the conditions

24. See Rajeev Bhargava, 'Introduction', in *idem* (ed.), *Secularism and Its Critics*, pp. 1-28, and Taylor, 'Modes of Secularism', on the impulse to secularism in different nation states.

25. Taylor, 'Modes of Secularism', p. 33.

26. Taylor, 'Modes of Secularism', p. 33.

27. Taylor, 'Modes of Secularism', p. 33. See also W.C. Smith on Grotius (de Groot) in *The Meaning and End of Religion*, p. 39.

28. Thomas Hobbes, *Leviathan* (Glasgow: Collins/Fontana, 1962 [first published 1651]). See also Taylor, 'Modes of Secularism', pp. 34-35; Bossy, 'Some Elementary Forms', p. 7; Stark, 'Atheism, Faith, and the Social Scientific Study of Religion', pp. 41-42.

29. Charles Taylor, *Varieties of Religion Today: William James Revisited* (Cambridge MA, and London: Harvard University Press, 2002), pp. 63-107; Abbey, *Charles Taylor*, pp. 197-209; Gilbert, *The Making of Post-Christian Britain*, Chapter 2, 'Secularization and Western Culture'. See also Caputo's playful account of Enlightenment secularisation, in Chapter 2, 'How the Secular World became Post-Secular' (*On Religion*, pp. 45-49); and Stark, 'Atheism, Faith, and the Social Scientific Study of Religion', pp. 42-53.

and processes involved in producing the secular. He rejects the argument that, just because church attendance is falling, religion must be declining, preferring the view that the secular age constitutes a plurality of beliefs, including those that are religious and spiritual. He gives only limited credence to the view that secularisation involves the steady retreat of religion from the public domain, as, in his opinion, 'rather than the complete eradication of God from public life, what we have seen is more a change in his mode of involvement'.[30] According to Taylor, religious beliefs are problematised in secular modernity because they co-exist with other beliefs, both religious and non-religious, and are wrought with doubt and instability.[31] Despite retaining a voice in this plural context, theism is nevertheless marginalised, and 'exclusive humanism' — with its focus on human flourishing without reference to the transcendent — is to the fore.[32] Preferring to explain secularity, not in relation to 'loss', but in terms of changing beliefs and their impact on 'the social imaginary', Taylor develops a Durkheimian typology to account for the apparent historical transition from a dispensation in which belief is informed and legitimised by the church, through its linkage with the state, national identity and civil society, to a focus and dependence in late-modernity on the authenticity of the individual's own experience, on 'expressive individualism'.[33] Taylor is clear that such changes do not constitute a straightforward linear development from belief to unbelief, a point to which we shall return shortly.

Following his discussion of the rise of Renaissance humanism and scientific thought and practice, and the this-worldly turn of the Protestant Reformation, Gilbert suggests that, by the early eighteenth century, 'while it remained *dominant*, the Christian worldview was no longer *normative*'.[34]

30. Charles Taylor from his Foreword to M. Gauchet, *The Disenchantment of the World: A Political History of Religion* (Princeton: Princeton University Press, 1997), quoted in Abbey, *Charles Taylor*, p. 197.

31. Taylor, 'Modes of Secularism', 1998.

32. Abbey, *Charles Taylor*, p. 199.

33. Abbey, *Charles Taylor*, pp. 201-202; Charles Taylor, *Sources of the Self: The Making of Modern Identity* (Cambridge: Cambridge University Press, 1989), p. 497; *idem*, *Varieties of Religion Today*, pp. 75-107, in which he discusses three ideal types of 'Durkheimian dispensation': paleo-Durkheimian, neo-Durkheimian, and post-Durkheimian. I accept that there is some operational value in distinguishing between these three types of dispensation, but find Taylor's tendency to conflate religion and the sacred unhelpful (not that Durkheim himself was always rigorous in articulating their difference). Taylor's principal concern in characterising these dispensations is in distinguishing changes in 'the imagined place of the sacred' (p. 93), whether in the church, the state, or the individual.

34. Gilbert, *The Making of Post-Christian Britain*, p. 36 (his italics). See also Wouter Hanegraaff, 'New Age Spiritualities as Secular Religion: A Historian's Perspective',

Certainly among the intelligensia a secular humanist outlook had primacy of place, especially in England where irreligion was given social and political respectability.[35] And there it might have stayed, suggests Gilbert, but for industrialisation, the process that—in Britain, at least—enabled the dissemination of secular culture and the secular transformation of society.[36] He cites the rise of a popular secularist tradition emerging in the working-class enthusiasm for Tom Paine's *Age of Reason* (1794), though acknowledges that such anti-religious fervour was less problematic for the churches in the long run than the more widespread 'religious ignorance and apathy'.[37] Nevertheless, a secularist, anti-religious campaign continued to be waged throughout the nineteenth and twentieth centuries by a minority of individual commentators and pressure groups (such as the Rationalist Press Association, the British Humanist Association, and the Secular Society).[38]

This political struggle over the allegiance of 'man' and nature, charted and argued over in newspapers and tracts, was also prevalent in the academy.[39] Durkheim's account of the consequences of modernity for religion, for example, was fiercely countered by his erstwhile colleague Gaston Richard in the 1920s. In his doctoral thesis (published in 1893) on the division of labour, Durkheim had written,

> ...If there is one truth that history teaches us beyond doubt, it is that religion tends to embrace a smaller and smaller sector of social life. Originally, it pervades everything; everything social is religious. The two words are synonymous. Then political, economic, scientific functions gradually free themselves from religious control, establish themselves separately and take on a more and more openly temporal character. God, if one may express

Social Compass 46.2 (1999), pp. 145-60: 'the Christian religion…lost its central position as the foundational collective symbolism of western culture' (p. 151).

35. Stark cites observations by Voltaire and Montesquieu to this effect ('Atheism, Faith, and the Social Scientific Study of Religion', p. 42). Hugh McLeod discusses the widespread working class disaffection with religion across Europe in *Religion and the People of Western Europe 1789–1989* (Oxford and New York: Oxford University Press, 2nd edn, 1997), pp. 84-85, 119.

36. See also McLeod, *Religion and the People of Western Europe*, p. 119.

37. McLeod, *Religion and the People of Western Europe*, p. 55. It is this indifference that proves central to debates about secularisation, rather than organised anti-religious activity. See Steve Bruce, *God is Dead: Secularization in the West* (Oxford and Malden, MA: Basil Blackwell, 2002).

38. Gilbert, *The Making of Post-Christian Britain*, p. 56; McLeod, *Religion and the People of Western Europe*, p. 119; Susan Budd, *Varieties of Unbelief: Atheists and Agnostics in English Society, 1850–1960* (London: Heinemann, 1977).

39. See Stark, 'Atheism, Faith, and the Social Scientific Study of Religion', for a discussion of religious and atheist views within the developing discourses of anthropology, sociology, and psychology.

the matter this way, was at first present in all human relations, but progressively withdraws from them; he abandons the world to men and their disputes.[40]

He described as 'temporal' those activities no longer associated with religion, noting the processes of functional differentiation and public religious decline (secularisation), ending with a statement of the modernist problem, God's abandonment of the world, or put conversely — as Zygmunt Bauman does — Western society's determination to do without God.[41] With some vitriol, however, he was accused, along with other scholars of *sociologie religieuse,* of dogmatic atheism. Gaston Richard, in 1923, penned an article on the incompatibility of sociology of religion 'with Christian faith…even with philosophical theism, and indeed with any belief that recognises, hypothetically at least, a divine personality'.[42] He criticised Durkheim for assuming a regressivist view of the role of religion in history, and of reducing religion to the social.[43] The individual, mystical, and transcendental aspects of religion were ignored.[44]

This is one example of the way in which the matter of the social location of religion — vis-à-vis the secular — and its modern fate were contested within sociological circles well before the emergence of the late-twentieth-century secularisation debate. Gaston Richard's ostensible concern was not, in fact, the atheism of his fellows so much as their ideological power (within public education).[45] What is clear then is that the political struggles in Europe over 'religion', 'the religious', and the 'secular' occurred not only between the churches and the state (or its representatives), but

40.   From *De la division du travail social* by Émile Durkheim, in Anthony Giddens (ed.), *Émile Durkheim: Selected Writings* (trans. Anthony Giddens; Cambridge: Cambridge University Press, 1972), p. 245. This should not be taken as a simple summary of Durkheim's understanding of the religious function as a whole or even in this early work. It is quoted here to illustrate, along with Gaston Richard's response (see below), an argument about the nature and reach of religion in an apparently secular age. However, see Stark ('Atheism, Faith, and the Social Scientific Study of Religion', pp. 46-47) on Durkheim's view of the irrationality of religion.

41.   Zygmunt Bauman, 'Postmodern Religion?', in Paul Heelas (ed.), with David Martin and Paul Morris, *Religion, Modernity, and Postmodernity* (Oxford: Basil Blackwell, 1998), pp. 55-78 (60) ('Modernity, or doing without God').

42.   Gaston Richard, 'L'Athéisme dogmatique en sociologie religieuse', *Revue d'histoire et de philosophie religieuse* (originally published 1923), translated by Jacqueline Redding and W.S.F. Pickering as 'Dogmatic Atheism in the Sociology of Religion', in W.S.F. Pickering (ed.), *Durkheim on Religion: A Selection of Readings with Bibliographies and Introductory Remarks* (London and Boston: Routledge & Kegan Paul, 1975), pp. 228-76 (229).

43.   Richard, 'Dogmatic Atheism, p. 236.

44.   W.S.F. Pickering, 'A Note on the Life of Gaston Richard and Certain Aspects of his Work', in Pickering (ed.), *Durkheim on Religion*, pp. 343-59 (351).

45.   Richard, 'Dogmatic Atheism', pp. 228-29.

also between scholars who debated their modern meaning and salience.[46] As Russell McCutcheon has pointed out,

> the very taxons 'religion' and 'faith', along with...'secular' and 'sacred', are themselves constituted as a political force when used as part of either a folk or scholarly discourse, a force which brings people under a certain system of classification, credibility, and thus control.[47]

Turning now to the contemporary situation, we can see, on the one hand, that certain political and legal arrangements are in place in different Western nations that constitute the formal relationship between religion, the religions, and the secular state. The exact relationship differs from country to country.[48] On the other, however, there is an informal and shifting relationship between the 'religious' and the 'secular', constituted by multiple discourses and practices in the spheres of politics, the media, the academy, and among religious and secular organisations and spokespersons. Within this informal struggle there are several types of debaters — those who confess and fight for a particular side (anti-religious secularists and anti-secular religious adherents), and those who claim some kind of scholarly or commentarial role on the tension between the two. Across the two types are many who concede that a process of secularisation has taken place (though they differ in their views about its extent, speed, and nature),[49] and plenty who would describe Western societies as 'secular'. However, there are increasingly those, particularly within the second type, who question the secularisation thesis and claim either that late-modernity (or post-modernity) is a time of re-enchantment, or that secularisation was a more limited process than was previously assumed (i.e. confined to Western Europe, and more evident in the north than the south).[50] In addition to those who claim the ascendancy of

46. For examples of other late-nineteenth-century debates, see Bryan S. Turner, *Religion and Social Theory* (London: Heinemann Educational Books, 1983).

47. McCutcheon, *The Discipline of Religion*, p. 235. See McCutcheon, *Manufacturing Religion* and *The Discipline of Religion* for examples of contemporary scholarly struggles on the subject of religion.

48. See the articles on Western secularisms in Bhargava (ed.), *Secularism and Its Critics*, and in Peter W. Edge and Graham Harvey (eds.), *Law and Religion in Contemporary Society: Communities, Individualism and the State* (Aldershot: Ashgate, 2000). For America, see Daniel O. Conkle, 'Secular Fundamentalism, Religious Fundamentalism, and the Search for Truth in Contemporary America', *Journal of Law and Religion* 12.2 (1995–96), pp. 337-70; for Europe, see also Davie, *Religion in Modern Europe*, and 'From Obligation to Consumption: Patterns of Religion in Northern Europe at the Start of the 21st Century', in R. Friedl and M. Schneuwly Purdie (eds.), *L'Europe des Religions: Eléments d'analyse des champs religieux européens* (Bern: Peter Lang, 2004), pp. 95-114.

49. See Bruce, *God is Dead*, for a discussion and pro-secularisation stance.

50. See Davie, *Religion in Modern Europe*; David Lyon, *Jesus in Disneyland: Religion in Postmodern Times* (Cambridge: Polity, 2000); and Heelas (ed.), with Martin and Morris, *Religion, Modernity, and Postmodernity*, for various views.

either the religious *or* the secular, there are commentators who postulate the political and moral *equivalence* of those who confess either a religious or secularist position.[51] The discussion about the territories of the 'religious' and the 'secular', the boundary between them, and their salience and reach continues.

It is in the nature of scholarship that what was once trumpeted is later critiqued, the two being followed by a third way, sometimes seeing the good in both. It is certainly possible to think of discourse about the 'religious' and the 'secular' dialectically, though it would be difficult to position such discourse with any historical accuracy:

Religious confessions	⇒	Secular confessions	⇒	Post-secular confessions

We might think of religious (Christian) confessions as having been broadly in the ascendancy in the West until the Enlightenment, then continuing in opposition and increasingly relegated to the private sphere. The secular confession in the nineteenth and twentieth centuries became the dominant order—in Western Europe, at least—but, with the rise of postmodern critiques, is under growing threat.

Although Gilbert does not define the 'secular' as such, he does offer us a way of distinguishing between 'secular' and 'religious' *modes*:

> In the 'secular' mode the world is conceived in terms of natural causation, interpreted in a matter-of-fact, objective way, and regarded as manipulable through physical agencies, human institutions and empirical logic. But viewed in 'religious' terms it remains a place of mystery, caught up in the supernatural order which is extra-empirical, arbitrary and personal, and which is open to human influence and manipulation only—if at all— through ritual, magic or religion. Obviously these are merely contrast-concepts. No individual worldview or cultural system ever has been entirely 'religious' or entirely 'secular' in these terms.[52]

His contrastive approach is useful for distinguishing the first two aspects of a dialectical process, but as he suggests, the 'religious' and the 'secular' are not either/or. As we saw in the brief account of their history and beliefs, they are within the same field and the boundary between them is not solid and defensible. Taylor, in discussing belief and unbelief, did not adopt 'a simple binary opposition' between the two, but instead saw a profusion of different positions.[53] The third aspect produced by the dialectic of the religious and the secular, the post-secular confession, is important here: the contemporary examples which demonstrate it are attempts to come to terms with *both* 'religious' and 'secular' in varying

51. Conkle, 'Secular Fundamentalism, Religious Fundamentalism'.
52. Gilbert, *The Making of Post-Christian Britain*, p. 9.
53. Abbey, *Charles Taylor*, pp. 209-10.

ways for the current age.[54] Ruth Abbey, in her account of Taylor's work, has suggested that he too envisages three aspects to the contemporary scene which he sees as 'triangulated between exclusive humanism, the immanent counter-Enlightenment and a capacious theism, one that entertains a variety of ways of believing in God and practising spirituality'.[55] The 'immanent counter-Enlightenment' position 'remains within the naturalist vista of humanism, repudiating any interest in theism and the transcendent realm', but nevertheless challenges an 'exclusive humanism' by stressing the darker side of human nature.[56] This critical, postmodern stance maps roughly onto my third confession. However, we should not be drawn into seeing the dialectic as composed of historically progressive stages—that itself would be a modernist concession—for the history of the struggle over the 'religious' and the 'secular' since the Enlightenment has simultaneously contained examples of various types of confession.[57] I shall return to the third confession shortly, after considering the postmodern critique that provides the context for such post-secular confessions.

Attempting to explain the phenomenon of the secular and its attendant ideology in contemporary Western Europe, Peter Berger posits as one cause a like-minded intellectual elite (the late-modern inheritors of Enlightenment humanism):

> [T]here is a thin but very influential stratum of intellectuals—broadly defined as people with Western-style higher education, especially in the humanities and social sciences. They constitute a secular *internationale*, whose members can be encountered in every country… I cannot here go into the question of why this kind of education has secularizing effects (I suspect that it is mainly because of the corrosive insight into the relativity of beliefs and values). But I would point out that this peculiar *internationale* helps to explain the continuing plausibility of secularization theory among many Western intellectuals: when they travel to, say, Istanbul, Jerusalem or New Delhi, they almost exclusively meet with other intellectuals—that is, people much like themselves—and they can then jump to the conclusion that this faculty club faithfully reflects the cultural situation outside—a fatal mistake indeed![58]

---

54. See Chapter 7.

55. Abbey, *Charles Taylor*, p. 210. See also Taylor on three Durkheimian dispensations in *Varieties of Religion Today*.

56. Abbey, *Charles Taylor*, p. 210.

57. The writings of Nietzsche and Kierkegaard could be said to demonstrate earlier post-secular or counter-Enlightenment stances. They were written at a time when avowedly secularist literature was being published, as well as religiously confessional and expository material.

58. Peter Berger, 'Secularization and De-Secularization', in Linda Woodhead, Paul Fletcher, Hiroko Kawanami and David Smith (eds.), *Religions in the Modern World* (London: Routledge, 2002), pp. 293-94 (my italics). This view is shared by John D.

Although Berger's remarks do not constitute a reasoned argument so much as an observation on the continuing, widespread popularity of a thesis that may be local (Western European) in character rather than global, they are nevertheless interesting. He suggests that the common secular beliefs shared by this elite arise from an education (in humanities and the social sciences) which—though he doesn't say so—would have been underpinned by an awareness of the views of certain key nine-teenth- and twentieth-century thinkers, such as Marx, Comte, Nietzsche, Durkheim, Darwin, Freud, Weber, and Sartre, views that, though they differ, saw religious beliefs, practices, and institutions as increasingly marginal or irrelevant, and of declining significance in a modern, rational world.[59] Perhaps Gaston Richard had reason to be fearful of the power of 'dogmatic atheism' within the public education system![60] However, what is also evident is that in recent years there has been some dissatisfaction with these views. John D. Caputo, accounting for what appears to be a post-secular turn, has suggested that, increasingly, a weariness among intellectuals with the verities of modernism has led 'to a break within their own ranks on the hot topic of religion, where even otherwise "secular" intellectuals have become suspicious of the Enlightenment suspicion of religion'.[61] Interestingly, Berger calls this elite an *'internationale'*, and Caputo refers to its 'ranks', both suggesting a more formal grouping than in fact exists, but thereby indicating the existence of shared beliefs and a common discipline.[62] Carrette refers to some of these beliefs—in so far as they pertain to religion—in his call for a renewal of scholarly interest in religion.

> Religion needs to be rediscovered outside the superstitions, misconceptions and illusions through which 'secular' academics have so far dismissed the subject. We need to find religion in the very fabric of the 'secular'—in the absence.[63]

Caputo who writes that 'religion was reported missing mostly by the intellectuals; no one outside the academy thought it had gone anywhere at all' (Caputo, *On Religion*, p. 66).

59.   Perhaps ironically, it is some of these same scholars, with other later theorists, who provided the theoretical insights that enabled the postmodern critique of modern-ism to gain ground.

60.   Richard King, in his discussion about the emergence of the secular discipline of religious studies, refers to the 'irreligious dogmatism of secular reductionism' and its institutionalisation in the Western academy, *Orientalism and Religion*, pp. 44-52 (49).

61.   Caputo, *On Religion*, p. 37.

62.   This idea is also expressed by Richard Webster who refers to 'the troops of secularism', picking up on Salman Rushdie's reference in *The Satanic Verses* to the battle lines between the religious and the secular. Richard Webster, *A Brief History of Blasphemy: Liberalism, Censorship and 'The Satanic Verses'* (Southwold: Orwell Press, 1990), p. 55.

63.   Carrette, *Foucault on Religion*, p. 152.

If the state, then, with the help of political philosophers and the churches themselves, relegated religion from the public to the private realm, it was secular scholars and commentators who relegated it to the intellectual margins by dismissing it as superstition, misconception, and illusion.

Carrette's call, though, is not just for religion to be put back on the intellectual agenda, but for it to be found 'in the very fabric of the secular'. That it is there to be found is a point made by Richard Webster in his account of the history of blasphemy in Britain when he reminds us of the 'profound internalisation of the religious consciousness which lies at the heart of our own continuing cultural revolution'.[64] Referring to the quasi-religious zeal of Salman Rushdie and his liberal supporters in the heat of the controversy surrounding the publication of *The Satanic Verses*, but more importantly to the 'idealisation of the writer's conscience as the ultimate authority on moral questions', Webster saw the cultural clash not as one between religious authoritarianism and freedom, but between 'two factions of the same religious tradition — the Judaeo-Christian tradition to which, ultimately, Islam itself belongs'.[65] The secularist response to Muslim uproar following the publication of the book represented 'liberalism's holy war' against Islam, a war in which the novel had sacred status and the freedom of the individual conscience was the right to be upheld.

That the 'religious' is held somehow within the 'secular' is an idea also explored within the 'post-secular confessions' I mentioned earlier when discussing the dialectical relationship between the two. 'Post-secular' should not be taken to mean anti-secular or a negation of the secular, but a form of confession or analysis which is only possible as a consequence of secularism — but within its context — and with the benefit of a knowledge of its contours. Two exponents of the 'post-secular' position are Don Cupitt and Richard K. Fenn.

Don Cupitt, who in Britain was perhaps the first to have his name associated with post-Christianity through his 1980s books *Taking Leave of God* and *Sea of Faith*, distinguishes the preservation of traditional religion in modernity — as values, limited to the private sphere, conceived as personal faith, and countercultural — from the possibility of a novel religion geared to the present postmodern age. This new faith would recognise 'that *we made it all up*' (our languages, religions, values etc.) and that it is legitimate to continue to do so in the light of our current experience: 'a new way of feeling and living our own relationship to the world of our common experience'.[66] Richard K. Fenn, an American sociologist of

---

64. Webster, *A Brief History of Blasphemy*, p. 57.
65. Webster, *A Brief History of Blasphemy*, pp. 57, 59.
66. Don Cupitt, *After God: The Future of Religion* (London: Phoenix Orion, 1997), pp. 126-28 (Cupitt's italics).

religion,[67] like Cupitt, wishes to see a break between the religions of the past and a way of integrity for the secular present and future. 'A truly secular society', he says, 'is one in which these cultural fictions are understood to be just that: not merely illusions with the capacity to motivate or even captivate, but ideas and beliefs that are better understood than venerated'.[68]

But there is nothing to fear from living in such a society, one that is '*not bound together by sacred memories and beliefs, by sacred institutions and practices, or by a religious culture that seeks to collect the various manifestations of the sacred into a single, coherent order'.*[69] Furthermore, according to Fenn, there is no less access to the sacred in a truly secular society than in a religious one.[70] His plea is, in fact, for society to embrace the secular with openness, and discover the sacred within it, rather than to confine it or reduce to manageable proportions, to idolise it, either out of fear or the desire to control or limit it. Indeed, 'to become secular is… to open oneself and one's society to a wide range of possibilities', to be open to the sacred.[71]

Given Fenn's penchant for the secular, am I right to cite his views as an example of the post-secular confession? Is Fenn in fact a *secularist*? Are both Cupitt and Fenn, in believing traditional religions to be out of place and time, anti-religious? How should we locate Cupitt's 'post-Christianity' and Fenn's 'religionless Christianity' in the field of 'the religious' and 'the secular'?[72] I would suggest that they are proponents of positions that benefit from an awareness and knowledge of religious confessions (particularly Christian) but that deem these to be unsuitable 'closures' for

67. But a sociologist in the intellectual tradition of 'religious sociology' or *sociologie religieuse*, that is, one who discusses and explores the possibility of the social religious or social sacred, rather than one who takes a more scientific stance on the study of religion/the sacred in society. As we shall see, however, Fenn's stance is not easily categorised as 'religious'.

68. Richard K. Fenn, *Beyond Idols: The Shape of a Secular Society* (Oxford: Oxford University Press, 2001), p. 23.

69. Fenn, *Beyond Idols*, p. 7 (my italics). Interestingly, the very things that Fenn suggests society should have no fear of, and must thus free itself from in order to participate fully in the 'secular', are those things which constitute the chain of memory that, according to Hervieu-Léger (*Religion as a Chain of Memory*), enable the 'religious' to continue (and that are endangered in late-modernity).

70. By 'Sacred' (with a capital 'S') Fenn means 'the world that lies alongside the one in which we ordinarily move, talk, imagine, and have what is left of our being' (*Beyond Idols*, p. 22); it is 'whatever lies behind the idols' (p. 45). He uses 'sacred' (with a small 's') to refer to society's attempts to *manage* the 'Sacred'.

71. Fenn, *Beyond Idols*, p. 5.

72. Fenn follows Bonhoeffer here. We might also include John D. Caputo's 'religion without religion' (*On Religion*, Chapter 5, 'On Religion – Without Religion').

late-modernity.[73] It is clear, however, that neither accepts in any straight-forward way those closures commonly associated with secular humanism that focus solely on the will, power, and needs of humanity at the expense of the sacred. Rather, they are postmodern and post-secular in their acknowledgment of the human hand in the construction of narratives, myths, and beliefs, in their embrace of plurality, choice, and risk, and in their return to the sacred. John D. Caputo, in his statement *On Religion* (2001), understands this *return* not as a simple imitation of an earlier position, but as a 'reiteration…for a post-secular time', an examination of 'an historical *how* not a transhistorical *what*'.[74]

These commentators are illustrative of the postmodern stance on 'the religious' and 'the secular'. As committed exponents of a post-secular perspective they necessarily find themselves embroiled in a struggle with those who hold other positions. They flesh out and argue their stances; they do not expect all their readers to agree with them as the field of the 'religious' and the 'secular' comprises multiple positions and viewpoints.[75] Apart from the obvious contenders—exponents of traditional religions or the openly secularist—a further challenge comes from those who question whether the 'religious', the 'sacred', or the 'spiritual' (a term with which I have yet to deal) can really be separated from religion/s. The attempt to do so is often criticised as trying to have the best of both worlds (e.g. the libertarian character of the secular and the experiential aspect of the religious) when real religion requires taking on the difficult bits—such as discipline and submission—not just those things that appeal to late-modern sensibilities.[76]

Where has this admittedly selective discussion of the 'religious' and the 'secular' got us? I have presented it in order to do two things: to show how the two are entangled in the same *field*, and how they are a matter of

---

73. Lawson, *Closure*.

74. Caputo, *On Religion*, pp. 131-32. In addition to Caputo himself, who, with Cupitt and Fenn, is an exemplar of the post-secular confession, there are those who contributed to his edited collection, *The Religious* (Malden, MA, and Oxford: Basil Blackwell, 2002). They have in common an interest in engaging with Continental philosophy in order to explore the postmodern religious. See also Phillip Blond (ed.), *Post-Secular Philosophy: Between Philosophy and Theology* (London and New York: Routledge, 1998).

75. That there are many post-secular perspectives is further evidenced by Blond (*Post-Secular Philosophy*), who presents a strong Christian realist critique of the limitations of the secular but is unequivocal about the need — in moving forward — to avoid 'the horrors of the sublime modern surrender to immanentism' and self-reference (pp. 54-55).

76. Tom W. Boyd, 'Is Spirituality Possible Without Religion? A Query for the Postmodern Era', in Ann W. Astell (ed.), *Divine Representations: Postmodernism and Spirituality* (New York: Paulist Press, 1994), pp. 83-101.

contention (of force relations) both outside and inside the academy.[77] Grace Jantzen aptly summarises this view:

> ...the religious/secular divide is a binary constitutive of modernity which cries out for radical questioning. Rather than seeing the secular and the religious as opposites, I suggest that they should be viewed as two sides of a coin, the coin itself being of peculiarly modern mint. Ever since the 'sacred canopy' of the mediaeval world was shattered, secularism and religion have often defined themselves over against one another; yet they are deeply implicated in each other in the discourses of modernity, especially obviously in the technologies of power surrounding gender, 'race', colonialism, and sexuality.[78]

I have suggested a dialectical relationship between what I have called religious confessions, secular confessions, and post-secular confessions as a way of locating the two sides of the coin within the same relational field. It is now left to me to show how this can be used to formulate the object to be investigated in a spatial analysis of religion, and to explain why it offers a better solution to the problem than would the adoption of a straightforward definition of religion.

Choosing an Approach to the 'Religious' and the 'Secular'

Earlier in the chapter I referred to the potential spaces of 'conventional religion', and implied that to use such a definition for this study would be to accept without question the commonly held view that religion inhabited a specialised social sphere and was in decline. I suggested that the complex, contested field of the 'religious' and the 'secular' deserved more careful scrutiny. Having looked at it in some detail, and become aware of the force relations that shape it, we may now examine various positions situated within this field, on the basis of which a spatial analysis of religion could be conducted. I have identified six positions (which may be further sub-divided), which fall into three pairs. Each of these will be characterised briefly, their limitations for the spatial location of religion discussed, and my own preference stated.

---

77. I have utilised Bourdieu's conception of a field of play for situating the relationship of power between different positions (Pierre Bourdieu and L. Wacquant, *An Invitation to Reflexive Sociology* [Cambridge: Polity, 1992], pp. 97-99). The notion of an 'epistemological field', which I have in mind here, is one used by Michel Foucault in the preface to *The Order of Things: An Archaeology of the Human Sciences* (London: Tavistock, 1970 [French edn 1966]), p. xxii.

78. Jantzen, *Becoming Divine*, p. 8. Although this quotation is positioned at the end of this discussion, in many ways it formed a starting point for thinking about it. I am in debt to Grace Jantzen and Jeremy Carrette, see below, for alerting me to the idea of the double-sided coin of the religious and the secular.

1.   Any attempt to locate 'religion', particularly in unconventional
        everyday spaces, demands that 'religion' be defined or at least
        demarcated. One way of doing this would be to adopt a commit-
        ted secularist perspective on religion that would understand the
        secular and the religious as mutually exclusive.[79] Such a stance
        would hold that the secular public sphere is an arena in which
        religion is absent and into which it should not trespass, except
        when invited in a formal representative capacity. This would
        result in a narrowing of the territory to be studied still further
        than in the conventional religion example that I presented earlier
        (in which it was accepted that conventional religions sometimes
        traversed the normal boundary between the religious and the
        secular without invitation, for instance in a spirit of mission or in
        order to claim space for public witness or public ritual). In terms
        of a study of religion and space, this would place severe limita-
        tions on the territory to be investigated. It would exclude study of
        all sites identified as 'secular' on the grounds that religion is
        generally absent from them. To take such a stance would be to
        fall in with the normative view of religious/secular differen-
        tiation. Certainly it would not invite me to consider Carrette's
        point, that 'we need to find religion in the very fabric of the
        secular'.[80]

2.   Alternatively, I could take an overtly religious view.[81] Although
        Western liberal Christians have themselves accepted a secularised
        account of modernity (but not a secular vision), exponents of
        religion do not generally give credence to secularism as such.[82]

79. In imagining 'a committed secularist view', I am distinguishing such a strong,
ideological viewpoint (probably also atheist) from a weak perspective which operates
pragmatically. There are, in fact, several types of secularism, see Bhargava, 'Introduction', p. 9.

80. Carrette, *Foucault on Religion*, p. 152.

81. There are a variety of committed religious positions on the issue of religious/
secular relations. They do not map neatly onto traditional doctrinal stances. Phenomenological approaches within the study of religions, whilst not being seen as religiously
confessional as such, are deemed to share with such stances an 'insider' perspective on
religion. See Russell T. McCutcheon (ed.), *The Insider/Outsider Problem in the Study of
Religion: A Reader* (London and New York: Cassell, 1999).

82. Peter L. Berger gives a short account of the acceptance of secularisation within
sociologie religieuse in Catholic Europe in the 1930s, in his article on 'Secularization and
De-Secularization', p. 292. Perhaps of greater significance, though, is the recognition
that the seeds of secularisation germinated *within* European Christianity and not
outside it, Christianity being 'its own gravedigger'; see Berger, *The Sacred Canopy*,
p. 129. See Gilbert, *The Making of Post-Christian Britain*; B.S. Turner, *Religion and Social
Theory*, p. 107; and Bryan Wilson, 'Secularization: The Inherited Model', in Philip E.

Secularisms are seen as a-theistic ideologies which hold that discourse and practice directed to the divine should be confined to the private domain and that eschew the potential public role of religions. This is an arrangement that most religious people tolerate in the West, but not one that they embrace warmly. Many of them feel besieged by secular beliefs and values, unheard by secular authorities, even ignored or discriminated against for being religious at all.[83] Under such circumstances, some religious extremists go as far as to deny secular claims for space, and assert or even use violence to enforce their views. They see public, so-called secular space as ripe for religious re-interpretation and repossession. At the other extreme, those of a liberal persuasion are accepting of the separation of the two spheres, and accommodate themselves within it. From the point of view of a study of space, a committed religious perspective—of whatever kind—has certain disadvantages, of reading the secular through a religious confessional lens, of prioritising religion over the secular, and also of asserting one religious perspective on space above others.

Both of these perspectives are outspokenly confessional, the first of ideological secularism, the second of a religious stance, whether anti-secularist or accommodationist. These perspectives affect the way everyday spaces are viewed, in terms both of how such spaces are defined and depicted, and of what opportunities they present for colonisation. Both are inadequate as a theoretical basis for this study, as they are oppositionally located vis-à-vis the other and to a greater or lesser extent ideologically reproduced with the other in mind.[84] They are already deeply implicated in the problem to be investigated, and, whilst it is unlikely that I shall fully avoid such 'implication' myself (see below), I prefer to start from a more disinterested, reflexive—if not neutral—position.

In addition to these there are a number of avowedly non-confessional perspectives on the 'religious' and the 'secular' (though I shall argue that they too are situated within the dialectical field of religious–secular relations). These also have implications for the study of spaces. Four of these

---

Hammond (ed.), *The Sacred in a Secular Age* (Berkeley: University of California Press, 1985), pp. 9-20 (17).

83. 'Ignorance and indifference towards religion were of widespread concern amongst research participants from all faith groups', states a report published by the British Government Home Office following a national study on religious discrimination. Paul Weller, Alice Feldman and Kingsley Purdam, *Religious Discrimination in England and Wales* (London: Home Office Research Study 220, 2001), p. vi.

84. A liberal religious stance might be the exception that proves the rule here.

will be considered briefly. The first pairing is predicated on the modern need to define the concept 'religion' in order to study it.[85] As Talal Asad has observed,

> It may be a happy accident that this effort of defining religion converges with the liberal demand in our time that it be kept quite separate from politics, law, and science—spaces in which varieties of power and reason articulate our distinctively modern life. This definition is at once part of a strategy (for secular liberals) of the confinement, and (for liberal Christians) of the defense of religion.[86]

A potential problem with this pairing then may well be that the perspectives that comprise it, though not formally confessional, have their very roots in the force relationships which, in modernity, confine or defend religion.

3.   The first takes a substantive view of religion, and defines it with reference to specific attributes of structure, belief or practice. We saw one such example earlier when we looked at religion in its conventional, institutional form. Others might focus upon belief in God or a supernatural force, or the collective practice of life cycle rites or sacraments. According to such views, religion generally does not contest or unsettle the notion of the secular, but is seen as existing in parallel, in the spaces allocated to it by secular authorities, both political and intellectual. A researcher adopting such a substantive and exclusive view of religion for an analysis of space would be limited to investigating those sites which bore out the adopted definition, of religion as 'conventional', 'official', as expressive of belief in God, or as the territory of 'World Religions'.

4.   Alternatively, a more inclusive functional view, that sees religion as having to do with ultimate problems or fundamental meanings, would be likely to breach what others see as the boundary between the religious and the secular because it envisages the

---

85. Definitions of religion arose in the modern period in the context of debates about the differentiation of the religious and the secular. They attempt to answer such questions as: What is the preserve of religion? Where is the boundary between the religious and the non-religious? What do religions do that other institutions and agencies do not? Scholars in the cognitive study of religion have distinguished between theories of religion and definitions of religion, arguing that only the former can provide a basis for scientific analysis. It is possible to theorise or conceptualise 'religion' whilst acknowledging that the real phenomena to which it refers are variable and contextual, and thus not clearly definable. Ilkka Pyysiäinen, 'Religion and the Counter-Intuitive', in Ilkka Pyysiäinen and Veikko Anttonen (eds.), *Current Approaches in the Cognitive Science of Religion* (London and New York: Continuum, 2002), pp. 110-32 (111).

86. Asad, *Genealogies of Religion*, p. 28.

category 'religious' as extending beyond conventional or official religions. Inclusivists hold differing views about the social functions of religion, and about which socio-cultural spaces, identities, and activities are 'religious', (whether invisibly, implicitly, or metaphorically 'religious'). The boundary between the religious and the secular shifts depending on the exact nature of the inclusive definition of religion offered—and it may even disappear altogether with the social being seen to be necessarily religious—but the space for religion is always both more expansive and more open than in the previous view.[87] The difficulty in analysing religion spatially from this perspective is in what, if anything, to eliminate as non-religious, and on what grounds to do so.

This definitional pairing, exclusive/substantive and inclusive/functional, 'constitute[s] a partial, yet radically limited, response to the question of the location of religion in modernity. Religion is nowhere, or else it is everywhere...'[88] Such positions owe their origins to modernist attempts to make sense of the changing face of religion in the West, and often bear the hallmarks of Christian beliefs and structures. It seems to be in the very nature of *defining* religion, however, that the definition selected, even if it was designed for a specific purpose, should bear the strain of being applicable beyond these circumstances, to other times, places, and religions, with the result that it may distort the very things it should make sense of. In order to avoid such misappropriation, we are better off confining ourselves to conceptualising 'religion' (or equivalent categories within other societies or cultures) within the terms of the time and place to be studied, and with due attention to the genealogy of the concept itself.[89]

In the work that follows, I am eager to treat 'religion' with a lighter touch, avoiding a specific definition in advance and preferring to see how the 'religious' and 'secular' are used, and how they are formed practically and discursively in the various spaces of the left hand.[90] To take an *a priori*

87. See Hervieu-Légér, *Religion as a Chain of Memory*, Chapter 2, 'The Fragmentation of Religion in Modern Societies', and the critique offered by Steve Bruce on inclusive definitions of religion in *God is Dead*, Chapter 10, 'Discovering Religion: Mistakes of Method', pp. 186-203.

88. Hervieu-Légér, *Religion as a Chain of Memory*, p. 38. Hervieu-Légér suggests that 'religion is nowhere' in an analysis which adopts an exclusive, substantive definition because religion is reduced to a declining differentiated and privatised existence in modernity (according to sociologists of secularisation who adopt such a definition).

89. Asad, *Genealogies of Religion*, Chapter 1, 'The Construction of Religion as an Anthropological Category'.

90. See James A. Beckford, *Social Theory and Religion* (Cambridge: Cambridge University Press, 2003), pp. 20-21, for a similar view.

definition of religion, designed for some earlier or other purpose, whether substantive or functional in type, would result I suggest in me *finding what I was looking for*. True, I might learn something about *how* religion (conventional, credal, official, invisible, implicit, or whatever) worked in and through space. However, in doing so I would not be giving full rein to space itself — and the particular places within it, whether bodies, things, communities, organisations or events — to tell me about religion, its presence and absence, its dynamism, its power and lack of it, its relations.[91] In my view then I need an alternative stance on religion at the outset. Two further views are possible, neither of which takes as its starting point either a commitment for or against the secular or the religious, or a formal definition of religion, whether exclusive or inclusive. This pairing places the 'religious' and the 'secular' within the same field, the positions being historically intertwined — but not necessarily evolutionary — and located in Western modernity. I prefer one to the other, as I shall now explain.

5.   The first view seeks to abandon the distinction between the religious and the secular by dissolving 'religion' into 'culture'. Exponents of this stance stress that the isolation and reification of the 'religious' and of 'religions' results from specific historical circumstances within European Christianity, later exacerbated by scholars within the tradition of liberal Christian theology who widened their intellectual horizons beyond the study of their own religion to incorporate the 'religions' of others. 'Religion' and 'religions' are Western categories which prove problematic when exported to non-Western societies. When deconstructed they turn out to be no more than ideologically weighted cultural constructions and should be studied as such. So the argument goes. A key exponent of this viewpoint is Timothy Fitzgerald who calls for the de-privileging and de-mystification of the category 'religion' and its treatment within the discipline of cultural studies (rather than within a distinctive discipline or field of religious studies).[92] I suggest, however, that in any study of contemporary Western spaces the *problem of religion* will continue to arise. The terms 'religion', 'religious', and 'religions' (as well as their secular counterparts) will be heard repeatedly, and will be brought into play

---

91. Namely, the inductive approach I discussed in the Introduction and in Knott, 'Community and Locality in the Study of Religion'.

92. Fitzgerald, *The Ideology of Religious Studies*, Chapter 11; *idem*, 'Religious Studies as Cultural Studies: A Philosophical and Anthropological Critique of the Concept of Religion', *Diskus: A Disembodied Journal of Religion* 3.1 (1995), pp. 35-47, at <http://www.uni-marburg.de/religionswissenschaft/journals/diskus>; *idem*, 'Problematising Discourses on Religion' (Review Symposium on Jeremy Carrette's *Foucault and Religion* and *Religion and Culture*), *Culture and Religion* 2.1 (2001), pp. 103-12.

by actors and commentators eager to name, claim, or denounce people, things, events, and places, and to explain their nature. We are not situated in pre-modernity, and must work with the language of our time, however ideologically charged, rather than seeking to abandon or deny it. So, whilst I appreciate Fitzgerald's analysis, I draw the same conclusion as Carrette who concludes that 'the idea of religion needs to be challenged…but it does not necessarily have to be eradicated'.[93] Its eradication from the disciplinary agenda might very well mask ideological forces—liberal theological—of the kind that Fitzgerald is keen to identify, as well as those inherent within the secularist discourse of cultural studies.[94] It would certainly remove a powerful—if contested—conceptual tool from the scholarly workshop.[95] The proposed construct 'culture' is itself ideologically charged and presents us with no less difficulty than does 'religion' for an examination of Western spaces.[96] Carrette calls for the strategic operation of 'religion' rather than its dissolution, on the grounds that the Western conception of religion provides 'a location for understanding a regime of knowledge-power'.[97] This brings me directly to my preferred perspective, one that elects to focus explicitly on the *tension between* the 'religious' and the 'secular', a major 'binary constitutive of modernity'.[98]

93. Jeremy R. Carrette, 'Foucault, Strategic Knowledge and the Study of Religion: A Response to McCutcheon, Fitzgerald, King, and Alles' (Review Symposium on Jeremy Carrette's *Foucault and Religion* and *Religion and Culture*), *Culture and Religion* 2.1 (2001), pp. 127-40 (127). See also R. King, *Orientalism and Religion*, p. 60; McCutcheon, *The Discipline of Religion*, p. 240.

94. R. King, *Orientalism and Religion*, p. 60. Ivan Strenski suggests that those who argue for the dissolution of 'religion' into 'culture' are clearly situated in the ideological field of religious-secular relations as 'despisers' of religion ('On "Religion" and Its Despisers', in Thomas A. Idinopulos and Bryan Wilson [eds.], *What is Religion?* [Leiden: E.J. Brill, 1998], pp. 113-32).

95. Arguments to retain the concept for scholarly use can be found, for example, in Idinopulos and Wilson (eds.), *What is Religion?*; Benson Saler, *Conceptualizing Religion: Immanent Anthropologists, Transcendent Natives and Unbound Categories* (New York: Berghahn Books, 2000 [1993]); Pyysiäinen and Anttonen (eds.), *Current Approaches in the Cognitive Science of Religion*; and the journal *Culture and Religion*.

96. In addition to Carrette on this subject, 'Foucault, Strategic Knowledge and the Study of Religion', see Gerd Baumann, *Contesting Culture: Discourses of Identity in Multi-Ethnic London* (Cambridge: Cambridge University Press, 1996), and Ayse Caglar, 'Hyphenated Identities and the Limits of Culture', in Tariq Modood and Pnina Werbner (eds.), *The Politics of Multiculturalism in the New Europe: Racism, Identity and Community* (London: Zed Books, 1997), pp. 169-85.

97. Carrette, 'Foucault, Strategic Knowledge', p. 129.

98. Jantzen, *Becoming Divine*, p. 8.

6.   In an insightful study of New Religious Movements in the 1980s, James Beckford proposed that controversies surrounding 'cults' '[threw] into sharp relief many of the assumptions hidden behind legal, cultural, and social structures'.[99] Such disputes and debates — between members, parents, anti-cult bodies, the police, the media, and so on — revealed a great deal about social norms and expectations, and what was deemed to be abnormal behaviour or 'beyond the pale'. In *Social Theory and Religion*, he states that, 'religion is…a particularly interesting "site" where boundary disputes are endemic and where well-entrenched interest groups are prepared to defend their definition of religion against opponents'.[100] It is precisely such a perspective that underpins the approach I intend to take in this study, through which I shall look at contested spaces to see what they reveal about the 'religious' and the 'secular' and people's experience of them. Rather than dissolve the boundary between them in favour of an analysis of 'culture', I intend to face it squarely, and to see the exponents of both and those who wittingly or unwittingly comply with them as participants in a complex struggle. In this view, all types of spaces, whether ostensibly religious or secular, private or public are deemed relevant for examination because they are all sites in which 'religion' and the 'secular' are, or have been, contested.[101] If they appear to be uncontested — either wholly religious or wholly secular — they are no less interesting in having successfully excluded the other. This very exclusion is of value in what it can tell us about religion in the late-modern West, 'in the very fabric of the secular'.[102] As McCutcheon has said, 'If post-modern criticism has taught us anything, it has taught us that the authority afforded one binary pole over another is highly tentative and tactical; its seemingly self-evident authority is the result of a number of ideological and rhetorical mechanisms that most often pass unnoticed'.[103] Some may object that this view does not

99.   James A. Beckford, *Cult Controversies: The New Societal Response to the New Religious Movements* (London: Tavistock, 1985), p. 11. See also his article, 'The Politics of Defining Religion in Secular Society: From a Taken-for-Granted Institution to a Contested Resource', *Studies in the History of Religions* 84 (1999), pp. 23-40.

100.   Beckford, *Social Theory and Religion*, p. 13.

101.   For discussions of recent contestation in the public sphere over the meaning of religion, see Beckford, 'The Politics of Defining Religion in Secular Society', and Nye, *Multiculturalism and Minority Religions in Britain*.

102.   Carrette, *Foucault on Religion*, p. 152.

103.   Russell T. McCutcheon, 'The Economics of Spiritual Luxury: The Glittering Lobby and the Parliament of Religions', *Journal of Contemporary Religion* 13.1 (1998), pp. 51-64 (57).

resolve the difficulty of *where to draw the line between* the 'religious' and the 'secular'. This is with good reason, as there is no static boundary between them.[104] How could there be, as ideas on 'both sides' (to concede the binary, for the sake of argument) differ and shift according to time and circumstance, and as exponents from either side periodically win minor battles which reposition the line of engagement?[105]

As we saw earlier, contests on the field of the 'religious' and 'secular' take place not only between overt exponents of the two, but within each camp (e.g. between different types of Christians or different types of secularists), and among commentators who observe and analyse the changing nature of the field (e.g. secularisation debaters).[106] It was in order to show the scale and complexity of the force relations within the field that I pointed to several intellectual debates that have taken place there. There are two additional issues that need raising in the light of this history and presence of contestation, however, one concerning terminology, the other standpoint.[107]

Terminology and Standpoint

The first point to note is the charged nature of some of the terms used within the struggle and their manner of usage. Obvious contested terms are those which characterise the field itself—the 'religious' and the 'secular', but also 'religion', 'religions', the 'sacred', and 'spirituality'. The Western history and ideological usage—the genealogy—of some of these has been discussed by religious studies scholars in recent years. In particular, the concepts 'religion', 'religions', and the 'sacred' have been interrogated.[108] More recently, 'spirituality' has emerged as a term in

104.   See also Beckford, *Social Theory and Religion*, p. 21.

105.   Note here my choice of metaphor, continuing the allusion to the battlefield of the religious and the secular. Bourdieu's conception of a field of play, from which the term 'field' is drawn, utilises the metaphor of a gameboard and the strategy of the game, but I prefer the language of battle and the strategy of warfare (with awareness of its gender politics) as it lends itself to the spatial struggles I wish to consider. Taylor, for example, sees theism within modernity as 'an embattled option' (see Abbey, *Charles Taylor*, p. 197); Conkle refers to the 'culture war' between secular and religious fundamentalisms (see Conkle, 'Secular Fundamentalism, Religious Fundamentalism', p. 338).

106.   See Figure 1, Chapter 5.

107.   The genesis of these observations occurred during a seminar discussion at the University of Stirling in 2002, and I am grateful to the students and staff for their thought-provoking questions and comments.

108.   See earlier references in this chapter to analysis of the terms 'religion' and 'religions'. On the 'sacred' see Veikko Anttonen, 'Sacred', in Willi Braun and Russell T.

popular parlance in Europe and America, not only among religious exponents but also secular professionals, and one thus worthy of careful
scholarly treatment rather than uninformed casual acceptance.[109] In the
second half of my study we will see at times how the way in which one or
other of these terms is used is suggestive of a commentator's desire to
position him- or herself within the field of 'religious' and 'secular' relations. Their usage may denote dominant values, but may also be indicative of changing priorities, a sense of loss, uncertainty, or desire. How, for
example, should we interpret the use of the term 'spirituality' within the
realm of the secular? Is this an attempt by those who have given up or
lost religion to appropriate its most amenable aspect (that which fits best
with the demands of a secular lifestyle)? Or is it a veiled acknowledgment
that even the 'secular' is at heart 'religious'? Does it indicate the re-
enchantment of the West, or simply another aspect of its gradual secularisation? And how are power and capital caught up in its consumer face?

Moreover, towards the end of the book, it will be necessary to return to
questions of the meaning of these terms and their interrelationship. Will a
spatial analysis of the left hand—the case to be examined in Part II—
clarify relations between the 'religious' and the 'secular'? Will we see the
emergence in post-secular accounts of references to 'spirituality' or John
D. Caputo's favoured term 'the religious', and what will that tell us about
how religion is located in late-modernity? Will it be necessary to re-
appropriate the term 'sacred' to explain what is happening in struggles
between different positions? With these questions in mind the work of
three scholars will be introduced at this point as it is their deliberations
on connections between these concepts that will help me at the end of the
book to explain contemporary 'religious', 'secular', and 'post-secular'
representations of the left hand, the values they express, and the force-
relations between them.

McCutcheon (eds.), *A Guide to the Study of Religion* (London: Cassell, 2000), pp. 271-82;
Thomas A. Idinopulos and Edward A. Yonan (eds.), *The Sacred and its Scholars:
Comparative Methodologies for the Study of Primary Religious Data* (Leiden: E.J. Brill, 1996),
in particular articles by William E. Paden, Veikko Anttonen and Stewart Guthrie;
William E. Paden, *Interpreting the Sacred: Ways of Viewing Religion* (Boston: Beacon
Press, 1992); W.S.F. Pickering, 'Locating the Sacred: Durkheim, Otto and Some
Contemporary Ideas', *British Association for the Study of Religions Occasional Papers* 12
(1994), pp. 1-14; and Terence Thomas, '"The Sacred" as a Viable Concept in the
Contemporary Study of Religions', *British Association for the Study of Religions Occa-
sional Papers* 13 (1994), pp. 15-37. See the discussion in Chapter 9.

  109. For a genealogy of 'spirituality', see Jeremy R. Carrette and Richard King,
Selling Spirituality: The Silent Takeover of Religion (London and New York: Routledge,
2004). This book was in press at the time my own study was being completed. Also see
Ann W. Astell (ed.), *Divine Representations: Postmodernism and Spirituality* (New York:
Paulist Press, 1994).

In *Religion as a Chain of Memory*, the sociologist Danièle Hervieu-Léger distinguishes between the 'sacred' (in both religious and secular modes), 'religions', the 'religious', and non-religious 'elective fraternities' in order to account for the changing nature of religion in contemporary Western societies. What is specific to religious activity and religious institutions, she argues, is their focus on 'the production, management and distribution of the particular form of believing which draws its legitimacy from reference to a tradition'.[110] This distinguishes it from the 'sacred', which may occur in either religious or secular contexts, but which refers to 'the experience of encountering a force and a presence that is stronger than self'.[111] Thus, whilst it is perfectly possible for the 'sacred' to be experienced in late-modern, secular societies, it does not always issue forth in religion because religion is contingent upon reference to a tradition that is capable of supporting a community or institution. A chain or lineage of belief must be in operation. Where it is not, whilst there will still be beliefs and social groups that hold them ('elective fraternities'), these need not become 'religious' unless there is a shared need for continuity beyond the group's present context and a move by the group to represent this to themselves in some fashion.[112] What we see in the work of Hervieu-Léger then is an attempt to understand not only the location of the 'religious' (as opposed to institutional religion) in Western modernity, but also its fundamental relationship to a lineage of beliefs. The focus on belief in her work links her to Charles Taylor whose ideas on secularity we encountered earlier.

Another scholar who defines and delineates terms that refer to the domain of religion in modern Western society is the historian Wouter Hanegraaff. In an article entitled 'New Age Spiritualities as Secular Religion', he offers clear definitions of 'religion', 'a religion', 'a spirituality', and then examines these in religious and secular contexts, particularly in relation to the New Age, arguing that his approach allows for a reassessment of the processes of modernisation and secularisation.[113] He focuses on myths and symbols (stories and images) rather than beliefs in order to account for his view that New Age 'may be defined as "secular religion" based on "private symbolism"' surrounding the foundational story of the Self '.[114] The strength of his work lies in his scholarly accommodation

---

110.   Hervieu-Léger, *Religion as a Chain of Memory*, p. 101.

111.   Hervieu-Léger, *Religion as a Chain of Memory*, p. 106.

112.   Hervieu-Léger, *Religion as a Chain of Memory*, p. 152.

113.   Hanegraaff, 'New Age Spiritualities', pp. 146-47, 152. For his definitions, see Chapter 9. See also Wouter Hanegraaff, *New Age Religion and Western Culture: Esotericism in the Mirror of Secular Thought* (Leiden: E.J. Brill, 1996).

114.   Hanegraaff, 'New Age Spiritualities', pp. 146, 158.

and use of the concept 'spirituality' in explaining the changing presence
of the religious within a secular context. His focus on the importance of
the myth of science, the story of the Self, private symbolism, and the disembedding of 'spiritualities' (their 'autonomisation') from 'religions' all
provide powerful tools for understanding religious change in modernity.

The third scholar is Veikko Anttonen, a scholar of religions who
engages ethnography, social theory, and cognitive studies in developing
'a general and empirically tractable theory of the "sacred" on the basis of
which varieties of attributions can be approached and explained'.[115] He
clarifies various distinctions, between the 'sacred' as an emic term and as
an etic category,[116] and between the 'sacred' as a *sui generis* ontological
category employed by twentieth-century phenomenologists of religion
such as Mircea Eliade, and the 'sacred' as a situationally and 'culturally
dependent cognitive category which at the same time "separates" and
"binds"'.[117] According to Anttonen, the 'sacred' is the boundary that is
generated in situations of category transformation (such as between life
and death, human and divine, pure and impure, animate and inanimate,
male and female).[118] This distinguishes it from the notion of 'religion', and
that to which the term 'religion' refers, and from other belief systems. As
he says, 'people participate in sacred-making activities...according to
paradigms given by the belief systems to which they are committed,
whether they be religious, national or ideological', and whether they take
old or new, religious or non-religious forms.[119] Like Hervieu-Léger, Anttonen sees the category of the 'sacred' as applicable within both religion
and non-religion, and to both religious and secular contexts. Whereas the
former is concerned with the sociological task of articulating the nature of
the 'religious' in late-modern Western societies, however, the latter is
interested in theorising a cognitive category that can be used to analyse
transformational situations irrespective of their time or place. Both, with
Hanegraaff—and Taylor and Gilbert from my earlier discussion—
contribute to defining and applying concepts of relevance for making
sense of the contemporary field of the 'religious' and the 'secular', and I
shall refer to them again towards the end of the book.

115.   Veikko Anttonen, 'Sacred Sites as Markers of Difference: Exploring Cognitive
Foundations of Territoriality', in Lotte Tarkka (ed.), *Dynamics of Tradition: Perspectives
on Oral Poetry and Folk Belief* (Helsinki: Studia Fennica Folkloristica, Finnish Literary
Society, 2003), pp. 291-305 (293). See also Anttonen, 'Rethinking the Sacred', and
'Sacred'.
116.   Anttonen, 'Rethinking the Sacred', p. 40.
117.   Anttonen, 'Rethinking the Sacred', pp. 43, 57, and 'Sacred', pp. 272-74.
118.   Anttonen, 'Rethinking the Sacred', p. 43 (my examples).
119.   Anttonen, 'Sacred', p. 281.

I said earlier that there were two final issues to be addressed, the second being that of standpoint. There is no neutral ground from which to view the field of struggle between the 'religious' and the 'secular', no position to take which is not implicated in its force relationships. As King makes clear in his discussion of the discipline of religious studies: 'The modern study of religion is not unaffected by the Christian heritage of Western culture and by the development of theology as an academic discipline in the West, nor is the apparently secular nature of religious studies a 'position from nowhere'.[120] This has been demonstrated, for example, by Fitzgerald in relation to Ninian Smart whose work was forged in the tradition of liberal Christian theology.[121] It would certainly be possible to analyse the spaces of religion in terms of Smart's now famous dimensions,[122] but some consideration would need to be given to the legacy and consequences of Smart's stance for the field of the 'religious' and the 'secular'. A different case, and one pertinent for the preceding discussion, is that of Charles Taylor whose religious standpoint has emerged increasingly during the period of his work on modernity and secularity.[123] He is outspoken, for example, towards the end of his groundbreaking study, *Sources of the Self*, in challenging 'a stripped-down secular outlook' and in hoping 'to bring the air back again into the half-collapsed lungs of the spirit', and still more open about his beliefs in *A Catholic Modernity?*[124] However, it is not only those who write about 'religion' whose positions within the field need to be made clear, but also those who rarely mention it, for example, those whose work I have drawn on in theorising space and place, such as Henri Lefebvre and Doreen Massey. Finally, of course, there is my own position.

In applying a spatial approach and considering the formation of spaces in Part II, attention will be given to the position within the field of the 'religious' and the 'secular' of both exponents *and* commentators. Intellectuals, including scholars of religion—as we have seen—participate in the interpretive reproduction of spaces, along with those actors who are more directly involved in their production. I shall not take time to consider their positions any further at this point. The positions of Lefebvre, Massey and others do need some attention, however, as it is from their ideas that the spatial terms for my analysis emerge. Lefebvre—despite a

120. R. King, *Orientalism and Religion*, p. 42.
121. Fitzgerald, *The Ideology of Religious Studies*, Chapter 3, 'Ninian Smart and the Phenomenology of Religion'.
122. Ninian Smart, *The Religious Experience of Mankind* (London: Collins, 1969), and *The Phenomenon of Religion* (London: Macmillan, 1973).
123. Abbey, *Charles Taylor*, p. 212.
124. Taylor, *Sources of the Self*, pp. 520-21; Charles Taylor, *A Catholic Modernity?* (ed. J.L Heft; New York: Oxford University Press, 1999).

Roman Catholic schooling—was part of the generation of French intellectuals trained in secular humanism (a product of the very system which troubled Gaston Richard).[125] As a long-standing member of the Communist Party (until 1958) and, later, a figure-head of the student demonstrations of 1968, he was profoundly influenced by Marx, Hegel, Nietzsche, Freud, but also by the Dadaists and surrealists. He was not outwardly religious, but the marks of an earlier exposure to mystical thought and interest in artistic spontaneity remained within his work, and contributed to his vision of the potential of social space to irrupt in 'moments' of resistance and revolution.[126] He was not without hope, though the source of that hope was not to be found in religious institutions or teachings.

The theorists of postmodern space on whose work I have drawn—Massey, Soja, Shields, and so on—cannot as yet be positioned biographically. It is not unreasonable, however, to assume a lack of significant knowledge or interest in religion on the basis of their near total silence on the subject. Like many other theorists of the postmodern they show an interest in 'culture' and 'identity', occasionally seeing religious ideas and symbols as components of a broader debate, but otherwise generally ignoring it. I would suggest that these scholars are informal members of Peter Berger's 'secular *internationale*', an observation, I admit, which is based on an absence of evidence to the contrary rather than on the presence of clearly articulated standpoints on the subject of the religious/secular. Although I make no judgment on this, it is important to take it into account in the application of an approach that derives its terms from the work of these scholars. Within religious studies in the period since the Second World War, the utilisation of vocabulary, tools, and methods from the social sciences has been widespread, and has generally gone unquestioned on the apparent assumption that they have no effect on the subject matter in hand:

> Scholars in the area of religious studies have often made the claim that the methodologies used in this discipline are objective and neutral in that they neither presuppose nor preclude any particular religious commitment. This claim, however, will only stand if it can be shown that studying religion from within a secular framework is objective and neutral and that such an orientation does not distort or misrepresent the object of study.[127]

125. Elden, 'Introduction' to *Understanding Henri Lefebvre*; Rob Shields, *Levebvre, Love and Struggle*. See also David Harvey, 'Afterword', in Lefebvre, *The Production of Space*, pp. 425-31.

126. For example, see Elden, *Understanding Henri Lefebvre*, pp. 117-20, 170-71.

127. R. King, *Orientalism and Religion*, p. 47. See also Robert N. Bellah, 'Religious Studies as "New Religion"', in Jacob Needleman and George Baker (eds.), *Understanding the New Religions* (New York: Seabury Press, 1978), pp. 106-12, cited in King.

This raises a potential difficulty, one that I do not have space to consider in depth but which readers should nevertheless be aware of, the possibility that the very terms of the interpretive framework to be applied in this study arise out of and are weighted towards a secular intellectual orientation which may mask religion altogether or may reproduce it according to secular humanist ideas (of its institutional character, decline, and public irrelevance).[128]

What about my own standpoint? Where am I situated in the field of the 'religious' and the 'secular'? I stated briefly in the introduction what led me to undertake a spatial analysis of religion, and, in the next chapter, will describe in more detail my recent work on religion and locality and its contribution to the present study. The work I carried out on gender and destiny has also been influential in the way I have envisaged social spaces, as constructed, dynamic, power-full, and the subject of struggles between normative and discrepant positions.[129]

Since being a young student I have struggled to understand the ideological underpinnings of the phenomenological tradition within religious studies in which I was trained,[130] and, though I expect that it continues to leave its mark on me and the way I see things, I have tried to step away from it here by developing a strategic interpretive approach which places the 'religious' with the 'secular' in the same field, on the understanding that they are historically interconnected and dialectically related. I have immersed myself in a body of theory—on space and place—that is new to me in order to identify terms and ideas which may contribute to the study of religion but that arise outside its normal boundaries. But I have suggested that these must be treated with the same suspicion that scholars of religion in recent years have applied with such zeal to the terms and ideas associated with the phenomenological approach. I remember as a postgraduate being told to be suspicious of the ideas of Durkheim because his views on religion were reductionist. Since then such 'reductionism' has been embraced by those (including myself) who prefer a social scientific approach to religion to a phenomenological one. I am now suggesting that we move to a greater understanding of the ideological position of 'reductionism' within modernist discourse, not in

128.   Whilst this is possible in general, I would suggest it is not the case with Lefebvre's triadic portrayal of space, which I have shown earlier in Chapter 2, is sufficiently open to make room for the religious.

129.   Kim Knott, 'Hindu Women, Destiny, and *stridharma*', *Religion* 26 (1996), pp. 15-35, and 'Notions of Destiny in Women's Self-Construction', *Religion* 28 (1998), pp. 405-11.

130.   See my reflections in Kim Knott, 'Women Researching, Women Researched: Gender in the Empirical Study of Religion', in Ursula King (ed.), *Religion and Gender* (Oxford: Basil Blackwell, 1995), pp. 199-218.

order to reject it but in order to use it strategically and reflexively to research and comment on religion in 'secular' modernity.

Finally, where do I stand personally on the 'religious' and the 'secular'? My upbringing and education place me squarely within the tradition of secular humanism. Whilst I share the postmodern desire to deconstruct this European master narrative, this is not because I wish to see it torn down in its entirety, but because deconstruction is a strong impulse within it, arising alongside the desire to acknowledge and do justice to difference. I value the spaces — ostensibly beyond religion — which secular discourse and politics have made possible. Would the movement and ideas of Western feminisms from which I have benefited and in which I share have come to fruition without it? But, in addition to my secular background, I also have an acquired religious identity as a liberal Quaker,[131] and admire Quakerism's critical dissenting approach to the institutions, beliefs, and practices of the historical churches and the laws and values of the secular nation state. Its urge to practise and think outward non-conformity (whilst being to some extent conservative in its traditions), to make a regular space to contemplate, doubt, and be challenged, and to favour a socially and religiously pluralist outlook are all aspects that situate it in part within the liberal and secular humanist tradition, and that will no doubt affect the way I see and interpret the spaces in which religion is located.[132]

The reflexive approach that I am advocating is easier said than done with integrity. Reflexivity itself has emerged as a late-modern strategy of identity, and may in the future be found to have its flaws as an intellectual outlook. Apparent openness to one's own and others' standpoints can mask other forms of closure and bias, especially in terms of selectivity. For example, like other bodies of theory, late-modern social and cultural theory is partial and favours certain voices over others. Furthermore, it reproduces itself by disciplining those who enter its ranks, to speak, write, and think in certain ways. Like other bodies of theory, it is at times

131.   Quaker, one who is associated with the Religious Society of Friends, a religious denomination with its origins in seventeenth-century English Protestantism.

132.   See Ben Pink Dandelion, 'Those Who Leave and Those Who Feel Left: The Complexity of Quaker Disaffiliation', *Journal of Contemporary Religion* 17.2 (2002), pp. 213-28. In discussing issues of disaffiliation he provides an interesting view of the position of English Quakers in the field of the 'religious' and the 'secular'. Also see Eleanor Nesbitt, 'Friend in the Field: A Reflexive Approach to Being a Quaker Ethnographer', *Quaker Studies* 4.2 (1999), pp. 82-112, and Elisabeth Arweck and Martin Stringer (eds.), *Theorising Faith: The Insider/Outsider Problem in the Study of Ritual* (Birmingham: Birmingham University Press, 2002), for observations on how scholars of religion who are also Quakers think their Quakerism affects their scholarship.

dismissive, thereby sidelining and sometimes silencing other approaches. Given this tendency, it seems all the more important to consider what previous studies of religion—almost all of which go unnoticed in the work of those theorists I have already focused on—may have contributed to a spatial analysis of religion.

Chapter 4

Religion and Space: The Scholarly Legacy

Within the study of religions, examinations of the role of space and of the relations between space and religion have been a minority interest, with the two most visible clusterings being the sub-discipline of geography of religion — which has a history dating back to the seventeenth century — and the theme of sacred space, which arose following the conceptualisation of the 'sacred' in the early twentieth century and was fostered within anthropological and phenomenological traditions of scholarship on society and religion. Neither the explicit focus of institutional religions in the former, nor the focus on the 'sacred' in the latter provides the starting point for this study. My aim is rather to focus on spaces themselves, irrespective of whether or not they appear to be religious or sacred, and to examine the location of religion within them by attending to the presence of the 'religious' and the 'secular' and the tensions in and between them. Despite the difference in our intentions, it remains likely that there is a good deal that I can learn from a consideration of previous studies in geography of religion and the 'sacred', as well as in two recent additions to scholarship on religion and space: globalisation and locality. It is worth reiterating the importance of attending to areas of study and debates which seem at first sight either tangential or even passé in the light of disciplinary — and dialectical — tendencies at work within the academy that lead to the marginalisation and subordination of alternative viewpoints and approaches (e.g. of ethnography and other empirical studies by those who favour theory, of various modernisms by postmodernism, of phenomenology of religion by those adopting reductive approaches, of studies of religion by secular studies in the humanities and social sciences, *and vice versa*).

In the discussion that follows, I have utilised the division noted above, though the four areas are best thought of as interrelated: space and the sacred, geography of religion, religion and globalisation, and religion and locality. In looking at each of these, I shall introduce several significant works and mention others in passing, though the general purpose will be to consider their value and limitations for my own project rather than to provide a thorough review.[1]

Space and the Sacred

The problematisation of the 'sacred' surely begins with Durkheim, and his discussions of the totem offer an early consideration of a place made sacred.[2] However, it is with Eliade that most accounts of sacred space begin.[3] Brereton acknowledges this in the bibliographical note to his entry on 'Sacred Space' in *The Encyclopedia of Religion*, and most scholars working on the subject have felt the need to engage critically with his thesis.[4] I shall come on to several of these shortly, but will look first not at Eliade's work, but at that of Belden C. Lane who seems to me to carry forward the poetic character and experiential approach of his forebear, but in the particular context of American spirituality.[5]

Writing as Professor of Theology and American Studies, and publishing with Paulist Press, Lane presents what, in scholarly terms, is a religious discourse on space (on the *sui generis* sacred) rather than a discourse on religion and space.[6] His restatement of Eliade's axioms makes this clear:

1.   I have surveyed the general field for the purpose of introducing issues in the study of religion and locality in 'Religion and Locality'.

2.   Émile Durkheim, *The Elementary Forms of the Religious Life* (London: George Allen & Unwin, 1976 [French edn 1912]).

3.   Mircea Eliade, *The Sacred and the Profane: The Nature of Religion* (San Diego: Harcourt Brace Jovanovitch, 1959 [1957]).

4.   Joel P. Brereton, 'Sacred Space', in Mircea Eliade (ed.), *The Encyclopedia of Religion* (16 vols.; New York: Macmillan, 1987), XII, pp. 526-35 (534). For example, Jonathan Z. Smith, 'The Wobbling Pivot' [1971], in *idem, Map is Not Territory: Studies in the History of Religions* (Chicago and London: University of Chicago Press, 1978), pp. 88-103; Larry E. Shiner, 'Sacred Space, Profane Space, Human Space', *Journal of the American Academy of Religion* 40 (1972), pp. 425-36; David Chidester and Edward T. Linenthal, 'Introduction', in Chidester and Linenthal (eds.), *American Sacred Space*, pp. 1-42.

5.   Belden C. Lane, *Landscapes of the Sacred: Geography and Narrative in American Spirituality* (New York: Paulist Press, 1988).

6.   McCutcheon, *Manufacturing Religion*, Chapter 5, 'The Category "Religion" in Recent Scholarship'; Timothy Fitzgerald, 'Problematising Discourses on Religion' (Review Symposium on Jeremy Carrette's *Foucault and Religion* and *Religion and Culture*), *Culture and Religion* 2.1 (2001), pp. 103-12; Anttonen, 'Sacred'. In this sense, Lane is unequivocally one of those phenomenologists of the sacred whose work falls within the category of 'religious confession', see Chapter 3.

1.   Sacred place is not chosen; it chooses.
2.   Sacred place is ordinary place, ritually made extraordinary.
3.   Sacred place can be trodden upon without being entered.
4.   The impulse of sacred place is both centripetal and centrifugal, both local and universal.[7]

Following J.Z. Smith, Lane acknowledges the ordinary as potentially holy, refusing to focus only on the exotic and special. In keeping with his other professional interests, however, he also focuses on the 'storied nature of place', seeing the process of sacralisation as one in which people form significant places through narratives of association, relationship, and memory.[8] As such, he considers the landscape of American literature, from Puritan journals and pamphlets to transcendentalist poetry, as well as photography and the built environment, considering what they suggest about 'God's elusive presence'.[9] Taking as a foundational view that God is mediated through place, Lane stands in the phenomenological tradition — vis-à-vis both religion and place — and this is borne out by his weddedness to Otto and Eliade, and, on the geographical side, to Heidegger and Yi-Fu Tuan. My own standpoint on religion and space is quite different to Lane's, but I have alluded to his work because it openly espouses an approach which is adopted (either wittingly or unwittingly) by many scholars in studies of sacred space and pilgrimage.[10] A strength of Lane's work for my own, however, is his interest in ordinary spaces, particularly domestic places such as homes and their furniture. Much literature on sacred space focuses on major sites — often those ordered by dominant political or religious groups — such as cities,[11] places of worship,[12] and pilgrimage sites.[13] Some recent studies, however, have begun

---

7.   Lane, *Landscapes of the Sacred*, p. 15.
8.   Lane, *Landscapes of the Sacred*, p. 20.
9.   Lane, *Landscapes of the Sacred*, 'Epilogue'.
    10.   And, as such, is criticised by theorists such as McCutcheon and Fitzgerald as confusing religion as part of the problem to be analysed with religion as an analytical tool. See McCutcheon, *Manufacturing Religion*, p. 129.
    11.   Paul Wheatley, *The Pivot of the Four Quarters* (Chicago: Aldine, 1971); Diana L. Eck, *Banaras: City of Light* (Princeton: Princeton University Press, 1982); F.E. Peters, *Jerusalem and Mecca: The Typology of the Holy City in the Near East* (New York and London: New York University Press, 1986). From a Christian theological perspective, see also Gorringe, *A Theology of the Built Environment*.
    12.   Stella Kramrisch, *The Hindu Temple* (2 vols.; Calcutta: University of Calcutta Press, 1946); Harold W. Turner, *From Temple to Meeting House: The Phenomenology and Theology of Places of Worship* (The Hague: Mouton, 1979); J.Z. Smith, *To Take Place: Toward a Theory in Ritual*.
    13.   S. Bhardwaj, *Hindu Places of Pilgrimage in India: A Study in Cultural Geography* (Berkeley: University of California Press, 1973); Victor Turner and Edith Turner, *Image and Pilgrimage in Christian Culture* (Oxford: Basil Blackwell, 1978); John Eade and

to focus on smaller-scale sites of the sacred, including icons, wayside and domestic shrines, religious objects, flowers and food, bodies and homes.[14] In addition to examining people's experience and use of such sites, some scholars have begun to contest their apparently settled nature, and it is both the interest in small-scale and popular objects and places, and their destabilisation that is of interest in relation to my own work.

Homes and bodies as sites of the sacred have attracted recent attention because of their association with private, over against public, space, and their identification with women. Are women's bodies and their homes the sites of religious experience? Are they open to sacralisation by women, and do they constitute alternative sites of sacred power for them? Mazumdar and Mazumdar, in an article on women's identity development in the context of Hindu domestic space,[15] strongly suggest that Hindu homes do function in these ways. This builds on the idea that homes offer a stable and protective, private domain for women—the traditional view—by adding that it provides them with creative opportunities for the development of self-identity and the exercise of power. Home has also been seen as a site of resistance where women can organise in order then to act in the public sphere.[16] Yet other scholars have stressed the ambivalence of bodies and homes as sacred spaces, sanctuaries, and places of spiritual growth for women by claiming them to be sites of their oppression. Judy Tobler explores this view in the context of a violent South Africa where 'a woman is raped every 23 seconds'.[17] 'At the core of idealised notions of "home" reside equally idealised images of woman, or more specifically, the maternal body.'[18] Tobler suggests that, at a scholarly level, both

Michael Sallnow (eds.), *Contesting the Sacred: The Anthropology of Christian Pilgrimage* (London: Routledge, 1991); but see also Ian Reader and Tony Walters (eds.), *Pilgrimage in Popular Culture* (London: Macmillan, 1993). More recently scholars have questioned the traditional focus on place in pilgrimage studies and moved to an investigation of 'motion'; see Coleman and Eade (eds.), *Reframing Pilgrimage*.

14. For example, Colleen McDannell, *Material Christianity: Religion and Popular Culture in America* (New Haven and London: Yale University Press, 1995); Crispin Paine (ed.), *Godly Things: Museums, Objects and Religion* (London and New York: Leicester University Press, 2000); Kay Turner, *Beautiful Necessity: The Art and Meaning of Women's Altars* (London: Thames & Hudson, 1999).

15. Shampa Mazumdar and Sanjoy Mazumdar, 'Women's Significant Spaces: Religion, Space and Community', *Journal of Environmental Psychology* 19 (1999), pp. 159-70.

16. hooks, *Yearning*, pp. 41-48; Pnina Werbner, 'Public Spaces, Political Voices: Gender, Feminism and Aspects of British Muslim Participation in the Public Sphere', in W.A.R. Shadid and P.S. van Koningsveld (eds.), *Political Participation and Identities of Muslims in Non-Muslim States* (Kampen: Kok Pharos, 1996), pp. 53-70.

17. Judy Tobler, '"Home is Where the Heart Is?": Gendered Sacred Space in South Africa', *Journal for the Study of Religion* 13.1/2 (2000), pp. 69-98. This is a conservative estimate from Rape Crisis based on reported rapes only (p. 69).

18. Tobler, '"Home is Where the Heart Is?"', p. 77.

phenomenologists of place and phenomenologists of religion have fallen prey to processes of idealisation and essentialisation in their accounts of home and place as sacred.[19] Badly needed then are critical analyses of the idea of domestic space as sacred which must equally interrogate 'notions about the maternal body that likewise produce the maternal body as sacred space', notions which may help to uncover what lies at the root of those attitudes that lead to or collude with violence.[20] Tobler seeks both to develop such a critique and to offer a feminist theoretical reoccupation of sacred space that neither obliterates nor contains women:[21]

> For male fear of the maternal body and the consequent domination and control of—and sometimes violence against—women to be transformed, perhaps we need both new spaces and transformation of old spaces, where the reality of human embodiments and mortality is confronted and accepted by women and men.[22]

Tobler utilises Luce Irigaray's *Divine Women* to show how—at a theoretical level—such a reoccupation of space can occur, as Irigaray calls for women to find a divine horizon in their own image that will then allow them to achieve their subjectivity.[23]

Tobler's work offers a reminder to us not only that domestic, private spaces need interrogating and unsettling, but that they are as much sites of power as are so-called public spaces. She shows us how, as sacred spaces, they are fundamentally gendered, and how this may be a double bind for women.

Her call for a feminist reoccupation of sacred space brings us on to the subject of the making of such space, whether theoretically conceived, as above, or practically accomplished. Central to this subject—an important theme in the literature on sacred space—is the idea that people construct such sites or environments through their imaginations, memories, actions, and speech. Such sites are materially produced and reproduced, though 'insiders' and 'outsiders' undoubtedly differ in their accounts of the constitution of the 'sacred'.[24] Those like Eliade and Lane see the sacred as irrupting or manifesting in space before being apprehended by people who then develop the site, whilst others, like Jonathan Z. Smith, and David Chidester and Edward T. Linenthal, see the sacred and sacred

19. Tobler, '"Home is Where the Heart Is?"', p. 75.

20. Tobler, '"Home is Where the Heart Is?"', p. 77

21. Tobler ('"Home is Where the Heart Is?"', pp. 90, 96) is indebted to Elizabeth Grosz for these ideas.

22. Tobler, '"Home is Where the Heart Is?"', p. 93.

23. Tobler, '"Home is Where the Heart Is?"', p. 92.

24. For a discussion of the insider/outsider question, see McCutcheon, *The Insider/ Outsider Problem in the Study of Religion*.

places as the outcome of the human activity of sacralisation. Chidester and Linenthal distinguish between these two views as 'substantial' and 'situational' approaches to the 'sacred'.[25]

In the second of these, sacred space is contested space, a point which Chidester and Linenthal note is absent from Eliade's analysis,[26] and as a consequence of which they subvert his axioms (see the discussion of Lane, above). They see sacred space as 'inevitably entangled with the entrepreneurial, the social, the political, and other "profane" forces'.[27] Its significant 'levels of reality' they see not as heaven, earth and hell, but as 'hierarchical power relations of domination and subordination, inclusion and exclusion, appropriation and dispossession', all of which, rather than marking it out as a sacred centre, connect it to wider systems of meaning and power relations.[28] Finally, they challenge Eliade's view that the sacred irrupts or manifests with a reminder of the human labour of choosing and creating a sacred place, and the 'symbolic violence' involved in establishing it.[29] And 'Why is sacred space contested?', they ask; because it is spatial and a site of struggle and competition (as Lefebvre made clear), and because it is open to 'a surplus of signification…to unlimited claims and counter-claims on its significance',[30] which the authors characterise as strategies of *appropriation, exclusion, inversion*, and *hybridisation*.[31] With Lefebvre's spatial aspects, these strategies of contestation have a value in differentiating the manipulation and experience of space by actors.[32]

It is Jonathan Z. Smith's work that is perhaps of most interest in relation to the process of the spatial sacralisation.[33] At the heart of it is his

25. Chidester and Linenthal, 'Introduction', p. 6.

26. Chidester and Linenthal, 'Introduction', pp. 15-16. They acknowledge that Jonathan Z. Smith rectified this lack in taking up the mantle of scholarship on sacred space.

27. Chidester and Linenthal, 'Introduction', p. 17.

28. Chidester and Linenthal, 'Introduction', p. 17. But see Mary M. McDonald (ed.), *Experiences of Place* (Cambridge, MA: Harvard University Press/Center for the Study of World Religions, 2003) for new perspectives from religious studies on heaven and the underworld.

29. Chidester and Linenthal, 'Introduction', p. 17.

30. Chidester and Linenthal, 'Introduction', p. 18.

31. Chidester and Linenthal, 'Introduction', p. 19. We will see such strategies at work in the case of the left hand. See Chapters 7 and 8.

32. The various case studies which follow Chidester and Linenthal's introduction to *American Sacred Space* illustrate and explore these themes in more detail, whilst other instructive contributions to the discussion of the contestation of sacred space include Bowman, 'Nationalising the Sacred'; Lily Kong, 'Negotiating Conceptions of "Sacred Space": A Case Study of Religious Buildings in Singapore', *Transactions of the Institute of British Geographers* NS 18 (1993), pp. 342-58; Barbara Bender, *Stonehenge: Making Space* (Oxford: Berg, 1999); Nye, *Multiculturalism and Minority Religions in Britain*.

33. See also Daly Metcalf (ed.), *Making Muslim Space*.

conviction that people strive to construct and organise a meaningful space by which they can live in the world, a process that requires all their powers of negotiation and creativity. That this is human work and not God's work is made very clear by Smith in the first chapter of his book, *To Take Place,* in which he brings anthropology rather than cosmology to the fore, and reminds us, as Geza Roheim put it, that 'environment is made out of man's activity'.[34] This was no less a theme in Smith's earlier work, and it was in his famous essay, *Map Is Not Territory,* that we met the dairy farmer from upstate New York who provided a pertinent, personal example of this process of spatial construction: 'He had made a world by gestures and words in which he, his family and farm gained significance and value'.[35] Smith referred to the farmer's creation as 'a locative map of the world',[36] distinguishing it from a 'utopian map',[37] characterised by rebellion and flight, and a third map, which, by holding the tension, allowed its creators 'to play between the incongruities'.[38] This interesting third map has not been pursued in depth by Smith or his commentators, but of the first two Chidester and Linenthal provide this clear summary:

> Locative space is a fixed, bounded, sacred cosmos, reinforced by the imperative of maintaining one's place, and the place of others, in a larger scheme of things. By contrast, utopian space is unbounded, unfixed to any particular location, a place that can only be reached by breaking out of, or being liberated from, the bonds of a prevailing social order.[39]

It is tempting to draw a parallel between these maps (it is important to remember that Smith saw them as representations and not geographical spaces as such) and the three aspects of Lefebvre's triad that I looked at in the previous chapter. Smith's locative map—which he also refers to as 'imperial'—is loosely akin to Lefebvre's 'representations of space' in being an attempt to order the unconnected, dominate the environment, and control through symbolisation. His utopian map, akin to Lefebvre's 'spaces of representation', expresses the desire to disrupt or reverse the ordered locative representation, and 'perceives terror and confinement in [its] interconnection, correspondence and repetition'.[40] It represents a flight to a new world. Smith's tentative third map, in being neither one thing (locative) nor the other (utopian), and in being 'third' might be said

34. J.Z. Smith, *To Take Place,* p. 11.
35. J.Z. Smith, *Map Is Not Territory,* p. 292.
36. J.Z. Smith, *Map Is Not Territory,* p. 292.
37. J.Z. Smith, *Map Is Not Territory,* p. 309.
38. J.Z. Smith, *Map Is Not Territory,* p. 309.
39. Chidester and Linenthal, 'Introduction', p. 15.
40. J.Z. Smith, *Map Is Not Territory,* p. 309.

to vie with the utopian map as a parallel to Lefebvre's 'spaces of representation'. However, in holding the incongruities of both other positions
in play and in working between the two of them (like a practical joke,
suggests Smith),[41] it is loosely akin to the role played by spatial practice in
Lefebvre's triad, though, like Smith's other maps, it is representational. It
would be wrong to draw this parallel too closely, particularly when it
comes to Smith's illusive third map. However, it is instructive to see,
through Smith's confident references to such apparently secular domains
as farming, imperial governance, and trade and exchange, the role that he
attributes to creative religious activity (through myth and ritual) in the
formation of these alternative maps of the world.

Before leaving the contribution of Smith, it is important to pursue the
theme of the making of sacred space into his later book, *To Take Place*, the
value of which for my work is twofold. First, Smith theorises 'place' for
the study of ritual, and, in doing so, engages critically with geographers,
sociologists, and anthropologists in rejecting both a Kantian and a humanistic geographical view. He concludes that 'place is not best conceived as
a particular location with an idiosyncratic physiognomy or as a uniquely
individualistic node of sentiment, but rather a social position within a
hierarchical system', following the English verbal form, 'to take place'.[42]
This accords generally with Lefebvre's view of space as social, and helped
to inform my use of 'place' in Chapter 1.

Secondly, Smith intriguingly brings together the three concepts of the
sacred (and its obsolete verbal form, *to sacrate*),[43] place (and its verbal
form, *to place*, specifically, *to take place*), and ritual. In doing so, he denies
two commonly held views, that the sacred is a substance, and that ritual
is an expression of the sacred:

> Ritual is not an expression of or a response to "the sacred"; rather, some-
> thing or someone is made sacred by ritual…divine and human, sacred and
> profane, are transitive categories; they serve as maps and labels, not
> substances; they are distinctions of office, indices of difference.[44]

He proposes that, through ritual, people sacralise (themselves, others,
objects, places). Ritual then becomes a central creative process by which
people make a meaningful world that they can inhabit. Following Durkheim, he states that things and people become 'sacred' because they are
identified with and used in the places where ritual is enacted.[45] Others

41. J.Z. Smith, *Map Is Not Territory*, pp. 300-302.
42. J.Z. Smith, *To Take Place*, p. 45.
43. J.Z. Smith, *To Take Place*, p. 105.
44. J.Z. Smith, *To Take Place*, p. 105.
45. J.Z. Smith, *To Take Place*, p. 106.

like them may not acquire such a label and power, and are identified as 'profane'. Crucially, then, 'ritual is…an assertion of difference' in so far as,

> …it represents the creation of a controlled environment where the variables (the accidents) of ordinary life may be displaced precisely because they are felt to be overwhelmingly present and powerful. Ritual is a means of performing the way things ought to be in conscious tension to the way things are.[46]

In addition to adding weight to those views expressed in the first chapter about the social nature of space and place, Smith goes further in investigating the role of ritual (sacralisation) in creating meaningful places, objects, and people, and in marking out a sphere of difference (in producing the 'sacred').

A related project is pursued by Veikko Anttonen, who also sees the sacred as transitive rather than substantial (see Chapter 3). He too writes about sacred-making behaviour and its spatialisation, but he does not confine himself to seeing space as the outcome of sacralisation. He states that space also plays a role in the production of the 'sacred' because human experience of the relationship between body and territory,[47] and the cognitive process of categorisation that arises from it, is instrumental in generating what we call the 'sacred' as a category boundary. According to Ilkka Pyysiäinen,

> Anttonen has shown how the notion of the sacred is essentially a concept by which people define and mark the boundaries between themselves as individuals (the body and its boundaries) and as a community (ethnicity and territorial boundaries), between auspicious and dangerous days and times, as well as between what is human and part of culture and what is outside of it (nature and transcendence as "the other").[48]

---

46. J.Z. Smith, *To Take Place*, p. 109. See also Bell, *Ritual Theory, Ritual Practice*, p. 74: 'Ritualization is a way of acting that is designed and orchestrated to distinguish and privilege what is being done in comparison to other, usually more quotidian, activities. As such, ritualization is a matter of various culturally specific strategies for setting some activities off from others, for creating and privileging a qualitative distinction between the "sacred" and the "profane", and for ascribing such distinctions to realities thought to transcend the powers of human actors.' See also p. 204.

47. Anttonen follows George Lakoff and Mark Johnson in his understanding of the relationship between body and mind: see the discussion and references to their work in Chapter 1. As he explains it, my experience of the boundary between the outside of my body and the territory that surrounds it (the inside of the territory) enables me to identify myself and others as different, and the experience of the territorial boundary (separating the inside and outside of the territory) identifies my group as different from others. Territories are meaningful only in their differentiation from one another. See Anttonen, 'Rethinking the Sacred', pp. 47-54, and 'Sacred Sites as Markers of Difference', p. 292.

48. Ilkka Pyysiäinen, *Belief and Beyond: Religious Categorization of Reality* (Åbo: Åbo Akademi, 1996), p. 22.

As such, the 'sacred' is a relational and situational category that 'becomes visible in beliefs and practices in which value-laden distinctions are negotiated' in relation to 'powers and dangers'[49] associated with things, places, or events on either side of a boundary: 'Human beings have the dispositional property to invest the boundary-points of categories of for instance time, space and the human body with special referential value and inferential potential. This capacity is activated in places set apart as sacred.'[50] According to Anttonen, then, space is fully implicated in the notion of the 'sacred' — in its generation in the cognitive unconscious and its conceptualisation, but also in its practice (ritual) and expression (representation). Body and territory are formative for conceiving of the 'sacred' and for marking off or separating things, places, and events; space — physical, mental, and social — is the arena in which the sacred operates, whether at fixed boundaries (walls and fences), in topographical features (such as openings or fissures), at points of temporal or social transition, the margins of social groups, or zones between inhabited and uninhabited areas.[51]

Anttonen's theoretical work on space and the 'sacred', in taking the same starting point as my own study — in the body and the regions that surround it — and engaging the concepts we use in the study of religions with the semantics of space (mental space) and real places (physical and social space), offers a methodology for identifying and comparing sacred-making practice and sites of the sacred that is particularly useful for this study, and to which I shall return towards the end of Part II.

The scholars whose work I have highlighted here have begun to turn the study of religion and space away from the insular concerns of the early phenomenological agenda of sacred space. In turning increasingly to issues of material production and practice, power and ideology, representation and strategy, the ordinary as well as the special, and in their problematising of notions such as 'sacred', 'place', and 'home', they are clearly situated *within the same debate* as many of the theorists whose work was reviewed in the first chapter. However, whilst Smith, Anttonen, Chidester and Linenthal, and Tobler have engaged actively with the work of theoretical geographers and social and feminist theorists writing about space and place, regrettably we would be hard-pressed to find any

49. Anttonen, 'Sacred Sites as Markers of Difference', p. 57. See Chapter 9.

50. Veikko Anttonen, 'Identifying the Generative Mechanisms of Religion: The Issue of Origin Revisited', in Ilkka Pyysiäinen and Veikko Anttonen (eds.), *Current Approaches in the Cognitive Study of Religion* (London and New York: Continuum, 2002), pp. 14-37 (31).

51. Anttonen, 'Sacred Sites as Markers of Difference', pp. 297-98; see also Anttonen, 'Rethinking the Sacred', pp. 47-54.

reverse engagement. This failure on the part of most scholars of space and place outside religious studies to read the work of Smith and others illustrates the blinkered approach adopted in general within academic disciplines and, I would suggest, the bias against religion and those who study it in the predominantly secular academy. This is a further demonstration of the force relations of the 'religious' and the 'secular' to which I referred earlier. There is an exception to this, however, and I shall consider it now: the geography of religion.

The Geography of Religion

It was Erich Isaac in an article in 1965 who distinguished between 'religious geography' and the 'geography of religion', suggesting the former to be the proper terrain of theologians and comparative religionists, and the latter the terrain of geographers.[52] Some later geographers, however, have called for scholars on both sides to be well acquainted with one another's work, even for an informed understanding and study of the dialectical reciprocity of religion and the environment.[53] Despite this theory of mutuality, however, relatively few geographers of religion are well versed in work on space, place, and geography by those in the field of religious studies per se. Chris Park, for example, in his major survey of geography and religion, *Sacred Worlds*, fails to cite the work of either Jonathan Z. Smith or Paul Wheatley, though Mircea Eliade and Ninian Smart (whose name is not particularly associated with the study of sacred space) are mentioned in passing.

It is unnecessary for me to undertake a survey of this field given the excellent reviews that already exist by Büttner, Sopher, Kong, Cooper, Park, Henkel, and Knott which together show the great range and scale of research undertaken on religion, quantitative and qualitative, in social and humanistic geography.[54] Rather, I shall concentrate on the agenda for

52. Erich Isaac, 'Religious Geography and the Geography of Religions', *Man and the Earth* (Series in Earth Sciences, 3; Boulder, CO: University of Colorado Press, 1960), pp. 1-14. See also Park, *Sacred Worlds*, pp. 18-19. Richard F. Townsend, from the side of religious studies, implicitly confirms this division of duties by focusing exclusively on 'sacred geography' in his entry on 'Geography', in Eliade (ed.), *Encyclopedia of Religion*, V, pp. 509-13.

53. Lily Kong, 'Geography of Religion: Trends and Prospects', *Progress in Human Geography* 14 (1990), pp. 355-71; Adrian Cooper, 'New Directions in the Geography of Religion', *Area* 24 (1992), pp. 123-29; Park, *Sacred Worlds*, but see also the early intervention by Manfred Büttner, 'Religion and Geography: Impulses for a New Dialogue between *Religionswissenschaftlern* and Geography', *Numen* 21 (1974), pp. 165-96.

54. Manfred Büttner, 'Survey Article on the History and Philosophy of the Geography of Religion in Germany', *Religion* 10.2 (1980), pp. 86-119; David E. Sopher,

new geographies of religion suggested by Lily Kong in her 2001 review of the subject.[55]

After summarising recent scholarship on the politics and poetics of the sacred (drawing on the work of Chidester and Linenthal which I discussed earlier),[56] and on identity and community, Kong calls for 'new geographies', relevant to the conditions of modernity, that reflect,

> 1) different sites of religious practice beyond the 'officially sacred'; 2) different sensuous sacred geographies; 3) different religions in different historical and place-specific contexts; 4) different geographical scales of analysis; 5) different constitutions of population; 6) different dialectics; and 7) different moralities.[57]

As these are relevant, to a greater or lesser extent, to my own objectives, they are worthy of further consideration.

In her call for the study of sites of religious practice beyond the officially sacred, Kong suggests such places as religious schools, communal halls, the routes (as well as the destinations) of pilgrims, religious objects, roadside and domestic shrines, religious processions, and virtual religious sites.[58] Thus, as with some of the scholars discussed earlier, she acknowledges the virtue of seeing beyond traditional sacred spaces. Like them, though, she stops short of suggesting non-religious sites for the geographical study of religions, the sites in which religion/the sacred is apparently absent. In earlier articles, however, in which she writes about religious buildings in Singapore, it may be said that she looks closely at the oppositional meanings and values evident in negotiations between religious people and representatives of the state about the siting of such buildings and their removal.[59] She is sensitive to the politics of symbolic

'Geography and Religion', *Progress in Human Geography* 5 (1981), pp. 510-24; Kong, 'Geography of Religion: Trends and Prospects'; Cooper, 'New Direction in the Geography of Religion'; Park, *Sacred Worlds*; Reinhard Henkel, 'Der Arbeitskreis Religionsgeographie in der Deutschen Gesellschaft für Geographie—Bilanz 1983 bis 1998', in H. Karrasch (ed.), 'Geographie: Tradition and Forschritt', *Heidelberger Geographische Gesellschaft* 12 (2000), pp. 269-72; Lily Kong, 'Mapping "New" Geographies of Religion: Politics and Poetics in Modernity', *Progress in Human Geography* 25.2 (2001), pp. 211-33; Knott, 'Religion and Locality: Issues and Methods', and 'Britain's Changing Landscape'.

55. See also the 2002 editorial by Julian Holloway and Oliver Valins, 'Placing Religion and Spirituality in Geography', *Social and Cultural Geography* 3.1 (2002), pp. 5-9.

56. Unlike many geographers, Kong is extremely well-informed about the work done on religion by those in other academic disciplines.

57. Kong, 'Mapping "New" Geographies', p. 228.

58. Kong, 'Mapping "New" Geographies', p. 226.

59. Kong, 'Negotiating Conceptions of Sacred Space', and 'Ideological Hegemony and the Political Symbolism of Religious Buildings in Singapore', *Environment and Planning D: Society and Space* 11 (1993), pp. 23-45.

meanings and values in a heterogeneous context in which a variety of religious as well as secular voices have an interest.[60]

One way in which religious practice — particularly through identity — is increasingly seen to transform space is through residential patterns. In his study of 'stubborn' ultra-Orthodox Jewish identities and their boundary-making capacities, Oliver Valins examines how perceptions by ultra-Orthodox 'of themselves as moral and pure…[lead] to a perceived need to defend their way of life against outside society, portrayed as impure and corrupt'.[61] This need contributes to and is informed by both residential concentration (in Manchester, England) and the imagination of sameness and difference.[62]

On her next subject, 'different sensuous sacred geographies', Kong is largely silent beyond calling for a shift from the focus on the visual, though we may note that she herself has written about the politics and moralities of music.[63] The oral and aural, however, is a significant theme in the collection edited by Barbara Daly Metcalf, *Making Muslim Space*, with several contributions discussing *nat* (hymns in praise of the Prophet Muhammad), *zikr* (the repetition of the name of Allah), and *azan* (the call to prayer),[64] perhaps showing the timeliness of Kong's call and its relevance, at least in the context of Islamic traditions. For my work, this plea is opportune. As I stated in the previous chapter with regard to people's experience of space — it is sensed, as well as thought and practised.

In her third agenda item Kong appeals for greater context-sensitivity in the study of a variety of religious groups, including those in multicultural locations. Whilst interesting studies have been conducted, she says, on places outside 'the traditional centres' (by which I take it she means the

60. Lily Kong, 'Re-Presenting the Religious: Nation, Community and Identity in Museums' (paper presented at the Royal Geographical Society — Institute of British Geographers Annual Conference, September 2003).

61. Oliver Valins, 'Stubborn Identities and the Construction of Socio-Spatial Boundaries: Ultra-Orthodox Jews Living in Contemporary Britain', *Transactions of the Institute of British Geographers* NS 28 (2003), pp. 158-75 (159).

62. See also the work of Debbie Phillips and Peter Ratcliffe on Muslim, Sikh, and Hindu mobility in the English cities of Leeds and Bradford, <http://www.geog.leeds.ac.uk/projects/mobility/> (accessed August 2003).

63. Lily Kong, 'The Politics of Music in Singapore: Moral Panics, Moral Guardians' (unpublished paper presented at the Institute of Australian Geographers' Conference, September 1999).

64. Barbara Daly Metcalf, 'Introduction: Sacred Words, Sanctioned Practice, New Communities'; Regula Burckhardt Qureshi, 'Transcending Space: Recitation and Community among South Asian Muslims in Canada'; Pnina Werbner, 'Stamping the Earth with the Name of Allah: Zikr and the Sacralizing of Space among British Muslims'; and John Eade, 'Nationalism, Community, and the Islamization of Space in London', in Daly Metcalf (ed.), *Making Muslim Space*, pp. 1-30, 46-64, 167-85 and 217-33, respectively.

major European countries and North America), the same critical discussions — inspired by post-colonial theory — have yet to be brought to bear on the 'centres' themselves. One exception she cites is Claire Dwyer, whose work on community and identity among young British Muslims suggests that they are forging 'some discursive, but also perhaps material, possibilities as a means to contest homogeneous constructions of "young Asian women" as passive and powerless and to resist parental authority within some contexts'.[65] The work of Christine Chivallon on African-Caribbean Christians in Britain, discussed in Chapter 2, provides a further example of the growing tendency in spatial studies of religion to examine critically the categories of religion, race, identity, and community. That this is occurring is confirmed by Ceri Peach who cites examples of work being conducted on new minority ethnic populations in Britain and the USA:[66]

> Religion is the new key to unravelling ethnic identity in the west. From the 1950s to the 1980s, the British discourse was about race. Non-European immigrants and minorities were compressed, willing or unwilling, into a 'black' category. In the 1990s, interest shifted from the outer skin of race to the inner onion of ethnicity, thence to multi-ethnicity and now to religion.[67]

My own work on the changing religious landscape, in addition to that of Simon Naylor, James Ryan and Richard Gale, demonstrates how this shift of emphasis is affecting the geography of religion in Britain.[68]

Kong's request for a consideration of different geographical scales chimes with my own interest in investigating the location of religion in the places of the body, things, events, communities, localities, and institutions.[69] Scale remains an important consideration in social and cultural geography: a recent textbook on social geographies is organised on this basis.[70] As Holloway and Valins note, 'geographers are beginning to

65. Claire Dwyer, 'Contradictions of Community: Questions of Identity for Young British Muslim Women', *Environment and Planning A* 31 (1999), pp. 53-68 (66), and *idem*, 'Veiled Meanings'. A further exception is the work of Naylor and Ryan, for example, 'The Mosque in the Suburbs'.

66. Ceri Peach, 'Social Geography: New Religions and Ethnoburbs — Contrasts with Cultural Geography', *Progress in Human Geography* 26.2 (2002), pp. 252-60. Note also the comparative work of Reinhard Henkel, 'Comparing the Religious Landscapes of the United States and Germany' (paper presented at the University of Connecticut, March 2001).

67. Peach, 'Social Geography', p. 255 (citations removed).

68. Knott, 'Britain's Changing Religious Landscape'; Naylor and Ryan, 'The Mosque in the Suburbs', and 'Tracing the Geographies of Religious Minorities in the UK'; Gale and Naylor, 'Religion, Planning and the City'.

69. The global and local scales she mentions will be discussed further in the next section.

70. Valentine, *Social Geographies*.

recognize more fully the powerful and contingent role of religion and spirituality on a range of geographical scales, from the corporeal, to the institutional, to the geopolitical'.[71] The examples they are able to give of those conducting such studies are small in number, however.

By 'different constitutions of population' Kong means groups, such as women, children, the elderly, and teenagers, whom she suggests require different geographies. She writes of 'the way in which religious place holds different meanings and exerts different influences' on these separate groups.[72] What she neglects to say, however, is how such constituencies have contributed to or been absent from the formation of religious places, and have thus been involved in their production as well as their reproduction. Issues discussed in Chapter 2, on Muslim women's use and interpretation of the *hijab* and on representations of the turban worn by Sikh men, provide examples of this. In addition, as we saw in Tobler's analysis of gendered sacred space and in Blum and Nast's critique of the work of Lefebvre (in Chapter 1), women in particular are caught up in the way places are perceived, conceived, and experienced.

Kong's sixth 'new geography' is 'different dialectics', and the particular dialectic which she attends to is the poetics and politics of space, following Chidester and Linenthal.[73] In terms of this pairing, poetics/politics, it is the latter rather than the former that is of most interest in this study, as is also the case in Chidester and Linenthal's work, where the thrust is towards examining the social and political engagement with and contest over sacred space rather than on developing an imaginative vocabulary for typologising sacred spaces. Kong also encourages the exploration of other dialectical pairings, such as private/public and social/spatial, and there is some evidence that other geographers of religion concur. Valins, for example, employs notions of same/different and in place/out of place.[74] In this study, as I showed in Chapter 3, a dialectical approach will be employed with regard to the religious/secular.

Kong's final agenda item is 'different moralities'. Citing the work of David Smith and David Harvey,[75] she refers to the recent moral turn in geography, and reflects that,

71. Holloway and Valins, 'Placing Religion and Spirituality', p. 5 (citations removed).

72. Kong, 'Mapping "New" Geographies', p. 227.

73. Chidester and Linenthal, 'Introduction', *American Sacred Space*. The term 'poetics of space' comes originally from Gaston Bachelard, *The Poetics of Space* (Boston: Beacon Press, 1969 [French edn 1957]).

74. Valins, 'Stubborn Identities'.

75. David M. Smith, *Geography and Social Justice* (Oxford: Basil Blackwell, 1994), and David Harvey, *Justice, Nature, and the Geography of Difference* (Oxford: Basil Blackwell, 1996).

[w]hile morality and social justice may exist apart from religion, often religion is the basis of morality and the impetus for social justice, as well as of intolerance and injustice. Yet, how different religions may inform the constructions of different moral geographies has not been explored, and how these constructed moral geographies contradict or are negotiated or reinforced by other secular agents of morality (for example, the state) requires examination.[76]

She invites a consideration of competing religious conceptions, and of religious and secular conceptions of good/bad, just/unjust, and also recognises how, through a process of dedifferentiation, the secular may itself become 'less obviously secular' as it is expressed through new social movements such as those focused on ecological issues.[77] Holloway and Valins support Kong in calling for work on the place of religion in 'systems of ethics and morality, architecture, systems of patriarchy and the construction of law, government or the role of the voluntary sector'.[78] They go on to ask, 'What role does religion play in "secular" notions of right and wrong, in the "correct" and "moral" ways to run societies, the practices (and ethics) of consumption, or in the (historical and contemporary) constructions of the relative places of men and women, straight and gay?'[79] In so doing, they note Foucault's point, which informed my discussion in Chapter 3, that religion has been instrumental in the construction of secular society.

Kong's new agenda raises important concerns for contemporary geography of religion, some of which, as I have shown, are pertinent to this study. Notable by its absence, however, is any explicit reference to the engagement of geography of religion with the social and cultural theory developed elsewhere within geographical studies. Indeed, it is clear from the reviews of the field by Park as well as Kong that geography of religion has largely taken the form of empirical studies, broadly in the four areas previously identified by Sopher: denominational geography, the landscapes and spatial organisation of particular religious groups, the development of sacred centres, and pilgrimage.[80] Kong's most recent review shows that the concerns of geographers of religion are broadening and are being affected by developments in postcolonial studies and postmodern

76. Kong, 'Mapping "New" Geographies', p. 228.
77. Kong, 'Mapping "New" Geographies', p. 228. She is indebted to Paul Heelas here in his 'Introduction on Differentiation and Dedifferentiation', in *idem* (ed.), with David Martin and Paul Morris, *Religion, Modernity, and Postmodernity* (Oxford: Basil Blackwell, 1998), pp. 1-18.
78. Holloway and Valins, 'Placing Religion and Spirituality', p. 6.
79. Holloway and Valins, 'Placing Religion and Spirituality', p. 6.
80. Sopher, 'Geography and Religion'; Park, *Sacred Worlds*, p. 20.

geography, even if they have further to go in contributing directly to those theoretical debates.[81]

Religion and Globalisation

Hearing the voices of those living transnational lives and reading the work of globalisation theorists has affected my thinking on the role of place and nature of space in human experience. The conservative verities of 'home', 'community', and one's own place, both as the starting point for understanding the other and as a stable retreat from the pressures of social change, have inevitably been brought into question by the late-modern processes—economic, political, social, and cultural—that we now refer to as 'globalisation'.[82] Defined by Robertson as 'both the compression of the world and the intensification of consciousness of the world as a whole',[83] this has had consequences for how both space and religion are experienced by actors and understood by commentators. It is not only that people's perceptions of space and religion are thought to be changing as a result of global processes, but that questions are raised about the adequacy of existing theories to explain previous perceptions. Perhaps places and communities, for example, have always been more porous and less settled than had been supposed. Certainly, many religions have had global as well as local aspirations and consequences. In fact religion was perhaps 'the original globalizer', an idea which, according to Lehmann, challenges the common assumption that markets occupy this role.[84] By referring to both global compression and global consciousness, Robertson has stressed the centrality of both spatial and cultural factors in world-system analysis. Late-modern processes are not only about the movements of capital, people, and information, but also about ideas, images, and feelings of global interconnectedness. These issues have been explored by a number of theorists,[85] including Robertson himself, who have pursued

81. See Holloway and Valins, 'Placing Religion and Spirituality', p. 6.

82. See the words of a young British Bengali, Justna, cited by Eade (ed.), *Living the Global City*, p. 159, on the meaning of 'home' in the context of globalisation: Justna has no home or first place from which to view and evaluate other places and cultures. See also Knott, 'The Sense and Nonsense of "Community"'; Casey, *The Fate of Place*.

83. Robertson, *Globalization*, p. 8.

84. David Lehmann, 'Religion and Globalisation', in Linda Woodhead, Paul Fletcher, Hiroko Kawanawi and David Smith (eds.), *Religion in the Modern World* (London and New York: Routledge, 2001), pp. 299-315 (299).

85. Giddens, *The Consequences of Modernity*; Michael Featherstone (ed.), *Global Culture: Nationalism, Globalization and Modernity* (London, Thousand Oaks, New Delhi: Sage, 1990); Featherstone, *Undoing Culture*; Appadurai, *Modernity at Large*; Ulf Hannerz, *Transcontinental Connections* (London and New York: Routledge, 1996); Martin Albrow, *The Global Age: State and Society beyond Modernity* (Cambridge: Polity, 1996). These

several lines of enquiry of potential importance for a study of religion and space: the development of a new vocabulary for conceptualising social and cultural space, and the investigation of the following themes, the impact of the new communications, the growth of transnational and diasporic identities and networks, the engagement of politics and religion, and the relationship of global and local cultures.[86] We should not think that religion is confined only to the penultimate of these. As I shall show in the brief survey that follows, it is implicated in them all.

On the cover of John Eade's edited collection, *Living the Global City*, several questions are posed which strongly suggest that the study of globalisation destabilises apparently traditional conceptions: What does 'home' mean in globalised conditions? Death of the 'local'? Death of the 'social'?[87] In fact, even a cursory examination of the theoretical literature on globalisation shows that, just as talk of death of God or death of religion by sociologists and philosophers of religion may have been premature, talk of the demise of such notions as home, local, social, as well as community and place is probably short-sighted and alarmist. But the spaces, institutions, and processes to which they refer have certainly changed, leading at times to a felt need for a new technical vocabulary. Hence we find scholars experimenting with terms such as 'scapes', 'spheres', 'flows', and 'milieux' in an attempt to describe and explain with precision the social and cultural formations and processes at work under conditions of globalisation.[88] These have been utilised increasingly within

works are of general relevance to a social and cultural analysis of globalisation. See below for references on specific aspects of the process.

86. Steven Vertovec also provides a list of themes in his discussion of global religious change: awareness of global religious identities; universalisation vs. localisation; what is essential in a religious tradition; politico-religious activity; reorienting devotion; the problem with the past; compartmentalisation; and trajectories. Steven Vertovec, 'Religion and Diaspora', in Peter Antes, Armin W. Geertz and Randi Warne (eds.), *New Approaches to the Study of Religion* (Berlin and New York: W. de Gruyter, 2004) (an electronic version of this paper is available as a Transnational Communities Programme working paper on <http://www.transcomm.ox.ac.uk/working%20papers/Vertovec01.pdf>).

87. Eade (ed.), *Living the Global City*.

88. This new terminology is attributable as follows: 'scapes' — Appadurai, *Modernity at Large*, and 'Disjunction and Difference in the Global Cultural Economy', in Featherstone (ed.), *Global Culture*, pp. 295-310; and Martin Albrow, 'Travelling Beyond Local Cultures: Socioscapes in a Global City', in Eade (ed.), *Living the Global City*, pp. 37-55; 'spheres' — Albrow, 'Travelling Beyond Local Cultures'; 'flows' — Manuel Castells, *The Informational City* (Oxford: Basil Blackwell, 1989); Appadurai, 'Disjunction and Difference'; and 'milieux' — Jörg Dürrschmidt, 'The Delinking of Locale and Milieu: On the Situatedness of Extended Milieux in a Global Environment', in Eade (ed.), *Living the Global City*, pp. 56-72. Other key globalisation terms have included those referred to in Chapter 1, 'time-space compression' (Harvey), 'distanciation' and

the study of religions to refer to the ways in which contemporary net-works and movements, ideas and practices operate.[89] Several scholars, for example, have critiqued and amended Arjun Appadurai's influential list of 'scapes' (ethnoscape, technoscape, finanscape, mediascape, and ideo-scape), adding 'sacriscape' (Waters), 'religioscape' (Dwyer), and 'sacred landscape' (Lyon).[90]

All these scapes are constituted by flows, of people, information, images, money, and culture, which are enabled and enhanced by new communications technologies. Religions — both traditional and new — have been as affected by this as other institutions (or scapes), sometimes being at the fore of specialist media developments, for example in tele-vangelism, virtual communities, or the provision of cyber pilgrimage or ritual. Ironically, many conservative religious groups have developed and employed 'the means of modernity [in order] to oppose its message'.[91] Global evangelicalism, Islamic revivalism (or Islamism), and new conser-vative religious movements do just this.[92]

Peter Beyer, in his book on religion and globalisation, states that religion itself is a 'certain variety of communication'.[93] Above all, relig-ions are systems which link the transcendent with the immanent, though their 'communicative contexts change'.[94] Perhaps unsurprisingly then

---

'disembedding' (Giddens), and 'power-geometry' (Massey), as well as the term popu-larised by Robertson, 'glocalisation', to which reference will be made towards the end of this section. The terms 'transnationalism' and 'diaspora' have also become popular in the depiction of late-modern global communications and consciousness. The word 'fundamentalism', which predates theoretical discussion of globalisation, has never-theless become a key term in its vocabulary. Many theorists with no interest in or knowledge of religion refer to it as an aspect of the globalising process.

89.   A recent study that applies globalisation theory to local religious conditions is Tuomas Martikainen's *Immigrant Religions in Local Society: Historical and Contemporary Perspectives in the City of Turku* (Åbo: Åbo Akademi University Press, 2004).

90.   Malcolm Waters, *Globalization* (London: Routledge, 1995); Rachel Dwyer, 'The Swaminarayan Movement', in Knut A. Jacobsen and P. Pratap Kumar (eds.), *South Asians in the Diaspora: Histories and Religious Traditions* (Leiden and Boston: E.J. Brill, 2004), pp. 180-99; Lyon, *Jesus in Disneyland*.

91.   Grace Davie, *Religion in Modern Europe: A Memory Mutates* (Oxford: Oxford University Press, 2000), p. 148.

92.   Gilles Kepel, *The Revenge of God* (Cambridge: Polity, 1994), and *Allah in the West* (Cambridge: Polity, 1997); Manuel Castells, *The Rise of the Network Society* (Cambridge. MA, and Oxford: Basil Blackwell, 1996); Davie, *Religion in Modern Europe*; Lyon, *Jesus in Disneyland*; Simon Coleman, *The Globalisation of Charismatic Christianity: Spreading the Gospel of Prosperity* (Cambridge: Cambridge University Press, 2000); John Wolffe, 'Evangelicals and Pentecostals: Indigenizing a Global Gospel', in *idem* (ed.), *Global Religious Movements in Regional Context* (Aldershot and Burlington, VT: Ashgate, in association with the Open University, 2002), pp. 13-108.

93.   Beyer, *Religion and Globalization*, p. 5.

94.   Lyon, *Jesus in Disneyland*, p. 59.

they utilise whatever means are at their disposal—within any theologi-
cally imposed limits (such as the teaching on the prohibition of music
within many Islamic traditions)—in order to facilitate communication
with believers, to convey teachings, and to attract newcomers or the
lapsed. In late-modernity these means include the frequent movement of
persons—whether charismatic leaders or bodies of adherents—electronic
as well as conventional transmission of information, e-communication as
well as telecommunication, the reproduction and circulation of visual
and aural images and sounds, the enactment of ritual and spiritual
community in cyberspace, and, more disturbingly, the mass promotion
of religious hatred.[95] These novel media themselves create new religio-
spatial possibilities, such as unforeseen connections between individuals
or groups, new audiences or types of adherence, unusual sites, forms and
textures in which to reproduce old or produce new religious practices,
ideas, or images, new global events or rituals, and new virtual spiritual
bodies. As Caputo has noted, 'religion shows every sign of adapting with
Darwinian dexterity...of flourishing in a new high-tech form, and of
entering into an amazing symbiosis with the "virtual culture" '.[96]

It is not only religions as systems of communication that are afforded
new possibilities in a compressed world connected by electronic and
digital technologies, but also socio-religious collectivities, including new
diasporic communities (such as the Khalistani Sikhs, Rastafarians, and
Baha'is), global pentecostal movements, and the network of New Age
interests. The communications that enable the repeated ideological and
practical reproduction of such collectivities is speeded up in late-modernity, in some cases reinforcing community where it might otherwise have
declined, in some enabling the development of new forms of sociality,
and, in others, opening them up to new audiences.

One of several ways in which the issue of religious community has
been discussed in the context of globalisation has been in terms of transnationalism and diaspora (another being fundamentalism, see below).

95. These are variously explored by J.K. Hadden and D.E. Cowan (eds.), *Religion on the Internet: Research Prospects and Promises* (Amsterdam, London, New York: JAI/Elsevier Science, 2000); Gary Bunt, *Virtually Islamic: Computer-Mediated Communications and Cyber Islamic Environments* (Cardiff: University of Cardiff Press, 2000); Coleman, Chapter 7, 'Broadcasting the Faith', in *The Globalisation of Charismatic Christianity*; Lyon, Chapter 4, 'Signs of the Times', in *Jesus in Disneyland*; Gwilym Beckerlegge, 'Computer-Mediated Religion: Religion on the Internet at the Turn of the Twenty-First Century', in *idem* (ed.), *From Sacred Text to Internet* (Aldershot and Burlington, VT: Ashgate, in association with the Open University, 2001), pp. 219-64; Anastasia Karaflogka, *Religion and Cyberspace* (London: Equinox, forthcoming).

96. Caputo, *On Religion*, pp. 67-68.

Lest we should confuse or conflate these, Steven Vertovec has provided a sensible distinction, showing also how they relate to migration:

> I consider migration to involve the transference and reconstitution of cultural patterns and social relations in a new setting, one that usually involves the migrants as minorities becoming set apart by "race", language, cultural traditions and religion. I refer to diaspora here especially as an imagined connection between a post-migration (including refugee) population and a place of origin and with people of similar cultural origins elsewhere... By transnationalism I refer to the actual, ongoing exchanges of information, money and resources — as well as regular travel and communication — that members of a diaspora may undertake with others in the homeland or elsewhere within the globalized ethnic community. Diasporas arise from some forms of migration, but not all migration involves diasporic consciousness; all transnational communities comprise diasporas, but not all diasporas develop transnationalism.[97]

It is evident from this that new spaces, in which religions may be active, repeatedly emerge from these migrational processes, and that these are physical (new landscapes and global geographical connections with places of origin), mental (having an imagined as well as actual form), and social.[98] Whilst these processes offer many opportunities for the study of religions in such transnational and diasporic contexts, these need not all involve looking at multiple geographical sites over several continents. Some may consider very specific places, people, or objects which focus these processes.[99] One study which takes a comparative view of two Muslim populations in an English city, one actively transnational, the other diasporic in its imaginative maintenance of global community, is Sarah Smalley's account of Pakistanis and Khoja Shi'a Ithna'asheris of East African Asian origin.[100] It distinguishes the two in their orientations to Britain and beyond, the Pakistanis being notable for their dual focus on Pakistan and Britain, expressed through marriage, visits, and dispersal of

---

97.   Vertovec, 'Religion and Diaspora'. For a study that considers both contemporary and early cases of religions in diaspora, see ter Haar (ed.), *Strangers and Sojourners*.

98.   That recent diasporas themselves produce new spaces of identity is discussed in various studies, including Avtar Brah, *Cartographies of Diaspora: Contesting Identities* (London and New York: Routledge, 1996); Chivallon, 'Religion as Space'; Pnina Werbner, 'The Place which is Diaspora: Citizenship, Religion and Gender in the Making of Chaordic Transnationalism', *Journal of Ethnic and Migration Studies* 28.1 (2002), pp. 119-33.

99.   Examples include studies of black African Arab foyers and Mouride hotel rooms in Daly Metcalf (ed.), *Making Muslim Space*; also Martikainen, *Immigrant Religions in Local Society*, on the Finnish city of Turku.

100.   Sarah Smalley, 'Islamic Nurture in the West: Approaches to Parenting amongst Second Generation Pakistanis and Khojas in Peterborough' (PhD thesis, University of Leeds, 2002).

finances, and the Khojas for a more single-minded focus on Britain as home, but within a global religious and social consciousness, maintained particularly through telephone and the Internet.

Such transnational and diasporic communities, in maintaining communications with kin in diverse locations and a consciousness of common geographical and religious origins and concerns, are not infrequently associated in the public mind with fundamentalism, often quite incorrectly. To make sense of this assumption, it is useful to cite the distinction offered by Bruce Lawrence, between literalist, terrorist, and political activist fundamentalisms.[101] Unlike Christian literalist fundamentalism, a form often associated with American evangelicalism, the other forms are generally identified with religions other than Christianity, and are often global in outreach, anti-modernist and anti-Western, sometimes marked by diasporic consciousness and/or nationalist sentiments, and political in character.[102] Above all, however, fundamentalism — of whatever kind — is religious, 'in that it derives from charismatic leaders who uphold a particular interpretation of scripture as the only fail-safe device for protesting against the phalanx of modernism', which is itself ideological and perpetuates global inequalities.[103] It is, what is more, 'a specifically post-modern form of religion'.[104]

But how do global religious politics, particularly in so-called fundamentalist forms, affect space and how it is conceived? Sometimes an actual physical site is contested, whether a territory or a symbolic place or object. Such a space may have profound theological significance for more than one group (such as Jerusalem), hence the fight for its ownership or control. It may become the target in an ideological struggle — the Babri mosque in Ayodhya and the World Trade Center being two examples.

Virtual spaces, as we saw earlier, are also central to the success of late-modern religious movements, not least of all those with a political agenda.

101.   Bruce B. Lawrence, 'From Fundamentalism to Fundamentalisms: A Religious Ideology in Multiple Forms', in Heelas (ed.), *Religion, Modernity, and Postmodernity*, pp. 88-101 (89). But see also Conkle on multiple secular fundamentalisms in 'Secular Fundamentalism, Religious Fundamentalism, and the Search for Truth in Contemporary America'.

102.   For a far-reaching study of fundamentalism, see the five volumes of the Fundamentalism Project, edited by Martin Marty and Scott Appleby and published by the University of Chicago in the 1990s. Lehmann offers a useful list of the characteristics of fundamentalist forms of globalisation in 'Religion and Globalisation', p. 306.

103.   Lawrence, 'From Fundamentalism to Fundamentalisms', p. 96.

104.   Bauman, 'Postmodern Religion?', p. 72. Lehmann suggests, however, that to be fundamentalist or charismatic is 'to be modern' ('Religion and Globalization', p. 312).

Such movements are willing to move into new cyberspaces, and to utilise electronic media to move information and capital in support of their cause. 'Fundamentalism has transplanted the advanced communications systems into its own body and, in order to tolerate the transplant, has suppressed its natural auto-immune systems', which one might have expected to reject such a modernist product.[105] As Bauman suggests, fundamentalists both have their cake and eat it.[106]

Additionally, Robertson's recognition that globalisation signals an intensification of consciousness of the world as a whole reminds us that the global space itself is of ideological significance for some movements. Revivalist Islamic groups stress membership of the worldwide *umma*; religious environmentalists an ethic of physical and social interconnectedness. Global space — whether physical, social, or mental — is religiously conceived anew, and such conceptions may themselves become influential beyond their movement of origin, or may lead to unforeseen consequences, such as humanitarian acts or, conversely, acts of terror.

What is sometimes neglected in accounts of worldwide religio-political movements inspired by globalisation is the history of colonialism which often informs them. Sociological and economic theories of globalisation are rarely engaged with the historical and cultural theories and data of colonialism and postcolonialism. Yet the two have much to say to one another. As we shall see in Chapter 8, the global spread of ideas and practices originating in the Indian subcontinent, and their reproduction and adaptation in new Western locations are a consequence of colonialist — and orientalist — engagement and cultural acquisition from the eighteenth to the twentieth century.[107] Postcolonialist — and also feminist — approaches, which seek to investigate the historical power relations inherent in the global economy and global social and cultural developments, bring a different theoretical perspective to the discussion of globalisation and its impact on both global and local scales.

As Robertson himself makes clear, however, consciousness of the world and the global spread of images and messages should not lead to the assumption that cultural homogeneity has triumphed at the expense of heterogeneity.[108] Neither the infectious Toronto Blessing,[109] nor the

---

105.   Following Jacques Derrida, Caputo, *On Religion*, p. 106.

106.   Bauman, 'Postmodern Religion?', p. 72.

107.   R. King, *Orientalism and Religion*. See also the work of Hugh B. Urban on Tantrism in the West cited in Chapter 8.

108.   Roland Robertson, 'Glocalization: Time-Space and Homogeneity–Heterogeneity', in Michael Featherstone, Scott Lash and Roland Robertson (eds.), *Global Modernities* (London, Thousand Oaks, New Delhi: Sage, 1995), pp. 24-44.

109.   Lyon, *Jesus in Disneyland*, Chapter 6.

popular rhetoric of worldwide *umma* signify an irrevocable turning away from locally distinctive cultural expressions. To quote Hannerz,

> There is now a world culture, but we had better make sure we understand what that means: not a replication of uniformity but an organization of diversity, an increasing interconnectedness of varied local cultures, as well as a development of cultures without a clear anchorage in any one territory.[110]

Globalisation then stimulates local as well as global cultures and the links between them, a process Robertson refers to as 'glocalization', following the Japanese business principle of micro-marketing or *dochakuka*.[111] The global success, for example, of the Hindu *Swaminarayan Movement* or the charismatic Christian *Word of Life* reaches back to their places of origin, in Gujarat, India, and Sweden, with flows of money, pilgrims, and cultural accretions from many distant parts of the world.[112] Additionally, new locations in which these movements take root contextualise them in their own ways. This confirms the point I made earlier, that attention to the processes of globalisation does not only invite a study of universal spaces and global connections, but also of particular places, persons, and objects that participate in and are affected by globalisation. In his study of the impact of globalisation on the religious field of Turku, Tuomas Martikainen illustrates the interconnection between the global and the local —in this case through the media flow of information—with a telling quotation from one Muslim migrant,

> If the newspaper says there is something bad in Islam, I will see this in the eyes of Finns tomorrow… When I live with this kind of condition, I am in a prison. Even when there are no walls around me… Because the sky is not just over Finland. The sky is over the whole world.[113]

The 'glocal reality' which such migrants experience has a profound impact not only on their own identity but on the nature of local social and religious life.[114] It is to the subject of the local that I shall now turn in concluding this examination of resources within the study of religions for a spatial analysis of religion.

---

110.   Hannerz, *Transcontinental Connections*, p. 102. This is also quoted by Coleman in his informative study of 'Word of Life', a global charismatic Christian movement with its roots in Sweden, which 'appears both to celebrate and to transcend' the Swedish context, *The Globalisation of Charismatic Christianity*, p. 16.

111.   Robertson, 'Glocalization', p. 28.

112.   R. Dwyer, 'The Swaminarayan Movement'; Raymond Brady Williams, *An Introduction to Swaminarayan Hinduism* (Cambridge: Cambridge University Press, 2001); Coleman, *The Globalisation of Charismatic Christianity*.

113.   Martikainen, *Immigrant Religions in Local Society*, pp. 234-35.

114.   Martikainen, *Immigrant Religions in Local Society*, p. 235.

Religion and Locality

Though only recently described as a distinct approach to studying religions, 'religion and locality' could be said to embrace previous studies
conducted in a variety of locations with a common concern for examining
the interrelationship between religious groups and their activities, and
their immediate environs.[115] I have discussed the contours, benefits, and
possible agenda of such an engagement and suggested several formative
questions:

> How is a particular, local religion formed by its context, and how does it
> grow and change as its context changes? How does it express itself
> through this context? This is not just a question of the effect of local
> demographic, social, economic, and political factors upon religion. Relig-
> ions and the institutions and individuals that constitute them do not arise
> passively from their local circumstances. They recruit and are built by
> local people with their own particular interests; they meet local needs.
> What, then, are the local forms and styles of these religious bodies, and
> how and why have they come about? How do local religions engage with
> one another and with other local agencies and institutions, meeting local
> needs and producing locally informed networks? To what extent do
> religions perceive their locales as sacred, or their people specially blessed
> or empowered? Do local religious bodies look outward to external
> national or global centres of activity and authority, or within to their own
> sources and resources? How do the local, national, and global interact,
> and with what consequences? ...And how, as students and scholars, are
> we to study these local forms? What is our place, having stepped beyond
> the confines of the library into the community?[116]

The value of beginning with the locally particular and seeking to
understand the reciprocity of the religious, social, (other) cultural,
political, and economic is one of the motivations behind this study, and
will be witnessed in Part II. It has a number of advantages, which I see as
having the potential to make it a useful approach within the study of
religions. One of these is the way in which—through its focus on specific
locations (whether physical, social, textual, or virtual), the particular
constellations of relations therein, and localised religious groups, places,
and activities—it challenges the 'World Religions' approach of religious

---

115.   A conference was held on this subject in 1998 at the University of Leeds,
papers from which appear in Knott, Ward, Mason and Willmer (eds.), *Religion and
Locality*. A panel was also held at the XVIIIth Congress of the International Association
for the History of Religions in 2000 in Durban, South Africa. For an account of the
history and examples of this approach, see Knott, 'Issues in the Study of Religions and
Locality', 'Community and Locality in the Study of Religions', and 'Religion and
Locality: Issues and Methods'.

116.   Knott, 'Community and Locality', pp. 99-100.

studies with its focus on discrete, generic traditions, and normative beliefs and practices. It does this not so much by arguing directly against it as by starting from the particular rather than the general and focusing on what happens to religion within a designated local space.[117] As I have said when describing a local religious mapping project I run with students, we encourage them to reason inductively from their examination of particular Methodist churches and Sikh gurdwaras rather than to reason deductively from a reading of textbooks about Christianity and Sikhism.[118]

Related to this is a second advantage, that is the movement away from the modernist regime of collecting, classifying, comparing, and typologising data on religion towards seeing religion as a dynamic and engaged part of a complex social environment or habitat, which is itself crisscrossed with wider communications and power relations. I have illustrated this previously with an extended reference to A.S. Byatt's story of a nineteenth-century naturalist, William Adamson, who suffered under the claustrophobic regime of ordering miscellaneous specimens for his aristocratic patron, and then sought release in the close observation of a colony of ants in his local wood.[119] The very title of the book Adamson compiled, with the assistance of the governess and children of the household, is instructive: *The Swarming City: A Natural History of a Woodland Society, its Polity, its Economy, its Arms and Defences, its Origin, Expansion and Decline*. It was a study of the production, reproduction, and relations of a local social space. I have argued that such close studies of the operation of religion in particular places can lead to the development of models and theories for use in other studies.[120]

Additional advantages pertaining to such localised studies of religion are as follows:[121]

- They require a multidisciplinary and polymethodic approach that brings a researcher into an arena of interest shared by scholars within and beyond the study of religions.

117.   Timothy Fitzgerald argues directly against a World Religions approach in 'Hinduism and the "World Religion" Fallacy', *Religion* 20 (1990), pp. 101-18, and in *The Ideology of Religious Studies* (New York and Oxford: Oxford University Press, 2000), Chapter 3.

118.   'The Religious Mapping of Leeds'. For an account of this, see Knott, 'Issues in the Study of Religions and Locality', pp. 281-82, 285-86.

119.   Knott, 'Community and Locality', pp. 87-90. From A.S. Byatt, *Angels and Insects* (London: Vintage, 1993).

120.   This presupposes what others have called a 'grounded-theory' approach; see A. Strauss and J.M. Corbin (eds.), *Grounded Theory in Practice* (London, Thousand Oaks, New Delhi: Sage, 1997).

121.   Knott, 'Community and Locality', and 'Issues in the Study of Religions and Locality'.

- They necessitate local engagement, negotiation, and accountability, and are often socially useful studies.
- Because of the nature of late-modern localities, such studies necessitate an investigation not only of local but also wider—national and global—communications and interconnections.
- Finally, they are of considerable pedagogical value as people of all ages, backgrounds, and competencies are able to observe and to a greater or lesser extent analyse local situations or those further afield. In addition to the practice in inductive reasoning that this provides, as well as in the development of hypotheses and models, an opportunity is opened up for researchers to observe and evaluate their own place in the locality and its effect.

It was my awareness of the shortcomings of such an approach to date—the need to give greater attention to the theorisation of space and place, and the ideological forces at work within them—that gave rise to the present study.

An example of a study that takes seriously the possibility of deriving an understanding of the religious and the social from local particularity is Timothy Jenkins's account of religion in English everyday life, notably the life witnessed in and through the Kingswood Whit Walk.[122] Although Jenkins takes an ethnographic rather than a spatial approach, and is arguably also open to the criticism noted earlier—of failing to theorise the space of the walk or of Kingswood—his method and objectives have contributed to the genesis of my own approach. At the outset of his book he suggests three interwoven questions that are not dissimilar to my own.

> First, what kind of social science is appropriate for studying religious events and forms of life? Then, what kind of understanding of religion emerges from the appropriate approach? And last, what are the implications of this approach and this understanding for the wider study of English society? Together, these themes constitute a claim as to how to comprehend our contemporary situation, broadly conceived: it is a claim as to the value of the ethnographic approach to understanding everyday life and, at the same time, as to the proper understanding of the place of religion both in that approach and in the object being considered.[123]

Despite the scale of his purpose, his approach is specific. It is social anthropological, and 'sheds—or at least defers—the whole business of prior definition and justification of its object', religion.[124] As he recognises,

---

122.   Jenkins, *Religion in English Everyday Life*. Kingswood is a working class district on the outskirts of the city of Bristol in the west of England. The Whit Walk is a procession held annually on the morning of Whit bank holiday (p. 6).

123.   Jenkins, *Religion in English Everyday Life*, p. 3.

124.   Jenkins, *Religion in English Everyday Life*, p. 5. It is not clear that he is entirely successful in achieving this. He does offer hints about how he sees religion, as the

some may say that he does this at the expense of 'reducing his ambition', by focusing on description rather than theory, and the locally particular rather than the general. However, he makes a compelling case for the value of studying particular events, moments, and contexts in order to understand people's 'habits for coping with reality',[125] and the way in which religion (e.g. the Whit Walk) may serve as a clue to the ordering of society.[126] In order to do this, he focuses on two themes: local particularity and respectability.[127] The first, which emerges from the engagement of territoriality, local history, and personality, is contingent upon the idea that local ways of doing things and thinking 'are tied in the actors' perceptions to the experience of that locality', creating an 'identity which relates to a particular place'.[128] The second, the stereotype of respectability, the 'locally recognised collective morality',[129] signals the social relationships and values of the area played out—exhibited, negotiated, challenged, contested—through a particular event, the activities and feelings of those involved, the perceptions of outsiders, and the misunderstandings that ensue.

Jenkins then stresses similar methodological issues and themes to those I have raised earlier, such as an interest in the everyday, the value of an inductive approach based on specific localities and contingent upon the principle of local particularity, and the idea that a space or event—and the place of religion within it—can contribute to an understanding of the wider social, economic, and cultural order. The difference between his thought-provoking and nuanced account and the one offered in Part II of this book is that his approach is ethnographic and the one adopted here is spatial. How great is this difference? After all, Jenkins considers—though not necessarily directly—the physical, mental, and social nature of the place of Kingswood and the role of insiders and outsiders in its construction. Additionally, he has a dynamic view of the place, and sees the aspiration to human flourishing (religion) woven through social, economic, and cultural concerns and issues. However, what I aim to do in this study that Jenkins does not is, *first*, take seriously the active role of

---

'human aspiration to flourish' (p. 13). He later criticises the definition adopted by Steve Bruce at the outset of his work on religion in modern Britain, which Jenkins argues is based on 'a teleology of individual consciousness' (p. 29) thus leading to a statistical approach to the issue of the salience of religion and, ultimately, to a view of its decline. Jenkins suggests that such a conclusion is not necessarily wrong, but is certainly incomplete (p. 30).

125. Jenkins, *Religion in English Everyday Life*, p. 19.
126. Jenkins, *Religion in English Everyday Life*, pp. 12-13.
127. Jenkins, *Religion in English Everyday Life*, p. 17.
128. Jenkins, *Religion in English Everyday Life*, p. 77.
129. Jenkins, *Religion in English Everyday Life*, p. 17.

the space itself in contributing to the nature and location of religion within it, enveloping social, cultural, religious, economic, and political factors, and making them available for focused study, and, *secondly*, take into account the role of theory as well as participant (insider and outsider) accounts in evaluating the location of religion in particular places.[130] My 'place' is very different to his in being a small body part rather than a geographical locale. Whilst it is my intention here to demonstrate the application of a spatial approach to this single case study (though to multiple examples within it), further studies will be conducted in due course.[131]

Conclusion

In order to establish the legacy for a spatial analysis of religion of previous studies — those produced not only within religious studies but also within the disciplines of geography, sociology, and anthropology — I have surveyed four areas — space and the sacred, geography of religion, globalisation, and locality — all of which gave rise to ideas, approaches, and conclusions relevant to this study. Some of these reinforced points made in the first chapter about the nature of space. In summary, the most important of these are as follows:

1.   Body and territory are formative for the notion of the 'sacred', that is, for marking off or setting apart things, places, and events;

2.   sacralisation (or ritualisation) produces distinctive spaces, that is, places, persons, objects, and events;

3.   spaces, including those that are religious or in which religion is situated, are constituted of power relations; they are sites of contestation;

4.   like other spaces, religious spaces are materially and ideologically produced and reproduced;

5.   late-modern conditions require new geographies of religion (which look beyond the officially religious, and are sensitive to differences in context, aesthetics, scale, constituency, dialectics, and morality);

---

130.   Arguably, Jenkins (*Religion in English Everyday Life*) does the second of these in his Chapter 1, 'Two Sociological Approaches to Religion in Modern Britain', but he does not refer to these approaches later in his investigation of Kingswood. They are seen as alternatives to his own social anthropological approach rather than contributions to the elucidation of religion in Kingswood.

131.   For example, studies conducted in association with 'Locating Religion in the Fabric of the Secular: An Experiment in Two Public Sector Organisations' (funded by the Arts and Humanities Research Board, 2004–2005).

6.   the understanding of late-modern social and cultural (including religious) processes benefits from the application of a new spatial terminology;

7.   globalisation gives rise to new religious spaces, and offers novel means for religious people, communities, ideas, practices, images, and symbols to migrate, stake claims, and establish themselves;

8.   global and local religious spaces mutually reinforce one another; both are stimulated by globalisation;

9.   local places, objects, persons, and events—in which religion is situated—are not merely particular and parochial as they often focus the conditions and processes evident at larger scales; some may even be exported and globalised;

10.   an investigation of particular, local spaces provides a different perspective on the location of religion to those approaches which take 'World Religions' and generic religious categories and dimensions as their objects of study.

Chapter 5

The Spatial Approach Summarised

The first part of this book has been devoted to the development of a spatial approach for locating religion within contemporary places. I began by assessing the theoretical literature on space, place, and location in order to identify and develop appropriate terms for a spatial analysis. I followed this, in Chapter 2, with a more detailed examination of a singular theory of the production of space, Lefebvre's dialectical model, which was used to illuminate some aspects of religion in Western modernity. Recognising that the task of locating 'religion' in spaces requires an understanding of what one is looking for, I then turned, in Chapter 3, to the development of a strategic approach to 'religion'. I discarded previous definitions in favour of a field of 'religious' and 'secular' force relations. I noted that struggles within the field involve scholars as well as overtly religious or secularist exponents, and, furthermore, that the spatial theorists on whose work I am dependent generally ignore religion (its empirical presence and theoretical possibilities, and the scholarship about it). It was important then, in Chapter 4, to examine the contribution to a spatial analysis of those scholars whose primary focus had been 'religion' or the 'sacred'.

It is the task of this chapter to summarise the conclusions of the previous four in such a way that they can be brought to bear as analytical tools for locating religion in a variety of places. What follows is a short reiteration of the *object* of the research, the *methodological approach* to be employed, and its *analytical terms*. A diagram and table are offered, which together form an *aide-memoir* for applying what has been developed in the first half of the book to a case study in the second.

Object: The Religious/Secular Field

It was established that the Western epistemological field of the 'religious' and the 'secular' constituted a site of struggle with multiple religious and secular positions, including those that sought to bridge the two or move beyond them. This field is shown below. As the relationship between the 'religious' and the 'secular' is dialectical and not merely oppositional, the field is shown to include a third camp, the 'post-secular'.

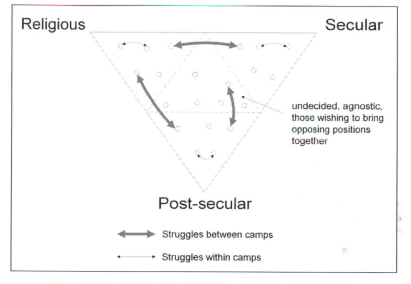

Figure 1: *The Religious/Secular Field, and its Force Relationships*

Within the field, four areas or camps can be seen: religious, secular, post-secular, and the middle ground — which includes the undecided, the deliberately agnostic, and those who desire to build bridges. Positions within the field are taken up by both confessors (of one or another camp) and commentators. It is held that there are no disinterested, external positions. There is no 'bird's eye view', though there are other epistemological fields beyond the Western one. The academy and its representatives, like those in the media and other professions, indeed like confessors of all kinds, are situated within the field, both historically and in terms of the contemporary cultural order. The field of the 'religious' and 'secular' is one in which knowledge-power is expressed and contested, and in which controversies between positions (either within a single camp or across different camps) reveal some of the deeply held views and values which constitute the field and mark out the territorial areas and lines of engagement within it. Investigating such controversies helps to uncover some of the unspoken norms of late-modernity regarding the 'religious' and 'secular'. They occur in space and, as such, the places they occupy are amenable to spatial analysis.

The following propositions comprise my operational approach to the focus or object of the research:

- The object is the field of the 'religious' and the 'secular' in the late-modern West.
- The field is dialectically constituted.
- It contains many positions within three broad areas or camps.
- It is a site of struggle.
- It provides a location for the analysis of knowledge-power.
- The controversies that occur on the field provide a means of observing and understanding the nature of the field, its internal and external boundaries, and the relationship between positions within and beyond it.
- Controversies are spatially located and thus open to spatial analysis.

A Critical Reflexive Approach

As I have stated previously that all confessors of the 'religious' or 'secular' and those who comment upon them—whether academic, literary, or popular—are within the field, then several methodological considerations must follow. Attention must be paid, for example, to the position and relations of myself and others, in terms of our personal stances on religion and secularism, and the theoretical positions we adopt, even those that we think are neutral. Generally, I shall endeavour to allow people, groups, and those who write about them, to position themselves within the field, but a certain amount of interpretation on my part in the matter of positioning will no doubt be necessary. It is important also for me to remember that any position is supported by an informing context. The territorial area of the 'religious', to take one of the three camps, includes those with differing religious and sectarian backgrounds, nationalities, ethnic allegiances, genders, generations, roles, life-styles, and levels of commitment. Furthermore, the controversies in which they and those from other camps engage emerge from historical contexts that affect both the parties involved and the terms of their engagement. As I suggested, in both the Introduction and Chapter 1, a spatial analysis cannot be divorced from a consideration of historical and other contextual factors.

As we saw in Chapter 3, neither the terms of the field itself or their close relatives—'religion', 'the sacred', 'spirituality'—nor the vocabulary of the spatial are neutral once used discursively. They evoke meanings in hearers, readers, and users as a result of their course through history, the context in which they are received or used, and the biographies and intentions of recipients and users. Furthermore, they may be applied directly or metaphorically, and conventionally or innovatively. These linguistic and ideological factors need consideration in the discussion that follows in Part II.

The final methodological reminder concerns the process of examining places. They too carry ideological weight. Some places are more dominant than others in modernity, as are some scales.[1] Shopping malls are hot places; the global is a hot scale. In this study, I have favoured a small scale, the body, and a particular marginal place within it, the left hand (though it is worth noting that the margin itself has become a popular postmodern standpoint). A reflexive engagement with the politics of a marginal place such as the left hand will be adopted.

The Terms of a Spatial Analysis

What were the key points raised in Chapters 1 and 2 from the work of spatial theorists on the constitution, experience, activity, and meaning of space for the location of religion? How have those scholars of religion whose work was discussed in Chapter 4 contributed to theorising space in order to study religion? The following issues are of significance.

First, the foundational nature of the body for the perception, conception, and production of space (including sacred space) was noted.[2]

Secondly, we ascertained that space is multi-dimensional, being physical, mental, and social, and that there is an intrinsic connection between social relations and space, the former having 'no real existence save in and through space'.[3]

Thirdly, we noted the properties of relational space, of configuration, simultaneity, extension, and power.[4] Things are brought together in space. Capital amasses there, whether social, cultural, or financial. 'Space envelopes the raw materials and products it brings together'.[5] But different places within space have different configurations of things. Space also has simultaneity. Multiple spaces/places exist within it, overlapping and interconnected. It has extension, being a moment in time, but situated at the interstices of various developments, occurrences, causes, and consequences. Any given place, furthermore, is spatially stratified, containing within it a complex history. And space is full of power, not only hegemonic power, but also the powers of resistance, strategic incursion, and ironic collusion. Places — including sacred places — are the result and expression of knowledge-power, yet remain contested.[6]

---

1. On 'scales' and their nature, see Valentine, *Social Geographies*, and Neil Smith, 'Homeless/Global: Scaling Places', in Bird, Curtis, Putnam, Robertson and Tickner (eds.), *Mapping the Futures*, pp. 97-116.
2. See the discussion of the body in Chapter 1, and of space and the sacred in Chapter 4.
3. Lefebvre, *The Production of Space*, p. 404.
4. See the discussion of Foucault and Massey in Chapter 1.
5. Lefebvre, *The Production of Space*, p. 410.
6. See the discussion of the work of Chidester and Linenthal in Chapter 4.

The way in which space is both encountered and enacted is dynamic, particularly given the circumstances of globalisation when time and space are compressed and different places increasingly interconnected (see Chapters 1 and 4). Global and local scales are interpenetrated, with the opening up of new cultural spaces and places that combine universalising and particularising trends. Virtual space and cyber-places, diasporic space and the outposts of transnational communities, and global evangelical networks and local house churches are examples of this.

Fourthly, space was seen to be practised, thought, and sensed, but not in a merely passive way. These activities bring space and its various places into being, and then repeatedly reproduce and adapt them. Similarly, sacralisation as a way of acting creates — both materially and ideologically — special places, in turn producing the 'sacred'.[7]

Fifthly, despite the identification in Chapter 1 of the bodily generation of space, its dimensions, properties, and activities, 'space' was recognised also to be socially constructed. The notion of 'space' is used in both material and metaphorical senses, and is repeatedly contested by those who apply it and study its meaning. Like 'religion', it has no single fixed meaning. Understood in this way, 'space' is what Hilary Lawson refers to as a compound *linguistic closure*.[8] Closure, in Lawson's sense, is what we do in order to make sense of a world that is open: 'It is through closure that openness is divided into things'.[9] In the case of the concept 'space', many preceding closures have occurred and either been incorporated or rejected in order for this one to be presented. Furthermore, as so many preceding acts of closure lie behind this one (e.g. 'dimension', 'property', 'social relations', 'power'), there are innumerable closure combinations that could lead to alternative constructions or closures of 'space'. This only highlights the contingency of my use of 'space' and the terms I have attached to it (or closed within it). By these acts of closure, alternative possible closures have necessarily been hindered or obscured.[10] The very decision to understand more about religion by analysing its location in various places is an attempt to focus the task, to make it manageable. The closure, not only of 'space', but also of 'place' and 'location', helps me to tackle the openness of the physical, social, and mental environment in which religion operates. However, as I shall suggest in the final points below, such closures are 'a means of *holding* openness as something', not of exhausting it.[11]

7. See the discussion of the work of J.Z. Smith and Anttonen in Chapter 4.
8. Lawson, *Closure*, Chapters 4, 5, and 6 on language and closure.
9. Lawson, *Closure*, p. 3.
10. In Chapter 3, following a discussion of the history and the usage of the terms, I have also enclosed the 'religious' and the 'secular'.
11. Lawson, *Closure*, p. 10.

This brief discussion of closure brings me to my sixth point, the aspects of space discussed in Chapter 2. In *The Production of Space*, Lefebvre presented three dialectically connected, mutually occurring aspects of social space in the form of a conceptual triad. He organised the experience of space into *spatial practice, representations of space,* and *spaces of representation* in order to show how he thought spaces were perceived, conceived, and lived. This conceptualisation, with which Lefebvre sought to hold the openness or dynamic activity of space whilst closing it for the purpose of ordering and structuring its meaning, has value in distinguishing the aspects of space produced and transformed by religious individuals and groups.

Finally, the active potential of space and place was stressed. Space is not merely a container in which activities take place, nor is it a backdrop against which they are played out. Like the places within it, it is more than the sum of its dimensions, properties, and aspects. Each place within space is *that very place*, a particular closure, as well as one of a type of closures. Writing of space, but of equal significance for the places within it, Lefebvre writes, 'It brings [materials and resources] all together *and then in a sense substitutes itself for each factor separately by enveloping it'*.[12] That very place, enveloping as it does the various properties, dimensions, and aspects of space, as well as embodying within it innumerable other places (alternative closures of the same place as well as separate, smaller places), then evokes practices, ideas, and sensual responses which are additional to those evoked by other similar places, places in general, or by smaller parts of this place. Whilst space cannot be said to exhibit agency itself, it affects agency in those who experience and participate in space. This is what I mean by space being active.

I have abbreviated and summarised these spatial terms in the following table:

Constitution of Space	Experience of Space	Activity of space	Meaning of 'Space'
• Foundation of space in the body • Dimensions of space • Properties of space	• Space as practised, thought and sensed • Lefebvre's three experiential aspects of social space	• Production and reproduction of space • The active potential of places within space	• The operational closure of 'space'

Table 1. *The Terms of a Spatial Analysis*

12. Lefebvre, *The Production of Space*, p. 410.

In Part II, in my case study of the left hand—which will comprise many examples, most of which are contemporary Western in origin, with others from mediaeval and early modern European religion and magic or from Indian and Tibetan Tantrism—I shall use these spatial attributes to analyse the location and relationship of the 'religious', the 'secular', and the 'post-secular'. In this analytical exercise spatial terms will not be applied systematically; rather they will operate as memory aids by means of which to think and rethink the left hand and the location of religion within it.

Part II

Applying a Spatial Approach: The Case of the Left Hand

Chapter 6

The Physical, Social, and Mental Space
of the R̶i̶g̶h̶t̶ Left Hand

My left hand…supporting my forehead as I think and write, holding the
edge of the paper, running its fingers through my hair, then at rest by my
side…whilst the right hand conveys the thoughts to the page, deftly
manipulating the pencil, ably forming the letters, poised in readiness, the
more active and dextrous of the two.[1]

The two hands—body parts that, for most of us, are vital to our identity as both independent agents and social beings. Hands, at once subject,
object, and tool,[2] a means by which we engage with things.[3] Touching,
sending the message of texture, temperature, size, shape, and movement
to the brain.[4] Active, creative, and communicative. With head and feet,
chest and back, defining the area around the body, the regions in space,
the directions.[5]

---

1.   I write here of the left hand as a right-hander; a left-hander would clearly have
a quite different view of the role of the two hands.

2.   Marcel Mauss, 'Techniques of the Body', *Economy and Society* 2 (1973), pp. 70-88;
Lefebvre, *The Production of Space*, p. 213.

3.   See Heidegger on the relationship between hands and things, on the 'ready-
to-hand', discussed in Richard Polt, *Heidegger: An Introduction* (London: UCL Press,
1999), Chapter 3, and Hilary Lawson, *Reflexivity* (La Salle: Open Court, 1985),
pp. 75-79.

4.   Ruth Finnegan, 'Communicating Touch', in *idem, Communicating: The Multiple
Modes of Human Interconnection* (London and New York: Routledge, 2002), pp. 194-212
(194, 196).

5.   Immanuel Kant, 'Concerning the Ultimate Foundation of the Differentiation of
Regions in Space' [1768], in G.B. Kerferd and D.E. Walford (eds.), *Kant: Selected Pre-
Critical Writings and Correspondence with Beck* (Manchester: Manchester University
Press, 1968), pp. 36-43, and see discussion of this essay in Chapter 1; Macrae, 'The
Body and Social Metaphor', pp. 64-65; Lefebvre, *The Production of Space*, p. 213.

The two hands, serving the self and others. The co-operative hands. Feeding and cleaning.[6] Making contact, grooming, honouring, embracing, stroking, stimulating.[7] Conveying a message, indicating a direction.[8] Reinforcing the verbal; producing the written. Telling the future, praying, blessing.[9] 'The hands may almost be said to speak.'[10]

The two hands, mirror image but asymmetric; apparently alike, but different. Incongruent counterparts, revealing an asymmetry that fosters hierarchy and inequality, that leads to the hegemony of the right and the mutilation of the left.[11]

The Physical, Social, and Mental Space of the Left Hand

Hands, as we see, are themselves places, having a dynamic physical form (e.g. one that may be open, fisted, pointing), being a related pair, a space of social relations and communication, and in being the focus for various meanings and values. As such, they are open to spatial examination. But may we expect this examination to reveal the location of religion within the hands? Can such commonplace body parts contain and express religion in the first place? If what we mean by place is that nexus in space in which social relations occur, which may be material or metaphorical, and which is necessarily interconnected (with other places) and full of power, then — as such a place — a hand has the potential to contain and express religion (religion being those social relations given meaning by a certain type of ideology, set of traditions, values, and ritual practices).

6.   Mary Douglas, *Purity and Danger: An Analysis of Concepts of Pollution and Taboo* (Harmondsworth: Pelican Books, 1970 [first published 1966]), pp. 41-53; Michael Barsley, Chapter 1, 'The Unclean Hand', in *The Left-Handed Book: An Investigation into the Sinister History of Left-Handedness* (London: Souvenir Press, 1966), pp. 8-16.

7.   Finnegan, *Communicating*, pp. 201-10.

8.   J.A.V. Bates, 'The Communicative Hand', in Jonathan Benthall and Ted Polhemus (eds.), *The Body as a Medium of Expression* (London: Allen Lane, 1975), pp. 175-94.

9.   Bates, 'The Communicative Hand'; Finnegan, *Communicating*, pp. 209-10; Robert Hertz, 'The Pre-Eminence of the Right Hand: A Study in Religious Polarity', in Rodney Needham (ed.), *Right and Left: Essays on Dual Symbolic Classification* (Chicago: University of Chicago Press, 1973), pp. 3-31 (15-17). Originally published as 'La prééminence de la main droite: étude sur la polarité religieuse', *Revue Philosophique* 68 (1909), pp. 553-80.

10.   Quintillian (c. 80 CE) quoted in Bates, 'The Communicative Hand', p. 175.

11.   On mirror image and incongruent counterpart, see Kant in Kerferd and Walford, *Kant*, p. 41; Casey, *The Fate of Place*, pp. 207-209; Bennett, 'The Difference between Right and Left'. Bennett discusses 'enantiomorphs' (things having contrary shapes), and uses this term interchangeably with 'incongruous counterparts'. He concludes that 'the right/left distinction (by which, always, I mean the distinction between any enantiomorphic pair) still differs enormously from every other spatial distinction' (p. 191). On hierarchy and inequality, and the mutilation of the left hand, see Hertz, 'The Pre-Eminence of the Right Hand', pp. 3, 21.

Furthermore, can the hands go as far as to produce and reproduce new spaces with significance for religion? Following Lefebvre, I shall ask to what extent the left hand, in particular, has been a productive and creative space for religion.

In his discussion of 'spatial architectonics', in which he examines the way the body generates space, Lefebvre considers hands and their role in gestural systems.[12] He notes the importance of space in such systems, high and low, and right and left, and acknowledges that 'gestural systems embody ideology and bind it to practice', with the examples of the clenched-fist salute and sign of the cross.[13] More importantly for this argument, he goes on to add that, 'organized gestures, which is to say ritualised and codified gestures, are not simply performed in "physical" spaces, in the space of bodies. Bodies themselves generate spaces, which are produced by and for their gestures'.[14] It is not the hands that provide his example here, but the feet and the everyday practice of walking, transformed through theology and ritual into contemplative mode, issuing forth in the space of the cloister, 'a space of promenade and assembly':

> What has happened here is that, happily, a gestural space has succeeded in mooring a mental space — a space of contemplation and theological abstraction — to the earth, thus allowing it to express itself symbolically and to become part of a practice, the practice of a well-defined group within a well-defined society.[15]

The body, through a spiritual gestural system, has produced a new space — one that is physical, social, and symbolic.

It would be unwise to assume from Lefebvre's example that the left hand is similarly effective as an active participant in gestural systems, and as producer of new spaces, whether of significance for religion or not. A separate case needs to be made for the left hand, the apparently passive partner of the two hands. Only by the end of the chapter will the case have been fully presented, and the reader must display considerable patience in hearing first about the dominant party, the dextrous hand, because, as is so often the case, it is only possible to understand the place of the 'other' by knowing the one that has presence, that does, that dominates, that has value.[16] First then, I shall discuss the left hand in rela-

---

12. Lefebvre, *The Production of Space*, pp. 213-17.

13. Lefebvre, *The Production of Space*, p. 215. Note that such systems exceed Lefebvre's notion of spatial practice (see Chapter 2 above) by being informed by ideas deriving either from dominant or alternative orders or spaces.

14. Lefebvre, *The Production of Space*, p. 217.

15. Lefebvre, *The Production of Space*, p. 217.

16. For contemporary data on the incidence of left- and right-handedness, see Chris McManus, *Right Hand, Left Hand: The Origins of Asymmetry in Brains, Bodies, Atoms and Cultures* (London: Weidenfeld & Nicolson, 2002), Chapter 9. 'The historical data in

tion to the role, status, and practice of the right hand, before turning to an examination of the work of Robert Hertz for whom the hands were the symbols of sacred and profane. Some useful theoretical ramifications of Hertz's work will then be discussed before I move on, in the next chapter, to a spatial analysis of contemporary Western representations of the left hand in which lie the remains of earlier totalities, vying with modern and postmodern values. I shall consider where these left hands lie within the field of the 'religious' and 'secular', and then ask whether any of them constitute new 'spaces of representation' with the capacity for criticism, resistance, or liberation. Or must they lie forever within the shadow of the right, the dominant order, whether religious or secular?

Frankly, it is hard to think of many gestural systems, to return to Lefebvre's phrase, which give a significant place to the left hand or which depend upon it—though there are many which involve both hands in play together, such as forms of dance, prayer, signalling, and non-verbal communication (such as signing for the deaf). Certainly the most important for informing behaviour and values is that system at work within Arab, African, and Indian cultures, that of the clean/unclean, of the separation of the hands and their corresponding duties for the purpose of maintaining order and avoiding defilement.[17] In this system, the left hand takes on the burden, in particular, of dealing with excrement and contact with the genitals, whilst the right is reserved for food.[18] That this distinction is maintained and practised by religious people is not in doubt, as we can see in this recent exchange on an Islamic Internet website:

> Q325 I am a 12 year old student, and I am left-handed. People have often reminded me not to eat or write with my left hand, because people who do so will not go to heaven; they will go to hell. I have tried to use my right hand for eating and writing, but I always feel that my right hand is weaker. I will be grateful for your advice.
>
> A325 Let me tell you straight away that no one will go to hell for using his left hand for eating, drinking, writing or indeed for any other purpose. Any

America and elsewhere in the West clearly show that left-handedness is more common now than it was a hundred years ago… In Canada and the UK, the proportion of left-handers is about 11.5 per cent. However, as one moves across Asia the proportion falls, becoming 7.5 per cent in the Emirates, 5.8 per cent in India and four per cent in Japan' (pp. 204-205).

17. Douglas, *Purity and Danger*, Chapter 2, 'Ritual Uncleanness'.

18. Douglas cites examples from Nigeria and India, pp. 42, 46; Barsley from Egypt and Morocco, *The Left-Handed Book*, Chapter 1, 'The Unclean Hand'. See also Louis Dumont, *Homo Hierarchicus: The Caste System and its Implications* (London: Paladin, 1972 [French edn 1966]), p. 87; essays by Wieschhoff, Chelhod, Needham, and Beck in Needham (ed.), *Right and Left*; and Serge Tcherkézoff, *Dual Classification Reconsidered: Nyamwezi Sacred Kingship and Other Examples* (Cambridge: Cambridge University Press; Paris: La Maison des Sciences de l'Homme, 1987 [French edn 1983]).

one who suggests otherwise...betrays a degree of ignorance of God, His compassion and fairness... God will not ask anyone why he is left-handed, because it is He who has created him. Besides using one's right hand for eating and most other purposes is recommended or a sunnah. This means that it is not obligatory. On the Day of Judgement, God will not ask any person why that person has not done something that is not obligatory...[19]

The importance of this to Muslims is further borne out in various books dealing with *hadith* and customary practices.[20] However, whilst it is well known from the *Qur'an* that a Muslim's destiny is spatially expressed according to regions to the right or left of Allah, there would seem to be no necessary link between Islamic eschatology and the aforementioned behavioural norms.[21] As the respondent suggested in answer to the young person's question, Allah's principal concern is in judging the intention behind actions rather than in punishing 'natural difficulties' such as left-handedness.[22]

For many people in the West, whether Muslim or Hindu, Arab, North African, or Indian, the advice on the separation of duties of the two hands remains important in matters of cleanliness. However, despite the significance postulated for it by at least one author writing on left-handedness

19. 'Left-Handedness', http://www.islamicity.com/dialogue/Q325.HTM (accessed 20 October 2002). Answers provided by *Arab News* in Jeddah (Chris McManus, *Hyper-note* 2.22 to *Right Hand, Left Hand*, <http://www.righthandlefthand. com>).

20. For example, in *Bihisti Zewar*, a late-nineteenth-century Urdu text, which continues to be circulated among Muslims in the Indian sub-continent and Britain, dedicated to the perfection of women through the encouragement of normative behaviour, we learn that many everyday acts requiring cleanliness should be done on or with the right (Barbara Daly Metcalf [trans. with commentary], *Perfecting Women: Maulana Ashraf 'Ali Thanawi's Bihisti Zewar* [Berkeley: University of California Press, 1990)], pp. 184-85). For other Muslim traditions associated with right or left see *hadith* cited in Alfred Guillaume, *The Traditions of Islam* (Oxford: Clarendon Press, 1924), pp. 118-19; and J. Chelhod, 'A Contribution to the Problem of the Pre-Eminence of the Right, Based upon Arabic Evidence', in Needham (ed.), *Right and Left*, pp. 239-62 (240). For Hindu tradition, see *Manusmrti* 5.136 in Edward W. Hopkins (ed.), *Hindu Polity: The Ordinances of Manu* (Ludhiana: Kalyani Publishers, 1972 [first published 1884]), p. 129. For recognition of the continued use of the right hand for eating and the left for cleaning, see D. Stoter, *Spiritual Aspects of Healthcare* (London: Mosby, 1995), p. 16.

21. *The Holy Qur'an: Text Translation and Commentary*, Yusuf Ali (Brentwood, MD: Amana Corporation, 1983), Sura 56 'Waqi'a or the Inevitable Event' in which the fate of the companions of the right and the left is described.

22. <http://www.islamicity.com/dialogue/Q325.HTM>. A reader of Salman Rushdie's *The Satanic Verses* (Harmondsworth: Penguin Viking, 1989), the book that was at the centre of heated and sometimes violent debate in the early 1990s, might be forgiven for assuming a direct link between the word of God and human regulation, including 'which hand to use for the purpose of cleaning one's behind' (p. 363). This erroneous conflation of Allah's will with traditions of customary practice infuriated many Muslims at the time of the book's publication.

in the modern West, there is no clear mandate for it within Western culture itself.[23] Rather, what we have are the traces of a complex system of etiquette in which different tasks were spatially allocated to the different hands not, it would seem, to mark an inviolable distinction between the clean right and unclean left, but in order to civilise and hierarchically organise social behaviour (for instance, we may note that, in humanist handbooks from sixteenth and seventeenth-century Europe, blowing one's nose and spitting were to be done behind the left hand, which was also to be used at table for the serviette and bread, whereas goblet and knife were to be placed within reach of the right).[24] What were initially presented as shaming prohibitions became internalised 'as self-controls', and ultimately emerged as irresistible and unquestionable habits associated with appropriate civilised behaviour.[25] As with all gestural systems, what we have here is an ideologically informed system of spatial practice, but one in which the underlying purpose and values have now become hidden.

Broadly speaking, then, in the Western gestural system of eating/ cleaning, the distinction between right and left hands is not as significant in terms of purity and impurity as it is in some other cultural contexts. Can we learn any more from the gestural system associated with marriage, as the only duty assigned to the left hand in some Western countries is the wearing of the wedding ring, the outward sign of the matrimonial contractual relationship?

Why is the wedding ring worn on the left, when it is the right hand that takes the lead in the majority of social activities?[26] It is the right hand that reaches out to shake another, the right that testifies to the swearing of an oath, that salutes, that concludes a contract, that makes a blessing, an offering, or the sign of the cross.[27] It is indeed right hands that are joined formally in matrimony (and a 'left-handed' or 'morganatic' marriage was one that, in earlier times, was not sanctioned by the Church, in which neither wife nor children had the right to inherit).[28] We find a clue to the

23.   Barsley, *The Left-Handed Book*.

24.   Norbert Elias, *The Civilising Process: Sociogenetic and Psychogenetic Investigations* (trans. Edmund Jephcott; Oxford: Basil Blackwell, rev. edn, 2000 [1939]), see particularly 'On Behaviour at Table' and following sections, pp. 76-77, p. 105, and p. 124.

25.   Elias, *The Civilising Process*, p. 160. See also Foucault's analysis of the 'disciplining' or training of docile bodies in *Disciple and Punish: The Birth of a Prison* (London: Penguin, 1977).

26.   The wedding ring is worn on the left in the USA, UK, and some other European countries, but not in Germany. McManus, *Right Hand, Left Hand*, p. 29.

27.   McManus, *Right Hand, Left Hand*, p. 29; Hertz, 'The Pre-Eminence of the Right Hand', pp. 15-17. This accords with Classical Greek practice, see Geoffrey Lloyd, 'Right and Left in Greek Philosophy', in Needham (ed.), *Right and Left*, pp. 167-86 (170).

28.   For 'left-handed' or 'morganatic' marriage, see McManus, *Right Hand, Left Hand*, p. 29; Hertz, 'The Pre-Eminence of the Right Hand', p. 17; Barsley, *The*

role of the left hand as bearer of the ring if we return to the Roman social world. There we find confirmation of *dextrarum iunctio*, the joining of the right hands, in the writing of Tertullian: at betrothal, virgin girls 'are mingled with the male body and spirit through a kiss and their right hands', it being the joining of the right hands that signified not only the key moments in betrothal and wedlock, but the sealing of contracts in general.[29] From Aulus Gellius, however, we learn that choice of ring finger—whether for marriage or any other reason—derived from the belief that a nerve ran from the third finger of the left hand direct to the heart.[30] Here we see that an early physiological idea led to the adoption of a socio-cultural practice which has been retained against the grain of dominant views about the importance of the right hand and side for conducting social affairs. For, as Hertz asked, 'How could the left hand conclude valid acts since it is deprived of prestige and spiritual power, since it has strength only for destruction and evil?'[31]

What we have witnessed in considering these two Western gestural systems of eating/cleaning and marriage practice is that the left hand does indeed act but in a secondary capacity to the right. It carries out more lowly tasks, whilst the right wields the knife and seals the contract. The normality of what are now routine spatial practices goes unquestioned, but, as we shall see when we turn to Hertz's account shortly, they are arguably the outward expression of a deep-seated dualistic order responsible for the symbolic organisation of Western culture. But first I shall conclude this opening account of the hands with a poem that focuses on the left hand in all its incapacity, otherness, and promise:

> I want to have my right hand,
> the hand I write with, the hand
> I use to eat and point with,
> the hand with which I shake hands,
> that hand, I want it chained.
> > Then
> I am left with my left hand,
> the dumb sinister one I
> keep about me but barely
> allow.

Left-Handed Book, pp. 108-109; and *Brewer's Dictionary of Phrase and Fable* (London: Cassell, centenary edn, 1970 [1870]), p. 633, and p. 100 on relevance of this for heraldry.

29. Tertullian, *de virginibus velandis* 11.4-5, cited in Susan Treggiari, *Roman Marriage: Iusti Coniuges from the Time of Cicero to the Time of Ulpian* (Oxford: Clarendon Press, 1991), pp. 150, 164-65.

30. Aulus Gellius, discussed in Treggiari, *Roman Marriage*, p. 149. This view was also aired in seventeenth-century England by Sir Thomas Browne: see McManus, *Right Hand, Left Hand*, p. 29; Barsley, *The Left-Handed Book*, p. 108.

31. Hertz, 'The Pre-Eminence of the Right Hand', p. 17.

It's gauche, it's faulty,
it paws and grabs, not always
getting things in hand: it can
break as well as hold.
          Leery
of that hand, I never know
what it has in it, but fright
excites me, I want to scare
myself silly, to give me
the creeps, to moan when I see
how my left hand, faltering,
handles itself.
   Though it can
hardly write two words, I'll let
it forge my signature, I'll
let it, if it wants, call it
-self me.
   Me, I want to live
on a dare, daring myself
to scrape through with one hand tied
and the other running wild.[32]

Whilst this poem looks ahead to a later discussion of the potential of the left hand to be a liberative space of representation and to produce other equally empowering new spaces, it also reiterates certain commonly held views about the left. The poet, Jack Anderson, reminds us of two familiar linguistic connotations, the French 'gauche' (in English signifying awkward, clumsy), and the Latin 'sinistra' (signifying unlucky, deviant, evil-looking, threatening). The English word 'left', with its origins in Old Dutch and Old German, has as its primary meaning 'weak, worthless'.[33] Anderson refers obliquely to the ideas—developed in folklore from advice given by Jesus in the Sermon on the Mount—that the two hands act independently of one another, the left being the more devious of the two, and that the one should not know what the other is doing or holding.[34] He notes that the left hand lacks dexterity, is present but silent. Furthermore, it is not the 'I', the self/subject, but some 'it' or 'other' (the forger) who is potentially frightening, exciting, erotic, and, ultimately,

---

32. Jack Anderson, *Toward the Liberation of the Left Hand* (Pittsburgh: University of Pittsburgh Press, 1977), reproduced in McManus, *Right Hand, Left Hand*, pp. 333-34.

33. *The Shorter Oxford English Dictionary of Historical Principles* (London: Guild Publishing, 3rd edn, 1983), I, p. 1195. For more on the linguistic meanings associated with the left and left-handedness, see McManus, *Right Hand, Left Hand*; Barsley, *The Left-Handed Book*.

34. Matthew 6.3. In Matthew it is the left hand that is to be kept in the dark about the charitable actions of the right. See also Hertz, 'The Pre-Eminence of the Right Hand', p. 10.

wild.[35] But, for this alien within to emerge, to be permitted to act, the subject-hand must be bound.

As we will see in the next chapter, Anderson's wary openness to the left is not untypical of its time. Nevertheless, his poem also draws effectively on deeply embedded ideas that resurface periodically today, but which had their chief expression in classical, mediaeval, and early modern Europe, associated variously with luck and ill-fortune, untamed spirits, demons, magic, deviant sexuality, and criminality.

From Organic Asymmetry to Religious Polarity

In 1909, Robert Hertz, a young member of Durkheim's circle, published a thought-provoking and elegantly written paper on the place of the right and left hands — and the pre-eminence of the former — in both designating and becoming a focus for the sacred and profane. Although Hertz's principal aim was to understand the prevalence and nature of religious polarity in terms of collective representations, he did not entirely espouse a socio-cultural explanation at the expense of the biological evidence.[36] Instead, like Kant, he began with the issue of organic asymmetry and considered the current scientific debate (on the relationship of handedness to the sides of the brain).[37] Concluding that 'the organic *cause* of right-handedness is dubious and insufficient', he was nonetheless reluctant to discount the organic basis completely on the logical grounds that there was indeed a congenital *disposition* to asymmetry and 'a vague disposition to right-handedness'.[38] But, for Hertz, organic asymmetry, though clearly 'a fact' was also 'an ideal', and it was to this aspect that he then turned.[39]

---

35.   Lefebvre, in writing about duality within the body, refers to 'its "other" within itself' (*The Production of Space*, p. 75).

36.   Durkheim, in the introduction to *The Elementary Forms of the Religious Life*, failed to acknowledge what Hertz was at pains to discuss — organic asymmetry and the dominance in nature of right-handedness. Durkheim wrote, 'the distinction between right and left...*far from being inherent in the nature of man in general*, is very probably the product of representations which are religious and therefore collective' (p. 12 [my emphasis]). As Tcherkézoff notes, Hertz does '[abandon] anatomy for sociology' (*Dual Classification Reconsidered*, p. 12), but not without giving credence to our congenital predisposition to right-handedness. See also Robert Parkin, *The Dark Side of Humanity: The Work of Robert Hertz and its Legacy* (Amsterdam: Harwood Academic Publishers, 1996), p. 60.

37.   The nineteenth-century work of Paul Broca, discussed in Hertz, 'The Pre-Eminence of the Right Hand', p. 4. See also McManus, *Right Hand, Left Hand*, Chapter 1, Dr Watson's Problem'.

38.   Hertz, 'The Pre-Eminence of the Right Hand', pp. 4-5 (my emphasis).

39.   Hertz, 'The Pre-Eminence of the Right Hand', p. 6. See B.S. Turner, *The Body and Society*, for a recent iteration of the biological and physiological facts of asymmetry and handedness (pp. 30-31) by a sociologist with a primary interest in theory and ideology.

Two significant issues were interwoven in his discussion of religious polarity and right and left.[40] One was that of dualism, which Hertz saw as 'essential to the thought of primitives [and as dominating] their social organisation', as influential in religious activity, and as governing both social and natural bodies.[41] The other was that of status and value, which, in terms of right and left, were inter-related: '…the right and the left are really of different value and dignity'.[42] At times Hertz focused on contrasting the sacred and profane, and right and left as balanced oppositions, especially in relation to gods and sinister powers, and religious and magical ritual.[43] He also associated right and left, particularly in Maori culture, with other oppositions, notably male and female, light and dark, day and night, and east/south and west/north, going so far as to say that 'the opposition of right and left has the same meaning and application as the series of contrasts, very different but reducible to common principles, presented by the universe'.[44]

However, he was repeatedly drawn back to the values associated with right and left, and the pre-eminence of the former. Early in the essay, he noted that, in cultural if not in anatomical terms, 'the preponderance of the right hand is obligatory, imposed by coercion, and guaranteed by sanctions; contrarily, a veritable prohibition weighs on the left hand and paralyses it', thus stressing the operation of power with regard to the two.[45] Later, he assertively linked the hierarchy of the hands with what he saw as an unchangeable and irreversible socio-religious order:

> No more than the profane is allowed to mix with the sacred is the left allowed to trespass on the right. A preponderant activity of the bad hand could only be illegitimate or exceptional; for it would be the end of man and everything else if the profane were ever allowed to prevail over the sacred and death over life. The supremacy of the right hand is at once an effect and a necessary condition of the order which governs and maintains the universe.[46]

Towards the end of this passage, Hertz drew us back to the material hand, as *condition* as well as effect, and then went on to reiterate the place of the body, its structure, indeed its basic asymmetry in facilitating the preferential representation of the right and its association with the sacred.[47]

---

40. Tcherkézoff develops these issues in *Dual Classification Reconsidered*.
41. Hertz, 'The Pre-Eminence of the Right Hand', p. 8.
42. Hertz, 'The Pre-Eminence of the Right Hand', p. 17.
43. Hertz, 'The Pre-Eminence of the Right Hand', pp. 15-17.
44. Hertz, 'The Pre-Eminence of the Right Hand', p. 14.
45. Hertz, 'The Pre-Eminence of the Right Hand', p. 6.
46. Hertz, 'The Pre-Eminence of the Right Hand', pp. 19-20.
47. Hertz, 'The Pre-Eminence of the Right Hand', pp. 20-21. See McManus for a contemporary view of the complex link between asymmetry in physics and genetics

Hertz's ideas have led to further discussions which not only have relevance for current thinking about dualism, but which will help us to understand the space of the contemporary left hand and the location of religion within it. Ironically, the logic of Hertz's position with regard to the categorical nature of sacred and profane (and right and left) in the collective consciousness might well have led me to reject the idea of the left hand as a space for religion altogether, for, if the left hand must be both a condition and effect of the *profane*, then what possible place can religion have within it?[48] On the one hand this brings us to the question of the relationship between the sacred and religion, to which I shall return in Chapter 9. On the other, it raises a question about dualism, about the nature of oppositional concepts and their boundaries, their fixity, fluidity, and relations. Although I consider this to be of some importance, I can discuss it only briefly at this point. But discuss it I must, because it takes further the question of how values can be located in a space that is both material and discursive, and also shows how the discussion of oppositional concepts can be used creatively to contest or critique the existing apparently unchangeable order, and thus to enable a place like the mutilated left hand to become a 'lived space' or 'space of representation', in Lefebvre's terms. Whether such forays constitute a radical or conclusively damaging breach of the old order is open to question. Perhaps the original rigid categories remain intact, our natural asymmetry always inclining us to favour the stronger one over the other. Alternatively, with the benefit of a critical, deconstructive approach to the dualistic order, perhaps it is possible to offer a different approach, one that is non-dualistic and rooted in different bodies and their experience.[49]

As I suggested earlier, Hertz treated two inter-related issues in his essay — dual classification, and the hierarchy and value of left and right — though he did not resolve the relationship between them. Other scholars, including anthropologists such as Lévi-Strauss, Dumont, Needham, Tcherkézoff, Maybury-Lewis and Almagor, and the historian Stuart Clark, have since pursued aspects of this problem.[50] The anthropological

and symbol and metaphor in language and culture, see 'The argument', *Right Hand, Left Hand* (pp. 361-62); Brian Goodwin, 'Why Groovy Hearts Lean Left', *The Times Higher Education Supplement* (25 April 2003), p. 27.

48. I have over-stated Hertz's position here in order to make this point. As Parkin notes in *The Dark Side of Humanity* (p. 62), Hertz was more interested in the impure sacred (the left) than in the profane as such. See also the discussion of Bataille on left and right sacred below.

49. See below for a discussion of Jantzen, and examples of contemporary postsecular religious left hands in Chapter 7, and Tantrism in Chapter 8.

50. See Parkin, *The Dark Side of Humanity*, pp. 65-86, for a discussion of reactions to Hertz's essay and the development of his ideas. Claude Lévi-Strauss, 'Do Dual

contribution to the debate is well summarised by Serge Tcherkézoff at
the outset to his reconsideration of dual classification. He distinguishes
'binary' from 'dualist' approaches, the former signalling a symmetrical
relationship where the two poles remain 'on one and the same plane', and
the latter a hierarchical and asymmetrical relationship where different
levels are possible. He concedes that it is feasible to derive both views
from Hertz's essay, but associates the former most particularly with the
work of Rodney Needham, in his edited work on right and left, and his
essay on the Meru, and the latter with the work of Louis Dumont in his
study of the caste system, hierarchy, and the values of purity and impurity.[51] He noted that it was Dumont who characterised the two perspectives underlying this distinction (between binary and dualist
approaches), the Western individualistic, egalitarian one, and the
traditional social hierarchical one.[52] The binary view gave equal status to
the two complementary sides of any opposition within a single plane,
and represented a modernist perspective. The dualist view accepted an
unequal hierarchical relationship between two poles in which one was
held to be superior in status and value, and in which different levels
could potentially be accommodated.[53] As such, it best described non-
Western and non-modern perceptions of social relations.

The importance of this distinction for this case study lies, first, in the
recognition of the significance of asymmetry, and thus of an approach to

Organisations Exist?', in *idem, Structural Anthropology* (New York: Basic Books, 1963
[French edn 1956]), pp. 132-63; Dumont, *Homo Hierarchicus*; Needham (ed.), *Right and
Left*; Tcherkézoff, *Dual Classification Reconsidered*; David Maybury-Lewis and Uri
Almagor (eds.), *The Attraction of Opposites: Thought and Society in the Dualistic Mode*
(Ann Arbor: University of Michigan Press, 1989), especially Maybury-Lewis, 'The
Quest for Harmony', pp. 1-17; Stuart Clark, *Thinking with Demons: Witchcraft in Early
Modern Europe* (Oxford: Clarendon Press, 1997).

    51.   Tcherkézoff, 'Introduction', in *Dual Classification Reconsidered*. He discusses the
way both binary and dualist aspects emerge within Hertz's essay (pp. 13-15), then
moving on to an account of Needham's binary symmetrical or 'equalitarian' perspective on pp. 15-26. He reserves a thorough discussion of the dualist, hierarchical
perspective for Chapter 6.

    52.   Tcherkézoff, *Dual Classification Reconsidered*, pp. 10-11, 121. Dumont, *Homo
Hierarchicus*, Introduction, Chapters 2 and 11. In his later work, Dumont commented
critically upon the binary perspective put forward by Needham in his 1973 work on
right and left (Louis Dumont, 'The Anthropological Community and Ideology', *Social
Science Information* 18.6 [1979], pp. 785-817). Needham's own approach was developed
in later books and articles. For further discussion of the work of Needham and
Dumont on opposition and hierarchy, see R.H. Barnes, 'Hierarchy without Caste', in
R.H. Barnes, Daniel de Coppet and R.J. Parkin (eds.), *Contexts and Levels: Anthropological Essays on Hierarchy* (Oxford: JASO, 1985), pp. 8-20, and Clark, *Thinking with
Demons*, Chapter 3, 'Dual Classification'.

    53.   Dumont, *Homo Hierarchicus*, pp. 93-96.

right and left poles which acknowledges hierarchy, value, and power, and, secondly, in Tcherkézoff's account (following Dumont) of a modernist binary approach to right and left which valorises complementarity and equality.[54] We shall soon see these approaches at work in various contemporary representations of the left hand (Chapter 7).

A related feature highlighted by Tcherkézoff is that of the possibility, within the Dumontian dualistic rather than the binary model, of varying value positions. Of Hertz's consideration of the sacred and profane as seen from variant insider/outsider standpoints, Tcherkézoff writes,

> Thus, if one is considering things from a profane perspective, the sacred appears to be double in nature, with a pure and an impure aspect. On the other hand, if one is considering things from a sacred perspective, the impure appears to be a feature of the profane, and this latter turns out to have a double aspect also.[55]

This double nature was exemplified — in his 1938 account of a funeral in a French village church — by Georges Bataille. In his work on the forces of attraction and repulsion, he developed a point made by Hertz in relation to taboo by considering the way in which apparently repulsive objects — 'such as corpses, blood, especially menstrual blood, menstruating women themselves' — might be impure and untouchable yet also sacred.[56] Using the language of left and right to clarify his meaning he wrote,

> In the sacred realm these objects do not occupy just any place: They belong to the left-hand side of this realm that is essentially divided into two parts, the left and the right, or in other words, the impure and the pure, or even unlucky and lucky. On the whole, that which is left entails repulsion, and that which is right entails attraction. This does not mean at all, by the way, that the various sacred objects are divisible into left objects and right objects... Also it must be added that the relatively right or left side of a given object is mobile: It varies in the course of ritual practices.[57]

Bataille shows how, from differing standpoints and at different times, objects might be seen to change from repulsive to attractive, from left-hand taboo to right-hand sacred, just as a corpse does during a funeral procession and ceremony.

---

54. For another discussion of the hierarchical conceptualisation of opposition and the weaker modern version, see Clark, *Thinking with Demons*, pp. 34-36.

55. Tcherkézoff, *Dual Classification Reconsidered*, p. 14. See Hertz, 'The Pre-Eminence of the Right Hand', pp. 7-8, 12.

56. Georges Bataille, 'Attraction and Repulsion II: Social Structure', in Denis Hollier (ed.), *The College of Sociology, 1937–39* (Minneapolis: University of Minnesota Press, 1988), pp. 113-24 (121).

57. Bataille, 'Attraction and Repulsion II'. See also Parkin, *The Dark Side of Humanity*, pp. 77-78; Carol E. Burnside, 'The Left Hand of the Sacred', *Method and Theory in the Study of Religion* 3 (1991), pp. 3-9; Paul Hegarty, 'Undelivered: The Space/Time of the Sacred in Bataille and Benjamin', *Economy and Society* 32.1 (2003), pp. 101-18.

Bataille made metaphorical reference to left and right to explain the way in which values might be associated with the same object according to time, place, and standpoint. The anthropologist Gregory Forth, also working with the idea that, when seen from different levels, things accrue different values, considered both the fact of left and right in cultural practice and their representational significance in his work on Eastern Sumbanese hairstyles. He noted that 'the Rindi state that the rule of movement to the right governs all matters connected with life...and defines correct order among the living'.[58] Movement to the left is associated with the dead. However, in the very different practical context of hairstyling, movement to the right is associated with men, whereas women tie their hair to the left. Yet clearly both men and women are within the realm of the living. Right and left have a different connotation *within* this practical level to what they have at the more general representational level of life and death.[59] Later, we shall see this interpretive mobility at work in contemporary representations of the left hand.

A final and related point of note concerns the issue of the interrelatedness of concepts on either side of a binary opposition. As we saw, Hertz drew attention to the conflation of meaning and reduction to common principles at work within Maori culture (e.g. of right, light, day, male, east/south); Tcherkézoff referred to it in relation to his discussion of the operation of homology within Needham's binary analysis.[60] For Tcherkézoff, the dualist model (which, because of its recognition of a hierarchy of levels, allows for changes and movement between these levels) avoids a rigid and necessary identification between the various concepts normally associated with the two poles (e.g. sacred/right/pure v. profane/left/impure).[61]

This problem of the conceptual linkage of different elements within a table of opposites has also been discussed by Grace Jantzen, not with sociological modelling in mind, but as part of a philosophical critique of the dominant Western symbolic and her case for a feminist pantheism.[62] Like Tcherkézoff, she observes the significance of hierarchy within a

58. Gregory Forth, 'Right and Left as a Hierarchical Opposition: Reflections on Eastern Sumbanese Hairstyles', in Barnes, de Coppet and Parkin (eds.), *Contexts and Levels*, pp. 103-16 (105). Forth's explicit aim in this paper is to examine the Rindi's ideas and use of right and left in relation to Dumont's work on hierarchical opposition.

59. Forth, 'Right and Left as a Hierarchical Opposition', pp. 100-101.

60. Hertz, 'The Pre-Eminence of the Right Hand', p. 14; Tcherkézoff, *Dual Classification Reconsidered*, p. 21. See also Catherine Bell for a discussion of the role of ritual in this process, in *Ritual Theory, Ritual Practice*, pp. 104-106.

61. Tcherkézoff, *Dual Classification Reconsidered*, pp. 124-31.

62. Jantzen, *Becoming Divine*. Jantzen begins (p. 266) by reminding readers of the Pythagorean table of opposites cited by Aristotle in the fourth century BCE.

polarised order (mind/spirit/goodness/maleness, over and above the subordinated body/matter/chaos/female), and the way in which the identities and boundaries of the primary concepts are normally established by the expulsion of their others or opposites.[63] She notes too, quoting Aristotle, that dualist concepts are expressive of value.[64] Jantzen — unlike Tcherkézoff, whose agenda was avowedly methodological — seeks to challenge the cultural order that is established so firmly on the basis of these traditional dualistic principles. For her, it is not enough merely to identify possible processes (such as reversal or exclusion) that overturn or transform the inherent symbolic linkages that form the binary order. Rather,

> ...a feminist deconstructive agenda does not seek a simple reversal, a mere changing places of oppressor and oppressed, but rather a dismantling of the whole oppressive system and the symbolic which holds it in place, opening the gap to make a way for a radical new symbolic and social order. Hence it is not enough for feminists just to valorize those poles of the dualist categories which have been belittled by patriarchy, lifting up matter, the earth, bodiliness, and women and putting down spirit, intellect, and men... What is needed instead is a strategy that overcomes the series of binaries and offers scope for integration...[65]

The strategy offered by Jantzen is the adoption of a pantheist symbolic which has its 'locus of being and truth' within the world not beyond it, not founded upon mind, spirit, and the notion of transcendence, but rooted in our different bodies and embodied experiences.[66] Whilst this feminist philosophical conclusion takes us into territory quite different to the sociological arguments stated previously, it is significant in suggesting that there is a body of opinion that is not content merely to observe the presence of hierarchy and value within a given dualistic order, but that must then critique it and seek to go beyond it. We shall see later in Part II how Jantzen's argument both falls within the field of religious/secular relations, and comments upon it by fulfilling a valuable critical role in challenging that very symbolic order of which left and right — and those concepts to which they are taxonomically linked — are a part.

In the first half of this chapter, I considered the physical, social, and mental dimensions of the general space of the left hand by looking at its relationship to the right hand in two Western gestural systems. This

---

63. Jantzen, *Becoming Divine*, p. 267, citing the work of Elizabeth Grosz.
64. Jantzen, *Becoming Divine*, p. 268.
65. Jantzen, *Becoming Divine*, p. 270.
66. Jantzen, *Becoming Divine*, p. 274. At one point Jantzen suggests that difference cannot be accommodated within a dualist account. This would certainly be contended by anthropologists such as Dumont, Tcherkézoff, and Forth on the basis that a hierarchically based dualistic order embodies the potential for different levels.

revealed how hands as spatial practitioners may simultaneously contain the traces of various worldviews (whether Arabic, early modern European, or Roman), and we shall see more of this pattern unfold in later chapters. By looking, in the second half, at the work of Robert Hertz and others I have also referred to the body — its inherent right/left asymmetry — as a condition for the development of a hierarchical and value-laden dualism in which the physical, social and mental space of the left hand, and those oppositional categories associated with it, become conceived as inferior and evil, but potentially no less powerful than the pre-eminent right. But to what extent can the left hand elude the grasp of its dominant partner to become a space of resistance or liberation, a space of the sacred? That question has been raised at several points, and will be reconsidered towards the end of Part II.

Chapter 7

The Location of Religion
Within Some Contemporary Left Hands

The world is all the richer for having a devil in it, *so long as we keep our foot upon his neck.*[1]

As I hope to show in what follows, this perceptive remark by William James suitably expresses the location of religion, even today, in both the place of the left hand and in spatial relations between the pre-eminent right and its inferior partner. The left hand continues, though often obtusely, to be associated with evil and its personification, and, as such, performs a vital purpose in facilitating the expression of those symbolic conditions at the heart of Western culture. Simultaneously, contemporary representations of the left hand hold within them the traces of earlier symbolic conditions and their associated values, and these appear at various points in telling metaphors, allusions, and images.

It is what our devils tell us about the society in which we live that is of most interest to the scholar (as distinct from the believer), and thus it is what the scurrilous left hand can reveal to us about what we hold dear, and consider normal, orderly, and appropriate that we must pursue. Revealing the space of the left, which as we saw earlier is seen as the more difficult of the hands to know and get a grasp of, will enable us to develop our understanding of the social and cultural order of the right, that defining, powerful order with its changing demeanour but entrenched moral fabric.

In order to achieve this we must now consider a range of contemporary representations of the left hand, many of them taken from the

---

1.   William James, *The Varieties of Religious Experience* (London: Penguin, 1982 [first published 1902]), p. 50. James alludes here to a picture by Guido Reni of St Michael with his foot upon the neck of Satan. Satan or the devil, in the form of Christ's anti-thesis, or Anti-Christ, has had an oppositional presence in Western culture from the second century CE.

Internet. In fact, if you were to have searched this resource for 'left hand' and 'right hand' at the time this chapter was first drafted (July 2003), you would instantly have been able to identify some of the prevailing pre-occupations with the left hand, left-handedness, and the left more generally. Among the many sites, you would have noted several generic websites providing wide-ranging information on all matters left-handed.[2] You would have seen the consumption needs of left-handers met (including everyday appliances, musical instruments, sports equipment, guns).[3] The issues of child development, special needs, and pedagogical considerations regarding left-handers could have been pursued, as could the relationship of handedness to brain lateralisation and genetics. Causal links between left-handedness and decreased longevity, stuttering, homosexuality, intelligence, creativity, underwater vision, alcoholism, diabetes, and many other conditions could have been investigated.[4] E-communities of left-handers — in America, Europe, Canada, and Japan — could have been accessed. Your search would also have revealed relations between God, the devil, right, and left. And it is with these that I shall begin.

In Chapters 3 and 5, I developed a strategic field of the 'religious' and the 'secular' in which power relationships within and between those two positions, and a third 'post-secular' position, could be mapped. It is the camps within this field that now become the focus for an examination of contemporary representations of the left hand.[5] In turn, I shall examine selected Christian representations, notably those relating to what I call a 'two destinies' approach, secular representations, featuring issues of equality and discrimination, and, finally, post-secular representations which build on but challenge religious and secular perspectives, and employ notions of reversal, reclamation, and liberation. During this examination I shall continue to think about the constitution, activity,

2.   For example, *Rosemary West's Left Handed World* <http://www.rosemarywest. com/left/>; M.K. Holder's primate handedness website <http://www.indiana.edu/ ~primate/left.html>); an archived page (9 January 2001) of frequently asked questions for left-handers <http://www.cs.uu.nl/wais/html/na-dir/lefty-faq.html>; *Lorin's Lefthandedness Site* <http://duke.usask.ca/~elias/left/>, Rik Smits' *Lefthanded Universe* <http://www. xs4all.nl/~riksmits/lhu/lhu.html>; Chris McManus's *Right Hand, Left Hand* site <http://www.righthandlefthand.com>. See bibliography for accession details.
3.   For example, an online store for left-handers <http://www.thelefthand.com> (accessed 7 April 2003).
4.   Rik Smits, *Nothing Left Unsaid: Facts and Fallacies of Left and Right Handedness*, Chapter 1, <http://www.xs4all.nl/~riksmits/lhu/lhu.html> (accessed 20 October 2002); see also McManus, *Right Hand, Left Hand*.
5.   Owing to their frequency in the following discussion, I have not used inverted commas to signify the representational and *etic* nature of the terms 'religious', 'secular', and 'post-secular'.

experience, and meaning of the place of the left hand (as a part of space), and the location of religion within it. I shall then move on in the following chapter to consider the force relations between and within various positions by means of an examination of the spatial properties of extension and simultaneity.

Religious Positions on the Left Hand: Two Destinies

'How do we practise right belief in a left-handed world?'[6] This is the question which lies at the heart of religious representations of right and left. It is contingent on a dualistic perspective, signified by right and left, in which the polar opposites juxtapose related value-laden categories. The author of the question, Martin Swanson, does not need to disclose these other categories, for merely by saying 'right' and 'left-handed', and by playing on the English linguistic ambiguity of 'right'—as both an orientational term and a term denoting 'correct' or 'proper'—he is able to convey the conventional opposition of sacred/profane, good/evil, and spirit/matter.[7] He is also able to give a sense of the difficulty of the task: 'right belief' runs counter to the world in which it must be pursued. A Christian—in this case, Orthodox—believer must be prepared to face this difficulty.

But what constitutes 'right' and 'left' in the eyes of this American Orthodox priest? First, he reminds us of God's judgment in separating the sheep to his right from the goats to his left, offering the former the kingdom and the latter 'the everlasting fire, prepared for the devil and his angels'.[8] He then states that 'many are on the left hand of Christ... [On] the right hand, we have the faithful who have made the church their abode. And on the left hand we have those who are separated from the church and have made the world their home', a world that is 'ruled by Satan'.[9] But the author is more specific still, for, by 'church' he means the Orthodox way of life, even then recognising that many Orthodox have allowed the world to infiltrate their lives and thus to draw them off the path. Certainly, he does not mean all Christians, nor all churches. By 'world', he means all that is 'heterodox', the root of which 'is the ancient

---

6.   Martin Swanson, 'Right Belief in a Left-Handed World', http://www.Orthodox.net/articles/right-belief-in-a-left-handed-world.html (accessed 10 January 2003).

7.   Hertz, 'The Pre-Eminence of the Right Hand', p. 14; Bell, *Ritual Theory, Ritual Practice*, pp. 105-106.

8.   Swanson's account here is based on 'Judging the nations' in the Gospel of St Matthew 25.31-46; <http://www.Orthodox.net/articles /right-belief-in-a-left-handed-world.html>.

9.   Swanson, 'Right Belief in a Left-Handed World'.

evil of humanism…man's preference for himself over God'.[10] This secular humanist concern, which he sees as originating in the serpent's temptation of Eve, and carried forward through the Renaissance and the Protestant Reformation, manifests in the modern world through the values of 'self-actualization, self-creation, and self-love', and notions of freedom and progress which endorse such practices as abortion, 'uncivilised sexual proclivities, and neo-paganism'.[11] What is recommended is a way of life insulated from the grip of secular society, its education system and evil life style. Such a way of life will attract the criticisms of un-Americanness and fanaticism because secularism will only tolerate Orthodoxy if it accommodates itself to the values of the wider society. On the left-hand then we are presented with the dominant secular humanist order, the 'broad way'; on the right, the 'narrow way', those Orthodox Christians who 'wage spiritual warfare against the sinister evil of our time' in pursuit of a reward in heaven.[12]

I have presented this in some detail for several reasons. First, it is an example of the two destinies genre which has developed from a passage in the Christ's Sermon on the Mount on the choice between the difficult path to life taken by the few, and the popular path to perdition followed by the majority.[13] Although no specific reference is made to right and left in Matthew 7.13-14, later exponents, particularly those who chose to represent the two ways pictorially,[14] felt bound to relate them to the (right and left hand) destinies of the sheep and the goats referred to later in the Gospel of Matthew.[15] Two contemporary illustrations show the continued popularity of depicting the choice between life and perdition since the original engraving commissioned by Charlotte Reihlen in the 1860s and distributed first by the German Evangelical Society in Europe and Africa and then by Gawin Kirkham in association with the Open Air Mission in England.[16] One, from 1991, by Peter N. Millward, inspired directly by Kirkham's nineteenth-century version, uses visual allusions to

---

10. Swanson, 'Right Belief in a Left-Handed World'.

11. Swanson, 'Right Belief in a Left-Handed World'.

12. Swanson, 'Right Belief in a Left-Handed World'.

13. Matthew 7.13-14. See also Deuteronomy 30.15, 19-20.

14. For the early history of pictorial representations, see Gawin Kirkham, *History and Explanation of the Picture: The Broad and the Narrow Way* (London: Morgan & Scott, 1886; reprinted by Peter N. Millward, 1997). For nineteenth- and twentieth-century versions of the broad and the narrow way, see Peter N. Millward's page in <http://picturemaker.safeshopper.com> (accessed 28 March 2003).

15. Matthew 25.33-34. In a popular multi-coloured version of the broad and the narrow way, probably from 1883, texts from Matthew 25.31-46 are cited within the picture: most telling is 25.41 (where God curses those on his left hand) which is placed on the top left side where hell is depicted.

16. Kirkham, *History and Explanation of the Picture*, pp. 5-6.

materialism, secular values, family break-up, prostitution, drugs, modern warfare, and violence to reflect the way to death and damnation (on the left), with a less colourful representation of the way to life and salvation (on the right) depicted chiefly by visual references to the resurrection, the living water, Christ's universal message, and its evangelical testimony.[17] In a second electronic version of the two destinies, again no literal reference is made to the left and right hands, but if we click on the left of two closed doors we face the judgment (Hebrews 9.27), wreathed in black and licked by flames; if we enter the right hand door, we face eternal glory with Jesus in a blue celestial landscape in which we approach the kingdom on a rainbow.[18] This association of left and right with freewill, judgment, and either damnation or salvation, which draws on Matthew 25.33-34, continues an eschatological tradition established by Plato in the cave narrative in which souls were thought to be sent at judgment into an opening to the left (and downwards), or to the right (and upwards), according to their deeds, the symbols of which they carried with them.[19] A later account is found in the Qur'an in which the fate of the companions of the right and the left is vividly described.[20]

Secondly, an issue raised by 'right belief in a left-handed world' but no less pertinent for other depictions of our two destinies is what exactly is represented by right, or salvation, and left, or damnation. In the Orthodox case, the right was reserved for those Orthodox who held out against the pull of secular American culture (including Christians of all persuasions who adopted an accommodationist stance). In the Protestant Evangelical illustrations (Kirkham, Millward), the left hand path is the broad way of worldliness, reflecting the period in which the picture was painted, with the narrow right being the way of the evangelical crusader, and, in Millward's case, the charismatic worshipper. Another version of the two destinies, non-Western in origin, underlines still further the issue of left and right representation. In an Iranian revolutionary poster from 1979, the right side portrays Ayatullah Khomeyni 'in the role of Moses victorious over the evil pharaoh, Mohammad Reza Shah Pahlavi', who is joined on the left by 'Uncle Sam with American, British, and Israeli insignia'.[21] The Ayatullah is surrounded by Qur'anic quotations and an

---

17. Peter N. Millward, 'The Broad and the Narrow Way', <http://picturemaker. safeshopper.com/images/g0zlblt.jpg> (accessed 28 March 2003).

18. 'The Broad and the Narrow Way (Matthew 7:13-14)', <http://www.gunhill. org.uk/opendoor/eternal/eternal.htm> (accessed 28 March 2003).

19. Plato, *The Republic* 10.614.

20. *The Holy Qur'an*, Sura 56.

21. Michael M.J. Fischer, *Iran: From Religious Dispute to Revolution* (Cambridge, MA, and London: Harvard University Press, 1980), p. 182. The poster artist must surely have known of the Christian evangelical version of 'The Broad and the Narrow Way'.

angel; the Shah by serpents and, in the top left of the picture, the tortures of hell. In this portrayal, the West, destined to damnation on the left, includes not only secular interests but Jewish ones, as the (Israeli) Star of David shows. Evidently, who and what is situated in the physical space of left or right is an ideological matter for the author or artist. In these depictions of two destinies left and right are shifting positions within the field of the religious and the secular, though right is always associated with the positive, religiously endorsed way and left with the negative, deviant way.

Thirdly, Swanson, in his Orthodox anti-humanist presentation, makes use of a language of struggle and warfare that is highly appropriate for understanding more about power relations between camps within this field. He calls on fellow Orthodox 'to wage spiritual warfare' against secular society and to struggle against the odds to maintain the Orthodox community and its way of life. In some of the pictorial accounts, images of violence, warfare and struggle are also used. War and physical violence—as opposed to spiritual warfare—are situated on the left. On the right, the difficulty of the path is shown, with steep steps and narrow bridges in Kirkham and a mountain to traverse in Millward. The struggle is heaven-bound, away from the attractions of worldliness, and indeed there are breaches in the boundary between the two ways, moments when a flagging spirit might fall back into the broad way of the sinister left.

Modern Western Christian portrayals of the choice facing humanity between life/salvation and suffering/damnation are constituted on the spatial polar opposites of right and left with their origins in the Classical Greek duality of *dexios* (literally, 'right-handed') and *euōnumos* (a euphemism for 'left' referring to [unlucky] omens), which, from the time of the early Greek writers, implied a hierarchical ordering with *dexios* superior to *euōnumos*.[22] Although hands are rarely mentioned explicitly in the two destinies accounts, the two are present therein by way of the two sides or regions to which they refer.[23] As the bodily condition, and cognitive categorisation, on which various values are established, they have both a shadowy presence in and symbolic correspondence to references to hell vs. heaven, Satan/serpent vs. Jesus/angel, broad way/damnation vs. narrow way/salvation, worldly vs. spiritual.[24] Furthermore, although left

His/her portrayal of hell is very similar, as is the use of the right and left sides to depict good and evil, and top right and left to indicate heaven and hell.

22. Lloyd, 'Right and Left in Greek Philosophy', pp. 170, 178. See also Jantzen, *Becoming Divine*, p. 268.

23. See my discussion of Kant's essay, 'Concerning the Ultimate Foundation of the Differentiation of Regions in Space', in Chapter 6.

24. I have not pursued the issue of right and left as cognitive categories here; see my references to metaphors of the body in the work of Lakoff and Johnson in Chapters

and right operate metaphorically in these accounts in relation to different life courses freely chosen, they are imagined as real spaces: the left constituted by worldly institutions, secular discourse and social conformity; the right by places of worship, preaching and prayer, biblical and Christian theological discourse, and the religious community, forged in struggle against the world and seen by the secular mainstream as fanatical and fundamentalist. In the pictorial versions of these two destinies the boundary between the two is clear, though breachable, but in Swanson's narrative it has to be constructed linguistically (hence the references to struggle and warfare, and to the oppositional nature of the values associated with the two sides).

The pictorial examples of the broad and the narrow ways range from the simple to the complex, but all contain within them, as does the Swanson version, evidence of earlier texts, whether related to destiny *per se* or to dualistic principles more generally. In particular I have drawn attention to relevant Greek and New Testament texts, but there are no doubt others I have yet to uncover. As de Certeau suggested, it is the contemporary text within the palimpsest that presents itself to us most forcibly, but fragments of earlier versions remain in part and provide evidence of the force and continuity of the hierarchical ordering of right and left and its relationship to other values.

Within the field of the religious and secular the left hand and side continue to be used by Christians to signify the world, death, and the devil, a path associated strongly with contemporary materialism and secular humanism. But how do those who espouse secular values and beliefs see the left hand and the region to which it refers?

Secular Positions on the Left Hand: Equality and Discrimination

In moving from religious to secular interests, we move from the left hand and side to left-handedness, the condition of that minority of the population (about 11.5% in the West) who have a predisposition to favour the use of their left hand.[25] We also move, as I shall show, from a discourse of hierarchy to one of equality.[26] This move is not achieved, however, by using grand political rhetoric or legal precision on the subjects of equality

1 and 9, and on the body and its role in the formation of boundaries in the work of Anttonen in Chapters 4 and 9.

25. McManus, *Right Hand, Left Hand*, p. 205.

26. See Louis Dumont on the move from a non-modern discourse of hierarchy to a modern, secularist discourse of individualism (and equality), in *Homo Hierarchicus*, Introduction and Chapters 2 and 11.

of opportunity, human rights, and the moral evil and social unaccept-
ability of individual and structural discrimination. Instead, it is presented
through parody. Why, within this secular camp, does the left hand and
left-handedness become the target for jokes and mocking narratives?
Because 'irony [is] the trope of contrariety'.[27] Thus, whilst there is a genuine concern—both pedagogical and material—to affirm and equip left-
handers for full social participation on a par with right-handers, their
greater value is in what such people, their condition, and identity may
signify. As we look at a variety of examples we shall see how the values
associated with the left hand and those that favour it continue to stand in
for other, often unnamed values. It is the representational capacity of this
hand and its users that is its primary importance, not least of all in relation to its opposite.

Our first parody, perhaps surprisingly, takes its subject matter directly
from Catholic tradition and assumes some knowledge of the place of the
right hand of God in scripture and liturgy.[28] *Dextera Domini: The Declaration of the Pastoral Care of Left-Handed Persons*, an anonymous text first
posted on the Internet in 1994, uses the left hand and left-handers as a
means by which to mock Catholic tradition, teachings, and practice.[29] It
takes the form of a humorous, literalist reading of selected biblical passages followed by a discussion of general principles, the chief of which is
that 'Catholic tradition has constantly taught that only the right hand
may properly engage in manual activities', and, finally, pastoral norms,
focusing on how Christians, particularly clergy, should treat 'sinistrals'.[30]
Ironic attention is drawn to the outward call for compassion by a Church
that nevertheless sees such people as deviant, depraved, and destined for
damnation. Despite the pastoral guise, discrimination against left-handers is legitimised by scripture and the Church's teachings.

27. Clark, *Thinking with Demons*, p. 82. See also pp. 26, 81-83.
28. The notion of *dextera domini* is repeatedly reinforced in the divine office of the
Catholic Church and in its festive calendar through the repetition of Psalm 118.15-16:
'With his right hand the Lord does mighty deeds, the right hand of the Lord raises up.
I shall not die but live'. For a contemporary example, see *'The Roman Breviary' of the Lay
Confraternity of Ss Peter and Paul*, <http://www.breviary.net/comment/comment1prim.
htm> (accessed 4 April 2003).
29. <http://www.users.csbsju.edu/~eknuth/rehu/dex-text.html> (accessed 10
January 2003). The website in which this parody is located belongs to Elizabeth T.
Knuth, herself an MTh, and presumably a Catholic. Although not the author herself,
her pleasure in this text raises the question of whether it is a parody by liberal Catholics of the more repressive aspects of their own tradition. Even if this is the case, the
parody, by raising the issues of the rights of left-handers and their active pursuit of
their claims, is underscored with liberal humanist values (hence my choice to discuss it
here with other secularist positions on the left hand).
30. *Dextera Domini*.

But, remember, this is a joke (or is it?). A parody uses mimicry to ridicule its subject,[31] and mimicry is fraught with ambiguity. Thus, *Dextera Domini* raises a number of issues with reference to the left hand that are central to both religious (in this case, Catholic) and secular causes and which emerge in the text as moments of anxiety. They return us to William James's quotation that 'the world is all the richer for having a devil in it, so long as we keep our foot upon his neck'. *Dextera Domini* is a parodic account in a religious idiom of the necessity for keeping the foot in place, whether by demanding that left-handers repress themselves or by containing and disabling them forcibly.[32] But what is the nature of the devil in the left hand (of left-handers) in this account?

We are told that the proper role of the left hand is to be passive and subservient to the right as in the case 'of a wife in relation to her husband'.[33] For the left hand to assert itself is for 'disorder' to ensue, 'a sin against nature', 'an intrinsic moral evil'.[34] The imaginary author of the declaration clearly associates the left with other negative symbols in the traditional binary pairings: evil, disorder, female. The dominant theme, however, is dexterity and its applications. The left hand acts out of turn in undertaking manual activity: '[A] left-handed activity... lacks an essential and indispensable finality'.[35] Furthermore, left-handers show their true nature by engaging in perverted and deviant practices with the left hand and in thinking 'left-handed thoughts'.[36] Although masturbation, bisexuality, and homosexuality are never directly mentioned, they are clearly alluded to in references to 'nasty thoughts', 'bi-manuals', 'a left-handed life-style', the need for 'a lifelong commitment to right-handedness', 'shockingly offensive manual options', and the instruction to 'sinistral and bi-manual individuals...to disguise their sinistrality by keeping it repressed, although under no circumstances are they to keep their left hands in their pockets'.[37] Sexual practices and thoughts outside heterosexual marriage emerge as a major concern in the text. As readers, we are invited to enjoy a joke at the expense of Catholic teachings on sexuality. But perhaps the centrality of this theme also tells us something about the preoccupations of the real author, as opposed to his/her traditionalist Catholic persona, an author whose identity is unknown but who is unsympathetic towards his or her subject? Why does a commentator —

31. *The Shorter Oxford English Dictionary of Historical Principles*, p. 1515.
32. For Clark's treatment of demonic irony and the religious idiom, see *Thinking with Demons*, pp. 82-83.
33. *Dextera Domini*.
34. *Dextera Domini*.
35. *Dextera Domini*.
36. *Dextera Domini*.
37. *Dextera Domini*.

presumably a liberal, possibly both secular and anti-Catholic—harp on about 'sinistral' sexuality? This will become clear in due course.

I shall now move on to two further texts which deal humorously with the space of the left-hander, and in which this theme is again present. The first is from a novel by Theodore Dalrymple, *So Little Done: The Testament of a Serial Killer*, in which it is not the Church but the political cause of left-handers and their rights that is the object of parody.[38] The plight of the left-hander is that s/he is situated 'in a right-handed world', an unsympathetic space in which the left-hander has for centuries been repressed by parents and teachers who have seen the condition of left-handedness as a matter of moral failure (rather than its true cause, neurology).[39] The right-handed world, though implied rather than formally identified or depicted, is a world of tradition, authority, moral judgment, and oppression. The left-hander in Dalrymple's account is certainly on the left, but the left is presented here, albeit in parody, as ideologically correct and scientifically affirmed.

The space of the left-hander is not only a mental one in Dalrymple's narrative. It is physical and social, and always contested. Its physical expression emerges with reference to the equipment of left-handedness—scissors and the handles of toilet cisterns—as well as the use of the left hand itself. But it is its social expression that is of most importance. It is the 'left-handed lobby' that is the ostensible butt of Dalrymple's joke, with its calls for equality of access and opportunity, for the righting of centuries-old wrongs, and the elimination of 'handedness—biased language'.[40] The lobby claimed,

> That a significant number of so-called right-handers were really left-handed, having been forced to change their preference in childhood, and that, with a modicum of official encouragement, they could be returned to their true identity, and hence to personal wholeness.[41]

This allusion to the oppression of homosexuals and to the process of encouraging them 'to come out' and declare their true identity, added to the veiled references to social and linguistic discrimination against women, attest to the source of the narrator's irritation, the political correctness and affirmative action associated with minority politics.

38. Thomas Dalrymple, *So Little Done: The Testament of a Serial Killer* (London: Andre Deutsch, 1995), quoted at length in McManus, *Right Hand, Left Hand*, pp. 282-83.

39. McManus, *Right Hand, Left Hand*, p. 282. We hear an echo here of Swanson's reference to the difficulties of living in the secular left-handed world, <http://www.Orthodox.net/articles/right-belief-in-a-left-handed-world.html>; see also 'Frequently Asked Questions', <http://www.cs.uu.nl/wais/html/na-dir/lefty-faq.html> (accessed 17 January 2003).

40. Dalrymple in McManus, *Right Hand, Left Hand*, p. 283.

41. McManus, *Right Hand, Left Hand*, p. 282.

Left-handers are on the same side as gays and lesbians, women, black people/people of colour, and members of other minorities. This side is the left, and its 'other' is the dominant right, 'the right-handed world' which oppresses, demands conformity, and takes the moral high ground. 'The tables are turned', those represented by the left are finding their voice, and asserting the need for equality, even at times for preferential treatment in order to correct an age-old imbalance.[42] The status of the two sides of the Western symbolic order with its polar opposites begins to be questioned, with the left being raised up in the discourse on equality and human rights to a position of parity with the right.

The final example of the secular left hand is 'The Lesbian of Darkness', whose author, Joel Rosenberg, makes a deliberate play on the analogy between homosexuality and left-handedness.[43] Rosenberg explores homophobia and its effects by imaginatively pursuing the consequences of left-hander phobia.[44] Again, the narrative touches on the three dimensions of space, the physical space of handedness, the ideological spaces of political correctness and anti-leftist bigotry and fundamentalism, and the ensuing social spaces, such as support groups for left-handers, left-handed coffee houses, and the opposing 'gangs of left-bashers' and anti-left groups:

> Imagine the persecution lefties could suffer. People could threaten to institutionalize confused lefty adolescents for writing in the 'perverted scriptstyle'. Parents would deny the early signs that their kids were sinister, and might well disown those who persisted in their left-handedness. Fundamentalist groups masquerading as research organizations would go on Nightline to explain how some lefties had been found to be child molesters or suicides, and suggest that it was all because of that 'left-handed lifestyle'; red-faced women could stand up in the Donahue audience and shriek at uncloseted left-handed parents that they were condemning their children to a life of evil left-handedness… We could have special schools for lefty teenagers who were tired of being beaten up, and right-handed bigots could complain about how that constituted special treatment.[45]

42. See Kenneth Jernigan, 'Blindness — A Left-Handed Dissertation', <http://www.empowermentzone.com/lefthand.txt> (accessed 2 November 2003), for a serious comparison of issues facing the blind and left-handers in relation not to disability but to public attitudes, myth-making, and bigotry.

43. Joel Rosenberg, 'The Lesbian of Darkness', <http://www.winternet.com/~joelr/leftles.html> (accessed 10 January 2003). In doing so he borrows and adapts the title of a novel by Ursula K. Le Guin, *The Left Hand of Darkness* (New York: Ace Books, 1969).

44. See also *Lefthandedness and Homosexuality*, <http://www.kenyon.edu/Depts/WMNS/Projects/Wmns21/left%20handedness.htm> (accessed 2 November 2003); Tammy C, 'My Brother is Left-Handed', <http://www.geocities.com/WestHollywood/stonewall/8505/sf_lefthand.html> (accessed 2 November 2003). The latter is a further satirical essay about homophobia which uses left-handers as its focus.

45. Rosenberg, 'The Lesbian of Darkness'.

Although allegorical, there is more than a hint of truth in this passage. Many left-handers *have* suffered at the hands of parents or teachers, and, as we have seen, the symbolic left hand *has* continued to be vilified as deviant, other, subordinate, and a representation of evil and depravity.[46] So, whilst Rosenberg's real aim is to alert readers to the pain experienced by lesbians and gays, he does so by alluding to that proclivity associated with one of our deepest cultural and physical signs of otherness, the left.

Whereas homosexuality was an implicit theme in the earlier parodies, here it is the explicit object of attention, though examined through the lens of imagined left-hander-phobia. Left-handers stand in for homosexuals in this account. And we do not have to look hard to see why. If we focus on the mental space of the left hand in terms of either its historical layering or its current associations, we witness the presence of what were deemed to be unnatural sexual acts, whether heterosexual but beyond the bounds of convention (e.g. incest, promiscuity, intercourse with the devil), or homosexual.[47] In the first half of the twentieth century it was the psychoanalytic tradition that highlighted this association: first Freud, following Stekel, who of right and left in dreams wrote, 'the right hand path always means the path of righteousness and the left hand one that of crime. Thus "left" may represent homosexuality, incest or perversion',[48] then Jung who noted that the joining of the left hands was indicative of incestuous betrothal.[49] The most explicit recent link between homosexuality and the left hand and left-handers is made by three Canadian

46. For serious examples of left-hander persecution, see McManus, *Right Hand, Left Hand*, pp. 268, 271-73, and M.K. Holder, 'The World of Sinistral Subterfuge', <http://www.indiana.edu/~primate/left.html> (accessed 10 January 2003).

47. For example, books on witchcraft (fifteenth–seventeenth centuries) describe as unnatural the sexual activities of witches with the devil or with incubi. Such relations were often marked by the use of the left hand. See passages from Martín del Río, *Tractatus de confessionibus maleficorum et sagarum* (first published 1591, in Julio Caro Baroja, *The World of the Witches* (Chicago: Chicago University Press, 1961), pp. 119-21; and Heinrich Kramer and James Sprenger, *Malleus Maleficarum* [first published c. 1486] (ed. Montague Summers; London: Hogarth Press, 1969), pp. 109-14. On sexuality and accusations of witchcraft, see Keith Thomas, *Religion and the Decline of Magic* (Harmondsworth: Penguin, 1973), pp. 678-79; and Robin Briggs, *Witches and Neighbours: The Social and Cultural Context of European Witchcraft* (London: Fontana Press, 1996), pp. 32, 250. Briggs notes that he only found one instance of homosexual relations with the devil in witchcraft trial records, homosexuality being 'outside their imaginative repertoire' (p. 250).

48. Sigmund Freud, *The Interpretation of Dreams* (London: George Allen & Unwin, 1954), pp. 357-58 (citing Stekel, 1909). See also his interpretation of Bismarck's dream, linking left with 'what is wrong, forbidden, sinful' (infantile masturbation) (pp. 378-81).

49. C.G. Jung, *The Practice of Psychotherapy*, in *Collected Works* (20 vols.; London: Routledge & Kegan Paul, 1954), XVI, p. 211.

scientists, Lalumière, Blanchard, and Zucher, in an article from 2000 in *Psychological Bulletin* in which they conclude that gays and lesbians are more likely to be left-handed than heterosexuals.[50] This is contested by another researcher, N. E. Whitehead, who doubts the significance of their findings, for methodological reasons, and states that 'most left-handed persons are not homosexual and most homosexual people are not left-handed'.[51] The symbolic connection between left-handedness and homosexuality is recognised and embraced in the title of a lesbian journal: *Sinister Wisdom.*[52]

This anxiety about the relationship of left-handedness to homosexuality demonstrates the continued use of the space of the left hand to signify those devils in our midst that are deemed to be most in need of social and ideological control.[53] That homosexuality is a modern devil is borne out by David Sibley in his account of geographies of exclusion where he discusses the moral panic in the West in the 1980s concerning 'the gay disease', AIDS.[54] He notes that 'homophobia will not go away while homosexuality is constructed as an 'other' which threatens the boundaries of the social self'.[55] Such deviance from normality, as we have seen, is often labelled 'left-handed' in an attempt to isolate it and contain its danger. As Sibley remarks, 'moral panics bring boundaries into focus by accentuating the differences between the agitated guardians of mainstream values and excluded others'.[56] However, the secular examples that we have examined suggest that there is a move by those identified as 'other' and placed on the left to fight back, at least to assert their identity and call for equal treatment.

The left hand, in these contemporary secular accounts, has become a space for humour, but one which simultaneously reveals a discourse on oppression, discrimination and inequality, and the late-modern reaction, the need for minority rights, equality of opportunity, political correctness,

50. M.L. Lalumière, R. Blanchard and K.L. Zucher, 'Sexual Orientation and Handedness in Men and Women: A Meta-Analysis', *Psychological Bulletin* 126 (2000), pp. 575-92. They conclude that gays are 31% more likely than male heterosexuals to be left-handed, and lesbians almost twice as likely than heterosexual women to be left-handed.

51. N.E. Whitehead, 'Is There a Link Between Left-Handedness and Homosexuality?', <www.narth.com/docs/lefthand.html> (accessed 18 October 2002).

52. *Sinister Wisdom: A Journal for Lesbians*, <http://www.sinisterwisdom.org/> (accessed 15 September 2003).

53. In November 2003, the Google search engine identified some 85,700 Internet references containing both homosexuality and the left hand.

54. Sibley, *Geographies of Exclusion*, pp. 41-43.

55. Sibley, *Geographies of Exclusion*, p. 42.

56. Sibley, *Geographies of Exclusion*, p. 43. He notes also the role of parody (and thus inversion) in this process (p. 44).

social and linguistic inclusion, identity politics, and single issue interest groups. As such, this space becomes a means by which the pre-occupations of the age can be explored, a process facilitated by its association with deviance and with the subordinate half of the Western symbolic order. However, whilst the Greeks and early Christians accepted and argued for the superiority of the right and its related values, in Western modernity the plea is for equality, in this case the need to acknowledge and correct the injustice wrought on left-handers and other oppressed peoples, and thus for binary symmetry.[57] Such may be the plea, but, as Dumont made clear in his allusions to racism in the West, 'Make distinctions illegitimate, and you get discrimination'.[58] A society may seek to abandon a hierarchical principle in favour of egalitarianism, but the old tendency to rank and discriminate re-emerges in new forms, such as homophobia.

Traditional religion, except in the first of my examples, was noteworthy by its absence. It was not Christian values or principles that came to the fore, but those associated with secular humanism. Indeed, equality has been called 'the religion of modernity'.[59] Equality and the other Enlightenment values connected with it are situated in the space once occupied by Christian values, not entirely separated from them, but in part a reaction to them and in part bound by them. And where religion formally appears in these three texts, it fulfils the role of the one to be mocked and despised: represented as the repressive traditional Church in *Dextera Domini*, and, briefly, as the fundamentalist extremist in 'The Lesbian of Darkness'.[60] As we saw earlier in this chapter, however, the 'other',

57.   Dumont, *Homo Hierarchicus*, Introduction. See also Serge Tcherkékoff, *Dual Classification Reconsidered*, on Needham and an 'equalitarian' position, pp. 15-26.

58.   Louis Dumont, 'Caste, Racism and Stratification', first published in French in *Cahiers Internationaux de Sociologie* 29 (1960), pp. 91-112, reprinted in English as an appendix in Dumont, *Homo Hierarchicus*, pp. 287-307 (303).

59.   A remark made by a scholarly commentator on the BBC Radio 4 programme *Thinking Allowed*, summer 2003. Dumont alludes to the valorisation of equality, along with individualism, in the work of modernist ideologues such as Rousseau and de Tocqueville, and to the notion of *Homo aequalis* (*Homo Hierarchicus*, p. 286). See also Phillip Blond who writes (in his 'Introduction' to *idem* [ed.], *Post-Secular Philosophy: Between Philosophy and Theology* [London and New York: Routledge, 1998], pp. 1-66 [2]), 'we are told there can be no discrimination in the secular city…equality names itself as the only value that cannot be devalued'.

60.   Swanson's recognition that the secular left-handed world would present the Church as old-fashioned, fanatical and un-American supports this idea (<http://www.Orthodox.net/articles/right-belief-in-a-left-handed-world.html>). See also Daniel O. Conkle on the use of the term 'fundamentalism' by American religious and secularist exponents of each other, in 'Secular Fundamentalism, Religious Fundamentalism'.

the enemy, was normally identified with the left: Would we not expect the secular cause to associate itself with the right, casting religion to the space of the left? This does not happen in this case for the reason that the terms were already established, the positions set long ago by those early Christians who absorbed the Greek traditions of Pythagorus, Aristotle, and Plato: the Church was, and continues to be, on the *right* hand of God, a non-negotiable position. Secular humanists have no choice, then, but to raise up the oppressed left and enable it to stand its ground against the oppressor right, the Church, its Christian traditions and values.

What can we learn about this struggle, and the significance of left and right within it, from the third of our camps, the post-secular position? How are the other positions, the Christian religious and liberal secular, presented by exponents of this third camp, and what devils need repressing or controlling in their accounts?

Post-Secular Positions on the Left Hand: Reversal, Reclamation, and Liberation

Turning to post-secular approaches to the left hand means to face squarely the devil in our midst because one of the principal positions is that of contemporary Satanism. With Tantra, Thelemic Magic, and some forms of feminist spirituality, Satanism follows the 'left hand path'.[61] We move then from the role of the left hand in issues of identity and rights back to its role in characterising and locating the sacred quest. This time, however, it is not the narrow right hand way that is prioritised, but the deviant left hand path. This path, as will soon become clear, does not map onto the broad worldly way represented by the left in the 'two destinies' approach, but is a self-selected, occult quest[62] which runs counter to the right hand path of organised religion and white magic. It is not antithetical to the world, or to the values of secularism, except in so far as it is self-consciously religious. As was the case with the secular hands, the

61. Other organising terms which are associated with the left hand path include ritual magic, black magic, and chaos magic, all aspects of the Western esoteric tradition. There is considerable debate about the origin of the idea of the 'left hand path'. Some attribute the first Western use to Helena Blavatsky of the Theosophical Society who, in turn, would have derived the term from Hindu and Buddhist Tantra (see Vexen Crabtree, 'The Origins of the Lerm LHP', in <www.dpjs.co.uk/lefthandpath. html> (accessed 20 October 2002). Sutcliffe also associates it explicitly with the tantric *vāma-mārga* (left path), but accredits Aleister Crowley with being its chief populariser (Richard Sutcliffe, 'Left-Hand Path Ritual Magick: An Historical and Philosophical Overview', in Graham Harvey and Charlotte Hardman [eds.], *Paganism Today: Wiccans, Druids, the Goddess and Ancient Earth Traditions for the Twenty-First Century* [London: Thorsons, 1995], pp. 109-37 [110]).

62. Sutcliffe, 'Left Hand Path Ritual Magick', p. 123.

left is raised up, but here it is embraced as a means to liberation. The use of the left as a signifier in both social and cultural criticism and personal empowerment continues to be important, however.

In focusing particularly on Satanism[63] I shall examine the use of the space of the left hand and the path associated with it, and consider its relationship to the religious and secular positions discussed previously. Key themes will be the reversal of the elements within the dualistic order, the deviant reclamation of the left, and the left as a space for emancipation or liberation. Within these contemporary post-secular religious spaces, as well as identifying the traces of earlier ideas, we will see the use of genealogical strategies which place left hand path movements in an ideological and romantic relationship with mediaeval and early modern magic and witchcraft. In the following chapter, reflecting on this earlier engagement between religious and magical practices, the process of demonising witches, and the role of the left hand in both will help me to analyse force relations in the *contemporary* field of religious, secular, and post-secular positions, and to explore the way in which left and right have been used to articulate various positions in the field, to demonise others, to resist oppressors, and to argue for liberation.

Our principal journey down the path of the left hand is with a young British Satanist and self-publicist, Vexen Crabtree.[64] Associating himself with the Church of Satan and the life and work of Anton LaVey, Vexen appears to be a prime mover in the British-based electronic dissemination and organisation of Satanism: as well as developing and maintaining several websites on both Satanism and religion, in 2003 he ran the e-mail list for London Satanists.[65]

---

63. On contemporary Satanism, see Anton LaVey, *The Satanic Bible* (New York: Avon Books, 1969); R.H. Alfred, 'The Church of Satan', in Eileen Barker (ed.), *Of Gods and Men: New Religious Movements in the West* (Macon, GA: Mercer University Press, 1983), pp. 180-202; Gordon J. Melton, *Encyclopedia of American Religions* (Detroit: Gale Research, 1993), pp. 854-57; Graham Harvey, 'Satanism in Britain Today', *Journal of Contemporary Religion* 10 (1995), pp. 283-96; James R. Lewis, 'Diabolical Authority: Anton LaVey, *The Satanic Bible* and the Satanist "Tradition"', *Marburg Journal of Religion* 7.1 (2002), available at <http://www.uni-marburg.de/religionswissenschaft/journal/mjr/lewis.pdf>.

64. Vexen Crabtree, born 1975, heterosexual, Goth, Satanist, Humanist, one time Computer Studies student, prolific writer. From 'About Vexen', <http://www.vexen.co.uk/vexen/index.html> (accessed 14 November 2003).

65. Vexen Crabtree, webmaster, 'Description, philosophy and justification of Satanism: Personal essay collection by Vexen Crabtree', <http://www.dpjs.co.uk/> ([established 24 February 2002], accessed 20 October 2002); 'The Bane of Monotheism', <http://www.vexen.co.uk/religion/index.html> (accessed 14 November 2003); and 'Holy Shit', <http://www.vexen.co.uk/holyshit/index.html> (accessed 14 November

Vexen is informative on the meaning, origins, and usage of the term 'left hand path' (LHP), the place of Satanism within it, and its relationship to what LaVey referred to as 'White Light religion'.[66] He notes the importance to the LHP of the individual and the focus on the self, the emphasis on independent thought and freedom from dogma, on relativism and a non-missionary spirit, thus reflecting the radical individualism of modern Western magical traditions and the rejection in LaVey's *Satanic Bible* of 'a herd mentality'.[67]

Satanism, says Vexen, is atheistic.[68] It is an 'un-religion', with no sacred objects or gods, no prayer, and no institution, but *is* religious, with a philosophy, imagery, ritual, and with Satan as its personification.[69] Furthermore, quoting the Council for Secular Humanism, he asks if Satanism is really just a form of Humanism, concluding that, while the two share a materialist and ethical outlook, the former is religious — in having symbolism, ceremony, ritual, and dogma — whilst the latter is not.[70] Vexen is particularly indebted to the ideas of LaVey in this respect. As James R. Lewis wrote of LaVey,

> [His] secularist world view [was] derived from natural science. This world view provided LaVey with an atheistic underpinning for his attacks on Christianity and other forms of supernatural spirituality... LaVey claimed that Satanism was a legitimate religion because it was rational. As a corollary, traditional religion was irrational (unscientific) and therefore illegitimate.[71]

Following LaVey, Vexen extols the virtues of the LHP, especially Satanism, over those of traditional religions, as reason over blind belief or faith, the embracing of our evil side as opposed to the rejection of evil in favour

2003). The e-mail list was founded in August 2000, with 151 members by November 2003.

66. Vexen Crabtree, 'The Meaning and Usage of the Term "LHP" in the West', <http://www.dpjs.co.uk/lefthandpath.html> (accessed 20 October 2002).

67. LaVey, *The Satanic Bible*; Lewis, 'Diabolical Authority', pp. 9-14; 'Satanism and Left Hand Path', <http://www.velvetdragon.com/spirit/lhp.htm> (accessed 17 January 2003); Magister Peter H. Gilmore, 'The Myth of the "Satanic Community" and Other Virtual Delusions', <http://www.churchofsatan.com> (accessed 17 January 2003); Sutcliffe, 'Left Hand Path Ritual Magick', p. 111.

68. Vexen Crabtree, 'A Description of Satanism', <http://www.dpjs.co.uk/modern.html#REL2> (accessed 14 November 2003).

69. Vexen Crabtree, 'A Description of Satanism'. The idea of Satan as the personification of the LHP is taken from LaVey, 'The Book of Lucifer', *The Satanic Bible* (p. 52). This has led to discussions about the nature of Satan for contemporary Satanists. See Lewis, 'Diabolical Authority', pp. 10-11. He notes that most of those who responded to his questionnaire retained LaVey's humanistic approach to Satan.

70. Vexen Crabtree, 'A Description of Satanism'.

71. Lewis, 'Diabolical Authority', p. 4.

of the good, the affirmation of the self and recognition of selfishness over the veneer of altruism, and the stress on individualism and the personal as opposed to the universal 'herd'. Whilst noting the common ground between Satanism and Humanism, he distinguishes them on the grounds that the former follows the LHP and is religious whereas the latter is neither. With reference to both 'others' — traditional, White Light religions and Humanism — Vexen states that Satanism raises up those very things that would be deemed within them to be vices. This strategy of reversal is derived directly from LaVey's principles in which Satan represents values and views that run counter to those of Christianity in particular.[72]

Vexen makes a point, in fact, of distinguishing the LHP from all religions which call themselves 'good' and which those on the LHP refer to as 'Right Hand' or 'White Light' religions. They include not only Christianity and other traditional religions, but also many New Age and Wicca movements. Vexen's critique of such paths is that they are 'unbalanced' in denying the evil within us, thus reinforcing a dualistic understanding of the person rather than recognising the whole self.[73]

This dualistic outlook is noted by other Internet writers on the LHP, particularly Haramullah whose aim is to reclaim some negative terms — notably black magic and left hand path — from the Western value system, which seeks to categorise them as representing malevolence and coercion.[74] As Haramullah says, 'the current popular interpretation [of these terms] follows a narrow, fundamentalist character that accepts moral absolutes and authoritarian biases'.[75] Preferring, on the one hand, a more informed understanding of the motivations of those who practise this path and, on the other, a reclamation of those aspects of the Western

72. LaVey, *The Satanic Bible*; 'Satanism and Left Hand Path'; Lewis, 'Diabolical Authority', p. 8, in which Lewis discusses LaVey's indebtedness to Ayn Rand.

73. Vexen Crabtree, 'The Meaning and Usage of the Term "LHP" in the West'.

74. 'Haramullah' is one of several personas of the American occultist, Tyagi Nagasiva. The name 'Haramullah' means 'Forbidden by/of Allah' and/or 'Woman of Allah', according to Haramullah himself (<http://stderr.org/pipermail/tariqas/2001-June/000870.html> [accessed 11 December 2003]), and signifies Tyagi Nagasiva in his Sufi magical guise. More generally, he is identified with Thelemic Magic, and his work is included in *The Occult Archive* and classified under 'Thelema', <http://www.beyond-the-illusion.com/files/Occult/Thelema/Haramullah/kathulu_magik ([first posted 14 August 1993], accessed 11 December 2003). Haramullah, 'Black Magick and the Left Hand Path', <http://www.luckymojo.com/avidyana/shaitan/blkmgk.html> ([first posted 1993], accessed 2 November 2003). The quotation from Aleister Crowley (*The Book of the Law*) at the outset of the article places Haramullah in the tradition of Thelemic Magic rather than Satanism. See also Paul Hine, 'Black Magic and the Left-Hand Path', <http://www.phhine.ndirect.co.uk/archives/ess_bmlhp.htm> (accessed 17 January 2003).

75. Haramullah, 'Black Magick and the Left Hand Path', Part Two: Reclaiming the terms.

symbolic order that are normally despised (e.g. dark, left, female, unconscious), Haramullah, like Vexen, makes a case for holism: 'Reclaiming the
left hand is an important step in realizing the value of not only the entire
body (through revaluing the feminine), but the many modes of consciousness which we may experience'.[76] This focus on the left hand then raises
up intuition, imagination, dreams and feelings, spontaneity, and artistic
growth rather than those skills and approaches associated with reason,
bureaucracy, and discipline. Unlike those who 'see negation as a force to
be combated, avoided or destroyed', Haramullah stresses the value of
embracing it as a valuable and integral part of nature in order to move
towards 'a synthesis of mind and body, intellect and emotion, self and
society, microcosm and macrocosm'.[77]

Although the primary focus here has been on Satanism, it is important
to note that this is only one of several Western ways on the path of the
left hand, others being Thelemic Magic (with its foundations in the work
of Aleister Crowley),[78] Hindu and Buddhist influenced Tantrism,[79] and
some but not all forms of feminist spirituality.[80] Though widely divergent
in many ways, they exhibit some common aspects as a result of their
identification with the left, such as a focus on the will and liberation
of the individual rather than the good of all,[81] on the 'behaviour of the
left' (involving the breaching of taboos),[82] as well as the drive to unify

76. Haramullah, 'Black Magick and the Left Hand Path'.
77. Haramullah, 'Black Magick and the Left Hand Path'.
78. Sutcliffe, 'Left Hand Path Ritual Magick'.
79. See the work of Hugh B. Urban, especially, 'The Cult of Ecstacy: Tantrism, the
New Age, and the Spiritual Logic of Late Capitalism', *History of Religions* 39.3 (2000),
pp. 268-304, and 'The Power of the Impure: Transgression, Violence and Secrecy in
Bengali śākta tantra and Modern Western Magic', *Numen* 50.3 (2003), pp. 269-308.
80. Feminist Wicca is seen by Vexen as a White Light or Right Hand movement
(Vexen Crabtree, 'The Meaning and Usage of the Term "LHP"'). This is supported by
Salomonsen's theory that 'generic Witches' often concede that there is an 'ideological
continuity' between Jewish and Christian traditions and Wicca. She refers to Wicca
(specifically Reclaiming Witchcraft) as 'a subcultural branch of Jewish and Christian
traditions' (Jone Salomonsen, *Enchanted Feminism: The Reclaiming Witches of San
Francisco* [London and New York: Routledge, 2002], pp. 97, 297). On the left hand/
right hand divisions in Western esoteric and magic traditions, see Sutcliffe, 'Left Hand
Path Ritual Magick', pp. 113-14.
81. For the place of the will in Thelemic Magic, see Sutcliffe on Aleister Crowley,
'Left Hand Path Ritual Magick', pp. 122-24, and US Grand Lodge, Ordo Templi Orien-
tis, 'Thelemic Rheology', <http://oto-usa.org/theology.html> (accessed 14 November
2003).
82. For 'behaviour of the left' in relation to women in Tibetan tantra, see Miranda
Shaw, *Passionate Enlightenment: Women in Tantric Buddhism* (Princeton: Princeton University Press, 1994), p. 45; in feminist Goddess spirituality, see Daly with Caputi,
Websters' First New Intergalactic Wickedary, p. 268.

opposing principles, restore balance, and challenge dualism.[83] This interest in reversing the normal cultural order (whether of patriarchy in the
case of goddess spirituality, of social etiquette in the case of Tantra, or of
Christian ritual practice and ethics in Satanism) by reifying the left is
important for understanding the LHP as the cultivation of an alternative
spiritual strategy that critiques the social and religious institutions from
which it arises.

What must be acknowledged in the case of all these branches of the
LHP—except perhaps Tantra with its roots in Indian society and religions—is that their chief 'other' is not secularism but the Western Judeo-
Christian tradition of which secularism is but a recent and important
development. In fact, as we saw in Satanism, there is a certain sympathy
with aspects of a secular worldview, though not with its anti-religious
stance.[84] This raises the question of the extent to which the positions
discussed here can justifiably be called 'post-secular'. Arguably, they fall
within the camp of the 'secular'. However, in being overtly 'religious',
they distinguish themselves from those secular stances which are either
antagonistic or indifferent to religion.

That self-consciously *post*-secular religious stances exist is not in doubt,
however. This has been argued by Wouter Hanegraaff for New Age
holism, which he suggests rejects dualism and reductionism: '[It] emerges
as a reaction to established Christianity, on the one hand, and to ration-
alistic ideologies, on the other'.[85] The standpoint of Grace Jantzen, whose
ideas about dualism and the Western symbolic order I discussed at the
end of the previous chapter, is a further example. Whilst those on the left
hand path espouse strategies of reversal and reclamation of the beliefs
and practices of the subordinate, negative side of the order, Jantzen seeks
a new position. This certainly involves the process of reclaiming that
which has been dominated, undervalued, and marginalised by a Western
order informed by Greek and early Christian dualistic thought. Developing Irigaray's conception of a 'sensible transcendental', she emphasizes
'mutuality, bodiliness, diversity, and materiality'.[86] But her position is
more than 'a simple reversal, a mere changing places of oppressor and

---

83. On the unification of opposing principles, see Kama Sutra Temple, *Tantra: The
Left Hand Path of Love*, <http://www.tantra.org/lefthand.html> (accessed 2 November
2003); on challenging dualism, see Christ on goddess spirituality in *Rebirth of the
Goddess*, pp. 100-101.

84. Hanegraaff ('New Age Spiritualities as Secular Religion', p. 153) makes a
similar point about New Age religion which he says, 'looks like a strange mixture of
secular and non-secular elements'.

85. Hanegraaff, *New Age Religion and Western Culture*, p. 515.

86. Jantzen, *Becoming Divine*, p. 269.

oppressed'.[87] Rather, it is a 'disruption of the dualistic and hierarchical western symbolic, which western secularism largely leaves in place'.[88] It is a *new* position—both pantheist and feminist—one that disrupts both classical theism and 'an already masculinized secularism', and seeks to '[bring] the god to life through us—through us and between us'.[89] This is achieved, not by reversing the hierarchical arrangements of the Western order, but by opening out 'what has hitherto been seen as a set of polarities into a play of diversities' and thus offering 'new horizons for becoming'.[90]

Jantzen longs to find and articulate a new position precisely because the old ones are mutually implicated in the Western symbolic itself with its masculinized, hierarchical, and unjust order, and in the acts of practising and sustaining it. She is interested in freedom from the old order, but a kind of freedom not posited solely on the liberation of the individual, whether by the grace of God or the exercise of the will—as we saw in the case of the left hand movements—but on the possibility of diverse new horizons for mutual realisation. Although she does not explicitly engage with the idea of the left, her critical position invites the question of whether a left hand path that is either underpinned by secularism or that merely exchanges the old order for a new, opposing order can be more than a space for resistance. Can it also be a space for the achievement of liberation? I shall return to this question in Chapter 9 after looking more closely at the nature of the religious and secular field in which these debates are occurring.

---

87. Jantzen, *Becoming Divine*, p. 270.

88. Jantzen, *Becoming Divine*, p. 275. See also Christ, *Rebirth of the Goddess*, p. 100, for a further rejection of the strategy of reversal. Arguably, the integrative approach offered by Taoism, and popularised in the West in association with Tai Chi and the *I-Ching* or *Book of Changes*, offers a further counter strategy to Western dualism. A contemporary exposition that explores oppositions but moves towards their integration is the novel by Ursula Le Guin, *The Left Hand of Darkness* (New York: Ace Books, 1969). See also Haramullah, 'Black Magick and the Left Hand Path'.

89. Jantzen, *Becoming Divine*, p. 275.

90. Jantzen, *Becoming Divine*, p. 272. Jantzen's stance is based on the feminist philosophy of Luce Irigaray.

Chapter 8

Spatial Properties, Distant Left Hands, and the Field of the Religious and Secular

---

Having considered the physical, social, and mental dimensions of the left hand in general in Chapter 6, and in a range of contemporary texts in Chapter 7, I shall now investigate the location of religion in the place of the left hand with reference to the spatial properties I discussed in Chapter 1. These properties—discussed by Foucault and later by Massey—were configuration, simultaneity, extension, and power. A social space is the sum of the things, activities, ideas, processes, relations that are brought together within it. It simultaneously envelopes and contains various spaces, and exists alongside and in relation to others. It extends backwards and forwards in time. It is infused with power, and is dynamic. The place of the left hand, as a part of social space, operates thus. It has been my task to see where religion lies within the social space of the left hand as it is currently understood and represented in the West. So far this has involved looking particularly at how religion is configured with other ideas and practices associated with left and right, and at how writers on the left hand have utilised left and right to oppose, favour, discriminate, and valorise certain destinies, identities, life choices, and spiritual paths at the expense of others. Already it is clear that a study of the location of religion in the left hand must acknowledge the operation of power therein, and the way in which such power is expressed in terms of hierarchy and values.

The principal task of this chapter is to consider the spatial properties of extension and simultaneity in order to gain a greater understanding of the workings of religion as a focus of knowledge-power (see Chapter 3) in relation to left and right. In the first half I shall pursue the traces of demons, witches, and magic evident in today's representations of the left hand back into mediaeval and early modern Europe. What lessons does that earlier period hold for understanding the relationship between contemporary religious, secular, and post-secular perspectives? In the second half, I shall consider non-Western representations and practices of the left in order to obtain a comparative view of the possibilities for locating religion in the left hand. Given Europe's historical relationship to South Asia—the source of the Indian Tantric perspectives on which I shall focus—a postcolonialist and neo-comparativist approach will be adopted.

By Extension: Mediaeval and Early Modern Religion and Magic and the Contemporary Field of the Religious and Secular

In the struggle between contemporary positions on the right and left hands, we noted traces of earlier oppositions, for example, classical Greek views on spirit and matter, Christian Platonic views of good and evil, mediaeval views on God and the devil, and early modern views on religion and witchcraft. Our contemporary positions are related to these earlier ones, not in a formal historical chain of cause and effect, but ideologically and emotionally. Existing in the space of the left both contemporary and earlier sinistrals may well occupy a similar relationship to the dominant culture. Furthermore, this very situation encourages among some contemporary exponents a feeling of identity with those marginalised for their beliefs and practices in earlier times.[1]

The first lesson with a contemporary resonance that we learn by turning back to religion, magic, and witchcraft in late mediaeval and early modern Europe is that these aspects of culture and society were inextricably interwoven. They partook of the same universe of meaning.[2] 'Only one world and only one language is involved.'[3] Jorge Arditi, following Foucault, makes it clear that, despite appearing from within a religious worldview to be contradictory and in opposition to one another, mediaeval religious and magical discourses were 'functions of the same epistemological field',[4] though each discursive camp contained various heterogeneous discourses. Together, they shared the same 'immense appetite for the divine', and 'although often representing opposite sides of the same coin, were, by the same token, congruent'.[5]

1. This is witnessed in the tendency among some within the Western esoteric tradition to establish lines of continuity between modern movements and their supposed forebears, whether necromancers or witches.
2. Arditi, *A Genealogy of Manners*, p. 10; see also K. Thomas, *Religion and the Decline of Magic*, p. 318; Eamon Duffy, *The Stripping of the Altars: Traditional Religion in England, c. 1400–1580* (New Haven and London: Yale University Press, 1992), p. 279; Richard Kieckhefer, 'The Specific Rationality of Medieval Magic', *American Historical Review* 99 (1994), pp. 813-36.
3. Clark, *Thinking with Demons*, p. 13.
4. Arditi, *A Genealogy of Manners*, p. 10.
5. Arditi, *A Genealogy of Manners*, p. 31 (on the ideas of Richard Kieckhefer).

A consideration of this relationship reveals a congruity between the beliefs informing both religious and magical practices. Duffy, for example, discussing the nature of charms as 'magical prayers', notes that,

> The worldview they enshrined, in which humanity was beleaguered by hostile troops of devils seeking the destruction of body and soul, and to which the appropriate and guaranteed antidote was the incantatory or manual invocation of the cross or names of Christ, is not a construct of the folk imagination. Such ideas were built into the very structure of the liturgy.[6]

Furthermore, specialists from both domains operated within a single orbit: 'Both the exorcist and the conjurer were engaged in spiritual matches with the demons'.[7]

And yet such antipathy and fear developed within religious circles against magic (or certain types of it) that they took on the appearance of ideological separation, indeed opposition. Arditi suggests that this was a function of the hegemony of ecclesiastical authorities. Those practices that 'were perceived as disrupting the order of ecclesias…as violating its collective self' were condemned; those that affirmed that collective self were encouraged:[8]

> The condoned practices were defined as curative, as divinely healing, as fomenting a restoration of the essence of Christianity, and were assimilated within the spaces of religion. The threatening ones were redefined as sorcery and witchcraft and consigned to the other side of the line, to a space of 'difference'.[9]

This is clear also in an examination of the significance of witchcraft in early modern Europe which was 'construed dialectically in terms of what it was not… The witch—like Satan himself—could only be a contingent being, always a function of another.'[10] This, then, is the second idea that can be drawn on from this earlier period for our consideration of the contemporary engagement between religious, secular, and post-secular positions, the idea of the emergence of difference within a single epistemological field.

The third is the attribution of values to differing positions by those with knowledge-power at the centre of the field, in the case of the late

---

6.   Duffy, *The Stripping of the Altars*, p. 279.
7.   Richard Kieckhefer, *Forbidden Rites: A Necromancer's Manual of the Fifteenth Century* (Stroud: Sutton Publishing, 1997), Introduction.
8.   Arditi, *A Genealogy of Manners*, p. 32. See also K. Thomas, *Religion and the Decline of Magic*, pp. 313-32.
9.   Arditi, *A Genealogy of Manners*, p. 32.
10.   Clark, *Thinking with Demons*, p. 9.

mediaeval period, the ecclesiastical authorities.[11] Practices and beliefs which accorded with their aims were considered good, as moving them closer to the centre and to God, as contributing to salvation, and thus deliverance from evil;[12] those which did not were counter-productive, evil, and contributed to damnation. Although the positions with which these practices and beliefs were associated were clearly demarcated and identified by the official Church, many lay people were clearly confounded when it came to differentiating what lay close to the line, and by what constituted the exact job specifications of priest and magician.[13] The field was indeed a 'blurred' one.[14]

A further aspect of the emergence of difference within this field of religion, magic, and witchcraft, and a fourth point for us to consider in reflecting on our contemporary concerns, is the principle of inversion.[15] Whilst certain values and ends were attributed by ecclesiastical authorities to beliefs, practices, and roles at the centre and the periphery of the field, what was the nature of the beliefs, practices, and roles themselves? How could good, observant people oriented towards the centre recognise the very things they were supposed to fear if they were advised on pain of their mortal lives and eternal souls to avoid them? As Clark asks of knowledge about witches and their activities, 'How...did they "know" witchcraft; how did they "think" it?'[16] They thought it 'in a world of meanings structured by opposition and inversion'.[17] The popular imagination was fuelled by the colourful accounts and 'scholarly pornography' of the authors of *Malleus Maleficarum* and later writers such as Jean Bodin and Martin del Río.[18] That imaginations were quick to pick up on these

11. In the early modern period, in parts of Europe, this power shifts to Protestant divines, religious scholars and jurists, as becomes evident in discourses on witchcraft.

12. See Arditi, *A Genealogy of Manners*, p. 39, on the practices of centeredness which brought people closer to God; see Bossy on 'salvation' and 'deliverance' in this period, John Bossy, *Christianity in the West 1400–1700* (Oxford and New York: Oxford University Press, 1985), pp. 72-73.

13. K. Thomas, *Religion and the Decline of Magic*, pp. 303-304, 326; Bossy, *Christianity in the West*, pp. 138-39; Clark, *Thinking with Demons*, p. 458.

14. Arditi, *A Genealogy of Manners*, p. 32.

15. That Europeans were familiar with notions and practices of inversion is borne out by their significance in carnival, masquerade, and other festivals in this period. Clark, *Thinking with Demons*, pp. 11-30, 69-79. We may note that inversion was one of several strategies identified by Chidester and Linenthal in their account of the contestation of sacred space: see Chapter 4.

16. Clark, *Thinking with Demons*, p. 26.

17. Clark, *Thinking with Demons*, p. 80.

18. Briggs, *Witches and Neighbours*, p. 32. *Malleus Maleficarum*, by Heinrich Kramer and James Sprenger (c. 1486); Jean Bodin, *De la Demonomanie des Sorciers* (1580); Martin del Río, *Disquisitionum Magicarum Libri Sex* (1599).

once they had filtered down to popular level was borne out by the testi-
monies of so-called witches and those who identified them.[19] These
accounts made sense — they did not seem irrational or ridiculous — because
they were recognisable within the familiar cognitive and cultural rules of
inversion.

If the values and ends of religion and witchcraft were perceived to be
in opposition then so were the beliefs and practices themselves. As John
Bossy suggests, 'To know how the Devil was worshipped, one needed
only to know what true religion was, and turn it inside out... Through
the looking-glass one passed...from sacraments to excrements.'[20] In his
account of the new, sixteenth-century model of sorcery, he continues by
identifying the activities and roles of the Devil and those who were held
to be in thrall to him:

> The behaviour of the new-model witch was the inverted image of a moral
> system founded on the Ten Commandments, and particularly of the first
> table. The Devil, who had been the mirror-image of Christ, the personified
> principle of the hatred of one's neighbour, became a mirror-image of the
> Father, the focus of idolatry, and hence of uncleanness and rebellion... The
> witch was one who worshipped the Devil, blasphemed the Lord and
> inverted the Sabbath, before inverting all the other commandments.[21]

Thus it was that the cognitive patterns of 'interchangeability, hierarchy,
and invertability' provided the basis for imagining and thinking about
witches.[22] If further evidence were needed to support the argument that
these apparently opposed beliefs and practices occupied a single epistemological field, this is it, that clerics, scholars, and, later, magistrates of
the period, in imagining the ritual world of those who challenged their
hegemonic position, created it in the inverted image of that which they
knew well, the ritual world of the Roman Catholic mass, with God at its
centre and Christ on his right hand.[23]

The left — especially the left hand — had an important symbolic function
in this mythic, inverted world. Spatially, it denoted the territory, relations,

---

19.   Briggs, *Witches and Neighbours*, pp. 33-34; James Sharpe, *Instruments of Darkness:
Witchcraft in England 1550–1750* (London: Penguin, 1997), p. 78.

20.   Bossy, *Christianity in the West*, p. 137.

21.   Bossy, *Christianity in the West*, p. 138.

22.   Clark, *Thinking with Demons*, p. 40.

23.   See Briggs on the witches' sabbat, 'a diabolical anti-world in which normal
polarities were reversed' (*Witches and Neighbours*, pp. 31-32); See also Clark, *Thinking
with Demons*, pp. 14-23; Margaret A. Murray, *The Witch-Cult in Western Europe* (New
York: Oxford University Press, 1921), pp. 124, 135; on inversion and its socio-political
role, see Sibley, *Geographies of Exclusion*, pp. 40-45. The politics of centre and periphery
were not static in Europe at this time. The act of inverting the mass had different
connotations for Catholics and Protestants, for example.

and practices of the Devil,[24] and often served to identify his servants.[25] In moral terms, it signified all that was evil, 'other', and dangerous. A 'hidden boundary' existed between the conceived world of righteousness and that of *maleficarum* and the Devil, all too easy for the unsuspecting person—not infrequently a woman—to cross,[26] a boundary that came more sharply into focus during periods of heightened activity directed against those identified as witches.

If we review this spatially, what we have is a single epistemological field at the centre of which, at the beginning of the period in question, are the ecclesiastical authorities with the power to conceive the terms and values of the field at both centre and periphery.[27] In this field, they are divided from those they perceive to be their enemies by a hidden and somewhat fuzzy boundary. Although the mythic and ritual world beyond the boundary—in the territory of the 'other'—was held to be inverted, close to the boundary the beliefs and practices of 'cunning folk',[28] of local healers and enchanters, were more ambiguous. They drew on the rituals, charms, and symbols of those at centre not for religious ends but for the magical purposes of healing, protection, divining, propitiation, gaining favours, and exorcism.

In this in-between space, left and right were deployed to signal—on the right hand—officially legitimated religious actions, such as making the sign of the cross, and—on the left—unofficial magical or divinatory ones, such as reading past events and identifying guilt.[29] In addition, they indicated 'self' and 'other', as in this rite for obtaining favours from a king or lord:

> Take your image in your right hand, and the other in your left, and join his image to yours, saying three times, 'He has subjected the nations to us, and the peoples under our feet' [Ps. 46.4 Vulg.]. Then take a small iron chain and bind it to the neck of his image, placing the other end in the right hand

24. Montague Summers (ed.), *Malleus Maleficarum* (London: Hogarth Press, 1969 [c. 1486]), Part 1, Question 16, p. 81; see various early seventeenth-century accounts, including woodcut illustrations from F.M. Guazzo's *Compendium Maleficarum* (1609), reproduced in Julio Caro Baroja, *The World of the Witches* (Chicago: Chicago University Press, 1961), p. 147, and the work of Henri Boguet cited in Michael Barsley, *The Left-Handed Book* (London: Souvenir Press, 1966), p. 67, and Jean Boucher and Ben Jonson discussed in Clark, *Thinking with Demons*, p. 15.

25. For example, see Baroja's example of two girls from Pamplona who revealed that witches could be recognised by their left eyes in which the sign of a frog's foot could be seen, *The World of the Witches*, pp. 145, 148.

26. Briggs, *Witches and Neighbours*, p. 105.

27. Arditi, *Genealogy of Manners*, p. 8.

28. K. Thomas, *Religion and the Decline of Magic*, Chapter 8; Briggs, *Witches and Neighbours*, pp. 71, 122-26; J. Sharpe, *Instruments of Darkness*, pp. 66-70.

29. Kieckhefer, *Forbidden Rites*, pp. 108, 110.

of your image. Then, when it is firmly bound, say, 'Just as you, O image formed in the name of so-and-so, are subject to my image, thus may so-and-so be bound to me utterly for all eternity.[30]

As we see here, the right hand of the self-image dominated and controlled the other-image.

Let me reiterate the five points that have emerged in this discussion of religion, magic, and witchcraft in late mediaeval and early modern Europe that have relevance for my enquiry into the place of the left hand in the field of the contemporary religious and secular:

1.   The apparently opposed knowledge-worlds of religion and magic in this period can be seen as functions of a single epistemological field.

2.   A single field need not imply homogeneity. Different positions emerge within the field as a means of marking social centrality or peripherality.

3.   Values are attributed by those in authority to these different positions which signal the extent to which the latter are endorsed and included or criticised and excluded.

4.   The excluded or 'other' world is conceived as an inversion of the known world.

5.   Left and right play a symbolic role in differentiating the two worlds, and the beliefs, practices, and values associated with them. They operate as particularly helpful markers in the fuzzy territory around the boundary where religion and magic were at their most similar.

What happens if we now apply these points to the field of central concern to this study, the field of the religious/secular, especially to the positions within that field that I discussed earlier?

Prior to doing so, we should note the genealogical relationship between the two fields at issue here. The earlier one, of religion, magic, and witchcraft, operates not only as an analogy and case-in-point for the religious and secular one, but is held within our field and recalled repeatedly, as we have seen, by its language and practices, and, indeed, by its references to right and left. The traces of the earlier universe of meaning are still evident within the contemporary manuscript.[31] That said, I do not wish to minimise the differences between the two historical periods or to over-interpret the analogy. The place of religion within the two fields, for example, is very different, as is the nature and operation of the dominant order within each. Nevertheless, the process of extending backwards in

---

30. From *The Munich Handbook of Necromancy*, a fifteenth-century text (see Kieckhefer, *Forbidden Rites*, p. 77).

31. De Certeau, *The Practice of Everyday Life*, p. 201.

time various elements associated with the contemporary left hand leads us into another age, the social relations, beliefs, and practices of which are intriguingly informative for our own.

In Chapter 3 I postulated a dialectical field of the religious and secular (including the post-secular) which, whilst operating with a single rationality, makes space within it for a range of ideological positions some of which appear to be diametrically opposed (e.g. religious theist vs. secular atheist) and others similar but irreconcilable (e.g. secular materialist and post-secular spiritual or religious). We have observed some of these positions in the preceding examples, including the right-handed Orthodox Christian perspective of Martin Swanson, the secular views of the parodists, and the contemporary spiritual accounts of those on the left hand path. None of these positions is value-free, however. Indeed, as we saw, their exponents shape and authorise their moral stances with reference to other positions within the field, whether different or similar. The two destinies accounts, for example, gain their power from the juxtaposition of the narrow, right hand way of the few who fully commit themselves to Christ, and the broad, left hand way of the world. Rosenberg, in his spoof on the lesbian of darkness, succeeds in making his point about discrimination and its consequences by linking two similar positions, of the left-hander and the homosexual. Vexen, in his attempt to characterise the Satanic path, distinguishes it absolutely from the 'White Light', right hand religious traditions, whilst exploring its similarities and differences to secular humanism.

The strategy of inversion is clearly at work in the two destinies tradition, the purpose of which was to win converts to the difficult narrow way despite some of the apparent attractions of its opposite (bars, nightclubs, consumerism etc.). It was important that both the superficiality of these attractions and the direness of their consequences were conveyed. In the pictorial representations, viewers were left in no doubt about the punishments associated with a journey down the morally depraved path of the left. Although the demons here are secular materialism, consumption, and the failure to heed the word of Christ and to follow the path of discipleship, the inversion is no less striking than the late mediaeval and early modern ones and the end is the same even if the nature of the path is different.

Inversion is also evident in those positions I identified as post-secular (most of which were seen to be thoroughly imbued with secular values). In fact, inversion is fundamental to their very identity. When we turned back to the Middle Ages and the authorising and demonising of positions by those at the dominant centre, we witnessed a hegemonic 'othering' of 'witches' and 'necromancers'. In the case of contemporary Satanists, Thelemic magicians, and some Goddess feminists, we see a positive embracing of the inverted world in a desire to sustain a strategic resistance to the conventional, dominant order, whether of Christianity or patriarchy. The intentionality and playfulness of this stance, as well as its genealogical relationship to earlier periods, is aptly expressed in Mary Daly's account of '*X-ing*':

> X is the symbol for the Unknown and Variable Qualities of Questing women... First, X-ing implies the Contrary-Wise activities of Be-Wildering Witches. It has long been known that Witches are Contrary. Knowledge of this fact persisted into christian times:
>
>> Even in Christian times, witches often had their plaits arranged on their heads anti-clockwise. Looking into their eyes, a person saw his image in their pupils upside-down. At the sabbat, they also danced in a reversed manner. [Footnote]
>
> X-ing women are, of course, Anticlock-Wise... X-ing Witches dance, look, speak, act the Wrong Way, that is, contrary to customary procedures... X-ing women indeed do all things 'contrary to the custome of Men,' that is, Naturally, Elementally, upending/ending the reversals of cockocracy/clockocracy. Such Wickedness requires Moving Widdershins.[32]

This reference to 'Moving Widdershins', and in other parts of Daly's account of X-ing to the left hand path, demonstrates the function of the left in establishing this owned position of difference. Along with other symbols of otherness, it expresses the acknowledged peripherality of the position and its reversal of the norms of that which is deemed to be dominant and conventional (which Daly refers to as 'cockocracy/clockocracy').

Whilst many ritual inversions celebrate the very order they overturn, thus tending towards integration rather than the disruption of hierarchical relations, the post-secular religious pleasure in that which is conventionally 'other' does not signal intentional re-incorporation. Rather it thrives on its marginality, seeking to '[unsettle] the very classification system that gives it meaning'.[33]

Right and left are also clearly at work as symbolic markers in the religious and secular texts discussed earlier. The notions of pursuing a right-handed course in a left-handed world (Swanson), of being a left-hander in a right-handed world (Dalrymple), or of the care of sinistrals by Catholic dextrals are means of both differentiating and ordering moral positions within the field. As we saw earlier, the moral high ground shifts from right to left with the move from religious to secular (and post-secular)

---

32. Daly with Caputi, *Websters' First New Intergalactic Wickedary of the English Language*, p. 268 (italics and capitalisation are Daly's own). Footnote to citation in Hans Peter Duerr, *Dreamtime: Concerning the Boundary Between Wilderness and Civilization* New York: Basil Blackwell, 1985), p. 248 n. 29.

33. Clark, *Thinking with Demons*, p. 28.

positions. In the former, right is right, good, superior. In the latter, the left is valued and raised up to a position of equality, ultimately being embraced by those on the left hand path as a symbol of that which is whole, balanced, true, realistic, ethical, and spiritually effective. This shifting from right to left seems to me to be a further affirmation of the common rationality underlying these ostensibly very different positions. Given our slight biological predisposition to right handedness, and the identification of the right with the sacred (Hertz), we might have expected the right to remain the symbol of choice for the signification of superior moral value. What we see, though, is that within our examples the right is generally identified with the neo-Platonic Christian order.[34] The space of the right has already been claimed for the Christian God (and associated with other positive aspects of the Greek dualistic system). We do not see attempts by those on the margins to re-situate the Christian God on the left for their own moral ends. His place is secure, and other positions must accommodate themselves to this fact.

This leaves those who wish to argue against the centrality of the Christian God and Christian beliefs, practices, and values (on either secular or post-secular religious grounds) to make the most they can of the left. As this is traditionally the space of the other, the marginal, the dangerous, and the Devil, the task is challenging. For those post-secular exponents who are familiar and comfortable with the language and practice of myth and ritual, the inverted world is ripe for spiritual exploration.[35] Even the Devil himself can be a source for spiritual self-examination and progress. The inverted world can provide the tools for a struggle against the old orders of Christianity, patriarchy, and secular materialism. For those occupying secular positions, however, the task is more difficult. Generally, it involves denying the 'religious' in all its aspects, except where it must be acknowledged as an enemy (whether in the guise of 'fundamentalism', abusive 'Satanism',[36] or 'cults'). In secular accounts (with the exception of *Dextera Domini*), then, the Judeo-Christian order is often notable by its absence. Remarkably little is said in them about what is situated in and what constitutes the space of the right, as if to name it is to continue to give it power and authority.

34. A key exception to this is the Iranian example depicting Ayatullah Khomeini—beyond this epistemological field—in which the right is identified with the Shi'a Islamic order.

35. For example, see Hugh Urban's examination of Aleister Crowley and his transgression and inversion of conventional religious and moral practice in 'The Power of the Impure'.

36. I would suggest that, ironically, for those in the secular camp, *all* overtly religious persuasions are associated with the right including Satanism (which identifies itself with the left).

A further observation to be noted in an attempt to learn from the earlier case study of magic and witchcraft concerns the issue of inversion within secular accounts of the left hand. If we pursue Stuart Clark's invitation to 'think with demons', we find them curiously absent in these accounts, at least in their supernatural forms. The left hand has come to represent those oppressed in the natural rather than the supernatural realm. Both God and the Devil have been demythologised. Thus, whilst the left hand is raised up, the Devil is not.

What seems to be the case is that there is an unresolved ambivalence within the secular. There is no doubt that, in general, it has triumphed over the religious and become socially and politically dominant. In the secular accounts we looked at, the left hand had been raised up in a moral and ideological strategy of 'equalitarianism' and in an effort to supersede what, though unacknowledged, continued to be represented by the right hand — the Judeo-Christian aspect of the Western order. Yet, secularism is still very much a part of this order. It may wish to 'blank out' or fight off its counterpart, or to see itself as its natural successor, but, as Jantzen suggests, it is not free of it, indeed it has hardly begun to critique the symbolic order in which *both* Western Christianity and secularism have their roots.

This state of affairs, of the moral shift from right to left within the field of the religious/secular, poses a question for my return in the next chapter to the work of Robert Hertz, and to the relationship between this field and the polarity of sacred and profane.

Simultaneity: *vāma* in Hindu and Buddhist Tantra as a Metaphorical Foil for the Contemporary Western Left Hand

In the first half of this chapter I noted that mediaeval and early modern religion, magic, and witchcraft were related to my own case study in several ways. Spatially, the contemporary case is an historical extension of the earlier one: traces of the former can be found in the latter. I have used the earlier case as an analogy, the study of which throws up various issues that can illuminate the current one. Furthermore, I have posited a genealogical relationship between the two on the grounds that they are ideologically and affectively related (in the minds of many contemporary exponents). Turning now to our second case, Indian Tantra, a different network of relations emerges that link it to my own case and make it a valuable comparator.[37]

37. I am indebted to Louise Child, whose doctoral dissertation I examined, for placing the idea of Tantra as a comparative case in my mind: Alice Louise Child,

The principal methodological purpose here is to acknowledge and benefit from what Foucault and, later, Massey referred to as spatial 'simultaneity'. At the same time as our Western religious, secular, and post-secular religious places of the left hand are making their electronic presence felt and are struggling for the moral and spiritual high-ground, other non-Western places of the left hand are at work. Even if these other places were entirely unconnected to the Western ones, they would remain interesting in offering an alternative epistemological perspective on our contemporary left hand, a view from elsewhere, from beyond the Western symbolic and moral order. Without doubt, the many Tantric left hands (Tantrism is a complex related cluster of traditions, texts, groups, beliefs, techniques, and other practices) provide such a view.[38] However, the processes of colonialisation and globalisation have led to a situation in which even these apparently separate Eastern and Western formations of the left hand are interwoven.[39] We cannot say that the left hand as it is treated within the field of Western religious, secular, and post-secular relations is unaffected by the Indian Tantric left hand.[40] As we saw in the last chapter, the Western left hand path is shaped in part by the Theosophical and Thelemic magical engagement with Tantra. Furthermore, as Hugh Urban shows in his extensive work on Tantrism in the West, other connections lie within nineteenth-century Orientalism, and, more recently, within the New Age 'cult of ecstasy'.[41] These connections, as well as being intriguing for the history of religions and the study of religious transplantation, are important for what they reveal about power relations between East and West. Ronald Inden and Richard King, in particular, have discussed the way in which 'Hinduism' and 'the Mystic East' provided a foil for Orientalists seeking to understand the origins and nature of their own society and religion.[42] Furthermore, they became

'Transformative Bodies, Communication, Emotions, and Illumination in Tantric Buddhism' (PhD thesis, University of Leeds, 2003). Hertz and the left hand are discussed in her final chapter.

38. Hugh B. Urban, 'The Extreme Orient: The Construction of "Tantrism" as a Category in the Orientalist Imagination', *Religion* 29.2 (1999), pp. 123-46 (126); David Gordon White, 'Introduction', in *idem* (ed.), *Tantra in Practice* (Princeton and Oxford: Princeton University Press, 2000), pp. 7-9.

39. See Massey on simultaneity in Chapter 1 and discussion of globalisation in Chapter 4.

40. I shall use the singular 'Tantric left hand' from now on, but in the full knowledge that it signifies a plurality of Tantric perspectives.

41. Urban, 'The Extreme "Orient"', 'The Cult of Ecstasy', and, 'The Power of the Impure'.

42. Ronald Inden, *Imagining India* (Oxford: Basil Blackwell, 1990), Chapter 3, 'Hinduism and the Indian Mind'; R. King, *Orientalism and Religion*, Chapter 4, 'Orientalism and Indian Religions'.

a means by which India, its people, and its religion were objectified, disempowered, and possessed (as passive, feminine, otherworldly, and emotional rather than rational) by both British colonialists and other European and American commentators.[43] Urban suggests that, for Western Orientalists, Tantra represented 'the extreme Orient', leading to abhorrence, but also to a deep fascination, as witnessed in the life and work of Sir John Woodroffe, or 'Arthur Avalon' as he later styled himself.[44]

Taking the Tantric left hand as a simultaneous space through which to gain further insight into my own case study is not, therefore, undertaken lightly. It will be done with an awareness of the 'networks of [colonial and] neo-colonial or neo-imperialist exchange'[45] that must inform any account of Tantra, and, indeed, on the understanding that the very categories of Tantra and Tantrism derive substantially from nineteenth- and twentieth-century Western scholarship[46] — as do the religions of 'Hinduism' and 'Buddhism' in which they participate.

Bearing these issues of knowledge-power in mind, how should I approach the simultaneous spaces of the left hand in Hindu and Buddhist Tantra? As Lawrence Sullivan has asked,

> [W]hat role will other cultures be allowed to play in answering these questions about the nature of different modes of knowing and the relations among them? Since the Age of Discovery, myriad cultures have appeared on the margins of Enlightenment awareness. Normally, they have been taken as objects of study, subject to the explanatory paradigms of the natural and human sciences, and thrust into typological schemes which were not of their own making… They have all been taken, in the main, as data to be explained rather than as theoretical resources for the sciences that study them.[47]

I cannot claim to be entirely indifferent to the conceptual and classificatory possibilities that Tantra offers, as I shall reveal. However, what is more important is that in this study Tantra will operate as a theoretical resource for making sense of and elaborating upon contemporary Western representations of the left hand. For the success of this approach to be

43. See also Anne McClintock, *Imperial Leather: Race, Gender and Sexuality in the Colonial Context* (New York: Routledge, 1995).

44. *Calcutta Review* 47 (1885), p. xxiv, cited in Urban, 'The Extreme Orient', p. 127; for Urban on Woodroffe, see pp. 134-37 of Urban's article. Woodroffe wrote *The Principles of Tantra* (1960), and *Shakti and Shakta* (1978).

45. Urban, 'The Power of the Impure', p. 272 (my insertion).

46. Urban, 'The Power of the Impure', p. 271, drawing on an assessment by André Padoux; see also 'The Extreme "Orient"', p. 129, and 'The Cult of Ecstasy', pp. 272-75.

47. Lawrence Sullivan, 'Body Works: Knowledge of the Body in the Study of Religion', *History of Religions* 30.1 (1990), pp. 86-99 (87), cited in Keller, *The Hammer and the Flute*, pp. 8-9.

maximised it is important that the logic and epistemological under-pinnings of Tantra be allowed as full a rein as possible. In order to 'understand' the physical, mental, and social space of the Western left hand, the Tantric left hand at this point will 'stand over' it, thereby helping to reveal its nature, priorities, limitations, and possibilities.

Ironically, this cannot be achieved without the help of Western scholars of religion. There are two reasons for this. First, Westerners have for centuries been fascinated by Eastern religious thought and practice, particularly Tantra, and, secondly, as a result of this, they have rendered Tantric texts into English and dialogued with both Tantric practitioners and scholars of Tantra writing in Indian languages as well as English. It is through such Western scholars that Tantra can be accessed in the West.[48] To reject their work on the grounds that they themselves are Westerners would be unhelpful not least of all because many of them have been active in making available and giving voice to the very agents—Tantric practitioners and commentators—that a postcolonialist approach to religion upholds.[49] However, it must also be acknowledged that, as Westerners, they share with me a disciplinary background, training, and intellectual priorities that propel them towards the definition, ordering, categorisation, and classification of Tantra. They seek to make available *emic* terms and ways of seeing and organising Tantra whilst often developing their own *etic* models.[50] This, in itself, is useful for this study as it assists me in engaging the logic of the Tantric other for a study of the Western left hand. The tendency that Western scholars on Eastern religions have had, to order, define, distinguish, and classify the objects of

48. For example, in David Gordon White's reader on *Tantra in Practice* (2000) all of the thirty-six contributors were Western scholars with the exception of one Indian who worked in the West. Two of the Western scholars were working in India and Nepal at the time of writing and at least one Western scholar was a Tantric practitioner.

49. Western scholars of Tantra have included Arthur Avalon, Mircea Eliade, H.V. Guenther, Agehananda Bharati, Alex Wayman, Teun Goudriaan, André Padoux, Douglas Renfrew Brooks, Miranda Shaw, David Gordon White, and Hugh B. Urban. Indian scholars of Tantra have included Prabodh Ch. Bagchi, Benoytosh Bhattacharya, Chintaharan Chakravarti, S.B. Gasgupta, Gopinath Kaviraj, and Sanjukta Gupta. To list them in this dichotomous manner falsely represents a situation in which much boundary crossing has occurred, by Westerners who have practised Tantra and Indians who have studied or worked in the West.

50. See Ronald Inden, *Imagining India*, pp. 7-36, on the Western Enlightenment impulse to order and classify Indian social and cultural phenomena. I do not mean to suggest that these practices have had no place in Indian thought in general or in Tantra more specifically (as we shall see), only that they have been to the fore in mod-ern Western scholarship. See N.J. Allen, *Categories and Classification: Maussian Reflections on the Social* (New York and Oxford: Berghahn Books, 2000), on the views of French sociologists and comparativists, including Mauss and Dumézil, on primitive classification and on *emic* and *etic* approaches to classification.

their enquiry, facilitates a comparison to be made between the place of the left hand in an Eastern Tantric context and a Western religious/ secular one. It enables the act of translation to occur.

A 'comparison'? Another potential methodological pitfall opens up before us in light of debates about the intellectual value and scholarly politics of comparative religion.[51] But let us be clear about what kind of a comparison is intended here, its purpose, and how the two things to be compared are to be used. There is no doubt that the process of identifying simultaneous cultural places of the left hand and applying them to the study of Western examples is a comparative one. Similarities and differences of epistemological, social, and religious context, as well as cultural practice, will be noted. Without this it would not be possible for the one — the Tantric left hand — to illuminate the other — the contemporary Western religious/secular left hand. But the aim is not to evaluate, to judge one according to the other, nor to prefer one at the expense of the other.[52] Rather, it is to see the Western left hand through a different epistemological and socio-cultural lens. In this respect, the Tantric perspective is valued precisely on its own terms with its own integrity, but for its difference. However, whilst I have noted the utility of a Western body of scholarship on Tantra — as a cultural bridge to the apparently esoteric and different domain of Tantra — there is also a drawback. The Western scholarly production of any system of classification, however much this is based on the terms used by Tāntrikas themselves and the way they appear to order their social and religious world, reflects Western interests of a disciplinary if not an overtly ideological or theological kind. This does not invalidate a cross-cultural approach, but it does limit it. Nothing is to be gained from drawing back from the act of comparison altogether,[53] but it can no longer be undertaken without due regard for the historical conditions and knowledge-power relations which affect, and indeed produce, the things to be compared, the context in which the comparison occurs, and the one who undertakes it.[54]

51.   See Kimberley C. Patton and Benjamin C. Ray (eds.), *A Magic Still Dwells: Comparative Religion in the Postmodern Age* (Berkeley: University of California Press, 2000).

52.   On the ideological and colonialist character of the study of religions, especially its comparative approach, see McCutcheon, *Manufacturing Religion*; R. King, *Orientalism and Religion*; Laura E. Donaldson and Kwok Pui-Lan, 'Introduction', in *idem* (eds.), *Postcolonialism, Feminism and Religious Discourse* (New York and London: Routledge, 2002), pp. 1-38 (14-28).

53.   Wendy Doniger, 'Post-Modern and -Colonial -Structural Comparisons', in Kimberley C. Patton and Benjamin C. Ray (eds.), *A Magic Still Dwells: Comparative Religion in the Postmodern Age* (Berkeley: University of California Press, 2000), pp. 63-76.

54.   See Kwok Pui-Lan's criticism of the work of the feminist scholar of religion, Rita Gross. Whilst applauding Gross for her honesty and self-critical stance, she

It is for these reasons that Richard King suggests a 'new comparativism' that is both 'beyond Orientalism' and that 'redirect[s] the intellectual trajectory of comparative study in the light of postcolonial and post-structuralist theories'.[55] In the course of articulating this he draws on the work of the Indian historian and subalternist, Dipesh Chakrabarty whose methodological strategy involves 'provincializing Europe'.[56] This is instructive for thinking about the Western left hand through the Tantric left hand, of 'othering' the former in the light of the latter. The process of 'provincializing' that which is dominant and familiar by recognising that it 'cannot be divorced from the unfolding of events beyond the "homeland"'[57] is precisely what the spatial properties of simultaneity and extension should invite. Western spaces are not autonomous and self-contained, but engaged historically, ideologically, and socially with non-Western ones. Writing of history rather than space, Chakrabarty asks for an approach 'that deliberately makes visible...its own repressive strategies and practices', and that 'look[s] towards its own death'.[58] At one stroke the scholar, whether historian or spatial theorist, should both reflexively practise his or her methodological approach whilst being attentive not only to its contextual limitations, but also to its very limit in the face of emerging critical possibilities from beyond its epistemological boundary. Chakrabarty does not deny the difficulty of this task.[59]

Hugh Urban, who employs a new comparativist, post-Orientalist approach in his article on the power of the impure in Bengali Śākta Tantra and modern Western magic, does not go this far. His critical engagement with the colonialist formation of 'Tantrism', the emergence of a Western Tantra, and the methodological limitations and possibilities of a comparative approach are informative and significant for understanding simultaneous religious spaces, their interrelationship, and mutual illumination.

suggests that '[Gross] has taken a culturally and religiously pluralistic approach without seriously interrogating the power differentials undergirding the West's fascination, re-presentation, assimilation, and alienation of the religious and cultural Other since the beginning of the comparative study in religion' (Donaldson and Kwok Pui-Lan, 'Introduction', p. 25).

55. R. King, *Orientalism and Religion*, pp. 6, 186, 215; see also Doniger 'Post-Modern and -Colonial -Structural Comparisons'.

56. Dipesh Chakrabarty, 'Postcoloniality and the Artifice of History: Who Speaks for "Indian Pasts"?', *Representations* 37 (1992), pp. 1-26 (20), cited in R. King, *Orientalism and Religion*, p. 188. Subalternist historians are associated with the Indian Subaltern Studies Collective. Their interests lie in divulging indigenous, non-elite historical voices, those silenced by dominant groups whether colonialist or indigenous. See the journal *Subaltern Studies*, particularly the writings of Ranajit Guha. See R. King, *Orientalism and Religion*, pp. 190-200, for a summary.

57. R. King, *Orientalism and Religion*, p. 189.

58. Chakrabarty in R. King, *Orientalism and Religion*, p. 190.

59. R. King, *Orientalism and Religion*, pp. 189-90, on attempting the impossible.

He acknowledges that, in juxtaposing two cases 'like a metaphor, playing upon both their striking differences and their surprising similarities', he is not making claims for their sameness nor for some 'transcendent archetype or universal pattern' that might produce them.[60] He sees himself working 'from the ground up', from the body and physical substances, using comparison as a heuristic device for shedding light on transgression and secrecy.[61] In this sense, his approach is highly instructive for my own. Chakrabarty would no doubt note, however, that, whilst Urban recognises the limitations of a traditional comparative approach and revises his own accordingly, he does not go as far as he might in acknowledging his own participation in the unwinding project of colonialism (as a Western commentator on Tantra and a scholar of the new comparativism). Neither does he write with the humility borne out of an awareness of the fragility and potential demise of the Western modernist scholarly approach. Urban—like the rest of us Western scholars of religion—is a powerful player *within* the field of Western religious/secular relations[62] who makes subtle and clever use of the complex and dynamic web of relations that is Tantra for secular scholarly ends. As a result of this, what he produces has authority and is compelling. It does not acknowledge its own limitations or see its own end, however.

It is indeed likely, given Chakrabarty's concession to the near impossibility of embracing the death of Western historiography (and, by implication, other aspects of the modernist scholarly project) at the same time as employing it, that I shall only fall short of the subaltern ideal in the same way that Urban does. It is much easier to see the weaknesses in another's work than in one's own. Weaknesses aside, however, Urban takes forward the idea of the metaphoric foil[63] moving it from an Orientalist location, as outlined by Ronald Inden, to a new comparativist one. In the process of acknowledging the synchronic presence of Indian Tantric and Western left hands, and in focusing on the former in order to understand and illuminate the latter, I shall follow Urban's process of metaphorical juxtaposition, informed as far as possible by a postcolonialist critique.

A number of questions confront us at this point. What is the nature of the physical, mental, and social space of the Tantric left hand? What values are associated with right and left in the Tantric worldview and in Tantric practice? How are right and left used to order and organise physical space, theological positions, and social relationships? What is the

60. Urban, 'The Power of the Impure', p. 300.
61. Urban, 'The Power of the Impure', pp. 300, 273.
62. See my discussion in Chapter 3.
63. He applies this idea to the sixteenth-century Bengali Śākta, Kṛṣṇānanda Āgamavāgīśa and the twentieth-century Western esotericist, Aleister Crowley.

nature of the boundary between right and left in this context, and how is it maintained? What does the Tantric order reveal about the significance within it of those key spatial conceptions on which the categories of left and right rest, namely polarity, duality, opposition, alterity, and inversion? These questions cannot be answered systematically because they are intertwined. Nevertheless, I shall address them in the following account before returning at the end to engage Tantrism with the contemporary Western examples presented in the last chapter. By juxtaposing Tantric and Western spaces of the left hand, I hope to learn more about the field of religious/secular relations and the meaning and values attributed to left and right within it. Further issues relating to the liberative potential of the left, to dominance and resistance, and the positions of right and left, to embodiment, sexuality, and spatial practice, and the relationship of the sacred to both right/left and the field of religious/secular relations will be raised for further consideration in the following chapter.

Although my own initial rationale for taking Hindu and Buddhist Tantrism[64] as a metaphorical foil for the contemporary Western left hand was its penetration of the field of religious/secular relations by way of the left hand path itself, what emerged quickly in my investigation of non-Western Tantrism was not the *vāma-mārga*, or left hand path itself, but *vāmācāra*, 'ways of conduct' of the left[65] or 'behavior of the left',[66] practices that cut across sectarian divisions or paths rather than identifying or reinforcing them.[67] Specifically, the term *vāmācāra* refers to the offering of the 'five Ms' or *pañcamakāra*—that is, wine (*madya*), meat (*māmsa*), fish (*matsya*), fermented grain (*mudrā*), and sexual intercourse (*maithuna*).[68] In India, prohibited in Vedic, Smārta, and even in many

64. Henceforth in this discussion, when referring to the system of philosophy, practice, texts, and organisation associated with Hindu and Buddhist Tantra, I shall adopt the term 'Tantrism' as it seems to be used by the majority of scholars not just to denote the Western appropriation of this body of knowledge, but also to refer to its social, religious, and historical development in India and Tibet (these being the two areas to which I shall refer, though Tantrism operates in many other Asian contexts). See Urban on the contribution of André Padoux in 'The Power of the Impure', p. 271.

65. Teun Goudriaan, 'Tantrism in History', in Sanjukta Gupta, Dirk Jan Hoens and Teun Goudriaan, *Hindu Tantrism* (Leiden: E.J. Brill, 1979), pp. 13-46 (44).

66. M. Shaw, *Passionate Enlightenment*, p. 45. Shaw also notes (p. 216 n. 32) that Debiprasad Chattopadhyaya reads *vāmācāra*, not as practice of the left, but as 'practice centering on women'.

67. I realise that, in my focus upon the left hand, I have ignored much that is important within Tantrism, such as the roles of gurus and kings, *mantra* and *mandala*, yoga, 'intentional language' and secrecy.

68. David Gordon White (ed.), *Tantra in Practice* (Princeton and Oxford: Princeton University Press, 2000), p. 629; Agehananda Bharati, *The Tantric Tradition* (New York: Samuel Weiser, rev. edn, 1975 [first published 1965]), pp. 228-78; Sanjukta Gupta,

Tantric forms of worship, the 'five Ms' and the practices that surround them are considered by the majority of Hindus to be impure, unconventional, and socially unacceptable: in fact, according to Agehananda Bharati, '"left-handed" (*vāmācāra*) is a term of abuse for all orthodox Hindus'.[69] For Tantric *Kaula*[70] practitioners, however, the ritual use of the 'five Ms' in *vāmācāra* — which deliberately violates Vedic ethical norms — leads to the creation of 'a proximate form of ultimate bliss' which, through repeated practice, becomes permanent, with the transcendent coming to be understood as located within the immanent, and with the 'incongruity' of the two worlds — mundane and ritual, exoteric and esoteric — enjoyed 'as part of the divine's playful and deliberate plan for creation'.[71] The extraordinary is understood to permeate the ordinary and impure; the ordinary and impure to hold the possibility for the *Kaula* of *ānanda* or bliss.

That *vāma*, left, opposes *dakṣina*, right, and that the two are part of a Tantric ritual system of classification (pertaining to the practices of the *Kaula*) is made clear by Teun Goudriaan.[72] He also notes the use of these terms, with others, in delineating schools and currents within both *Śaiva* and *Śākta* traditions (those that focus on the worship of *Śiva* and *Śakti* respectively).[73] The potential of left and right for identifying and describing branches within broader Tantric traditions is clearly demonstrated by Alexis Sanderson.[74] Having separated the ascetic from the householder

---

'Tantric sādhanā: pūjā', in Gupta, Hoens and Goudriaan, *Hindu Tantrism*, pp. 121-62 (147); Douglas Renfrew Brooks, *Auspicious Wisdom: The Texts and Traditions of Śrīvidyā Śākta Tantrism in South India* (Albany: State University of New York Press, 1992), p. 155.

69.   The terms 'Vedic' and 'Smārta' refer to Hindu categories, the former to the religion of the *Veda*, early Indian scriptures which continue to have a central ritual and authoritarian significance for many Hindus. *Smārta* refers to the elite conventions of those Brahmins who consider themselves to be the guardians of Vedic religion. Quotation from Bharati, *The Tantric Tradition*, p. 241.

70.   Those initiated into the 'family' or *kula* of the goddess Śakti. See *Kulānava Tantra* for an account of Kaula teachings. Arthur Avalon, *Kulānava Tantra* (Delhi: Motilal Banarsidass, 1965); Douglas Renfrew Brooks, 'The Ocean of the Heart: Selections from the *Kulānava Tantra*', in White (ed.), *Tantra in Practice*, pp. 347-60; Paul Muller-Ortega, *The Triadic Heart of Śiva: Kaula Tantricism of Abhinavagupta in the Non-Dual Shaivism of Kashmir* (Albany: State University of New York Press, 1989).

71.   Brooks, *Auspicious Wisdom*, pp. 185-86; Bharati, *The Tantric Tradition*, p. 18; see also David R. Kinsley, *Tantric Visions of the Divine Feminine: The Ten Mahāvidyās* (Berkeley: University of California Press, 1997), p. 55. Kinsley suggests a process leading to the perception of a unified world in which division and fracture disappear whilst Brooks suggests that 'congruity' and 'holism' are eschewed (p. 185).

72.   Goudriaan, 'Tantrism in History', pp. 44-45.

73.   Goudriaan, 'Tantrism in History', pp. 40-41.

74.   Alexis Sanderson, 'Śaivism and the Tantric Traditions', in Friedhelm Hardy (ed.), *The World's Religions: The Religions of Asia* (London: Routledge, 1990), pp. 128-72.

path, Sanderson further subdivides the latter with reference to indigenous — *emic* — categories. His diagrammatic representation of the relationship between these cultic subdivisions makes use of the Tantric categories of *vāma* and *dakṣina* in order to distinguish gradations by level of initiation, esoteric practice, and the power and independence of the feminine divine or *Śakti* (culminating in her form as *Kālī*). In his diagram of cultic hierarchical relations,

> whatever is above and to the left sees whatever is below it and to the right as lower revelation. It sees itself as offering a more powerful, more esoteric system of ritual through further initiation (*dikṣa*). As we ascend through these levels…we find that the feminine rises stage by stage from subordinate to complete autonomy.[75]

This association between the left and the feminine is further evident in Tibetan Buddhist theory and its categories as Alex Wayman shows in his examination of female energy and symbolism in Tantric texts.[76] In his discussion of correspondences in the writings of Tson-kha-pa, the fourteenth-century founder of the Gelug-pa school, Wayman notes the association in 'fruitional time correspondences' (as opposed to basic, profane time correspondences) between 'Prajñā, the form of woman' (*prajñā*, insight or wisdom) and the left, as well as body, birth, moonlight, and several other categories.[77] The form of man, *upāya* (means or method), is associated with the right, with speech, the intermediate state, and sunlight, whilst the androgyne forms a cluster with the middle, with mind, death, and fire. As Western readers, however, we should resist placing any uninformed interpretation or value judgment upon such associations.[78] As Wayman suggests,

> the form of man and the form of woman are two superficial commonplace aspects that according to the Tantras conceal two mysteries of heightened consciousness. These two forms are not less worthy than their two mysteries and to the extent that a society realizes this worthiness, indeed sacredness, that society is civilised, removed from the brutes.[79]

Furthermore, the two mysteries are, it would seem, permeable at a higher state of consciousness (in fruitional time, that is) when a male *yogin* or

75. Sanderson, 'Śaivism and the Tantric Traditions', p. 137.

76. Especially in the body of texts known as the *Anuttara-yoga-tantra*, Alex Wayman, *The Buddhist Tantras: Light on Indo-Tibetan Esotericism* (New York: Samuel Weiser, 1973), p. 164.

77. Wayman, *Buddhist Tantras*, pp. 179-83 (182).

78. See M. Shaw, *Passionate Enlightenment*, pp. 9-10, for a discussion on inappropriate Western assumptions about the status of women and the category 'woman' in Tibetan Buddhism.

79. Wayman, *Buddhist Tantras*, p. 165.

female *yoginī* may actualise and attain the other, the recessive female or male within.[80]

In the field of Tibetan Buddhist ritual practice, the left retains this symbolic association with the female, with 'behavior of the left', according to Miranda Shaw, referring to a male Tantric practitioner's etiquette in focusing on,

> the left side in all his interactions with women: when walking with a woman, staying to her left and taking the first step with the left foot; when circumambulating her, doing so in a counter-clockwise fashion; using his left hand to make the secret signs; making offerings and feeding her with his left hand; and embracing her with his left arm.[81]

Indeed, in Tantrism, *vāma* seems to be associated routinely with both woman *and* the feminine divine. It is the left side of the androgynous Śiva-Ardhanārīśvara that takes the form of Śakti (and the right, Śiva).[82] Vāmā, or the goddess of the left, is also the name attributed to the consort of Brahmā who, as one of the three powers of Tripurā—the goddess as creator, preserver, and destroyer—is depicted within the *Śrīcakra*, 'a triadic symbol of the cosmos' used by South Indian Tantrikas in the ritual and imaginational process leading to liberation.[83]

In Bengal, it is with two of the many aspects (*mahāvidyā*) of Devi, with Kālī and Tārā, that the left is particularly associated. June McDaniel's Śākta informants see Kālī as the goddess who liberates her followers from this transitory world, and Tārā as the goddess of supreme knowledge.[84] Both are worshipped with 'reverse' magical rituals in which traditionally impure products (the 'five Ms') are used, and which feature practices normally deemed to be polluting, involving corpses, the cremation ground, and sexual acts.[85] Citing various Tantric texts such as the *Kalitantra* and the *Māyā-tantra*, as well as examples offered by her Śākta informants and Tantric autobiography, McDaniel offers accounts of corpse ritual (*śava-sādhanā*) and secret sexual ritual (*latā-sādhanā*).[86] She

---

80. Wayman, *Buddhist Tantras*, p. 183.

81. M. Shaw, *Passionate Enlightenment*, p. 45, and n. 33, pp. 216-17.

82. David Gordon White, *The Alchemical Body: Siddha Traditions in Medieval India* (Chicago and London: Chicago University Press, 1996), pp. 252-53.

83. Brooks, *Auspicious Wisdom*, p. 78.

84. June McDaniel, *The Madness of the Saints: Ecstatic Religion in Bengal* (Chicago and London: University of Chicago Press, 1989), p. 115.

85. For details of *pūjā* ritual to Kālī and Tārā, see Gupta, 'Tantric sādhanā', pp. 147-57 (147, 154-57). See also Bharati's quotation from the *Rudrayāmala* in *The Tantric Tradition*, p. 230.

86. McDaniel, *Madness of the Saints*, pp. 120-27. See also June McDaniel, 'Interviews with a Tantric Kālī Priest: Feeding Skulls in the Town of Sacrifice', in White (ed.), *Tantra in Practice*, pp. 72-80 (78-79).

then recounts the life story of the nineteenth-century devotee of Tārā, 'the mad or crazy...follower of the left-handed path', Vāmakṣepā.[87] Focused on the form of Tārā at Tārāpīth in rural Bengal, later becoming her priest there, Vāmakṣepā was renowned for what was, by any conventional standards, inappropriate behaviour. Stories abound that,

> he drank liquor and ate human flesh from corpses, that he had super-natural power...[that] he would share the food offered to him with dogs, jackals, crows, and low-caste people... He would smoke hashish and drink liquor from the broken neck of a bottle or from a skull.[88]

Furthermore, he would seem to insult Tārā by showing her a lack of respect and hurling abuse at her. Nevertheless, his behaviour was accepted by those around him because he was deemed to be divinely mad, perpetually entranced by Tārā, in continuous *bhava* or ecstasy; he 'became the symbol of devotion for millions of Bengali Śāktas'.[89]

Still at Tārāpīth, but looking both backwards and forwards from the time of Vāmakṣepā, David Kinsley recounts the myth of Vasiṣṭha-muni whose divine revelation led to the 'reverse' or left-hand practices still associated with the worship of Tārā at this site: daily blood sacrifice and *śmaśāna sādhanā*, the spiritual practices of the cremation grounds.[90] Believing himself instructed to worship Tārā with wine and women, the sage sought the advice of Vishnu in his Buddha form and was instructed in the *kula-mārga*, the way of forbidden things. He was told, 'With this ritual, and on this path, one can live in the midst of good and bad things while remaining aloof from them'.[91] Dwelling in the tradition established by Vasiṣṭha and popularised by Vāmakṣepā, Śāktas at Tārāpīth continue these practices with Tārā on the burning grounds, purifying their minds, stripping away attachments, and practising the equanimity of the *kula-mārga*.[92]

From this review of the meanings and uses of *vāma*, the left, in Indian Tantra, it has emerged that, whilst the left is clearly and uncompromisingly associated with that which is normally considered impure and

87. McDaniel, *Madness of the Saints*, pp. 127-33. The quotation is from Kinsley, *Tantric Visions*, p. 111.
88. McDaniel, *Madness of the Saints*, pp. 130-31; see also Kinsley, *Tantric Visions*, pp. 97, 108-11.
89. McDaniel, *Madness of the Saints*, p. 133.
90. Kinsley, *Tantric Visions*, pp. 97, 108-11; see also interview with Śākta informant in McDaniel, *Madness of the Saints*, p. 127.
91. Kinsley, *Tantric Visions*, p. 97.
92. Kinsley, *Tantric Visions*, p. 108. 'Equanimity' and 'equipoise' are noted as vital within a system that engages polar opposites (impure/pure, female/male, left/right, Śakti/Śiva). See White, *The Alchemical Body*, p. 252.

inauspicious (in the form of corpses, forbidden foods, wine, blood sacrifice, and women), it is also seen as having the potential to lead to knowledge and, ultimately, to liberation from that which is transitory and illusory. In terms of the spatial dimensions I have repeatedly discussed, *vāma* in these Tantric contexts refers concurrently to a space that is physical, mental, and social. Ritual behaviour may be enacted by the left hand or left side of the body, or in a counter-clockwise direction—in reverse of what would be practised in conventional Vedic ritual performance. Moreover, certain physical substances and objects, notably those linked with blood (meat, fish, wine, women) and death (corpses, cremation grounds, skulls) are, by metaphorical association and correspondence, placed on the left, with other substances and objects—which need not detain us here—on the right. They are conceptually clustered within and around the left because of their mutual relation to blood or death and the values they signify, of impurity and inauspiciousness.[93] However, whilst in the Vedic Hindu value system, in particular, these substances, objects, and values are seen as fundamentally polluting, profoundly limiting, counter-productive, and directed towards the profane and rebirth rather than the sacred and liberation, within Tantrism they acquire a new meaning and possibility, as we shall see shortly with reference to South Indian Śrīvidyā Śākta Tantrism. In terms of Tantric social space, left and right correspond to female and male and are terms used to denote relations between them (and also between the 'female' and 'male' aspects within an individual). Although some Tantric texts and practices evidently stress equality but difference between male and female on the spiritual path, they exist within an Indian social milieu of hierarchical relations between men and women, high caste and low caste.[94] Within this social milieu right and left continue to represent male and female and also (relatively) high and low in terms of caste ranking.[95]

93. See Brooks, *Auspicious Wisdom*, pp. 153-54, on impurity and power in relation to wine and blood.

94. The issue of women in Tantrism is complex, especially given the stress on the power relations of ritual sexuality. Several scholars have debated this issue; see M. Shaw, *Passionate Enlightenment*, pp. 5-8, for a survey; McDaniel, *Madness of the Saints*, pp. 171-75; Urban, 'The Power of the Impure', pp. 283, 286, 303-304; Frédérique Apffel Marglin, 'Refining the Body: Transformative Emotion in Ritual Dance', in Owen M. Lynch (ed.), *Divine Passions: The Social Construction of Emotion in India* (Berkeley: University of California Press, 1990), pp. 212-36 (215-16).

95. White, in *The Alchemical Body*, refers to 'an Indian (if not human) commonplace that a woman's place is on the distaff, the left side of her husband' (p. 253); on left and right in relation to caste divisions, see Brenda E.F. Beck, 'The Right-Left Division of South Indian Society', in Rodney Needham (ed.), *Right and Left: Essays on Dual Symbolic Classification* (Chicago and London: University of Chicago Press, 1973), pp. 391-426.

Before moving on, we might note Miranda Shaw's point that what we are seeing is,

> a cultural realm that is animated by dualities that are entirely different from those shaping the western interpretations of Tantra. Indian society and religion revolve on the axial values of purity and pollution and auspiciousness and inauspiciousness; they do not share the prevalent western dualisms of nature and culture, matter and spirit, and humanity and divinity.[96]

It is important then that we resist applying Western dualistic conceptions of left and right, woman and man, and so on, in our assessment of Tantric values. This investigation into comparative simultaneity requires that we do our utmost to understand the Tantric left hand within its own symbolic system before we see what light it can shed upon the Western case. Whilst we must surely note the polar relationship between certain substances, objects, and genders within Indian social life and its ritual and symbolic order (as demonstrated in the opposition between the Vedic and Tantric worldviews), we should not assume a naïve relationship, but rather expect a subtle and intentional interplay between them, as Douglas Renfrew Brooks indeed makes clear, using the analogy of the two hands to do so. For the male South Indian Tantric brahman, he suggests,

> the Vedic and Tantric worlds relate to one another like the two hands of a single person: they are complementary inversions of one another, bound by the same structural similarities and purposes and yet separate in both substance and function… Their sometimes puzzling relationship is an expression of certain ongoing and irreconcilable conflicts in the Hindu tradition, conflicts from which there is no flight and for which there are no easy solutions.[97]

Whilst many writers on Tantrism describe its unusual characteristics and its marginality within Hinduism, Brooks focuses on its relationship to Vedism in the historical and social experience of the South Indian brahman community. This *structural* relationship—which is both fundamental to their character and *modus operandi* and a continuing source of ideological tension between them—is witnessed in symbolic, ritual, and social terms.

As Shaw notes, 'Indian society and religion revolve on the axial values of purity and pollution and auspiciousness and inauspiciousness',[98] values which inform and structure the hierarchical relationships, discursive strategies, and ritual behaviour of both *Kaula* Tantric and Vedic

96. M. Shaw, *Passionate Enlightenment*, p. 9.
97. Brooks, *Auspicious Wisdom*, p. 187.
98. M. Shaw, *Passionate Enlightenment*, p. 9.

practitioners. Conceptions of purity and impurity, in particular, are vital for the two groups in the deployment and control of ritual power, but they are viewed and manipulated somewhat differently.[99] Vedic or non-Tantric brahmans maintain a separation between profane and sacred arenas by marking certain substances and actions as pure and others as impure. Tantrics understand and accept this distinction, but 'assert their difference...by inverting or reversing the criteria that determine the dichotomy of pure/impure within the confines of ritual'.[100] They 'deliberately introduce' those things which are conventionally impure (the 'five Ms') into a setting which demands the greatest purity in order 'to assert complete control over the categories that govern ritual',[101] and to create the conditions for the attainment of bliss through the 'exaggeration' of those differences that normally separate the mundane from the ritual.[102] In doing so, they challenge the Vedic distinction between the transcendent and the immanent by locating the former within the latter, thus turning a conflict into an opportunity.

Kaula Tantrics do not deny the polluting potential of substances and actions such as wine and relations with menstruating women. Within ordinary experience they see them as dangerous and uncontrollable. They become 'polluting when they are either misplaced or misused'.[103] However, in the Tantric ritual environment, their power can be contained, and used transformatively: 'ritual creates a means by which the power (*śakti*) inherent in a given action or object can be brought to its fullest potential'.[104]

So, notions of purity and impurity are accorded importance by Tantrics and non-Tantrics alike, but they differ in the way they utilise those substances normally deemed to be polluting. This is possible because of another aspect of similarity and difference in evidence between the two groups. South Indian brahmans — whether Tantric or non-Tantric — have in common their acceptance of ritual 'for obtaining the four human aims' and its centrality in enabling them to fulfil their inherited role as

99.   See Gupta, 'Tantric sādhanā', pp. 123-24.

100.   Brooks, *Auspicious Wisdom*, p. 152.

101.   Brooks, *Auspicious Wisdom*, p. 152.

102.   Brooks, *Auspicious Wisdom*, p. 186. This play on difference is also discussed by Mircea Eliade in relation to the Tantric 'conjunction of opposites', in *Yoga: Immortality and Freedom* (Princeton: Princeton University Press, 2nd edn, 1969), pp. 267-73.

103.   Brooks, *Auspicious Wisdom*, p. 153; cf. Douglas, *Purity and Danger*, Chapter 10, 'The System Shattered and Renewed', based on ideas from William James, *The Varieties of Religious Experience* (1902), on matter out of place, and the possibility that the 'ritual mixing up and composting of polluting things would provide the basis of "more complete religion"' (Douglas, *Purity and Danger*, p. 195).

104.   Brooks, *Auspicious Wisdom*, p. 155.

'religious virtuousi' with specialised knowledge.[105] However, for Tantrics ritual is not a domain which keeps the worlds of the transcendent and immanent, esoteric and exoteric apart, rather it is the place where their incongruity can first be recognised, then enjoyed as the source of knowledge and as ultimately divine. Where incongruity — of being-in-the-world and achieving other-worldly goals — is an uncomfortable fact that Vedic ritual attempts to negotiate and resolve, for Tantrics it is welcomed as the means to solving those very problems that non-Tantric ritual fails to deal with. Tantric ritual does this by drawing together the transcendent and the immanent, and by producing that state of bliss and fulfilling those goals in this lifetime that are promised but not accomplished in Vedic ritual.[106]

In addition to existing within a common cultural environment in which they differentiate themselves in terms of their interpretation and performance of values and rituals, Tantric and non-Tantric brahmans share their formal position within the caste system. The former believe it is possible to obtain freedom within such a structure; the latter that freedom requires renouncing one's position within it and becoming an ascetic. The Tantric view, as Brooks suggests, is about having it 'both ways': remaining an in-caste householder within the normal boundaries of purity/impurity for much of the time, but also 'defying' caste through Tantric initiation and ritual practice.[107] This 'dual norm' enables them to live with the distinctions of purity/impurity, caste/castelessness, and mundane world/ritual world, and allows them to manipulate these distinctions in order to become socially and spiritually powerful.[108] Having it 'both ways' is contingent upon *not* doing what others — namely non-Tantric brahmans — are bound to do: 'Fundamentally, Tantrics adopt and then invert the opposition of pure/impure to establish an oppositional relationship with non-Tantrics'.[109]

In summary, *Kaula* Tantrics operate within the same epistemological and structural order as their non-Tantric peers, but, in ritual, invert substances, actions, principles, and the values identified with them in order to develop a space of knowledge and ritual power, social privilege and hierarchy, and ultimate bliss. Whilst Brooks does not formally organise

---

105. Brooks, *Auspicious Wisdom*, p. 182. This mutual immersion of Tantric and non-Tantric brahmans in ritual activity is also noted by Sanderson, 'Śaivism and the Tantric Traditions', p. 130.

106. Brooks, *Auspicious Wisdom*, pp. 185-86; Brooks, 'The Ocean of the Heart', p. 350.

107. Brooks, *Auspicious Wisdom*, pp. 155-56.

108. See also Urban's account of the 'dual norm' in the life of the sixteenth-century Tantric Brahman, Kṛṣṇānanda Āgamavāgīśa, 'The Power of the Impure', pp. 277-78.

109. Brooks, *Auspicious Wisdom*, p. 159.

his account of these complex relations around the opposition between left and right, it is evident from what we have seen already with regard to the meaning and value of the left in Tantrism that the distinctions to which he refers are contiguous with left and right (just as we saw in relation to other distinctions and values within the dualistic symbolic system of the West). In Brooks's analysis the key oppositional categories are Vedic/Tantric, pure/impure, and mundane/ritual. The first pair relate to one another within a common structural framework, as Brooks suggests, 'like the two hands of a single person', a complementary inversion of Vedic and Tantric, akin to right hand and left hand. What soon becomes clear, however, is that pure and impure substances and actions cannot be attributed straightforwardly to Vedism and Tantrism respectively. The reason is that, even for Tantrics, impure substances and actions—the 'five Ms'—remain polluting *except* when transformed and controlled in a Tantric ritual environment. We need to employ a more nuanced model than the conventional polar one to depict these relationships.[110]

One way of understanding the inter-relationship between these oppositional categories is to return to the work of Robert Hertz on the perspectival relations between right and left that I discussed in Chapter 6. As Hertz suggested, and Tcherkézoff clarified, from the perspective of the profane, 'the sacred appears to be double in nature, with a pure and an impure aspect'.[111] However, from the perspective of the sacred, the impure looks like an aspect of the profane, which thus seems to be two-fold. Bataille made the explicit left–right connection by referring to the right and left sacred (as well as pure and impure).[112]

Taking such a perspectival view of the Indic oppositions, from the perspective of the ordinary social world (Brooks refers to this as 'mundane' rather than profane) the Tantric and Vedic together constitute the 'ritual world' (Hertz's 'sacred'), but the former represents the impure sacred or left taboo (because of its use of the 'five Ms') whilst the latter represents the pure or right aspect of the sacred.

From within the ritual world, the perspective differs between Vedic and Tantric, though both acknowledge the division between mundane and ritual domains. From the Vedic perspective, substances, actions, and principles are distinguished according to purity and impurity, and those that are impure are prohibited—taboo—within a ritual context; they

110.   Brooks (*Auspicious Wisdom*, p. 157) offers just such a model for the structure of Tantric Hinduism, but I have not used it here as it employs more variables than are needed for my purposes.

111.   Hertz, 'The Pre-Eminence of the Right Hand', pp. 7-8; Tcherkézoff, *Dual Classification Reconsidered*, p. 14.

112.   Bataille, 'Attraction and Repulsion II', p. 121.

endanger its purity. From the *Kaula* Tantric perspective, whilst this distinction between pure and impure holds in the mundane world, in ritual, though impure things never become pure as such, they may be introduced and their power may be harnessed and controlled for ritual ends.

It seems that Vedic and Tantric perspectives are in agreement in attributing the term *vāmācāra* to the Tantric ritual use of the 'five Ms': it is not that the two groups have differing views about what should be designated 'right', *dakṣina*, or 'left', *vāma*.[113] Where they differ is in their understanding of the value and purpose of pursuing a left-current or path[114] for achieving life's goals.

As we saw in the discussion of late mediaeval and early modern religion, magic, and witchcraft, a single epistemological field contains a dominant and conventional camp and its complementary, inverted, and socially marginal counterpart. In the Indian case, unlike the Western one, although the left is associated with impurity, danger, and a deviant path, within Tantrism it is embraced as having the potential for liberation, not by the conversion or sanitisation of the impurity which is its trademark, but by the realisation and control of the power inherent within impure substances and activities.

How can this apparently very different case of the left (hand) illuminate relations within the Western field of the religious/secular? Using a wide range of sources — and acknowledging their relationship to Western scholarly discourse and interests — I have endeavoured to give voice to the meanings and uses attributed to *vāma*, *vāmācāra*, and *vāma-mārga* (the left [hand] and its associated practices and path) in Indian, and sometimes Tibetan, Tantrism. Some of the general issues which have emerged in this discussion are akin to those I examined in the previous section on religion, magic, and witchcraft. They include the way in which beliefs and practices deemed normative or deviant and attributed to the right or left are epistemologically and structurally related despite being presented as antithetical; the role of reversal/inversion in designating social and cultural differences and attributing values; the way in which left and right are used as markers in relation to key organising principles, such as purity/impurity and male/female; and their role in denoting an important boundary within the ritual world separating Vedic and conventional

---

113. Although it is certainly the case that the terms *vāmācāra* and *vāma-mārga* are used disparagingly by non-Tantrics, to such an extent that Tantrics do not refer openly to their use of the 'five Ms'. Brooks, *Auspicious Wisdom*, pp. 179-80; McDaniel, 'Interviews with a Tantric Kālī priest', pp. 78-79.

114. Brooks refers to 'left-current' rituals rather than left-hand path (*Auspicious Wisdom*, p. 185).

from Tantric and deviant practices. I shall not rehearse these points of similarity.

The process of examining in some detail a simultaneous, non-Western space by means of those same spatial analytical terms used for understanding Western spaces of the left hand allows differences between the two to come to the fore.[115] I shall note just three of these.

First, whilst left and right signify female and male, as in the West, in Tantrism they are part of a different cultural spectrum in which the principles of impure/pure and inauspicious/auspicious, rather than evil/good, matter/spirit etc., are central.[116]

Secondly, the link between divinity and left and right in an Indian religious context is very different to their relationship in the West. The left is associated with certain important goddesses (forms of Śakti), notably Kālī and Tārā, who are worshipped principally by Tāntrikas. However, these goddesses are also revered by non-Tantrics. With the Christian figure of Satan they share an association with power and danger, but they are not identified with evil or a fall from grace. As with other goddesses and gods, worship and service directed to them lead followers towards liberation, even though the journey may be unorthodox (e.g. involving blood sacrifice and the use of the 'five Ms').

Thirdly, as this discussion about left and right, female and male, and Tantric and Vedic has shown, in the Indian religious context it is not necessary to see the poles within each of these pairings as mutually exclusive. As the divine figure of Śiva-Adhanārīśvara (Śiva/Śakti in one body) suggests—and Wayman in his account of the forms of man and woman, and Brooks with his analogy of the two hands confirm—the two poles are as two sides of a single being, counterparts, two within one body. Eliade, in his work on Tantra, referred to this as 'the conjunction of opposites',[117] and Brooks has more recently gone on to state that such a conjunction is not merely the dissolving of differences but their acknowledgment, enjoyment, and mutual productivity. In our Western examples of left and right we witnessed not a conjunction but a diametrical opposition at work—left and right as mutually exclusive categories. These

115.   I have not drawn repeated attention to the spatial dimensions, properties, and aspects outlined in the first half of the book in my depiction of the Tantric left hand. However, a re-reading with them in mind will show that I have considered physical, mental, and social spaces, the properties of configuration, simultaneity, and power, and the relationship between *conceived* and *lived* spaces (Lefebvre's 'representations of space' and 'spaces of representation').

116.   M. Shaw, *Passionate Enlightenment*, p. 9; Brooks, *Auspicious Wisdom*, p. 152; Urban, 'The Power of the Impure'.

117.   Eliade, *Yoga*, p. 267.

categorical relations operated within the social body, but not within the human body (except directly in terms of the two hands themselves).[118]

In Tantrism, the centrality of the human body and its internal dualities, as both the site and means of self-realisation, knowledge, and power, is instructive for understanding more about Western religious/secular relations and their apparent lack of rootedness in human bodies. In the West, individuals are normally marked as 'either/or', rather than an amalgam of both. They are either male or female, destined for heaven or hell, religious or secular/non-religious. It is only with the development of critical discourses of androgyny, bi-sexuality, the hyphenation of identity, hybridity, third-space, and post-secular religiosity that we begin to see the creative exploration of the embodied engagement of differences, of having it 'both ways'. The question remains, however, whether such explorations constitute the opening up of a new third option or alterative space, a 'space of representation', which is more than just the sum of two parts or a critique of two former positions or poles.[119]

In the Western religious examples of left and right, it was clear that the opposition of positions and the values associated with them was itself instrumental for spiritual progress. Seeing the evil in the 'broad way' of the left was motivational for choosing the 'narrow' or right way with its heavenly goal. What was difficult on the narrow Western religious way was staying firm on the one path and excluding the other by resisting its attractions (whilst in Tantrism difficulty arises from holding differences in tension). In the secular examples in which the status of the left is raised, and it becomes identified with the modernist value of equality, the right is curiously silenced (except in the case of *Dextera Domini*) and the supernatural, on both right and left, disappears from view within a materialist humanist account. Ironically, this discourse of equality and the acknowledgment of differences admits not of the transcendent or of those who proclaim it, and tends to disparage all religious people and institutions as backward, unenlightened, and 'fundamentalist'.

Within the third camp, the post-secular, we see the drawing together of the religious and secular (an acceptance of transcendence, the efficacy of ritual, and the value of spiritual discipline, with the prioritisation of secular humanist values such as individualism, self-centredness, and reason). However, with the wholehearted embracing of the left, including its personification of Satan, we witness a rejection of the old guard of the

---

118.   It is possible to envisage cases where the human body becomes the site of such a diametrical opposition, between good and evil, for instance. The character of 'Jekyll and Hyde' would be one example, and Christians who submit themselves to exorcism for the removal of demonic spirits or forces might be another.

119.   For a discussion of 'spaces of representation', see Chapters 2 and 9.

right, the 'White Light' religions, particularly Judeo-Christian traditions and institutions. The irony here is the emergence of a rhetoric of holism (and the incorporation of selected elements of Hindu, Buddhist, and Sufi teaching and practice, including Tantrism) with a strong antithetical approach to the right hand path.

Does the growing awareness and presence in the West of those religious paths, such as Tantrism, that delight in the conjunction of opposites and the paradox of transcendence in immanence and liberation through the body signal a move within contemporary Western religiosity, and the symbolic order that drives it, away from the diametrical opposition of dualism? Any answer must be tempered by three cautionary notes. Taking Tantrism as a case in point, we must first recall that such a system cannot be exported from India or Tibet to the West without change. As Hugh Urban has shown, this historical process has produced two forms of Western Tantrism: the deodorised version of Arthur Avalon, and the contemporary 'cult of ecstasy' or Sexual Tantra, a form forged in the crucible of late-capitalism.[120] Secondly, in the process by which Tantrism becomes embedded in the West, does it not become 'Protestant Tantrism',[121] not merely a Westernised form of an Eastern religion, but a new form of Western (Protestant) religion shaped by some of the characteristics of Indian or Tibetan Tantrism? Thirdly, what happens to Tantra's ritual play of opposites, and its consequent production of embodied knowledge and, ultimately, liberation, once it enters Western epistemological space with its dualistic structure? Can it survive in the new social and cultural body, or does it necessarily metamorphose into a hybrid conditioned by oppositional thinking and Western values? What can Tantrism mean when performed in a context informed by the Western oppositions of matter/spirit, immanence/transcendence, female/male, and evil/good?

These are difficult questions on the Western engagement with Tantrism that I am not competent to answer: Hugh Urban is ploughing this field with greater knowledge and authority that I can. Rather, my purpose is to consider—in the next chapter—whether the left and its associated hand can really constitute a space for liberation? Is it possible *from within* what appears to be a closed field of religious/secular relations to create a space that effectively challenges the very symbolic order on which that field is constituted? Or does it require the breaching of the boundaries of this field by an outsider, such as Tantrism, and can such a breach provide the conditions necessary to mount such a challenge?

120.   Urban, 'The Extreme "Orient"', and 'The Cult of Ecstasy'.
121.   I am borrowing an idea employed by Philip Mellor in his discussion of Western Buddhisms ('Protestant Buddhism?').

Chapter 9

Beyond the Field?
The Left, Transformation, and the Sacred

The left hand has been at the centre of our attention for three chapters now, and it is easy for us to forget its 'place'. It is time to remind ourselves of its subaltern status, its relative insignificance in social life, and — for right-handers — its physical inferiority and underdevelopment. The left hand is firmly 'put in its place' by the dominant, dextrous, and developed right.[1] Probably because of 'a failure of conservation of parity' at the sub-atomic level and the predominance of L-amino acids — which result by a complex genetic process in our left-sided hearts and our disposition to right-handedness — the asymmetry between right and left emerges disproportionately into social and cultural life.[2] And then,

> To the right hand go honors, flattering designations, prerogatives: it acts, orders, and *takes*. The left hand, on the contrary, is despised and reduced to the role of a humble auxiliary: by itself it can do nothing; it helps, it supports, it *holds*.[3]

Whilst Robert Hertz and later anthropologists have provided the evidence of this polarity and the dual system of classification of which it is a part for non-Western cultures,[4] I have illustrated it for the West.[5] By focusing on contemporary Western representations of the left hand (and its pre-eminent counterpart), I have shown not only how Christian, secular, and post-secular religious exponents have used the hands as a

---

1. J.Z. Smith on the social and hierarchical meaning of 'place' in *To Take Place*, p. 45, and Elizabeth Grosz on the expulsion of inferior opposites in Jantzen, *Becoming Divine*, p. 267.
2. I am indebted for an explanation of this process to McManus, *Right Hand, Left Hand*, pp. 361-62, and Goodwin, 'Why Groovy Hearts Lean Left', p. 27.
3. Hertz, 'The Pre-Eminence of the Right Hand', p. 3.
4. Hertz, 'The Pre-Eminence of the Right Hand', and other contributors to Needham (ed.), *Right and Left*.
5. See also Lloyd, 'Right and Left in Greek Philosophy'.

means to wrestle with one another, but also how their accounts have held the traces of earlier ideas and values in which right and left hands, and the relationship between the two, have played a significant symbolic role.

The continued salience of the hands and the regions to which they refer for distinguishing, categorising, classifying, and ordering things, people, spiritual beings, values, places, paths, and goals is explained by the embodied nature of our minds and the fact that reason—and everything that stems from it—arises within and from the body.[6] The concepts we use for relentlessly organising the world, nature, society, our relationships, and our identity are shaped by the body:

> Our bodies are symmetric in some ways and not in others. We have faces and move in the direction in which we see. Our bodies define a set of fundamental spatial orientations that we use not only in orienting ourselves, but in perceiving the relationship of one object to another.[7]

The asymmetry of left and right, instantiated in the hands, is foundational for metaphorical thinking.[8] These body parts, worked on by the cognitive unconscious,[9] become available for articulating difference, denoting hierarchical relationships and distinguishing self and other, as well as one group from its neighbours. 'The hidden hand'—which must surely be a left one—itself becomes a metaphor for 'the functioning of our unconscious conceptual system'.[10]

This left hand—the 'other' within the body—has proved to be extremely useful as a metaphorical tool for containing alien, dangerous, impure, disordered entities, whether animals, humans, other beings, values, feelings, substances, or things.[11] In this regard, it is inseparable in

6.   Lakoff and Johnson, *Philosophy in the Flesh*, p. 5, and further, 'The mind is not merely corporeal, but also passionate, desiring and social' (p. 565). For an account of the relationship of this cognitive systems approach to others in the physical and social world, and examples of their mutual application, see Fritjof Capra, *The Hidden Connections: A Science for Sustainable Living* (London: Flamingo, 2003). On the mind, language, culture, and dualism, see Aram A. Yengoyan, 'Language and Conceptual Dualism: Sacred and Secular Concepts in Australian Aboriginal Cosmology and Myth', in David Maybury-Lewis and Uri Almagor (eds.), *The Attraction of Opposites: Thought and Society in the Dualistic Mode* (Ann Arbor: University of Michigan Press, 1989), pp. 171-90.

7.   Lakoff and Johnson, *Philosophy in the Flesh*, p. 34.

8.   Lakoff and Johnson, *Philosophy in the Flesh*, Chapter 3, 'Metaphor and Truth'.

9.   For a definition and explanation of 'cognitive unconscious', see Lakoff and Johnson, *Philosophy in the Flesh*, pp. 10-12.

10.   Lakoff and Johnson, *Philosophy in the Flesh*, p. 13. See also Pascal Boyer, who uses the phrase 'invisible hand' to denote the 'multiple inferential systems in the mind' that produce religion (supernatural concepts etc.) as a side effect, in *Religion Explained: The Human Instincts that Fashion Gods, Spirits and Ancestors* (London: William Heinnemann, 2001), p. 379.

11.   Veikko Anttonen on the 'sacred' as a category boundary and its generation within the body and mind, and the neo-Durkheimian notions of 'right-hand' and

its function from its dominant and more familiar partner, the right, which operates for us as a zone of safety, a known world, in representing all that we need to survive and thrive.[12] The boundary between left and right, and between the other categories to which they refer, generates concern and anxiety. Its potential for transgression from both sides requires it to be fortified, policed, fought over, and constructed repeatedly in order that the other beyond it may be recognised and kept out, and the formation, ideology, and spirit of those within maintained. The attraction of the hands as metaphors for articulating the territories on either side of a problematic and contested boundary is that their difference is assured and fixed, even if the actual regions and boundary to which they refer are not. Left and right hands cannot become one another; they cannot merge. As incongruent counterparts, they remain separate and different. Used metaphorically, they suggest a sure and unbreachable boundary separating two distinct worlds or spheres. In point of fact, the boundaries we construct within the human environment, the social world, the public square, and private life are not like that. They are situational, unstable and permeable. We are vulnerable in the face of them. They have the power to terrify, though — if only we creatively celebrate them and familiarize ourselves with them through practice and controlled crossings — they can become exciting, even awe-inspiring.

If we review the narrative on the location of religion within the left hand in Part II, we see, in retrospect, that a spatial analysis has revealed its central themes to be duality, asymmetry, and boundary. When we scrutinised these themes in the course of an examination of contemporary Western representations of the hands, we saw an array of interlocking debates about,

- binary and dualistic approaches to dual classification with their differing principles of equality and hierarchy;
- opposition, juxtaposition, complementarity, conjunction, reversal, and inversion as ways of managing difference;
- classification and the use of order, characterisation and values in the marking of difference;
- the nature, construction, and negotiation of boundaries between ideological and value-laden positions;
- the Western dualistic symbolic order, its history and modern face, and its role in the field of the 'religious' and the 'secular';
- non-modern dualistic systems in relation to religion in the contemporary West.

'left-hand' sacred; Anttonen's 'Sacred' and 'Identifying the Generative Mechanisms of Religion'.
12. See also Hertz, 'The Pre-Eminence of the Right Hand', p. 13.

These are major intellectual preoccupations, some of which are general philosophical and anthropological concerns, whilst others are historically and geographically specific. As we have seen, religion in the broadest sense is implicated in them all;[13] it is quite definitely not just a thing of the past, a minority interest, or just an irrelevance in a modernist secular discourse. The left hand—a bit like religion to the contemporary secular, the devalued one of the pair—and its socio-spatial study has revitalised these themes and debates and brought them to our attention afresh. The sinister hand, through its relationship with the right, has thus proved to be a productive and dynamic space.

But there is still work to be done and some questions to be answered in applying a spatial analysis to the lesser hand in order to locate religion. Whilst the dimensions and properties of space have been considered in relation to the place of the left hand in previous chapters, the aspects— Lefebvre's spatial triad—have not been discussed explicitly.[14] However, if we think back to Chapter 6, we see that the aspect of spatial practice was treated there, in relation to the gestural systems of eating/cleaning and marriage. Furthermore, in Chapters 7 and 8, where the focus was on representations, Lefebvre's second aspect of conceived space was to the fore in discussions about attempts to authorise and give legitimacy to various religious, secular, and post-secular positions (as well as mediaeval and early modern religious and magical, and Indian Vedic and Tantric ones). The part played by the dominant order (whether ecclesiastical, secular political or judicial, or brahmanical) in controlling discourse, practice, and social space was present throughout as a major expression of the significance of power in representations of the space of the left hand. And, in each of the three chapters, the attendant issues of resistance and liberation arose. Could the left hand be productive as a space of representation (Lefebvre) within the field of the religious/secular? Is it indeed possible for such an apparently closed field to contain such a space at all? Could transgressions of the field's boundaries from beyond provide the necessary impetus for such a space, even for transformation of the field itself?[15]

A second issue also needs further attention. As I suggested earlier by quoting directly from his essay on the pre-eminence of the right hand, Robert Hertz has a special place in any study of the symbolic role of the hands for religion. His particular concern was not the engagement

13. I will come back to the issue of the meaning of religion, its relationship to the secular and the sacred shortly.

14. See Chapter 2 for discussion of Lefebvre's triad of spatial practice (*espace perçu*), representations of space (*espace conçu*), and spaces of representation (*espace vécu*).

15. See the end of Chapter 8 in particular for a discussion of these questions.

between the 'religious' and 'secular' worlds of early twentieth-century Europe, however. It was the polarity — attributable first to Durkheim — of the 'sacred' and the 'profane'. It would be unhelpful if we were now to conflate these two conceptual pairings, and I shall attempt to resolve their relationship below. The role of left and right hands in marking differences within the 'sacred' and between 'sacred' and 'profane', and in setting apart non-negotiable values and principles, will be discussed further. I shall return to the work of Danièle Hervieu-Léger, Wouter Hanegraaff, and Veikko Anttonen, discussed at the end of Chapter 3, in giving final consideration to the relationship between the 'sacred' and the field of religious/secular relations.

Lefebvre's Spatial Aspects, the Field, and the Left Hand

Given that the principal task in Part II has been the examination and analysis of a selection of contemporary representations of the left hand — the majority of which were material, electronic texts — for the purpose of understanding more about the field of religious/secular relations, it would be fair to assume that our preoccupation has been with what Lefebvre referred to as conceptualised or conceived space: *representations of space*.[16] This is not to say that *spatial practices* of the left hand have been entirely absent, or that the desire to create emancipatory *spaces of representation* has not been witnessed. However, in the illustrations on which I focused in Chapter 7, both spatial practice and emancipatory spaces were presented through the medium of the text, thus becoming part of the realm of representation. So, for example, the worldly practices of the broad way in the 'two destinies' examples were conceived by religious exponents to constitute a left hand path to damnation; the actions of left-handers in the secular parodies were represented as the spatial praxis of a newly self-conscious political minority. These were not the habitual, unreflective, and commonsense practices intended by Lefebvre in the first aspect of his triad. We must return to Chapter 6, to the role of the hands in social and cultural behaviour, to apply that aspect more properly.

However, in returning to those gestural systems of eating/cleaning and marriage in which the hands play so active a part, we are presented with a potential problem. From the perspective of an actor from North Africa or India, reserving one hand for the practices of the toilet and another for those of the dining room is an everyday matter, taken for granted. However, such behaviour is culturally normative. Although we

---

16. According to Lynn Stewart ('Bodies, Visions, and Spatial Politics', p. 610), Lefebvre held that 'representation precedes' in the modern period, with practice displaced by 'a world of representations'.

may not know its cultural origins and certainly cannot hold any particular social or religious group responsible for it, this separation of roles for the hands is a powerful idea, one that has transcended the commonplace and become part of the lore and norms of certain cultural groupings for civilised life. Its appearance in texts on the practice of tradition, such as commentaries on Islamic *hadith*, suggests that it is *conceived* rather than *perceived*. It is hard in such a case to separate the two.

And this is no less true with the practice of the left hand in customs of marriage, my other example in Chapter 6. The fact that I wear a ring on my left hand because I am married—and think nothing of it—does not mean that, as a spatial practice, it has no ideological significance. Evidently, as we saw, this practice holds within it a tradition that goes back to Roman marriage customs at least, that may have its roots in the physiological notions of that period in history. The ring could itself be said to be a representation of space, not only in carrying the traces of an earlier culture, but in signifying the married status of the individual wearing it. Thus, there is a body of Western folklore about flashing one's ring to discourage unwelcome sexual attention, or noting whether the person one fancies is wearing a wedding ring and is thus 'unavailable'. The ring worn on this hand holds within it and communicates to others a moral position and code of practice.

There is a difficulty, then, in both these cases of separating unreflective, taken-for-granted spatial practice from representations of space. This is more evident in gestural systems than in other kinds of spatial practice because, as Lefebvre himself notes, the former are necessarily linked to beliefs that they encapsulate and communicate.[17]

However, we find that, if we think hard about many everyday spatial practices, there seems to be more to them than first meets the eye: I repeatedly flick my hair back in a certain way; I shut the bathroom door behind me; like many of my neighbours I take a certain short-cut to the local shops; I go quiet or whisper as I walk through a graveyard; when in some countries—though not my own—I wait for the lights to change before crossing the road. I don't give much thought to any of these things, but—on reflection—I can give an explanation for why I and others act in these ways. These actions seem themselves to represent some unspoken cultural code, norm, or fashion.

This problem, of drawing a clear boundary between spatial practice and the representation of space, is partially explained by what Lakoff and Johnson have to say about perception and conception, and the role of metaphor. In rejecting the Cartesian mind and proposing the embodied

17. Lefebvre, *The Production of Space*, p. 214.

mind, they question the separation of the two. From the Cartesian perspective,

> there is assumed to be an absolute dichotomy between *perception* and *conception*. While *perception* has always been accepted as bodily in nature, just as movement is, *conception*—the formation and use of concepts—has traditionally been seen as purely mental and wholly separate from and independent of our abilities to perceive and move... The embodied-mind hypothesis...radically undercuts the *perception/conception* distinction.[18]

According to these authors, the body actually shapes conceptualisation and the very concepts we use. Conception, then, is not so different from perception after all. Furthermore, commonsense, everyday understandings are no less metaphorical than more sophisticated representations: unconscious metaphors cross-cut both.

The fact that Lefebvre's space-as-perceived and space-as-conceived may differ more in appearance than fact—one seeming to be largely unreflectively subversive, and the other self-conscious, normative, and dominant—is not in itself a reason to abandon the distinction.[19] Lefebvre's approach was both experimental and useful. He was interested in getting a better understanding of the nature and production of social space, and devised models and concepts for this purpose. The triad was one way of distinguishing aspects or modes of space, but he never suggested that it was the only way of doing so. Lefebvre himself noted that relations between the three aspects were unstable, and that they overlapped and interpenetrated one another.[20] Irrespective of this difficulty, as I showed in Chapter 2, the aspects have operational power for the study of religion. It was possible, using the triadic model, to discuss the different ways in which space is practised and represented by religious people.

The clearest modern examples of Lefebvre's second aspect are the theoretical and technical constructions of planners, architects, and engineers. The material effects for which they are responsible—buildings, bridges, rail networks, communication systems—'have the capacity to remain undiluted and so impose themselves as dominant representations', those that are *conceived* rather than *lived* according to Lefebvre's analysis.[21] We will return to the notion of lived space in a moment, but first I shall summarise what a study of contemporary representations of the left hand and their ideological underpinnings revealed.

18. Lakoff and Johnson, *Philosophy in the Flesh*, p. 37.

19. For Lefebvre on perception and conception in relation to the three aspects, see Elden, *Understanding Henri Lefebvre*, pp. 189-90.

20. Lefebvre, *The Production of Space*, pp. 86-87.

21. Chivallon, 'Religion as Space for the Expression of Caribbean Identity in the United Kingdom', p. 476.

In Chapter 7 we saw the way in which particular places of the left hand were created by various religious, secular, and post-secular exponents and used to mark their positions vis-à-vis those in the other camps. Two discourses were seen to have particular ideological weight, the Christian and the secular humanist.[22] The once-dominant, Christian worldview was present in many of our examples, either pronounced unequivocally as the 'right' way[23]—both correct and on the right hand—or denounced as wrong—but still on the right hand. Post-secular religious exponents saw it as an unhealthy and erroneous tradition of self-deception, sought to resist it critically, and to articulate a counter-strategy by reversing many of its central tenets. The left hand for them was synonymous with a healthy and holistic, but nevertheless religious, counter-path focused on the self and the will. However, the Christian right hand presence was notable by its absence in some of the secular examples. In *Dextera Domini*, it was unequivocally associated with the Roman Catholic Church whose authoritarian voice was satirically mocked for marginalising and demon-ising the left hand and those with a disposition to favour its use. In another example (Dalrymple), it was implicitly rather than explicitly part of the dominant, hierarchical right hand world that neglected the needs and interests of minorities; in Rosenberg's *Lesbian of Darkness*, it was represented as the red-faced 'fundamentalist' determined to fight the moral fight against deviant sinistrals (gays and lesbians).

The other equally strong worldview was secular humanism which, despite its ideological supremacy, was unable to take its 'rightful place' on the normally dominant right because of the usurpation of that position by Christianity (on God's right hand). Secular humanism was also vari-ously represented. In the religious examples it was cast on the left, seen as the *bête noire* of a powerful and attractive 'left-handed world' (Swanson); by post-secular religious exponents it was appreciated for its values, of equality, individuality, and an appreciation of plurality, but seen to be flawed in failing to engage with myth, symbol, and ritual, and thus in being non-religious (Vexen). Both secular and post-secular examples were gathered on the left, though only the latter reified it, secularists seeking only to 'right the balance', to provide an even and equal playing field for all.

These textual representations of the spaces of the right and left hands reinforce the idea that space is social and politically charged. Right and left are used repeatedly in order to represent particular moral positions

22. Lefebvre, *The Production of Space*, p. 44, for Lefebvre on ideology and space.
23. Please excuse my use of puns in the following paragraphs. They are un-avoidable given the metaphorical range of the terms 'right' and 'left' in the English language.

and ideological views and to challenge others. They are used variously to authorise and resist.

If we turn now to Lefebvre's third aspect, spaces of representation, we find we have a different problem to confront with regard to the relationship between the various aspects. When is a space really a space of representation rather than merely a representation of one? Lefebvre himself was cautious about this, despite his desire to distinguish the *lived* from the *conceived*. He was dubious, for example, about late-modern leisure spaces, seeing them as the arena of capitalist consumption, as an attempt to contain, control, and define desire, fantasy, and the imagination.

What did Lefebvre mean by a space of representation? It is 'space as directly *lived* through [those] associated images and symbols' which overlay physical space but which refer to objects within it.[24] It is unlike conceived space insofar as it 'does not produce order because the representations that come from it are not bound to logic any more than to coherence'.[25] It is the space that bursts forth as a creative response to the dominant context. Rob Shields refers to it as 'a dis-alienated moment', as 'space as it might be'.[26] As such, it emerges as a site of symbolic resistance which offers the possibility — albeit temporary — of gathering people and enabling them to escape or transcend their oppressive, routine, and meaningless experience. As '"moments" of presence', such spaces puncture the banality of everyday life.[27]

The symbolic potential of the left hand suggests that it could indeed generate a lived space or 'moment' within the dominated space of normal life.[28] We might even suggest that it is ideal for such a purpose given its categorical connection to other classically marginal and devalued principles and concepts such as body, woman, dark, and evil. Elizabeth Grosz noted that, in Western dualism, primary concepts are normally established by means of the expulsion of their opposites.[29] The Western mind, then, in forging 'right' as superior, higher, truer, and more central to power (arguably on the basis of bodily asymmetry), has produced an opposite with the symbolic capacity to represent resistance to authority and domination, and thus the potential for emancipation from alienation or liberation from suffering.

24. Lefebvre, *The Production of Space*, p. 39.
25. Chivallon, 'Religion as Space for the Expression of Caribbean Identity', p. 476; the second half of the quotation is a translation from Lefebvre, *La production de l'espace* (p. 54).
26. Shields, *Lefebvre, Love and Struggle*, p. 161.
27. Shields, *Lefebvre, Love and Struggle*, p. 60
28. See Chapter 6. Lefebvre's definition of a 'moment' is 'the attempt to achieve the total realization of a possibility' (*Critique of Everyday Life*, II, p. 348).
29. Grosz in Jantzen, *Becoming Divine*, p. 267.

Was this potential borne out in any of the examples we considered in Chapter 7? For religious exponents the left hand path was one of worldliness, itself a space of suffering. For those of a secularist persuasion, the left hand—and the one predisposed to use and identify with it—was associated with the interests of minorities in their plea for equal treatment and an end to discrimination. Insofar as their aim was full social participation with others in the existing order, it is arguable whether the left hand constituted for them a space of representation. It could be said, however, that, in admitting them, the dominant order would have been transformed in the process through the realisation of the potential vested in its primary value, equality. Whether such a process really constitutes the kind of resistance or emancipation envisaged by Lefebvre seems unlikely given that what was sought was a better version of the same world—the existing order—not the imagination of a different world.

At the end of Chapter 7, I suggested that post-secular positions on the left hand—those that favour the left hand path in opposition to 'White Light' or 'Right Hand religions'—might be said to fall within the secular camp in sharing so many of its values. Such positions were not antithetical to the secular or a negation of it, though they distinguished themselves from it on the grounds that they were 'religious' in respect of their use of ritual, symbol, and myth, and—in the case of Satanism—the figure of Satan. Satanists, as opposed to others on the left hand path, claim to live through the symbols of both the left and Satan. In theory, these interconnected symbols offer the possibility for those who live imaginatively through them of liberation from the stranglehold of the beliefs and values of the dominant religion, Christianity. Furthermore, Satanism, as *a network of individuals* who share an affirmation of the power of the will, the centrality of the self, the acceptance of the evil side of human nature, and the persona of Satan, is a movement of its time, and arguably an elective fraternity rather than a religious community.[30] The ironic notion of the 'Church of Satan' is enjoyed by its global contingent: Magister Peter Gilmore actively discourages conformity and over-identification with the social body, firmly stressing the need for individuals to follow their own paths and be true to their own experiences.[31] There is no model Satanist to become, and no body that can endorse an individual's experience: the Church of Satan is not so much a strategic and organised attempt to overturn Right Hand religions as *a cabal of non-joiners* 'who find unique ways of applying [its] philosophy towards their own personal goals'.[32]

30. The term 'elective fraternity' is used by Hervieu-Léger, *Religion as a Chain of Memory*, p. 149 and following.
31. Gilmore, 'The Myth of the "Satanic Community" and Other Virtual Delusions', <http://www.churchofsatan.com/> (accessed 17 January 2003).
32. Gilmore, 'The Myth of the "Satanic Community"'.

I have used the case of Satanism here to illustrate how Lefebvre's third aspect might be applied to one band of seekers who use the left hand as a symbol of resistance with emancipatory possibilities. A very different case has been presented by Christine Chivallon in her study of Caribbean identity in a diasporic context. Quoting from Steve Pile, she states that resistance 'not only takes place in places, but also seeks to appropriate space, to make new spaces'.[33] In the case of African Caribbeans in the UK, it takes the form of Christian pentecostal experience 'which implies criticism of the established order' but without strategic purpose.[34] The aim is not to bring about a new order with the aim of overturning the existing one—it would not constitute a space of representation if this were the case—but to imagine a space free from the confining distinctions of race and ethnicity, 'to reach an alternative vision of self'.[35] She suggests that this is not achieved by denying the very real social boundaries experienced by black people in Britain, but by finding 'ways and means of making [these] permeable, and thus less violent and constraining'.[36]

Returning once again to the end of Chapter 7, the further question raised there was whether a movement like Satanism, which settled for reversing the beliefs and practices of the existing religious order and accepting many of the values of its secular partner, could evoke a different 'horizon for becoming'.[37] Could such a movement—through its use of the left hand—really point beyond the field of religious/secular relations? The left hand is able to operate as a non-strategic space of resistance and growth (one that Lefebvre might have appreciated given his awareness that left and right were rich in meaning[38] and that gestural systems 'bring into play all segments of the limbs, even the finger tips, and invest them with symbolic (cosmic) significance'[39]), but can that same hand, as a space of representation, play a role in allowing a group to transcend the very field in which it is situated and, from that position, transform it?

In Chapter 8, I considered this issue comparatively with reference to the earlier case of religion, magic, and witchcraft in mediaeval and early modern Europe, and the contemporaneous one of Indian and Tibetan Tantrism. Did an analysis of those cases shed any light on the nature of

---

33. Steve Pile from Keith and Pile (eds.), *Geographies of Resistance*, p. 16, quoted by Chivallon, 'Religion as Space for the Expression of Caribbean Identity', p. 477.
34. Chivallon, 'Religion as Space for the Expression of Caribbean Identity', p. 477.
35. Chivallon, 'Religion as Space for the Expression of Caribbean Identity', p. 477. See also Soja, *Thirdspace*.
36. Chivallon, 'Religion as Space for the Expression of Caribbean Identity', p. 480.
37. Jantzen, *Becoming Divine*, p. 272.
38. Lefebvre, *The Production of Space*, p. 215.
39. Lefebvre, *The Production of Space*, p. 214.

our own field of religious/secular relations? Both were fields of force-relations in which struggles for ideological, social, and moral supremacy were fought, and in which those with power used right and left to organise and order various values, beliefs, and social positions. In both cases we observed how those identified with right or left interpreted their own and others' positions and how they saw and negotiated both the boundary between them and the field as a whole. The urge to see religion and magic—or Vedism and Tantrism—as separate domains was resisted; they were understood to constitute related parts of a single epistemological field (in the case of Vedism and Tantrism, this is also structural). Left and right were seen as significant markers for differentiating positions within each field and thereby understanding its contours rather than as a means to point beyond it. They were used to represent the known world, not to postulate something unknown. Certainly, within the Tantric/Vedic field, as with the religious/secular one, the left hand stood for the attempt to resist the established order and the promise of emancipation from its clutches, but not for an intervention from beyond the field.

In the previous chapters two further points emerged about the nature and boundary of a field of force-relations. First, Grace Jantzen questioned whether recent attempts to reverse traditional dualistic pairings and raise up those values marginalised in Western philosophy were able in any meaningful sense to disrupt the Western dualist order. Jantzen herself argued for a new space—a pantheist symbolic—in which she sought to take seriously the 'recognition of alterities' and the inseparability of matter and spirit, by transforming 'a set of polarities into a play of diversities'.[40] What can such a stance, which emerges within the field but in critical response to the order which underlies it, achieve? Following Irigaray, Jantzen ends her book by reminding us of the *strategic* nature of identifying a new horizon. The aim is not to *fix* a new position within or beyond the field as such, but to imagine and practice a horizon for becoming that then allows the terms of the field to be revisited.

In Chapter 8 a deliberate attempt was then made to observe the field of the religious/secular and its dualistic structure from the outside, with questions being raised about what contribution, if any, a neighbouring epistemological and structural field could make to our own. Could it infiltrate our field and change it, or are the particular dualistic characteristics of our own field so strong that they tranquillize the effect of its difference?

These two points concern the nature and boundaries of our epistemological field and its symbolic order. An in-depth discussion of such matters is both beyond my abilities and the scope of this project, though,

40. Jantzen, *Becoming Divine*, pp. 272-74.

on the basis of this study, several observations can be made. The first states the obvious that, despite historical developments, the Western symbolic order is remarkably durable. Its current face—which I have looked at briefly through representations of the left hand—is clearly related to earlier forms through its dualistic order. That scholars are able to subject this order to critical comparative study is positive because it allows all of us who operate within it to know something of its power, reach, and limit, even if bringing about change is difficult and conditional upon the order itself and its associated beliefs and values. Secondly, it is possible, as we have seen, to forge new critical and imaginative spaces of representation that effect change, though such spaces are products of minds and imaginations tempered by the field itself, its nature, conditions, and traditional symbols (or any from beyond its borders that can successfully be accommodated and interpreted within its terms). Many new, progressive spaces may be imagined or lived but few will have sufficient symbolic purchase and resonance to have a significant lasting impact on the nature of the field itself. Hope for change within the field is an intrinsic and perennial aspect of our order, rooted in our religious traditions, and, arguably, in our biological and cognitive nature. But what about a plea for change that critiques the field itself and the order which governs it? Is such a call only possible because we are now connected beyond our field with other cultures and societies, an engagement that has reinforced our sense of ourselves, our limits and alternative possibilities? Taking our earlier case as an example, what has Tantrism done for us?

As the work of Hugh Urban has shown, our meeting with Tantrism is complex.[41] Colonial relations with India in the nineteenth century provided the context and opportunity for a scholarly engagement—of both horror and fascination—through which Western spiritual seekers were able to extend their esoteric interests. More recently, through the writings of these early seekers in conjunction with the teachings of Indian and Tibetan gurus and lamas who have seen a market for Tantric ideas and practices in the West, Tantrism has emerged as a late-modern capitalist spirituality.[42] The focus of this spiritual form has been Tantric sex; its medium, the Internet.[43]

41. See the discussion and references in Chapter 8.
42. Urban, 'The Cult of Ecstasy', and 'The Power of the Impure'.
43. For example, Kama Sutra Temple, 'Tantra: The Left Hand Path of Love', <http://www.tantra.org/lefthand.html> (accessed 2 November 2003): 'Sexual union is thus a form of meditative discipline with profound psycho-mental and spiritual effects' (from the section on 'Sanctified sexuality').

As Urban suggests, in coming West, Tantrism has been honed to meet our needs, and now tells us more about ourselves than it does about the complex conceptual and ritual system of South Indian Śrīvidyā Tantrism or Tibetan Buddhist Tantrism. However, even though those meanings and values that we saw associated with the left in an Indian or Tibetan context have been adulterated in their journey westwards into a non-Vedic, non-Buddhist socio-religious context in which the values of purity and auspiciousness give way to those arising from the Judeo-Christian tradition and its secular offspring, the presence of Tantrism in the West is nonetheless revealing. It informs us about what our own order lacks but we desire (admittedly on our own terms). What Westerners identify in Tantrism that is largely unavailable in their own traditions is as follows,

- access to that which is beyond (transcendent) within the immanent;
- pleasure in those things that are normally frowned upon or seen as worldly or dangerous;
- achieving bliss and gaining meaning within this life, in this world, through our own bodies, and within our own socio-economic and cultural positions;
- thus, the possibility of having it 'both ways'.

Arguably, it is not Tantrism as such that is sought, but the impulse that it stimulates in those outside it—in this case, Westerners—to re-evaluate the opposites within their own symbolic order.

The ritual use and interpretation of the polarities of purity/impurity and auspiciousness/inauspiciousness within Indian and Tibetan Tantrism support the anthropological case that human groups organise their thinking and behaviour in dual systems using oppositions, sometimes extrapolating a third position involving the combination of the two.[44] But the Vedic/Tantric case was interestingly different to the religious/secular one. Right and left were employed in different ways to mark different values. Furthermore, the stress was not always on opposition, or even on complementarity, but on conjunction, the play of opposites, holding the two in tension and enjoying the incongruity. My third observation, then, is that seeing the deployment of the left hand in this other relational field helps us to understand our own field, its beliefs, values, and boundary, the way these are internally constructed and organised, and the desire that may then arise within this field for what is absent—a new and different path and goal.

Finally, there is the issue of my representation of force-relations between the 'religious' and the 'secular' as a *field*. Does this conception

44. See Maybury-Lewis and Almagor (eds.), *The Attraction of Opposites*.

itself limit the way I have thought and described the Western symbolic order and its capacity for transformation? Arguably, my conception of the field is grounded to too great an extent in the agricultural metaphor, with too little concession to alternative notions of the field.[45] Magnetic fields and fields of water, for example, are metaphors which offer us different ways of thinking about a field's boundaries and the process of change which it may undergo in reproducing or reconstituting itself. Consideration of this matter must await further study, however.

The Field, Boundaries, and the Sacred

One further issue remains to be resolved: What is the relationship between the field of religious and secular relations, and the 'sacred'? How are they configured in the left hand?

My principal focus here will be on the *etic* terms that scholars have used to discuss religion in Western modernity (though I recognise that the same terms are also in commonsense, everyday usage).[46] First, it is necessary to reiterate what has been established about the field of religious and secular relations and to summarise what I mean by 'religious' and 'secular' and their relationship. I shall return to the work of Wouter Hanegraaff and Danièle Hervieu-Léger in this process. Then I shall reconsider the contribution of Robert Hertz and those Durkheimian scholars who have seen right and left hands as useful tools in explaining the 'sacred' and 'profane'.

In previous chapters, I have proposed and then explored by means of different representations of the left hand an epistemological field of religious/secular relations, one that is made up of an array of knowledge-power positions. In bringing together knowledge and power in this way I am following Michel Foucault, but with particular reference to Jeremy Carrette's reading of his work on religion:

> Religion for Foucault was always part of a set of force relations and discursive practices which order human life…a reading that does not position religion in some separate realm but inside a political struggle of knowledge-power. In this way Foucault provides a radical framework to question the politics of all religious and theological thinking. He brings religion back into history and back into the immanent struggle of identity and subjectivity.[47]

---

45. I am indebted to Martin Hobson for this criticism and for suggesting alternatives.

46. Beckford, *Social Theory and Religion*, pp. 19-21.

47. Carrette (ed.), *Religion and Culture: Michel Foucault*, p. 32. Foucault preferred the conjunction 'knowledge and power' to 'ideology'. He found the latter problematic for several reasons including the implication that it stood in opposition to truth. See Michel Foucault, 'Truth and Power', in Paul Rabinow (ed.), *The Foucault Reader: An*

Carrette goes on to say that Foucault saw 'religion, alongside ideologies, philosophies and systems of metaphysics, as part of the mechanism for controlling the function of human life'.[48] Secular discourse would have been seen by Foucault as both containing traces of earlier religious traditions and as operating in a similar way to its religious forebears. I suggest that exponents of such knowledge-power positions bear a family relationship to one another, though they variously portray others in the same field as opponents, rivals, competitors, fellow travellers, supporters, or friends. They draw on various symbols, including the left hand, in order to represent their views about their neighbours and their inter-relationships.

This epistemological field is the current form of the Western political and cultural order with its roots in classical thought, patriarchal social organisation, and Judeo-Christian beliefs, traditions, and values, with a recent history informed in particular by the Enlightenment and colonialism.[49] It is fundamentally dualistic in its structure and operates in the mode of opposition rather than complementarity, parallelism, or conjunction. The modern face of this dualistic order is weaker than it was in earlier periods—more egalitarian than hierarchical—with a rhetorical stress on equality, diversity, and freedom of speech that has at times masked a deep-seated antipathy toward religion.

If we keep this notion of knowledge-power to the fore in thinking about exponents of the 'religious' and the 'secular', we can see why, though they are part of the same field with a common genealogy (see Chapter 3), they see each other as opponents. Within this temperate ideological war zone, each camp struggles for the right and opportunity to write history and laws, control the centre of power and its institutions, dictate behaviour, values, and tenets, and shape traditions and rituals of incorporation, exclusion, and passage.

We can see these struggles at work in various debates and controversies. The argument about secularisation, for example, far from being simply a neutral and objective scholarly discussion about the place of religion in modern society, is a struggle between various types of exponents—religious, secularist, clerical, scholarly—over whether religion

Introduction to Foucault's Thought (London: Penguin, 1984), pp. 51-75 (60-61), originally in Colin Gordon (ed.), *Power/Knowledge: Selected Interviews and Other Writings 1972–77* (Hemel Hempstead: Harvester Press, 1980), pp. 109-33.

48. Carrette, *Religion and Culture*, p. 38.

49. In his discussion of the '*episteme* of Western culture', Foucault notes the points of discontinuity which interrupt the development of our order, one being the entry of 'man' at the beginning of the nineteenth century (*The Order of Things*, p. xxii). See also Asad, *Genealogies of Religion*; R. King, *Orientalism and Religion*.

has been, can be, or should be erased from public institutions, laws, education, and ethics, and limited to the private domain. As part of this process of struggle, religion and its secular counterpart are defined.[50] Attempts are made to close these terms in various ways for political or intellectual ends.[51] Defining religion precisely according to a substantive definition—linked either to institutional structures, a focus on God, or particular beliefs—limits its power and reach; defining it broadly and inclusively is tantamount to saying that it is not open to containment, is fluid, and thus likely to find new ways of expressing itself in belief, practice, or social organisation. The more knowledge—in the form of evidence—that can be cited in support of an argument for or against secularisation, the more convincing it will seem to be, the more power it will have, and the more frequently cited by other scholars, media pundits, politicians, clerics, and lawyers. This ideological struggle does not only have 'religion', and its associated institutions, traditions, symbols, and representatives, in its sights. It focuses on the 'secular' too. Arguing that secularism—and its attendant ideological partners, modernism and humanism—is a belief system whose time has passed is itself a counter-strategy of containment.[52] Hailing the late-modern 'return of the sacred' or the rise of a post-secular critical commentary on the intellectual and spiritual poverty of modernism are other examples of skirmishes in the secularisation struggle.[53] Thus it is that scholars, as well as those who confess religion or secularism more overtly, are part of the field.

With James Beckford, I suggest that the more enlightening task at present is not establishing another definition of 'religion' in a secular age, but investigating the boundary between the 'religious' and the 'secular' and the way in which it is constructed, negotiated, and policed by those firmly on one side or the other, and transgressed by others, for example, those of a post-secular religious persuasion.[54] Evidently, this boundary—

50. James A. Beckford explores the contested nature of 'religion' in modern Europe in 'The Politics of Defining Religion in Secular Society'. His focus is controversy over 'religion' in public institutions. I suggest that defining religion is no less political an exercise in scholarly debates. See Chapter 3.

51. See Chapter 5 on 'closure', and Lawson, *Closure: A Story of Everything*.

52. For example, see the reference in Chapter 2 to the Vatican's readiness to side with postmodern critics and declare modernism outdated (David Harvey).

53. Daniel Bell, 'The Return of the Sacred', *British Journal of Sociology* 28.4 (1977), pp. 419-49; Phillip E. Hammond (ed.), *The Sacred in a Secular Age: Toward Revision in the Scientific Study of Religion* (Berkeley: University of California Press, 1985). See also Phillip Blond's cynical depiction of the intellectual climate in the contemporary polis, 'a time of failed conditions', no faith, 'the violence of denial', in Blond (ed.), *Post-Secular Philosophy*, 'Introduction', pp. 1-3.

54. Beckford, 'The Politics of Defining Religion', pp. 24, 39; *idem, Social Theory and Religion*, pp. 20-21.

which I argue separates camps within a single epistemological field not different fields — has a chimerical quality. From some positions, it appears substantial and impenetrable, separating insiders within the camp from aliens outside it; from others, it seems hardly a boundary at all, easy to cross, with those around it having much in common. It comes into focus at the time of public controversies about the place of 'religion' or the 'religious' in contemporary society — as in *The Satanic Verses* controversy in the early 1990s, or the more recent debate about the wearing of *hijab* in French schools — when the meaning of these and their relationship to secularism and the 'secular' become a matter of dispute and negotiation.[55]

Two other means of exploring the boundary between the 'religious' and the 'secular' are offered by Wouter Hanegraaff and Danièle Hervieu-Léger, both of whom seek to explain the nature of religion and its changing place in contemporary Western societies. As both are concerned with the dynamics of religion, it is necessary for them to define it and to distinguish it or close it off from other related concepts. Hanegraaff defines 'religion', 'a religion', and 'a spirituality' in relation to symbolic systems and action or practice, and examines the post-Enlightenment impact of individualism on religion and spirituality; Hervieu-Léger distinguishes the 'sacred' from the 'religious' on the basis of whether each exhibits chains of memory and inspires a lineage of believers, and considers how religions and the sacred fare in modern Western societies where such chains are often broken.

Through an historical account of both collective symbolism and spiritualities, Hanegraaff examines the boundary between religious and secular spheres, a boundary he sees emerging from the watershed of the Enlightenment which gave rise for the first time to 'a human society, the common culture of which was not religious'.[56] As he puts it, 'secular western society can be regarded as a historical "anomaly"'.[57] In one sense, then, for Hanegraaff the boundary between the 'religious' and the 'secular' is a temporal one, though he does not claim that religions cease operating in the West after the Enlightenment, only that it becomes possible to give meaning to things without recourse to the symbolic systems that religions provide. In another sense the boundary is based on the thought and practice made possible by the Enlightenment, in particular the disembedding of meaning from religion and the rise of individual approaches to its construction and practice.

---

55. See also examples discussed by Beckford in 'The Politics of Defining Religion'.
56. Hanegraaff, 'New Age Spiritualities as Secular Religion', p. 152.
57. Hanegraaff, 'New Age Spiritualities', p. 152. Necessarily this calls for a new account of secularisation (pp. 151-52).

Hanegraaff's chief 'analytic instrument' for examining this process of change is 'the distinction between religions and spiritualities'.[58] His choice of the latter term is instructive, it being one that has become popular in recent decades.[59] He defines 'a spirituality' as 'any human practice which maintains contact between the everyday world and a more general meta-empirical framework of meaning by way of *the individual manipulation of symbolic systems*'.[60] Furthermore,

> 'Spiritualities' and 'religions' might be roughly characterized as the individual and institutional poles within the general domain of 'religion'. A religion without spiritualities is impossible to imagine. But...the reverse—a spirituality without a religion—is quite possible to imagine.[61]

After the Enlightenment we witness the rise of non-religious as well as religious spiritualities. New Age—and no doubt the post-secular examples I cited in Chapter 7—offers 'a complex of spiritualities which emerges on the foundation of a pluralistic secular society'.[62] Whilst, for Taylor, it was this last aspect—the pluralistic—that characterised the secular (see Chapter 3), for Hanegraaff, the secular age is one in which not only is Christianity displaced as the foundational symbolic system, but a common culture arises—itself capable of generating spiritualities—which is not religious at all.

How is the boundary between the 'religious' and the 'secular' understood by the sociologist Danièle Hervieu-Léger? She makes two telling distinctions, one between 'religions' and the 'religious', and the other between the 'religious' and the 'sacred'. She does not dwell on the notion of the 'secular' as such, but she does identify secularisation in retrospect as the process whereby the 'religious' has been radically de-institutionalised.[63] The idea of the 'religious' can now be differentiated from

58. Hanegraaff, 'New Age Spiritualities', p. 152.

59. Arguably, the frequency with which it is now used, for example, with reference to health care, education and the workplace, is evidence of a need within the secular domain to indicate that what Hanegraaff calls 'a more general meta-empirical framework of meaning' (p. 147) is still taken seriously even if this is negotiated individually. As the term 'spirituality' has not emerged as significant within the examples used in this study, I shall not consider it to the same extent as other terms, though I expect to return to it in forthcoming publications arising from my research on 'Locating Religion within the Fabric of the Secular: An Experiment in Two Public Sector Organisations' (Arts and Humanities Research Board, 2004–2005).

60. Hanegraaff, 'New Age Spiritualities', p. 147 (my italics). His definition of 'religion' is 'any symbolic system which influences human action by providing possibilities for ritually maintaining contact between the everyday world and a more general meta-empirical framework of meaning' (p. 147).

61. Hanegraaff, 'New Age Spiritualities', p. 151.

62. Hanegraaff, 'New Age Spiritualities', p. 156.

63. Hervieu-Léger, *Religion as a Chain of Memory*, pp. 167-68.

'religions' in the conventional sense. She examines the process by which a group emerges as 'religious' through a discussion of 'elective fraternities, that is, 'a community of values and references which has developed through shared interests, experience and hardships'.[64] Such a community is not intrinsically religious. It becomes so, she suggests, when it 'takes on permanence and, seeking to legitimate its existence beyond the inevitable routinization of the emotional experiences that led to the sense of forming a single heart, needs to call upon a common spirit that transcends its individual members'.[65] The idea of continuity (tradition, memory) and the need for its representation (in beliefs) are central in distinguishing an elective fraternity from the religious group it becomes in undertaking such a process.

The other contribution Hervieu-Léger makes which is helpful for understanding the boundary between the 'religious' and the 'secular' concerns the 'sacred'. She claims that 'the gradual separation between the sacred and religion is a process that started long ago with the emergence of modernity' but that is fully realised in 'more advanced modern societies in which the two are no longer synonymous'.[66] Like Hanegraaff then she suggests that something occurs in modernity that changes the face of Western society and culture in enabling non-religious (secular) forms, symbols, beliefs, practices, and experiences to emerge and run in parallel with religious ones. The sacred does not disappear as the religious becomes de-institutionalised: elective fraternities and moments of 'corporate emotional awareness' continue to arise without reference to religions, their traditions, beliefs, and organisations.[67] She asserts that there is a barrier which divides 'the experience of the sacred, namely the experience of encountering a force and a presence that is stronger than self, and religion, which has to do with the constitution of a chain of belief'.[68]

The work of these two scholars helps us to clarify the nature of the 'religious' and the 'secular' and the boundary between them. Historical developments, associated primarily with the Enlightenment and modernity, are identified as important in allowing a non-religious space to emerge in Western societies, co-existent with various religious spaces. The concepts of 'spirituality' (Hanegraaff) and the 'sacred' (Hervieu-Léger)

64. Hervieu-Léger, *Religion as a Chain of Memory*, p. 150.
65. Hervieu-Léger, *Religion as a Chain of Memory*, p. 152.
66. Hervieu-Léger, *Religion as a Chain of Memory*, p. 108.
67. Hervieu-Léger, *Religion as a Chain of Memory*, p. 103. See also Fenn (*Beyond Idols*, p. 5) on the continued possibility of the 'sacred' in secular society.
68. Hervieu-Léger, *Religion as a Chain of Memory*, p. 106. She argues this in relation to the case of football using studies by Marc Augé and Grace Davie (pp. 102-106).

are shown to be applicable in both 'religious' and 'secular' contexts.[69] They cross the boundary, though they have different points of reference on either side.[70]

The third scholar whose work I introduced at the end of Chapter 3 also deals with the subject of the 'sacred', and it is with him that we are able to return to the left hand and the influential ideas of Robert Hertz. Veikko Anttonen's focus is not the place or fate of religion in modern, secular Western societies, but rather the development of the notion of the 'sacred' as an analytical tool (an *etic* category) that can be applied in a variety of times, places, and situations.

Again—as in the work of Hervieu-Léger—the bond with 'religion' is cut. With William Paden, Anttonen states that 'the sacred is not a uniquely religious category, although its religious meanings and the history of its use dominate the popular as well as scholarly discourse'.[71] Rather, it is a cognitive category which both separates and binds, 'the representations of which are culture-dependent'.[72] Returning to the issue of what the 'sacred' does in a moment, let us first consider its cultural dependency as it is this that both explains the error we make if we conflate the 'sacred' with 'religion', and that sets us free from the need to do so. 'Religion' is the term we have come to use in the West for that area of activity, thinking, and organising that is associated with the 'sacred', but this does not mean that the reverse is true, that the 'sacred' is what is religious.[73] The notion of the 'sacred' has a different and broader remit. Nothing is inherently sacred, but things, places, persons, and events are attributed with that quality by societies, groups, or individuals according to their own cultural context.[74] So, for example, in Western religious thought the 'sacred' has been used as,

69. These are *emic* as well as *etic* terms insofar as they are in common usage among religious and non-religious people.

70. Although I have not chosen to discuss his work in detail here, as an exponent of the secular sacred, Fenn (*Beyond Idols*, p. 5) offers one of the most intriguing perspectives in arguing that 'to become secular is…to open oneself and one's society to a wide range of possibilities' some of which are conducive to liberation and human aspiration, others to dread and danger: 'In their totality they constitute the Sacred… A truly secular society is therefore one that is wholly open to the Sacred.'

71. Anttonen, 'Sacred', p. 274; William E. Paden, 'Before "The Sacred" became Theological: Rereading the Durkheimian Legacy', *Method and Theory in the Study of Religion* 3.10 (1991), pp. 10-23; and *idem, Interpreting the Sacred*. See also T. Thomas, '"The Sacred" as a Viable Concept', p. 31.

72. Anttonen, 'Rethinking the Sacred', p. 43; Anttonen, 'Sacred', p. 277.

73. T. Thomas on Paden in '"The Sacred" as a Viable Concept', p. 19, and Paden, *Interpreting the Sacred*, pp. 71-72.

74. Durkheim, *The Elementary Forms of the Religious Life*, p. 122. See also discussion on space and the sacred in Chapter 4.

> An attribute of situations and circumstances which have some reference to
> the culture-specific conception of the category of God, [but] in non-theo-
> logical contexts, to some supreme principle of life such as love, freedom,
> equality or justice.[75]

As Anttonen goes on to say, 'people participate in sacred-making activities and processes of signification according to paradigms given by the
belief systems to which they are committed, whether they be religious,
national or ideological'.[76]

From the point of view of the field of religious/secular relations, then,
'sacred-making activities and processes of signification' may be said to be
at work in the different camps of the religious, the secular, and the post-
secular, according to their own paradigms. Moreover, what is at stake in
designating something as 'sacred' is the identification and protection of
'things with non-negotiable value' as distinct from 'things whose value is
based on continuous transactions', things that are repeatedly negotiated.[77]
The religious, secular, and post-secular camps, as we saw in Chapter 7, all
have values that they rank highly and others that they demean. Anttonen
has mentioned one that we noted in particular: equality. Said by a media
commentator to be 'the religion of modernity',[78] the value of equality —
along with freedom, diversity, and the centrality of the individual — is
non-negotiable for secular culture.

This takes us back to the issue of what the 'sacred' does, irrespective of
its cultural context. It 'separates and binds'.[79] The 'sacred' is that which is
set apart.[80] Sacred-making activity is that which sets things apart, which
creates a place for those things of value, separating them out from profane or impure things that are negotiable or may contaminate.[81] Such
activity 'binds' in uniting a society or group around whatever it is that is
of supreme value. The process of representing and experiencing the force
of that which is set apart is a collective one.[82]

---

75. Anttonen, 'Sacred', pp. 280-81.
76. Anttonen, 'Sacred', p. 281.
77. Anttonen, 'Sacred', p. 281.
78. In *Thinking Allowed*, BBC Radio 4, summer 2003. This phrase is telling. The
speaker wished to signal the non-negotiability of equality for modern secular culture,
and thus called it 'a religion'. He chose this term because, as I have suggested, it is the
one commonly used in the West to denote sacrality; in doing so, he suggested that
modernity, like other cultures, could not exist without 'religion' or a functional equivalent to it. Following recent scholars of the 'sacred', we may say that what modernity
cannot do without is the cognitive-cultural process of sacred-making activity.
79. Anttonen, 'Rethinking the Sacred', p. 43.
80. Durkheim, *Elementary Forms*, pp. 40-41, 47.
81. Anttonen, 'Sacred', p. 281; J.Z. Smith, *To Take Place*, p. 26, and on Lévi-Strauss,
n. 2, on pp. 121-22; Paul Hegarty on the space of the sacred, 'Undelivered', p. 102.
82. Durkheim, *Elementary Forms*, pp. 45-47, 172. Durkheim and others also considered what happens to the 'sacred' in the face of individualism.

The processes of separating and binding return us at last to the hands, the focus of our attention in preceding chapters, and to the work of Robert Hertz. The separation of some things as 'sacred' from others that are 'profane' is achieved by means of representations, which may take a variety of forms, whether iconic, symbolic, mythic, conceptual, or ritual. For Hertz, the right and left hands were primary examples of the collective representation—in many different cultural settings—of the sacred and the profane. Hertz described the universe as 'divided into two spheres' with two poles around which the principles of sacred and profane gravitate.[83] 'On the one side there is the pole of strength, good, and life; while on the other there is the pole of weakness, evil, and death...on the one side gods, on the other demons'.[84] This universal principle of dualism—which is asymmetrical—applies also to the body. Hertz asks, 'How could man's body, the microcosm, escape the law of polarity which governs everything?'[85] However, Hertz did not, as this question perhaps implies, see the social and cultural world as the cause of right-handedness and the pre-eminence of the right: '*If* organic asymmetry had not existed, it would have had to be invented'.[86] But it did exist. As we have seen elsewhere in this study, it is on the basis of the body—our hands, in particular—that cultural acts of separation and signification can be achieved.

Anttonen confirms this: 'Ethnographic evidence'—which he provides for prehistoric Finland, Estonia, and the Baltic area, and some examples of which I have given in relation to contemporary Western accounts of the left hand—'suggests that the human body and its locative dimensions, the notion of place, forms the cultural grammar on which sacred-making behaviour is based'.[87] Right and left (hands) are semantic tools used in the process of sacralisation. With other corporeal and territorial features—such as front/back, inside/outside, up/down—they operate as 'constraining structures of knowledge' which are reproduced metaphorically for various ends, including the separation of things with or without social value.[88]

As we saw earlier in the chapter, the particularity of left and right hands arises from their difference—they are incongruent counterparts—

---

83. Hertz, 'The Pre-Eminence of the Right Hand', p. 8.
84. Hertz, 'The Pre-Eminence of the Right Hand', p. 9.
85. Hertz, 'The Pre-Eminence of the Right Hand', p. 10.
86. Hertz, 'The Pre-Eminence of the Right Hand', p. 10 (my italics).
87. Anttonen, 'Sacred', p. 278; for evidence, see *idem*, *Ihmisen ja maan rajat. 'Pyhä' kultuurisena kategoriana* (Helsinki: Suomalaisen Kirjallisuuden Seura, 1996), and 'Sacred Sites as Markers of Difference'.
88. Anttonen, 'Sacred', p. 278, and 'Rethinking the Sacred', pp. 39-43. See also Lakoff and Johnson, *Metaphors We Live By*, and *Philosophy in the Flesh*.

and is endorsed by the asymmetry that emerges in their physical and genetic development. As cognitive concepts, left and right are frequently deployed to communicate difference and asymmetry, separation and hierarchy. They come into their own when they are used by 'cultural agents…[to] make distinctions between spaces, mark them for specific uses, create visible and invisible boundaries, and establish cultural conventions of behaviour to deal with those boundaries'.[89] However, their boundary-making potential—as we saw in Chapter 6, in relation to Bataille's discussion of a French village funeral, and in Chapter 8, on Tantrism and Vedism—is not confined to the straightforward signification of 'sacred' and 'profane'. When used in conjunction with other polarities, particularly pure/impure, their asymmetry produces a double effect, further separating things within the domain of the 'sacred'. As a concept, the 'sacred' comprises, on the one hand, order, unity, conformity, and, on the other, impurity, and that which is forbidden or dangerous.[90] And—as the words in the previous sentence suggest—it is the hands that mark this heterogeneity within the 'sacred', with 'right hand sacred' denoting religion, Bataille's village church, and Vedism, and 'left hand' reserved for contagious and impure aspects of the sacred associated with death, blood, and that which is prohibited, such as Bataille's corpse and the *vāmācāra* or left hand behaviour of Tantrism.[91] As Carol Burnside has shown, not only have the hands been used by practitioners (in an *emic* sense) to distinguish things considered to be sacred from those that are of lesser value, but scholars have found the metaphors of 'left' and 'right' (in an *etic* capacity) helpful in dealing with the ambiguity of the 'sacred'.[92]

Recognition of this ambiguity and the appropriation of a terminology of handedness for making distinctions within the 'sacred' is evident, as we have seen, within Western esotericism. It is probable that the Indic separation of left and right disciplines (*vāma-mārga* and *dakṣina-mārga*) was adopted by influential exponents of Theosophy in the late-nineteenth century, popularised by Aleister Crowley, and used since then to distinguish the left hand occult path from the right hand path of conventional religions (thus denoting a separation within the 'sacred').[93]

Let me conclude this discussion of the 'sacred' by returning to the subject of devils, explicitly to the unnamed demon of modernity that

89. Anttonen, 'Sacred Sites as Markers of Difference', p. 302. Anttonen was not referring specifically to right and left in this passage, but he could well have been.

90. Anttonen, 'Sacred', p. 279.

91. Bataille, 'Attraction and Repulsion II', p. 121; Burnside, 'The Left Hand of the Sacred'; Hegarty, 'Undelivered', pp. 107-108, 112.

92. Burnside, 'The Left Hand of the Sacred', pp. 1-8.

93. See Chapter 7 for references.

raised its head in secular representations of the left hand. In what way is homosexuality a 'sacred' matter, and why does it emerge as such in the modern West? I can only touch briefly on these questions here, beginning with the second.

Homosexuality is a *modern* devil—at the centre of the moral panic of HIV/AIDS in the 1980s[94]—because 'homosexuality' as a condition and 'homosexual' as an identity only began to be formally conceived in the late-nineteenth century.[95] As Jonathan Katz informs us, we may refer to the earlier 'acts or desires [of men] as gay or straight, homosexual, hetero-sexual, or bisexual, but that places their behaviours and lusts within our own sexual system, not the system of their time'.[96] Since then, the con-struction and differentiation of a range of approaches to sexuality and sexual identity, and the rise of insecurity about sexual self-identification and gender relations have reinforced one another. Homophobia is one aspect of this insecurity (as we saw in Chapter 7), along with fear about 'outing', comedy on sexual orientation, and, ultimately, the debate about a rights discourse and legal provision for gays and lesbians.

But what has this to do with the 'sacred'? The demons of the age tell us something about what is non-negotiable in our society: We saw in Chapter 7 how the values of equality and diversity were highlighted in parodies about left-handers and minority rights. In an example of the 'sacred' as an analytical category, Anttonen suggests there is more for us to consider in thinking about the categories and boundaries that are revealed by the wave of insecurity about sexuality and sexual relations. He cites the modern Western case of 'the heavily debated issue concerning the legalization of homosexual marriages'.[97] The ostensible anxiety about the role of marriage for reproduction and species continuity is not the only one of importance here: 'What is primarily at issue is the fundamen-tal significance that gender difference has as the moral foundation of society'.[98] The issue of gender difference has been so taken for granted in Western society that, until recent decades, its precariousness was not

---

94. Sibley, *Geographies of Exclusion*, pp. 41-43.

95. Michel Foucault, *The Will to Knowledge: The History of Sexuality*, I (London: Penguin, 1990 [French edn 1976]), pp. 38-39, 101; Jonathan Ned Katz, *Love Stories: Sex Between Men Before Homosexuality* (Chicago: University of Chicago Press, 2001), pp. 9-12. The ground-breaking book, *Sexual Inversions*, by Havelock Ellis and John Addington Symonds, was not published until 1896 (in German). The notion of 'sexual inversion' is itself interesting in the light of my earlier discussion about social and cultural inversion in Chapter 8. See also Michel Foucault, *The Use of Pleasure: The History of Sexuality*, II (London: Penguin, 1992 [French edn 1984], p. 18.

96. Katz, *Love Stories*, p. 9.

97. Anttonen, 'Sacred', p. 277.

98. Anttonen, 'Sacred', p. 277.

realised.[99] Homosexuality—especially the idea that same-sex relations could provide the basis for legally endorsed married relationships and family life—threatens the boundaries of the social self:[100]

> Homosexual marriages are opposed and seen as sacrilegious and impure because an acceptance of intercourse between spouses of the same sex is seen as threatening gender difference as a fundamental category-boundary in Judeo-Christian cultures.[101]

What this reveals is the way in which, in modern, mixed Judeo-Christian/secular cultures, what we call the 'sacred' is still at work. The 'fundamental category boundary' of gender difference (on the basis of which heterosexual relations are posited) continues to be invested with special value. Its 'sacred' quality, which goes unnoticed much of the time, comes to the fore when the boundary is publicly under threat, in this case from the contagion of homosexuality.

However, if we take seriously the earlier discussions in this chapter about permeable boundaries and the ambiguity of the 'sacred', we must not stop at this point. In writing about Bataille's views on the sacred and categorical contagion, Paul Hegarty makes an important point about boundary transgression that is applicable in this case:

> The transgression occurs where the taboo is, but in so doing, shows that it has always already occurred—the line has always been crossed, and therefore transgression is no longer simply the transgressive act and taboo the repression of it. Transgression is the movement that is continually in operation.[102]

The taboo in this case is homosexual intercourse: it violates the sanctity of gender difference and heterosexual relations.[103] The act of transgression of the category boundary occurs—or is postulated—in the call for same-sex marriage, but that merely brings to the fore the precariousness of the gender boundary and its transgressive nature. The conditions of gender and sexual difference are in fact commonly and repeatedly examined in a process of experimental transgression whether publicly performed or

99. See Anttonen, 'Sacred Sites as Markers of Difference', p. 4, on Mary Douglas, social consensus, and the 'sacred'; on the precariousness of gender difference and its subversion, see Butler, *Gender Trouble*.

100. Sibley, *Geographies of Exclusion*, p. 42.

101. Anttonen, 'Sacred', p. 277.

102. Hegarty, 'Undelivered', p. 107. Hegarty refers to Foucault in coming to this conclusion.

103. I have identified the taboo here as homosexual intercourse, but see the discussion in Butler (*Gender Trouble*, pp. 35-78) on 'Prohibition, psychoanalysis, and the production of the heterosexual matrix', especially on the relationship between interdictions on incest and homosexuality.

privately enacted (in peripheral and secret places, behind closed doors, on covered bodies, in desire, dreams, and the imagination).

As we saw in Chapter 7, homosexuality, a modern demon, joins the well known cluster of negative principles on the left hand side of the West's dualistic symbolic order. Its relationships with heterosexuality and gender difference, both of which are fundamental to the Western social self, make it a cause for anxiety and a contagious condition which is seen to threaten collective order and survival.

What I have endeavoured to show by looking at the boundaries that have come to light in this study of the hands — whether in-field boundaries between religious, secular, and post-secular camps, or category boundaries such as magic/religion, Tantrism/Vedism, impure/pure, female/male, homosexual/heterosexual — is how the field of religious/secular relations is a single epistemological arena the members of which use common cognitive-cultural resources (emerging from the body and its regions) to mark internal differences based on values which are held to be non-negotiable. Irrespective of the camps to which they belong, they participate in sacralising practices and often represent what is 'sacred' metaphorically by means of the hands. That which we refer to as the 'sacred' is not exhausted by the contemporary forms of traditional religions or post-secular religious movements. The activities and processes of signification associated with it occur also in non-religious (or secular) contexts.

In conclusion, what can we say about the location of religion within the contemporary Western space of the hands?[104] We noted those traces of early, mediaeval, and nineteenth-century Christian culture — as well as Roman and Greek — still evident within the current palimpsest. We saw the contemporary face of various traditional religions, such as Orthodox and evangelical Protestant Christianity, expressed in the right hand, as well as the antipathy directed at them by secular and post-secular critics. As well as 'the violence of [its] denial', we also noted the marked absence of religion.[105] The location of post-secular religious movements in the left hand was also evident. And we saw hosts of angels on the narrow, right hand way, and Satan and his servants on the left hand path.

Furthermore, in all our examples — whether religious, secular or post-secular — we saw the hands employed as markers to denote the highest principles. We do not need to name secular culture as ultimately 'religious' or secular institutions or traditions as 'surrogate religions' in order

---

104.   By the phrase 'contemporary space of the hands' I mean the summation of all those representations of the hands and those gestural systems associated with them that we considered in Chapters 6 and 7.

105.   Blond, 'Introduction', p. 3.

to find matters of interest to the scholar of religion in everyday, ostensibly non-religious or secular spaces. Conventional 'religions' in both their past and present forms, the post-secular 'religious', secular ideologies (sometimes anti-religious in tone), and what we refer to as the 'sacred' are all very much in evidence.

Conclusion

As the two parts of this book have contained their own conclusions, in Chapters 5 and 9, the aim here is not to summarise what has gone before, but to review the research process and to evaluate the spatial approach and field of religious/secular relations as transferable tools.

My original intention in this project was to find a way of locating religion in everyday spaces. This began with my frustration at being confined, when thinking about researching religion in my own locality, to the ostensibly religious, to places of worship and other outwardly religious sites and symbols. Inspired by Michel de Certeau's analysis of the practice of everyday life, ordinary, apparently secular spaces began to beckon as potential cases for the examination of religion. At that point I did not realise what major intellectual challenges this would throw up. As the research process unwound, these began to present themselves.

First there was the question of *how* to locate religion in such spaces. Initially, I thought this might just involve gaining a sound understanding of the meaning, constitution, and internal relationships of the actual places I might be interested in, and perhaps of 'place' in more general terms. Hearing a lecture given by Doreen Massey changed by mind.[1] As the subject was gender, I asked her from a feminist perspective why she had chosen to make the theoretical move from the groundedness of 'place' to the abstraction of 'space'. As she made clear in her answer, post-modern 'space' had been released from its dominant Cartesian shackles and re-presented as dynamic and full of power. I realised then that I needed to know more about how space was theorised in order to understand real 'places' and then to be able to examine the location of religion therein. As a result of this research I was able to identify what I have referred to as the terms for a spatial analysis of religion.

The second difficulty to emerge was what it was that I was actually looking for. What was this thing called 'religion'? Without a definition or some other operational approach I would not be able to distinguish the

1. The Annual Lecture of the Centre for Interdisciplinary Gender Studies, University of Leeds, November 2001.

object of my enquiry from other things I might see along the way. Settling for a conventional, substantive definition would be straightforward, but also counter-productive given that my interest lay in looking at non-religious places. Inclusive definitions of religion turned out to be no less problematic, though there the issue was how to distinguish religion from other social and cultural movements, activities, and ideas. I began to see that all definitions served interests of one kind or another. They had the effect of making the religious object either smaller or bigger, but no easier to relate to its apparently secular context. It would only be through seeing the two — the 'religious' and the 'secular' — in mutual engagement that a strategic approach could be identified for locating religion in late-modern Western places. I began to formulate a field of religious/secular relations.

In considering the matter of scholarly definitions and theories of religion it became increasingly obvious that their creators and users were no less part of this field than the avid and outward exponents of various religions and secularisms. This forced me to consider where the scholars whose work I was using (not only those writing on religion) were positioned within the field, and the extent to which they gave credence to one another's positions. As a result of the origins and history of religious studies vis-à-vis Christian theology, scholars working in this discipline are aware, to a greater or lesser extent, of the issue of religious/secular standpoint. As we know, there continue to be heated debates, for example, about closet theology, cultural baggage, and insider/outsider positions. But what about the other social and cultural theorists whose work I was using? Did they show any interest, knowledge, or awareness of religion and the secular? They were often highly aware of the issue of political standpoint, but were largely products of our secular age when it came to the matter of culture in general and religion in particular. Those who had been raised and schooled before the Second World War showed some knowledge and awareness of religion, even though most of them were highly secularised. Most younger scholars never referred to it, thus supporting Peter Berger's contention that a secular *internationale* exists that has so fully imbibed the values and rhetoric of secularism that it no longer recognises religion as a significant force or institution or even as an interesting phenomenon. (In the first decade of the twenty-first century, this is beginning to change.) For this reason it was important for me to retain a certain degree of scepticism about both the analytical tools I had developed on the basis of contemporary theory, and the effect of conducting a spatial analysis in the field of religious/secular relations. It was also necessary to consider what scholars of religion — most of whom are themselves highly secularised — have contributed that might be of value for such a spatial enquiry.

Considering the place of scholars within the field of religious/secular relations also made me think about the nature of this particular field — and such fields in general — its internal and external boundaries, and its relationship to what lies outside it, that is, to other epistemological fields. It was only as I undertook the study of contemporary Western left hands that this issue began to emerge in full. Thinking spatially — that is, using the spatial properties of extension, simultaneity, and power — about religion in the left hand encouraged me to investigate an earlier form of the Western epistemological field (religion/magic) and a non-Western one, the Vedic/Tantric field. Both of these helped me to analyse the Western religious/secular field, its nature, struggles, and boundaries.

As scholars we repeatedly become aware of our current limitations and generally seek to deal with them, either by identifying them and acknowledging that they are too big for us, or by bringing them to the fore and working hard at them. There was one major flaw that began to open up as I worked on developing a spatial approach, but that I neglected until almost too late. It was the body.

As you read the book, you will find the body very much in evidence, in both my account of the spatial theory and — of course — my study of the left hand. But this wasn't clear from the beginning of the project. It proved to be the most difficult issue for me to face, not least of all because it meant dealing with the subject of social constructionism and the extent to which I had imbibed this theoretical stance unquestioningly.[2] What is it that enables us to conceive of space and religion in the way we do? Construction on the basis of what? It became difficult to avoid these questions. But my other failing was laziness. I thought I could postpone the body until I began work on the left hand — and I did just that, only to find that the unresolved issues about the nature of the body for our perception and conception of space and for culture in general (including religion) threatened to undo the approach I had worked so hard to develop. It took me many months to sort out my thoughts and to reassess my approach before returning to the left hand.[3] Even though this was a difficult time and one that extended the duration of the project, it was invaluable for sorting out some fundamental theoretical and practical issues.

The remaining questions that arose in the course of the research were how many case studies to undertake, and on what? This is a classic example of how we, as scholars, 'bite off more than we can chew'. I sought to do just this, imagining that I would be able to undertake four case studies,

2.   I am indebted to my colleague Philip Mellor for pointing out this dilemma to me in the first place.

3.   As will be evident from earlier chapters, I was helped in an unlikely way by Kant and his work on bodily asymmetry, but in particular by the contributions of Mark Johnson and George Lakoff, Luce Irigaray, Grace Jantzen and Veikko Anttonen.

on the location of religion at different scales, in a body part, a thing, a community, and a locality. It remains my hope that I will achieve this, but it was certainly too ambitious an intention for this book. In the end the left hand proved to be just too productive a place to restrict to one among several case studies. I had not imagined that a spatial study of a range of its contemporary Western representations would open up so many fascinating questions, not only about the object of the research itself – the field of religious/secular relations – but about the Western cultural order, its dualistic nature, and dynamic resilience. The power of the left hand, not only to represent that which is marginal, deemed to be demonic, and feared within the order, *but also* to provide a space for resistance and the possibility of emancipation was remarkable. It would have been folly, in light of the range and importance of the emerging issues, to cut short this study.

This brief review of the research process brings to the fore some of the major issues that I have faced in preparing and writing this book, and should be read in association with the acknowledgments at the beginning, as such issues are not resolved alone. Why have I included this? Is it just an example of the self-indulgence of a reflexive approach? I see it rather as a necessary contribution to education about the scholarly process and scholarly product – about books and what lies behind them. With my final comments in Chapter 3 about my own position, this is an attempt to demystify what lies between the covers of the book, to show not only that I am situated within the very field that I have written about, but also that there is more to a book than the printed word. Graduate education and the process of producing a doctoral thesis is all about learning how to research, think, and write, but the process does not end there. All scholarly books, as well as being creative products that present more or less coherent arguments and evidenced conclusions, are the outcomes of personal and intellectual struggles, mine no less than others.

I turn now to an evaluation of the method and theory developed in the first half of the book and applied in the second. Does the spatial approach work? Does it reveal the location of religion within the taken-for-granted body part of the left hand? Is the conception of religion in Western modernity as a field of religious/secular knowledge-power relations a helpful one? Does it have strategic worth for locating that domain of human affairs that we refer to as 'religion' in the context of contemporary everyday life and its expressions?

Ultimately, it will be for others to answer these questions as I am too close to the process and too involved to be properly critical. There are some strengths and weaknesses of the method and theory that I am able to comment upon, however, and then several neglected issues to which I should draw the reader's attention.

In my opinion, the spatial approach has two benefits for locating religion in everyday spaces. One is that, as a methodological approach, it coheres with both the research intention and its context, that is to say, to the purpose of *locating religion within particular places*. It is for this reason that I provided an account of the nature and production of space, and its relationship to location and place in Chapter 1. There is an affinity, then, between the spatial approach, the task in hand, and the particular sites to be investigated. Another of its major strengths is related to a weakness. Using a spatial approach for the location of religion in the left hand was not a question of applying a systematic method to a well defined research object in a scientifically precise context. It was an analytical process which required thinking repeatedly — hermeneutically — about the place of the left hand in relation to the various dimensions, properties, aspects, and activities of space. The complexity of 'space' and its 'places' made this a time-consuming but rewarding process. I hope that Chapters 6 to 9 demonstrate how much it is possible to learn about one place through a spatial investigation of its various representations. So, although I would have liked to bequeath a clear and manageable research method to the study of religion, I find I am instead commending an interpretive approach which takes time and patience to grasp and then apply.

Can other people use it, whether in relation to religion or other scholarly objects? Yes, I am sure they can, if they acknowledge these limitations in advance. I see no reason why such a spatial approach may not be used for investigating other things, groups, ideas, institutions, and practices that gather or take place in space. Furthermore any types of place and at any scale may be chosen for such an analysis, though local particularity is an important consideration. The more specific one is about selecting a place or places for investigation, the more manageable the research process becomes. It is much easier, for example, to focus this spatial approach on a single textual representation of the left hand than on the Western left hand in general. Finally, given the strength of the secular *internationale*, I shall be interested to see whether those from beyond the study of religion are willing to consider using an approach that was devised initially for examining subject matter that for much of the twentieth century in Europe was seen by scholars as anathema, outdated, and irrelevant for social and cultural life. The very purpose of Lefebvre's work on space was to reconnect disparate disciplines and their approaches to space. It is time now for scholars of religion and their object of study to come in from the cold.

What about the theoretical construct I developed in Chapters 3 and 5 and investigated in the place of the left hand in Part II? My initial aim in devising a field of religious/secular relations was operational. It was related to my intention to locate religion in everyday, ostensibly secular places, and was less problematic for this purpose than the alternatives (see Chapter 3). However, the fortuitous choice of the hands as places to be investigated led me to dwell on unforeseen issues relating to the Western cultural order and its dualistic conceptual structure which in turn strengthened my understanding of the dialectical nature of the field I had proposed. What had begun in my mind as an operational device began to take shape as a way of seeing knowledge-power relations in Western modernity. Of course, in this process I am indebted to Foucault in particular and to the many other scholars whose work on the history and conception of religion and secularity I used (in Chapters 3, 8, and 9). It seems likely, though I have not investigated this myself, that Western modernity is indeed anomalous in its epistemological character, in so far as it is not only centred on humanity and the self but internally pluralistic in allowing both religious and non-religious confessions to run in parallel.[4]

A final challenge was offered by the hands themselves and their principal social theorist, Robert Hertz, who had discussed their role as collective representations not for the religious and secular, but for the sacred and profane. A different choice of case study might have allowed me to escape without needing to consider how my proposed field of religious/secular relations might be related to the idea of the 'sacred'. In the end this unsought opportunity has been beneficial in helping me to understand that the 'sacred' does not respect the difference between the 'religious' and the 'secular'. What we mean by 'sacred' is not confined to religious ideologies, practices, and institutions. In fact, as we have seen in Chapter 9, it refers to that very boundary between the 'religious' and the 'secular', and the many other boundaries within the field that separate out non-negotiable values, principles, places, and activities. There is a great deal more to be read and thought about the adequacy of this field for understanding the nature of its three camps—the 'religious', the 'secular', and the 'post-secular'—the dynamism of their inter-relationships, and the way these reveal themselves in boundary disputes and controversies.

The book offers readers *a spatial methodology*, *a theoretical framework* for considering religious/secular relations in Western modernity, and *a case study* of the left hand in which religion in its many guises is seen to be located variously in a range of contemporary representations. In being resolute about focusing on these developments, I have treated several important themes in a more cursory way than perhaps I should have done in the light of their importance for understanding space and power. The issue of gender has gone in and out of focus. Despite my interest in it,

4.   Foucault, *The Order of Things*; Taylor, *Varieties of Religion Today*; Hanegraaff, 'New Age Spiritualities as Secular Religion'.

I have been unable to keep it at the centre of my theoretical deliberations. The congruity of male and female, right and left, for example, was worthy of more attention. Time — so crucial for Lefebvre's ideas about the *production* of space — has been considered here in relation to the spatial stratification and historical extension of the hands, but, with more direct attention, it might have revealed other important issues. Also, given that the representations of the left hand chosen for investigation in Part II were mostly electronic texts, my lack of consideration of cyberspace in relation to the location of religion in the hands was inexcusable. These are serious gaps that arose from having an excess of plates to spin simultaneously. Finally, an unforgivable weakness, considering the subject matter of the book, has been my failure to discuss in depth the spatial nature of my own scholarly language. Every page has been replete with spatial metaphors: field, boundary, poles, positions, asymmetry, opposition, religions, margins, hands, to name just a few. To understand how and why I have used these concepts, I can do no more at this point than add my voice to the call for 'a philosophy in the flesh', which takes seriously the body and its spatial logic for the production of culture — language, space, and religion.[5]

5.   Lakoff and Johnson, *Philosophy in the Flesh.*

Bibliography

Abbey, R., *Charles Taylor* (Teddington: Acumen, 2000).

Ackroyd, P., *London: The Biography* (London: Vintage, 2001).

Albrow, M., *The Global Age: State and Society beyond Modernity* (Cambridge: Polity, 1996).

— 'Travelling Beyond Local Cultures: Socioscapes in a Global City', in Eade (ed.), *Living the Global City*, pp. 37-55.

Alfred, R.H., 'The Church of Satan', in E. Barker (ed.), *Of Gods and Men: New Religious Movements in the West* (Macon, GA: Mercer University Press, 1983), pp. 180-202.

Allen, N.J., *Categories and Classification: Maussian Reflections on the Social* (New York and Oxford: Berghahn Books, 2000).

Anderson, J., *Toward the Liberation of the Left Hand* (Pittsburgh: University of Pittsburgh Press, 1977).

Anttonen, V., 'Identifying the Generative Mechanisms of Religion: The Issue of Origin Revisited', in I. Pyysiäinen and V. Anttonen (eds.), *Current Approaches in the Cognitive Study of Religion* (London and New York: Continuum, 2002), pp. 14-37.

— *Ihmisen ja maan rajat. 'Pyhä' kultuurisena kategoriana* (Helsinki: Suomalaisen Kirjallisuuden Seura, 1996), with a summary in English, 'The Making of Corporeal and Territorial Boundaries: The Sacred as a Cultural Category'.

— 'Rethinking the Sacred: The Notions of "Human Body" and "Territory" in Conceptualizing Religion', in T.A. Idinopulos and E.A. Yonan (eds.), *The Sacred and its Scholars: Comparative Methodologies for the Study of Primary Religious Data* (Leiden: E.J. Brill, 1996), pp. 36-64.

— 'Sacred', in W. Braun and R.T. McCutcheon (eds.), *A Guide to the Study of Religion* (London: Cassell, 2000), pp. 271-82.

— 'Sacred Sites as Markers of Difference: Exploring Cognitive Foundations of Territoriality', in L. Tarkka (ed.), *Dynamics of Tradition: Perspectives on Oral Poetry and Folk Belief* (Helsinki: Studia Fennica Folkloristica, Finnish Literary Society, 2003), pp. 291-305.

Appadurai, A., 'Disjunction and Difference in the Global Cultural Economy', in Featherstone (ed.), *Global Culture*, pp. 295-310.

— *Modernity at Large: Cultural Dimensions of Globalization* (Minneapolis: University of Minnesota Press, 1996).

Arditi, J., *A Geneaology of Manners: Transformations of Social Relations in France and England from the Fourteenth to the Eighteenth Century* (Chicago and London: University of Chicago Press, 1998).

Arweck, E., and M. Stringer (eds.), *Theorising Faith: The Insider/Outsider Problem in the Study of Ritual* (Birmingham: Birmingham University Press, 2002).

Asad, T., *Genealogies of Religion: Disciplines and Reasons of Power in Christianity and Islam* (Baltimore and London: The Johns Hopkins University Press, 1993).

Astell, A.W. (ed.), *Divine Representations: Postmodernism and Spirituality* (New York: Paulist Press, 1994).

Augé, M., *Non-Places: Introduction to an Anthropology of Supermodernity* (London and New York: Verso, 1995 [French edn 1992]).

Avalon, A., *Kulānava Tantra* (Delhi: Motilal Banarsidass, 1965).

Bachelard, G., *The Poetics of Space* (Boston: Beacon Press, 1969 [French edn 1957]).

Barnes, R.H., 'Hierarchy without Caste', in Barnes, de Coppet and Parkin (eds.), *Contexts and Levels*, pp. 8-20.

Barnes, R.H., D. de Coppet and R.J. Parkin (eds.), *Contexts and Levels: Anthropological Essays on Hierarchy* (Oxford: JASO, 1985).

Baroja, J.C., *The World of the Witches* (Chicago: Chicago University Press, 1961).

Barsley, M. (ed.), *The Left-Handed Book: An Investigation into the Sinister History of Left-Handedness* (London: Souvenir Press, 1966).

Bataille, G., 'Attraction and Repulsion II: Social Structure', in D. Hollier (ed.), *The College of Sociology, 1937–39* (Minneapolis: University of Minnesota Press, 1988), pp. 113-24.

Bates, J.A.V., 'The Communicative Hand', in Jonathan Benthall and Ted Polhemus (eds.), *The Body as a Medium of Expression* (London: Allen Lane, 1975), pp. 175-94.

Bauman, Z., *Intimations of Postmodernity* (London: Routledge, 1992).

—'Postmodern Religion?', in Heelas (ed.), with Martin and Morris, *Religion, Modernity, and Postmodernity*, pp. 55-78.

Baumann, G., *Contesting Culture: Discourses of Identity in Multi-Ethnic London* (Cambridge: Cambridge University Press, 1996).

—*The Multicultural Riddle: Rethinking National, Ethnic, and Religious Identities* (Cambridge: Cambridge University Press, 1999).

Baumann, M., 'Sustaining Little Indias: Hindu Diasporas in Europe', in ter Haar (ed.), *Strangers and Sojourners*, pp. 95-132.

Beck, B.E.F., 'The Right-Left Division of South Indian Society', in Needham (ed.), *Right and Left*, pp. 391-426.

Beckerlegge, G., 'Computer-Mediated Religion: Religion on the Internet at the Turn of the Twenty-First Century', in *idem* (ed.), *From Sacred Text to Internet* (Aldershot and Burlington, VT: Ashgate, in association with the Open University, 2001), pp. 219-64.

Beckford, J.A., *Cult Controversies: The New Societal Response to the New Religious Movements* (London: Tavistock, 1985).

—'The Politics of Defining Religion in Secular Society: From a Taken-for-Granted Institution to a Contested Resource', *Studies in the History of Religions* 84 (1999), pp. 23-40.

—*Social Theory and Religion* (Cambridge: Cambridge University Press, 2003).

Bell, C., 'Pragmatic Theory', in Jensen and Rothstein (eds.), *Secular Theories on Religion*, pp. 9-20.

—*Ritual Theory, Ritual Practice* (New York and Oxford: Oxford University Press, 1992).

Bell, C., and H. Newby, *Community Studies* (London: George Allen & Unwin, 1971).

Bell, D., 'The Return of the Sacred', *British Journal of Sociology* 28.4 (1977), pp. 419-49.

Bellah, R.N., 'Religious Studies as "New Religion"', in J. Needleman and G. Baker (eds.), *Understanding the New Religions* (New York: Seabury Press, 1978), pp. 106-12.

Bender, B., *Stonehenge: Making Space* (Oxford: Berg, 1999).

Bennett, J., 'The Difference between Right and Left', *American Philosophical Quarterly* 7 (1970), pp. 175-91.

Benthall, J., and T. Polhemus (eds.), *The Body a a Medium of Expression* (London: Allen Lane, 1975).

Berger, P., *The Sacred Canopy: Elements of a Sociological Theory of Religion* (New York: Anchor Books, 1990 [first published 1967]).

—'Secularization and De-Secularization', in L. Woodhead, P. Fletcher, H. Kawanami and D. Smith (eds.), *Religions in the Modern World* (London: Routledge, 2002), pp. 293-94.

Bermann, K., 'The House Behind', in Nast and Pile (eds.), *Places through the Body*, pp. 165-80.

Berquist, J.L., 'Critical Spatiality and the Uses of Theory' (paper delivered at the AAR/SBL Annual Meeting, 2002), available at <http://www.cwru.edu/affil/GAIR/papers/>.

—'Theories of Space and Construction of the Ancient World' (unpublished paper delivered at the AAR/SBL Annual Meeting, 1999), available at <http://www.cwru.edu/affil/GAIR/papers/>.

Beyer, P., *Religion and Globalization* (London, Thousand Oaks, New Delhi: Sage, 1994).

Bhabha, H., *The Location of Culture* (London and New York: Routledge, 1994).

Bharati, A., *The Tantric Tradition* (New York: Samuel Weiser, rev. edn, 1975 [first published 1965]).

Bhardwaj, S., *Hindu Places of Pilgrimage in India: A Study in Cultural Geography* (Berkeley: University of California Press, 1973).

Bhargava, R., 'Introduction', in *idem* (ed.), *Secularism and Its Critics*, pp. 1-28.

Bhargava, R. (ed.), *Secularism and Its Critics* (New Delhi: Oxford University Press, 1998).

Bird, J., B. Curtis, T. Putnam, G. Robertson and L. Tickner (eds.), *Mapping the Futures: Local Cultures, Global Change* (Futures, New Perspectives for Cultural Analysis; London and New York: Routledge, 1993).

Blond, P., 'Introduction', in Blond (ed.), *Post-Secular Philosophy*, pp. 1-66.

Blond, P. (ed.), *Post-Secular Philosophy: Between Philosophy and Theology* (London and New York: Routledge, 1998).

Bloom, I., J.P. Martin and W.L. Proudfoot (eds.), *Religious Diversity and Human Rights* (New York: Columbia University Press, 1996).

Bloul, R., 'Engendering Muslim Identities: Deterritorialization and the Ethnicization Process in France', in Daly Metcalf (ed.), *Making Muslim Space*, pp. 234-50.

Blum, V., and H. Nast, 'Where's the Difference? The Heterosexualization of Alterity in Henri Lefebvre and Jacques Lacan', *Environment and Planning D: Society and Space* 14 (1996), pp. 559-80.

Bossy, J., *Christianity in the West 1400–1700* (Oxford and New York: Oxford University Press, 1985).

—'Some Elementary Forms of Durkheim', *Past and Present* 95 (1982), pp. 3-18.

Bourdieu, P., *The Logic of Practice* (Cambridge: Polity, 1990).

Bourdieu, P., and L. Wacquant, *An Invitation to Reflexive Sociology* (Cambridge: Polity, 1992).

Bowman, G., 'Nationalising the Sacred: Shrines and Shifting Identities in the Israeli-Occupied Territories', *Man* 28 (1993), pp. 431-60.

Boyd, T.W., 'Is Spirituality Possible Without Religion? A Query for the Postmodern Era', in A.W. Astell (ed.), *Divine Representations: Postmodernism and Spirituality* (New York: Paulist Press, 1994), pp. 83-101.

Boyer, P., *Religion Explained: The Human Instincts that Fashion Gods, Spirits and Ancestors* (London: William Heinnemann, 2001).

Brah, A., *Cartographies of Diaspora: Contesting Identities* (London and New York: Routledge, 1996).

Brenner, N., and S. Elden, 'Henri Lefebvre in Contexts: An Introduction', *Antipode* 33.5 (2001), pp. 763-68.

Brereton, J.P., 'Sacred Space', in Eliade (ed.), *The Encyclopedia of Religion*, XII, pp. 526-35.

Brewer's Dictionary of Phrase and Fable (London: Cassell, centenary edn, 1970 [1870]).

Briggs, R., *Witches and Neighbours: The Social and Cultural Context of European Witchcraft* (London: Fontana Press, 1996).

Brooks, D.R., *Auspicious Wisdom: The Texts and Traditions of Śrīvidyā Śākta Tantrism in South India* (Albany: State University of New York Press, 1992).

—'The Ocean of the Heart: Selections from the *Kulānava Tantra*', in White (ed.), *Tantra in Practice*, pp. 347-60.

Bruce, S., *God is Dead: Secularization in the West* (Oxford and Malden, MA: Basil Blackwell, 2002).

Budd, S., *Varieties of Unbelief: Atheists and Agnostics in English Society, 1850–1960* (London: Heinemann, 1977).

Bunt, G., *Virtually Islamic: Computer-Mediated Communications and Cyber Islamic Environments* (Cardiff: University of Cardiff Press, 2000).

Burckhardt Qureshi, R., 'Transcending Space: Recitation and Community among South Asian Muslims in Canada', in Daly Metcalf (ed.), *Making Muslim Space*, pp. 46-64.

Burnside, C.E., 'The Left Hand of the Sacred', *Method and Theory in the Study of Religion* 3 (1991), pp. 3-9.

Butler, J., *Gender Trouble: Feminism and the Subversion of Identity* (New York and London: Routledge, 1990).

Butler, R., and H. Parr (eds.), *Mind and Body Spaces: Geographies of Illness, Impairment and Disability* (London: Routledge, 1999).

Büttner, M., 'Religion and Geography: Impulses for a New Dialogue between *Religionswissenschaftlern* and Geography', *Numen* 21 (1974), pp. 165-96.

— 'Survey Article on the History and Philosophy of the Geography of Religion in Germany', *Religion* 10.2 (1980), pp. 86-119.

Byatt, A.S., *Angels and Insects* (London: Vintage, 1993).

Caglar, A., 'Hyphenated Identities and the Limits of Culture', in T. Modood and P. Werbner (eds.), *The Politics of Multiculturalism in the New Europe: Racism, Identity and Community* (London: Zed Books, 1997), pp. 169-85.

Capra, F., *The Hidden Connections: A Science for Sustainable Living* (London: Flamingo, 2003).

Caputo, J.D., *On Religion* (London and New York: Routledge, 2001).

Caputo, J.D. (ed.), *The Religious* (Malden, MA, and Oxford: Basil Blackwell, 2002).

Carens, J.H., and M.S. Williams, 'Muslim Minorities in Liberal Democracies: The Politics of Misrecognition', in Bhargava (ed.), *Secularism and Its Critics*, pp. 137-76.

Carrette, J.R., *Foucault and Religion: Spiritual Corporality and Political Spirituality* (London and New York: Routledge, 2000).

— 'Foucault, Strategic Knowledge and the Study of Religion: A Response to McCutcheon, Fitzgerald, King, and Alles' (Review Symposium on Jeremy Carrette's *Foucault and Religion* and *Religion and Culture*), *Culture and Religion* 2.1 (2001), pp. 127-40.

Carrette, J.R. (ed.), *Religion and Culture: Michel Foucault* (New York: Routledge, 1999).

Carrette, J.R., and R. King, *Selling Spirituality: The Silent Takeover of Religion* (London and New York: Routledge, 2004).

Casey, E.S., *The Fate of Place: A Philosophical Enquiry* (Berkeley: University of California Press, 1997).

— 'How to Get from Space to Place in a Fairly Short Stretch of Time: Phenomenological Prolegomena', in S. Feld and K.H. Basso (eds.), *Senses of Place* (Santa Fe: School of American Research Press, 1996), pp. 13-52.

Castells, M., *The Informational City* (Oxford: Basil Blackwell, 1989).

— *The Rise of the Network Society* (Cambridge, MA, and Oxford: Basil Blackwell, 1996).

Certeau, M. de, *The Practice of Everyday Life* (Berkeley: University of California Press, 1984).

Chakrabarty, D., 'Postcoloniality and the Artifice of History: Who Speaks for "Indian Pasts"?', *Representations* 37 (1992), pp. 1-26.

Chelhod, J., 'A Contribution to the Problem of the Pre-Eminence of the Right, Based upon Arabic Evidence', in Needham (ed.), *Right and Left*, pp. 239-62.

Chidester, D., and E.T. Linenthal, 'Introduction', in Chidester and Linenthal (eds.), *American Sacred Space*, pp. 1-42.

Chidester, D., and E.T. Linenthal (eds.), *American Sacred Space* (Bloomington and Indianapolis: Indiana University Press, 1995).

Child, A.L., 'Transformative Bodies, Communication, Emotions, and Illumination in Tantric Buddhism' (PhD thesis, University of Leeds, 2003).

Chivallon, C., 'Religion as Space for the Expression of Caribbean Identity in the United Kingdom', *Environment and Planning D: Society and Space* 19 (2001), pp. 461-83.

Christ, C., *Rebirth of the Goddess: Finding Meaning in Feminist Spirituality* (Reading, MA: Addison-Wesley, 1997).

The Church at Gun Hill, *The Broad and the Narrow Way (Matthew 7:13-14)*, <http://www.gunhill.org.uk/opendoor/eternal/eternal.htm> (accessed 23 March 2003).

Clark, S., *Thinking with Demons: Witchcraft in Early Modern Europe* (Oxford: Clarendon Press, 1997).

Coleman, S., *The Globalisation of Charismatic Christianity: Spreading the Gospel of Prosperity* (Cambridge: Cambridge University Press, 2000).

Coleman, S., and J. Eade (ed.), *Reframing Pilgrimage: Cultures in Motion* (London and New York: Routledge, 2004).

Conkle, D.O., 'Secular Fundamentalism, Religious Fundamentalism, and the Search for Truth in Contemporary America', *Journal of Law and Religion* 12.2 (1995–96), pp. 337-70.

Cooper, A., 'New Directions in the Geography of Religion', *Area* 24 (1992), pp. 123-29.

Coward, H., J. Hinnells and R.B. Williams (eds.), *The South Asian Diaspora in Great Britain, Canada, and the United States* (Albany: State University of New York Press, 2000).

Crabtree, Vexen, *About Vexen*, <http://www.vexen.co.uk/vexen/index.html>)accessed 14 November 2003).

— *The Bane of Monotheism*, <http://www.vexen.co.uk/religion/index.html> (accessed 14 November 2003).

—'A Description of Satanism', <http://www.dpjs.co.uk/modern.html#REL2> (accessed 14 November 2003).

— *Description, Philosophy and Justification of Satanism: Personal Essay Collection by Vexen Crabtree*, <http://www.dpjs.co.uk/> ([first posted 24 February 2002] accessed 20 October 2002).

— *Holy Shit*, <http://www.vexen.co.uk/holyshit/index.html> (accessed 14 November 2003).

— *The Meaning and Usage of the Term LHP in the West*, <www.dpjs.co.uk/lefthandpath.html> (accessed 20 October 2002).

Crang, M., and N. Thrift (eds.), *Thinking Space* (London and New York: Routledge, 2000).

Cupitt, D., *After God: The Future of Religion* (London: Phoenix Orion, 1997).

Dalrymple, T., *So Little Done: The Testament of a Serial Killer* (London: Andre Deutsch, 1995).

Daly, M., *Beyond God the Father* (London: The Women's Press, 1986 [first published 1973]).

— *Outercourse: The Dedazzling Voyage* (London: The Women's Press, 1992).

Daly, M., with J. Caputi, *Websters' First New Intergalactic Wickedary of the English Language* (London: The Women's Press, 1987).

Daly Metcalf, B., 'Introduction: Sacred Words, Sanctioned Practice, New Communities', in Daly Metcalf (ed.), *Making Muslim Space*, pp. 1-30.

— (trans. with commentary) *Perfecting Women: Maulana Ashraf 'Ali Thanawi's Bihisti Zewar* (Berkeley: University of California Press, 1990).

Daly Metcalf, B. (ed.), *Making Muslim Space in North America and Europe* (Comparative Studies on Muslim Societies, 22; Berkeley: University of California Press, 1996).

Davie, G., 'From Obligation to Consumption: Patterns of Religion in Northern Europe at the Start of the 21st Century', in R. Friedl and M. Schneuwly Purdie (eds.), *L'Europe des Religions: Eléments d'analyse des champs religieux europeéns* (Bern: Peter Lang, 2004), pp. 95-114.

— *Religion in Britain Since 1945: Believing Without Belonging* (Oxford: Basil Blackwell, 1994).

— *Religion in Modern Europe: A Memory Mutates* (Oxford: Oxford University Press, 2000).

Dextera Domini: The Declaration of the Pastoral Care of Left-Handed Persons, <http://www.users.csbsju.edu/~eknuth/rehu/dex-text.html> ([first posted 1994] accessed 10 January 2003).

Donaldson, L.E., and Kwok Pui-Lan (eds.), *Postcolonialism, Feminism, and Religious Discourse* (New York and London: Routledge, 2002).

Doniger, W., 'Post-Modern and -Colonial -Structural Comparisons', in Patton and Ray (eds.), *A Magic Still Dwells*, pp. 63-76.

Douglas, M., *Purity and Danger: An Analysis of Concepts of Pollution and Taboo* (Harmondsworth: Pelican Books, 1970 [first published 1966]).

Duerr, H.P., *Dreamtime: Concerning the Boundary Between Wilderness and Civilization* (New York: Basil Blackwell, 1985).

Duffy, E., *The Stripping of the Altars: Traditional Religion in England, c. 1400–1580* (New Haven and London: Yale University Press, 1992).

Dumont, L., 'The Anthropological Community and Ideology', *Social Science Information* 18.6 (1979), pp. 785-817.

— 'Caste, Racism and Stratification', first published in French in *Cahiers Internationaux de Sociologie* 29 (1960), pp. 91-112 (reprinted in English as an appendix in Dumont, *Homo Hierarchicus*, pp. 287-307).

— *Homo Hierarchicus: The Caste System and its Implications* (London: Paladin, 1972 [French edn 1966]).

Durkheim, É., *The Elementary Forms of the Religious Life* (London: George Allen & Unwin, 1976 [French edn 1912]).

Dürrschmidt, J., 'The Delinking of Locale and Milieu: On the Situatedness of Extended Milieux in a Global Environment', in Eade (ed.), *Living the Global City*, pp. 56-72.

Dwyer, C., 'Contradictions of Community: Questions of Identity for Young British Muslim Women', *Environment and Planning A* 31 (1999), pp. 53-68.

— 'Veiled Meanings: Young British Muslim Women and the Negotiation of Differences', *Gender, Place and Culture* 6.1 (1999), pp. 5-26.

Dwyer, R., 'The Swaminarayan Movement', in Knut A. Jacobsen and P. Pratap Kumar (eds.), *South Asians in the Diaspora: Histories and Religious Traditions* (Leiden and Boston: E.J. Brill, 2004), pp. 180-99.

Eade, J., 'Nationalism, Community, and the Islamization of Space in London', in Daly Metcalf (ed.), *Making Muslim Space*, pp. 217-33.

Eade, J. (ed.), *Living the Global City: Globalization as a Local Process* (London and New York: Routledge, 1997).

Eade, J., and M. Sallnow (eds.), *Contesting the Sacred: The Anthropology of Christian Pilgrimage* (London: Routledge, 1991).

Eck, D.L., *Banaras: City of Light* (Princeton: Princeton University Press, 1982).

— *A New Religious America: How a 'Christian Country' has Become the World's Most Religiously Diverse Nation* (San Francisco: HarperSanFrancisco, 2001).

Edge, P.W., and G. Harvey (eds.), *Law and Religion in Contemporary Society: Communities, Individualism and the State* (Aldershot and Burlington, VT: Ashgate, 2000).

El Guindi, F., *Veil: Modesty, Privacy, and Resistance* (Oxford: Berg, 1999).

Elden, S., 'Politics, Philosophy, Geography: Henri Lefebvre in Recent Anglo-American Scholarship', *Antipode* 33.5 (2001), pp. 809-25.

— *Understanding Henri Lefebvre: Theory and the Possible* (London and New York: Continuum, 2004).

Eliade, M., *The Sacred and the Profane: The Nature of Religion* (San Diego: Harcourt Brace Jovanovitch, 1959 [French edn 1957]).

— *Yoga: Immortality and Freedom* (Princeton: Princeton University Press, 2nd edn, 1969).

Eliade, M. (ed.), *The Encyclopedia of Religion* (16 vols.; New York: Macmillan, 1987).

Elias, N., *The Civilising Process: Sociogenetic and Psychogenetic Investigations* (trans. Edmund Jephcott; Oxford: Basil Blackwell, rev. edn, 2000 [1939]).

Evans, M.D., 'Religion, Law and Human Rights: Locating the Debate', in Edge and Harvey (eds.), *Law and Religion*, pp. 177-97.

Featherstone, M., *Undoing Culture: Globalization, Postmodernism, and Identity* (London, Thousand Oaks, New Delhi: Sage, 1995).

Featherstone, M. (ed.), *Global Culture: Nationalism, Globalization and Modernity* (London, Thousand Oaks, New Delhi: Sage, 1990).

Fenn, R.K., *Beyond Idols: The Shape of a Secular Society* (Oxford: Oxford University Press, 2001).

Finnegan, R., *Communicating: The Multiple Modes of Human Interconnection* (London and New York: Routledge, 2002).

Fischer, M.M.J., *Iran: From Religious Dispute to Revolution* (Cambridge, MA, and London: Harvard University Press, 1980).

Fitzgerald, T., 'Hinduism and the "World Religion" Fallacy', *Religion* 20 (1990), pp. 101-18.

— *The Ideology of Religious Studies* (New York and Oxford: Oxford University Press, 2000).

— 'Problematising Discourses on Religion' (Review Symposium on Jeremy Carrette's *Foucault and Religion* and *Religion and Culture*), *Culture and Religion* 2.1 (2001), pp. 103-12.

— 'Religious Studies as Cultural Studies: A Philosophical and Anthropological Critique of the Concept of Religion', *Diskus: A Disembodied Journal of Religion* 3.1 (1995), pp. 35-47, also available at <http://www.uni-marburg.de/religionswissenschaft/journals/diskus>.

Flood, G., *Beyond Phenomenology: Rethinking the Study of Religion* (London and New York: Cassell, 1999).

Fog Olwig, K., and K. Hastrup (eds.), *Siting Culture: The Shifting Anthropological Object* (London and New York: Routledge, 1997).

Forth, G., 'Right and Left as a Hierarchical Opposition: Reflections on Eastern Sumbanese Hairstyles', in Barnes, de Coppet and Parkin (eds.), *Contexts and Levels*, pp. 103-16.

Foucault, M., *Discipline and Punish: The Birth of the Prison* (London: Penguin, 1977 [French edn 1975]).

— 'The Eye of Power: Conversation with J.-P. Barou and M. Perrot', in Gordon (ed.), *Power/Knowledge*, pp. 146-65.

— 'Of Other Spaces' (Des espaces autres)', *Diacritics* 16.1 (1986), pp. 22-27.

— *The Order of Things: An Archaeology of the Human Sciences* (London: Tavistock, 1970 [French edn 1966]).

— 'Questions on Geography: Interview with the Editors of *Hérodote*', in Gordon (ed.), *Power/Knowledge*, pp. 63-77.

— 'Space, Knowledge and Power', in Paul Rabinow (ed.), *The Foucault Reader: An Introduction to Foucault's Thought* (London: Penguin, 1991), pp. 239-56.

— 'The Subject and Power', in H.L. Dreyfus and P. Rabinow (eds.), *Michel Foucault: Beyond Structuralism and Hermeneutics* (Chicago: University of Chicago Press, 2nd edn, 1983), pp. 208-26.

— 'Truth and Power', in Paul Rabinow (ed.), *The Foucault Reader: An Introduction to Foucault's Thought* (London: Penguin, 1984), pp. 51-75, originally in Gordon (ed.), *Power/Knowledge*, pp. 109-33.

— *The Use of Pleasure: The History of Sexuality*, I (London: Penguin, 1992 [French edn 1984]).

— *The Will to Knowledge: The History of Sexuality*, II (London: Penguin, 1990 French edn 1976]).

Franks, M., 'Crossing the Borders of Whiteness? White Muslim Women Who Wear the *Hijab* in Britain Today', *Ethnic and Racial Studies* 23.5 (2000), pp. 917-29.

—*Women and Revivalism in the West: Choosing 'Fundamentalism' in a Liberal Democracy* (Basingstoke and New York: Palgrave, 2001).

Frequently Asked Questions for Left Handers, archived on 9 January 2001, <http://www.cs.uu. nl/wais/html/na-dir/lefty-faq.html> (accessed 17 January 2003).

Freud, S., *The Interpretation of Dreams* (London: George Allen & Unwin, 1954).

Gale, R., and S. Naylor, 'Religion, Planning and the City: The Spatial Politics of Ethnic Minority Expression in British Cities and Towns', *Ethnicities* 2 (2002), pp. 387-409.

Gauchet, M., *The Disenchantment of the World: A Political History of Religion* (Princeton: Princeton University Press, 1997).

Giddens, A., *The Consequences of Modernity* (Cambridge: Polity, 1990).

—*The Constitution of Society* (Cambridge: Polity, 1984).

—*Émile Durkheim: Selected Writings* (trans. Anthony Giddens; Cambridge: Cambridge University Press, 1972).

—*Modernity and Self-Identity* (Cambridge: Polity, 1991).

Gilbert, A., *The Making of Post-Christian Britain* (London and New York: Longman, 1980).

Gilliat-Ray, S., 'Civic Religion in England: Traditions and Transformations', *Journal of Contemporary Religion* 14.2 (1999), pp. 233-44.

Gilmore, Magister P.H., 'The Myth of the "Satanic Community" and Other Virtual Delusions', <http://www.churchofsatan.com> (accessed 17 January 2003).

Goldenberg, N., *Resurrecting the Body: Feminism, Religion and Psychoanalysis* (New York: Crossroad, 1990).

Goodwin, B., 'Why Groovy Hearts Lean Left', *The Times Higher Education Supplement* (25 April 2003), p. 27.

Gordon, C. (ed.), *Power/Knowledge: Selected Interviews and Other Writings, 1972–77, by Michel Foucault* (Hemel Hempstead, Herts.: Harvester Press, 1980)

Gorringe, T., *A Theology of the Built Environment: Justice, Empowerment, Redemption* (Cambridge: Cambridge University Press, 2002).

Goudriaan, T., 'Tantrism in History', in Gupta, Hoens and Goudriaan, *Hindu Tantrism*, pp. 13-46.

Gregory, D., and J. Urry (eds.), *Social Relations and Spatial Structures* (Basingstoke: Macmillan, 1985).

Gross, R.M., *Buddhism After Patriarchy: A Feminist History, Analysis, and Reconstruction of Buddhism* (Albany: State University of New York Press, 1993).

Grosz, E., *Space, Time, and Perversion* (New York and London: Routledge, 1995).

—'Women, *chora*, Dwelling', in S. Watson and K. Gibson (eds.), *Postmodern Cities and Spaces* (Cambridge, MA, and Oxford: Basil Blackwell, 1995), pp. 47-58.

Guillaume, A., *The Traditions of Islam* (Oxford: Clarendon Press, 1924).

Gupta, A., and J. Ferguson, 'Discipline and Practice: "The Field" as Site, Method, and Location in Anthropology', in A. Gupta and J. Ferguson (eds.), *Anthropological Locations: Boundaries and Grounds of a Field Science* (Berkeley: University of California Press, 1997), pp. 1-40.

Gupta, S., 'Tantric sādhanā: pūjā', in Gupta, Hoens and Goudriaan, *Hindu Tantrism*, pp. 121-62.

Gupta, S., D.J. Hoens and T. Goudriaan, *Hindu Tantrism* (Leiden: E.J. Brill, 1979).

Haar, G. ter (ed.), *Strangers and Sojourners: Religious Communities in the Diaspora* (Leuven: Peeters, 1998).

Haberman, D.L., *Journey Through the Twelve Forests: An Encounter with Krishna* (New York and Oxford: Oxford University Press, 1994).

Hadden, J.K., and D.E. Cowan (eds.), *Religion on the Internet: Research Prospects and Promises* (Amsterdam, London, New York: JAI/Elsevier Science, 2000).

Haider, G., 'Muslim Space and the Practice of Architecture: A Personal Odyssey', in Daly
    Metcalf (ed.), *Making Muslim Space*, pp. 31-45.
Hall, S., 'The Question of Cultural Identity', in S. Hall, D. Held and A. McGrew (eds.),
    Modernity and Its Futures (Cambridge: Polity; Milton Keynes: Open University Press,
    1992), pp. 300-11.
Hammond, P.E. (ed.), *The Sacred in a Secular Age: Toward Revision in the Scientific Study of
    Religion* (Berkeley: University of California Press, 1985).
Hampson, D., *After Christianity* (London: SCM Press, 1996).
Hanegraaff, W., *New Age Religion and Western Culture: Esotericism in the Mirror of Secular
    Thought* (Leiden: E.J. Brill, 1996).
—'New Age Spiritualities as Secular Religion: A Historian's Perspective', *Social Compass*
    46.2 (1999), pp. 145-60.
Hannerz, U., *Transcontinental Connections* (London and New York: Routledge, 1996).
Haramullah, 'Black Magick and the Left Hand Path', <http://www.luckymojo.com/
    avidyana/shaitan/blkmgk.html> [first posted 1993], accessed 2 November 2003.
Harrison, P., *'Religion' and the Religions in the English Enlightenment* (Cambridge: Cambridge
    University Press, 1990).
Harvey, D., 'Afterword', in Henri Lefebvre, *The Production of Space* (Oxford and Cambridge
    MA: Basil Blackwell, 1991), pp. 425-31.
—*The Condition of Postmodernity* (Oxford: Basil Blackwell, 1990).
—'From Space to Place and Back Again: Reflections on the Condition of Postmodernity', in
    Bird, Curtis, Putnam, Robertson and Tickner (eds.), *Mapping the Futures*, pp. 3-29.
—*Justice, Nature, and the Geography of Difference* (Oxford: Basil Blackwell, 1996).
Harvey, G., 'Satanism in Britain Today', *Journal of Contemporary Religion* 10 (1995), pp. 283-96.
Heelas, P., 'Introduction on Differentiation and Dedifferentiation', in *idem* (ed.), with David
    Martin and Paul Morris, *Religion, Modernity, and Postmodernity* (Oxford: Basil Black-
    well, 1998).
Hegarty, P., 'Undelivered: The Space/Time of the Sacred in Bataille and Benjamin', *Economy
    and Society* 32.1 (2003), pp. 101-18.
Heidegger, M., 'Building, Dwelling, Thinking' (1951), in David Farrell Krell (ed.), *Martin
    Heidegger: Basic Writings* (London: Routledge, rev. edn, 1993), pp. 343-63.
Henkel, R., 'Comparing the Religious Landscapes of the United States and Germany'
    (unpublished paper presented at the University of Connecticut, March 2001).
—'Der Arbeitskreis Religionsgeographie in der Deutschen Gesellschaft für Geographie—
    Bilanz 1983 bis 1998', in H. Karrasch (ed.), 'Geographie: Tradition and Forschritt',
    Heidelberger Geographische Gesellschaft 12 (2000), pp. 269-72.
Hertz, R., 'The Pre-Eminence of the Right Hand: A Study in Religious Polarity', in Needham
    (ed.), *Right and Left*, pp. 3-31. Originally published as 'La prééminence de la main
    droite: étude sur la polarité religieuse', *Revue Philosophique* 68 (1909), pp. 553-80.
Hervieu-Léger, D., *Religion as a Chain of Memory* (Cambridge: Polity, 2000).
Hetherington, K., *Expressions of Identity: Space, Performance, Politics* (London, Thousand
    Oaks, New Delhi: Sage, 1998).
Hine, P., 'Black Magic and the Left-Hand Path', <http://www.phhine.ndirect.co.uk/
    archives/ess_bmlhp.htm> (accessed 17 January 2003).
Hobbes, T., *Leviathan* (Glasgow: Collins/Fontana, 1962 [first published 1651]).
Holder, M.K., *The World of Sinister Subterfuge*, <http://www.indiana.edu/~primate/left.
    html> (accessed 10 January 2003).
Holloway, J., and O. Valins, 'Placing Religion and Spirituality in Geography', *Social and
    Cultural Geography* 3.1 (2002), pp. 5-9.
The Holy Qur'an: Text Translation and Commentary, Yusuf Ali (Brentwood, MD: Amana
    Corporation, 1983).

hooks, b., *Yearning: Race, Gender, and Cultural Politics* (Boston: Southend Press, 1990).

Hopkins, E.W. (ed.), *Hindu Polity: The Ordinances of Manu* (Ludhiana: Kalyani Publishers, 1972 [first published 1884]).

Idinopulos, T.A., and E.A. Yonan (eds.), *The Sacred and its Scholars: Comparative Methodologies for the Study of Primary Religious Data* (Leiden: E.J. Brill, 1996).

Inden, R., *Imagining India* (Oxford: Basil Blackwell, 1990).

Irigaray, L., 'Divine Women', in Joy, O'Grady and Poxon (eds.), *French Feminists on Religion: A Reader*, pp. 40-48.

— *An Ethics of Sexual Difference* (Ithaca, NY: Cornell University Press, 1993).

— *Sexes and Genealogies* (New York: Columbia University Press, 1993 [French edn 1987]).

Isaac, E., 'Religious Geography and the Geography of Religions', *Man and the Earth* (Series in Earth Sciences, 3; Boulder, CO; University of Colorado Press, 1960), pp. 1-14.

Jackson, P., 'Rematerializing Social and Cultural Geography', *Social and Cultural Geography* 1.1 (2000), pp. 9-14.

Jackson, R., *Religious Education: An Interpretive Approach* (London: Hodder & Stoughton, 1997).

Jacobus, J.M., Jr, 'USA', in *Encyclopedia of Modern Architecture* (London: Thames & Hudson, 1963), pp. 301-10.

James, W., *The Varieties of Religious Experience* (London: Penguin, 1982 [first published 1902]).

Jameson, F., *Postmodernism, Or the Cultural Logic of Late Capitalism* (London: Verso, 1991).

Jantzen, G., *Becoming Divine: Towards a Feminist Philosophy of Religion* (Manchester: Manchester University Press, 1998), pp. 45-46.

Jenkins, T., *Religion in English Everyday Life: An Ethnographic Approach* (New York and Oxford: Berghahn Books, 1999).

Jensen, T., and M. Rothstein (eds.), *Secular Theories on Religion: Current Perspectives* (Copenhagen: Museum Tusculanum Press, 2000).

Jernigan, K., 'Blindness — A Left-Handed Dissertation', <http://www.empowermentzone.com/lefthand.txt> (accessed 2 November 2003).

Johnson, M., *The Body in the Mind: The Bodily Basis of Meaning, Imagination and Reason* (Chicago and London: Chicago University Press, 1987).

Jordy, W.H., 'Mies van der Rohe', in *Encyclopedia of Modern Architecture* (London: Thames & Hudson, 1963), pp. 198-99.

Joy, M., K. O'Grady and J.L. Poxon (eds.), *French Feminists on Religion: A Reader* (London and New York: Routledge, 2002).

Jung, C.G., *The Practice of Psychotherapy*, in *Collected Works* (20 vols.; London: Routledge & Kegan Paul, 1954).

Kama Sutra Temple, *Tantra: The Left Hand Path of Love*, <http://www.tantra.org/lefthand.html> (accessed 2 November 2003).

Kant, I., 'Concerning the Ultimate Foundation of the Differentiation of Regions in Space' [1768], in G.B. Kerferd and D.E. Walford (eds.), *Kant: Selected Pre-Critical Writings and Correspondence with Beck* (Manchester: Manchester University Press, 1968), pp. 36-43.

Karaflogka, A., *Religion and Cyberspace* (London: Equinox, forthcoming).

Katz, J.N., *Love Stories: Sex Between Men Before Homosexuality* (Chicago: University of Chicago Press, 2001).

Kearnes, M.B., 'Geographies that Matter — The Rhetorical Deployment of Physicality', *Social and Cultural Geography* 4.2 (2003), pp. 139-52.

Keith, M., and S. Pile, 'Introduction, Part 2: The Place of Politics', in Keith and Pile (eds.), *Place and the Politics of Identity*, pp. 22-40.

Keith, M., and S. Pile (eds.), *Place and the Politics of Identity* (London: Routledge, 1993).

Keller, M., *The Hammer and the Flute: Women, Power, and Spirit Possession* (Baltimore and London: The Johns Hopkins University Press, 2002).

Kennedy, A., 'Place and Space in an Age of Immanence', in Knott, Ward, Mason and Willmer (eds.), *Religion and Locality*, n.p. (forthcoming).

Kepel, G., *Allah in the West : Islamic Movements in America and Europe* (Cambridge: Polity, 1997).

—*The Revenge of God* (Cambridge: Polity, 1994).

Kerferd, G.B., and D.E. Walford (translation and introduction), *Kant: Selected Pre-Critical Writings and Correspondence with Beck* (Manchester: Manchester University Press; New York: Barnes & Noble, 1968).

Kieckhefer, R., *Forbidden Rites: A Necromancer's Manual of the Fifteenth Century* (Stroud: Sutton Publishing, 1997).

—'The Specific Rationality of Medieval Magic', *American Historical Review* 99 (1994), pp. 813-36.

King, R., *Orientalism and Religion: Postcolonial Theory, India and 'The Mystic East'* (London and New York: Routledge, 1999).

King, U. (ed.), *Religion and Gender* (Oxford: Basil Blackwell, 1995).

—*Women and Spirituality* (London, Macmillan, 2nd edn, 1993).

Kinsley, D.R., *The Sword and the Flute* (Berkeley: University of California Press, 1975).

—*Tantric Visions of the Divine Feminine: The Ten Mahāvidyās* (Berkeley: University of California Press, 1997).

Kirkham, G., *History and Explanation of the Picture: The Broad and the Narrow Way* (London: Morgan & Scott, 1886; reprinted by Peter N. Millward, 1997).

Knott, K., 'Britain's Changing Religious Landscape: Drowning or Waving?', *Berichte zur deutschen Landeskunde* 78.2 (2004), pp. 213-29.

—'Community and Locality in the Study of Religions', in Jensen and Rothstein (eds.), *Secular Theories on Religion*, pp. 87-105.

—'Hindu Women, Destiny, and *stridharma*', *Religion* 26 (1996), pp. 15-35.

—'Issues in the Study of Religions and Locality', *Method and Theory in the Study of Religion* 10 (1998), pp. 279-90.

—'Notions of Destiny in Women's Self-Construction', *Religion* 28 (1998), pp. 405-11.

—'Religion and Locality: Issues and Methods', in Knott, Ward, Mason and Willmer (eds.), n.p. (forthcoming).

—'The Sense and Nonsense of Community', in Steven Sutcliffe (ed.), *Religion: Empirical Studies* (Aldershot and Burlington, VT: Ashgate, 2004), pp. 67-90.

—'Women Researching, Women Researched: Gender in the Empirical Study of Religion', in U. King (ed.), *Religion and Gender* (Oxford: Basil Blackwell, 1995), pp. 199-218.

Knott, K., K. Ward, A. Mason and H. Willmer (eds.), *Religion and Locality* (Leeds: Community Religions Project, University of Leeds, forthcoming).

Kong, L., 'Geography of Religion: Trends and Prospects', *Progress in Human Geography* 14 (1990), pp. 355-71.

—'Ideological Hegemony and the Political Symbolism of Religious Buildings in Singapore', *Environment and Planning D: Society and Space* 11 (1993), pp. 23-45.

—'Mapping "New" Geographies of Religion: Politics and Poetics in Modernity', *Progress in Human Geography* 25.2 (2001), pp. 211-33.

—'Negotiating Conceptions of "Sacred Space": A Case Study of Religious Buildings in Singapore', *Transactions of the Institute of British Geographers* NS 18 (1993), pp. 342-58.

—'The Politics of Music in Singapore: Moral Panics, Moral Guardians' (paper presented at the Institute of Australian Geographers' Conference, September 1999).

—'Re-Presenting the Religious: Nation, Community and Identity in Museums' (unpublished paper presented at the Royal Geographical Society—Institute of British Geographers Annual Conference, September 2003).

Kramrisch, S., *The Hindu Temple* (2 vols.; Calcutta: University of Calcutta, 1946).

Kristeva, J., *In the Beginning was Love: Psychoanalysis and Faith* (New York: Columbia University Press, 1987 [French edn 1985]).

—'Stabat Mater', in Joy, O'Grady and Poxon (eds.), *French Feminists on Religion*, pp. 114-38.

Lakoff, G., and M. Johnson, *Metaphors We Live By* (Chicago and London: University of Chicago Press, 1980).

—*Philosophy in the Flesh: The Embodied Mind and its Challenge to Western Thought* (New York: Basic Books, 1999).

Lalumière, M.L., R. Blanchard and K.L. Zucher, 'Sexual Orientation and Handedness in Men and Women: A Meta-Analysis', *Psychological Bulletin* 126 (2000), pp. 575-92.

Lane, B.C., *Landscapes of the Sacred: Geography and Narrative in American Spirituality* (New York: Paulist Press, 1988).

LaVey, A., *The Satanic Bible* (New York: Avon Books, 1969).

Lawrence, B.B., 'From Fundamentalism to Fundamentalisms: A Religious Ideology in Multiple Forms', in Heelas (ed.), *Religion, Modernity, and Postmodernity*, pp. 88-101.

Lawson, H., *Closure: A Story of Everything* (New York and London: Routledge, 2001).

—*Reflexivity* (La Salle: Open Court, 1985).

Le Guin, U.K., *The Left Hand of Darkness* (New York: Ace Books, 1969).

Lefebvre, H., *Critique of Everyday Life: Foundations for a Sociology of the Everyday* (London and New York: Verso, 2002 [French edn 1961]).

—*The Production of Space* (Oxford and Cambridge, MA: Basil Blackwell, 1991 [French edn 1974]).

—*The Survival of Capitalism* (London: Allison & Busby, 1976 [French edn 1973]).

The Left Hand: Your Source for Left-Handed Products, <http://thelefthand.com> (accessed 7 April 2003).

'Left-Handedness', http://www.islamicity.com/dialogue/Q325.HTM (accessed 20 October 2002).

Lefthandedness and Homosexuality, http://www.kenyon.edu/Depts/WMNS/Projects/Wmns21/left%20handedness.htm (accessed 2 November 2003).

Lehmann, D., 'Religion and Globalisation', in L. Woodhead, P. Fletcher, H. Kawanawi and D. Smith (eds.), *Religion in the Modern World* (London and New York: Routledge, 2001), pp. 299-315.

Lemert, C.C., and G. Gillan, *Michel Foucault: Social Theory as Transgression* (New York: Columbia University Press, 1982).

Lévi-Strauss, C., 'Do Dual Organisations Exist?', in *idem, Structural Anthropology* (New York: Basic Books, 1963 [French edn 1956]), pp. 132-63.

Lewis, J.R., 'Diabolical Authority: Anton LaVey, *The Satanic Bible* and the Satanist "Tradition"', *Marburg Journal of Religion* 7.1 (2002), available at <http://www.uni-marburg.de/religionswissenschaft/journal/mjr/lewis.pdf>.

Lied, L.I., 'Approaching Heavenly Promised Lands: Jewish Eschatological Geography from Edward W. Soja's Thirdspace Perspective' (paper presented at the European Association for the Study of Religion Conference on Localisation and Globalisation, Bergen, May 2003).

Lloyd, G., 'Right and Left in Greek Philosophy', in Needham (ed.), *Right and Left*, pp. 167-86.

Lorin's Lefthandedness Site, <http://duke.usask.ca/~elias/left/>.

Lyon, D., *Jesus in Disneyland: Religion in Postmodern Times* (Cambridge: Polity, 2000).

Lyotard, J.F., *The Postmodern Condition* (Manchester: Manchester University Press, 1984).

Macrae, D.G., 'The Body and Social Metaphor', in J. Benthall and T. Polhemus (eds.), *The Body as a Medium of Expression* (London: Allen Lane, 1975), pp. 59-73.

Marglin, F.A., 'Refining the Body: Transformative Emotion in Ritual Dance', in O.M. Lynch (ed.), *Divine Passions: The Social Construction of Emotion in India* (Berkeley: University of California Press, 1990), pp. 212-36.

Martikainen, T., *Immigrant Religions in Local Society: Historical and Contemporary Perspectives in the City of Turku* (Åbo: Åbo Akademi University Press, 2004).

Martin, D., *A General Theory of Secularization* (Oxford: Basil Blackwell, 1978),

—'Some Utopian Aspects of the Concept of Secularisation', *International Yearbook for the Sociology of Religion* 2 (1966), pp. 86-96.

Mason, A., 'Jenkinson and Southcott', in Alistair Mason (ed.), *Religion in Leeds* (Stroud: Alan Sutton, 1994), pp. 141-60.

Massey, D., 'Politics and Space/Time', in Keith and Pile (eds.), *Place and the Politics of Identity*, pp. 141-61.

—'Power-Geometry and a Progressive Sense of Place', in Bird, Curtis, Putnam, Robertson and Tickner (eds.), *Mapping the Futures*, pp. 59-69.

— *Space, Place and Gender* (Cambridge: Polity, 1994).

Massey, D., and P. Jess (eds.), *A Place in the World? Places, Cultures and Globalization* (London: Oxford University Press and The Open University, 1995).

Mauss, M., 'Techniques of the Body', *Economy and Society* 2 (1973), pp. 70-88.

Maybury-Lewis, D., 'The Quest for Harmony', in Maybury-Lewis and Almagor (eds.), *The Attraction of Opposites*, pp. 1-17.

Maybury-Lewis, D., and Uri Almagor (eds.), *The Attraction of Opposites: Thought and Society in the Dualistic Mode* (Ann Arbor: University of Michigan Press, 1989).

Mazumdar, S., and S. Mazumdar, 'Women's Significant Spaces: Religion, Space and Community', *Journal of Environmental Psychology* 19 (1999), pp. 159-70.

McClintock, A., *Imperial Leather: Race, Gender and Sexuality in the Colonial Context* (New York: Routledge, 1995).

McCutcheon, R.T., *The Discipline of Religion: Structure, Meaning, Rhetoric* (London and New York: Routledge, 2003).

—'The Economics of Spiritual Luxury: The Glittering Lobby and the Parliament of Religions', *Journal of Contemporary Religion* 13.1 (1998), pp. 51-64.

— *Manufacturing Religion: The Discourse on Sui Generis Religion and the Politics of Nostalgia* (New York and Oxford: Oxford University Press, 1997).

McCutcheon, R.T. (ed.), *The Insider/Outsider Problem in the Study of Religion: A Reader* (London and New York: Cassell, 1999).

McDaniel, J., 'Interviews with a Tantric Kālī Priest: Feeding Skulls in the Town of Sacrifice', in White (ed.), *Tantra in Practice*, pp. 72-80.

— *The Madness of the Saints: Ecstatic Religion in Bengal* (Chicago and London: University of Chicago Press, 1989).

McDannell, C., *Material Christianity: Religion and Popular Culture in America* (New Haven and London: Yale University Press, 1995).

McDonald, M.M. (ed.), *Experiences of Place* (Cambridge, MA: Harvard University Press/ Center for the Study of World Religions, 2003).

McLeod, H., *Religion and the People of Western Europe 1789–1989* (Oxford and New York: Oxford University Press, 2nd edn, 1997).

McManus, C., *Hypernotes*, <http://www.righthandlefthand.com>.

— *Right Hand, Left Hand: The Origins of Asymmetry in Brains, Bodies, Atoms and Cultures* (London: Weidenfeld & Nicolson, 2002).

Mellor, P.A., 'Protestant Buddhism? The Cultural Translation of Buddhism in England', *Religion* 21 (1991), pp. 73-92.

Mellor, P.A., and C. Shilling, *Reforming the Body: Religion, Community and Modernity* (London, Thousand Oaks, New Delhi: Sage, 1997).

Melton, G.J., *Encyclopedia of American Religions* (Detroit: Gale Research, 1993), pp. 854-57.

Mernissi, F., *The Veil and the Male Elite* (New York: Addison-Wesley, 1991).

—*Women and Islam: An Historical and Theological Enquiry* (trans. Mary Jo Lakeland; Oxford: Basil Blackwell, 1991).

Merrifield, A., 'Henri Lefebvre: A Socialist in Space', in Crang and Thrift (eds.), *Thinking Space*, pp. 167-82.

— 'Place and Space: A Lefebvrian Reconciliation', *Transactions of the British Institute of Geographers* NS 18 (1993), pp. 516-31.

Millward, P.N., *The Broad and the Narrow Way*, http://picturemaker.safeshopper.com/images/g0zlblt.jpg (accessed 28 March 2003).

Mitchell, K., 'Different Diasporas and the Hype of Hybridity', *Environment and Planning D: Society and Space* 15 (1997), pp. 533-53.

Muller-Ortega, P., *The Triadic Heart of Śiva: Kaula Tantricism of Abhinavagupta in the Non-Dual Shaivism of Kashmir* (Albany: State University of New York Press, 1989).

Murray, M.A., *The Witch-Cult in Western Europe* (New York: Oxford University Press, 1921).

Nast, H.J., and S. Pile (eds.), *Places Through the Body* (London and New York: Routledge, 1998).

Naylor, S., and J. Ryan, 'The Mosque in the Suburbs: Negotiating Religion and Ethnicity in South London', *Social and Cultural Geography* 3 (2002), pp. 39-59.

— 'Tracing the Geographies of Religious Minorities in the UK: Using Surveys and Case-Studies', in Knott, Ward, Mason and Willmer (eds.), *Religion and Locality*, n.p. (forthcoming).

Needham, R. (ed.), *Right and Left: Essays on Dual Symbolic Classification* (Chicago and London: Chicago University Press).

Nesbitt, E., 'Friend in the Field: A Reflexive Approach to Being a Quaker Ethnographer', *Quaker Studies* 4.2 (1999), pp. 82-112.

Nye, M., *Multiculturalism and Minority Religions in Britain: Krishna Consciousness, Religious Freedom, and the Politics of Location* (Richmond: Curzon, 2001).

Oberoi, H.S., *The Construction of Religious Boundaries: Culture, Identity and Diversity in the Sikh Tradition* (Delhi: Oxford University Press, 1994).

The Occult Archive, 'Haramullah', <http://www.beyond-the-illusion.com/files/Occult/Thelema/Haramullah/kathulu_magik> (first posted 14 August 1993 [accessed 11 December 2003]).

Paden, W.E., 'Before "The Sacred" became Theological: Rereading the Durkheimian Legacy', *Method and Theory in the Study of Religion* 3.10 (1991), pp. 10-23.

— *Interpreting the Sacred: Ways of Viewing Religion* (Boston: Beacon Press, 1992).

Paine, C. (ed.), *Godly Things: Museums, Objects and Religion* (London and New York: Leicester University Press, 2000).

Parekh, B., *Rethinking Multiculturalism: Cultural Diversity and Political Theory* (London: Macmillan, 2000).

— 'Some Reflections', *New Community* 20.4 (1994), pp. 603-20.

Park, C., *Sacred Worlds: An Introduction to Geography and Religion* (London and New York: Routledge, 1994).

Parkin, R., *The Dark Side of Humanity: The Work of Robert Hertz and its Legacy* (Amsterdam: Harwood Academic Publishers, 1996).

Patton, K.C., and B.C. Ray (eds.), *A Magic Still Dwells: Comparative Religion in the Postmodern Age* (Berkeley: University of California Press, 2000).

Peach, C., 'Social Geography: New Religions and Ethnoburbs—Contrasts with Cultural Geography', *Progress in Human Geography* 26.2 (2002), pp. 252-60.

Peters, F.E., *Jerusalem and Mecca: The Typology of the Holy City in the Near East* (New York and London: New York University Press, 1986).

Pevsner, N., *Pioneers of Modern Design: From William Morris to Walter Gropius* (Harmondsworth: Penguin, rev. edn, 1960 [1936]).

Phillips, Debbie, and Peter Ratcliffe, *Asian Mobility in Leeds and Bradford,* http://www.geog.leeds.ac.uk/projects/mobility/, (accessed August 2003).

Philo, C., 'Foucault', in Crang and Thrift (eds.), *Thinking Space*, pp. 205-38.

Pickering, W.S.F., 'Locating the Sacred: Durkheim, Otto and Some Contemporary Ideas', *British Association for the Study of Religions Occasional Papers* 12 (1994), pp. 1-14.

—'A Note on the Life of Gaston Richard and Certain Aspects of his Work', in Pickering (ed.), *Durkheim on Religion*, pp. 343-59.

Pickering, W.S.F. (ed.), *Durkheim on Religion: A Selection of Readings with Bibliographies and Introductory Remarks* (London and Boston: Routledge & Kegan Paul, 1975).

Pink Dandelion, B., 'Those Who Leave and Those Who Feel Left: The Complexity of Quaker Disaffiliation', *Journal of Contemporary Religion* 17.2 (2002), pp. 213-28.

Polt, R., *Heidegger: An Introduction* (London: UCL Press, 1999).

Pyysiäinen, I., *Belief and Beyond: Religious Categorization of Reality* (Åbo: Åbo Akademi, 1996).

—'Religion and the Counter-Intuitive', in I. Pyysiäinen and V. Anttonen (eds.), *Current Approaches in the Cognitive Science of Religion* (London and New York: Continuum, 2002), pp. 110-32.

Raphael, M., *Thealogy and Embodiment: The Post-Patriarchal Reconstruction of Female Sacrality* (Sheffield: Sheffield Academic Press, 2001).

Reader, I., and T. Walters (eds.), *Pilgrimage in Popular Culture* (London: Macmillan, 1993).

Relph, E.C., *Place and Placelessness* (London: Pion, 1976).

Rich, A., *Blood, Bread, and Poetry: Selected Prose 1979–85* (London: Norton & Co., 1986).

—'Notes Towards a Politics of Location', in *idem, Blood, Bread and Poetry: Selected Prose 1979–85* (London: Virago Press, 1986), pp. 210-31.

Richard, G., 'L'Athéisme dogmatique en sociologie religieuse', *Revue d'histoire et de philosophie religieuse* (originally published 1923), translated by Jacqueline Redding and W.S.F. Pickering as 'Dogmatic Atheism in the Sociology of Religion', in Pickering (ed.), *Durkheim on Religion*, pp. 228-76.

Roberts, R.H. (ed.), *Religion and the Transformations of Capitalism: Comparative Approaches* (London: Routledge, 1995).

Robertson, R., 'Globalization, Politics, and Religion', in R. Beckford and T. Luckmann (eds.), *The Changing Face of Religion* (Beverly Hills: Sage, 1989), pp. 10-23.

—*Globalization: Social Theory and Global Culture* (London, Thousand Oaks, New Delhi: Sage, 1992).

—'Glocalization: Time-Space and Homogeneity–Heterogeneity', in M. Featherstone, S. Lash and R. Robertson (eds.), *Global Modernities* (London, Thousand Oaks, New Delhi: Sage, 1995), pp. 24-44.

Rojek, C., *Ways of Escape: Modern Transformations in Leisure and Travel* (Lanham, MD: Rowman & Littlefield, 1994).

'The Roman Breviary' of the Lay Confraternity of Ss Peter and Paul, <http://www.breviary.net/comment/comment1prim.htm> (accessed 4 April 2003).

Rose, G., *Feminism and Geography: The Limits of Geographical Knowledge* (Cambridge: Polity, 1993).

—'The Interstitial Perspective: A Review Essay on Homi Bhabha's *The Location of Culture*', *Environment and Planning D: Society and Space* 13 (1995), pp. 365-73.

Rosenberg, J., 'The Lesbian of Darkness', <http://www.winternet.com/~joelr/leftles.html> (accessed 10 January 2003).

Rushdie, S., *The Satanic Verses* (Harmondsworth: Penguin Viking, 1989).

Sack, R.D., *Place, Modernity, and the Consumer's World: A Relational Framework for Geographical Analysis* (Baltimore: The Johns Hopkins University Press, 1992).

Saler, B., *Conceptualizing Religion: Immanent Anthropologists, Transcendent Natives and Unbound Categories* (New York: Berghahn Books, 2000 [1993]).

Salomonsen, J., *Enchanted Feminism: The Reclaiming Witches of San Francisco* (London and New York: Routledge, 2002).

Sanderson, A., 'Śaivism and the Tantric Traditions', in F. Hardy (ed.), *The World's Religions: The Religions of Asia* (London: Routledge, 1990), pp. 128-72.

Satanism and Left Hand Path, <http://www.velvetdragon.com/spirit/lhp.htm> (accessed 17 January 2003).

Saxer, S., 'Sacred Spaces and Planning Law: Property Rights and the Regulation of Religious Activities in the United States', in Edge and Harvey (eds.), *Law and Religion*, pp. 115-27.

Scott, G.G., *A Plea for the Faithful Restoration of Our Ancient Churches* (London: John Henry Parker, 1850).

Sharpe, E., *Comparative Religion: A History* (London: Gerald Duckworth, 1975).

Sharpe, J., *Instruments of Darkness: Witchcraft in England 1550–1750* (London: Penguin, 1997).

Shaw, M., *Passionate Enlightenment: Women in Tantric Buddhism* (Princeton: Princeton University Press, 1994).

Shaw, R., 'Feminist Anthropology and the Gendering of Religious Studies', in U. King (ed.), *Religion and Gender* (Oxford: Basil Blackwell, 1995), pp. 65-76.

Shields, R., *Lefebvre, Love and Struggle: Spatial Dialectics* (London and New York: Routledge, 1999).

—*Places on the Margin: Alternative Geographies of Modernity* (London and New York: Routledge, 1991).

Shiner, L.E., 'Sacred Space, Profane Space, Human Space', *Journal of the American Academy of Religion* 40 (1972), pp. 425-36.

The Shorter Oxford English Dictionary of Historical Principles (London: Guild Publishing, 3rd edn, 1983).

Sibley, D., *Geographies of Exclusion: Society and Difference in the West* (London and New York: Routledge, 1995).

Sinister Wisdom: A Journal for Lesbians, <http://www.sinisterwisdom.org/> (accessed 15 September 2003).

Smalley, S., 'Islamic Nurture in the West: Approaches to Parenting amongst Second Generation Pakistanis and Khojas in Peterborough' (PhD thesis, University of Leeds, 2002).

Smart,N., *The Phenomenon of Religion* (London: Macmillan, 1973).

—*The Religious Experience of Mankind* (London: Collins, 1969).

Smith, D.M., *Geography and Social Justice* (Oxford: Basil Blackwell, 1994).

Smith, J.Z., *Map is Not Territory: Studies in the History of Religions* (Chicago and London: University of Chicago Press, 1978).

—*To Take Place: Toward a Theory of Ritual* (Chicago and London: University of Chicago Press, 1987).

—'The Wobbling Pivot' [1971], in *idem, Map is Not Territory*, pp. 88-103.

Smith, N., 'Homeless/Global: Scaling Places', in Bird, Curtis, Putnam, Robertson and Tickner (eds.) *Mapping the Futures: Local Cultures, Global Change* (London: Routledge, 1993), pp. 97-116.

Smith, N., and C. Katz, 'Grounding Metaphor: Towards a Spatialized Politics', in Keith and Pile (eds.), *Place and the Politics of Identity*, pp. 67-83.

Smith, S.G., 'Buddhism and the Postmodern: The Nature of Identity and Tradition in Contemporary Society' (PhD thesis, University of Leeds, 1997).

Smith, W.C., *The Meaning and End of Religion* (London: SPCK, 1978).

Smits, R., *The Lefthanded Universe*, <http://www.xs4all.nl/~riksmits/lhu/lhu.html> (accessed 20 October 2002).

Soja, E.W., *Thirdspace: Journeys to Los Angeles and Other Real-and-Imagined Places* (Cambridge, MA: Basil Blackwell, 1996).

Sopher, D.E., 'Geography and Religion', *Progress in Human Geography* 5 (1981), pp. 510-24.

Starhawk, *The Spiral Dance: A Rebirth of the Ancient Religion of the Great Goddess* (San Francisco: HarperSanFrancisco, tenth anniversary edn, 1989 [1979]).

Stark, R., 'Atheism, Faith, and the Social Scientific Study of Religion', *Journal of Contemporary Religion* 14.1 (1999), pp. 41-62.

Starr Sered, S., *Priestess, Mother, Sacred Sister: Religions Dominated by Women* (New York: Oxford University Press, 1994).

Stewart, L., 'Bodies, Visions, and Spatial Politics: A Review Essay on Henri Lefebvre's *The Production of Space*', *Environment and Planning D: Society and Space* 13 (1995), pp. 609-18.

Stoter, D., *Spiritual Aspects of Healthcare* (London: Mosby, 1995).

Strauss, A., and J.M. Corbin (eds.), *Grounded Theory in Practice* (London, Thousand Oaks, New Delhi: Sage, 1997).

Strenski, I., 'On "Religion" and Its Despisers', in T.A. Idinopulos and B. Wilson (eds.), *What is Religion?* (Leiden: E.J. Brill, 1998), pp. 113-32.

Sullivan, L., 'Body Works: Knowledge of the Body in the Study of Religion', *History of Religions* 30.1 (1990), pp. 86-99.

Summers, M. (ed.), *Malleus Maleficarum* [c. 1486] (London: Hogarth Press, 1969).

Sutcliffe, R., 'Left-Hand Path Ritual Magick: An Historical and Philosophical Overview', in G. Harvey and C. Hardman (eds.), *Paganism Today: Wiccans, Druids, the Goddess and Ancient Earth Traditions for the Twenty-First Century* (London: Thorsons, 1995), pp. 109-37

Swanson, M., 'Right Belief in a Left-Handed World', <http://www.Orthodox.net/articles/right-belief-in-a-left-handed-world.html> (accessed 10 January 2003).

Tammy C, 'My Brother is Left-Handed', <http://www.geocities.com/WestHollywood/stonewall/8505/sf_lefthand.html> (accessed 2 November 2003).

Taylor, C., *A Catholic Modernity?* (ed. J.L Heft; New York: Oxford University Press, 1999).

—'Modes of Secularism', in Bhargava (ed.), *Secularism and Its Critics*, pp. 31-53.

— *Sources of the Self: The Making of Modern Identity* (Cambridge: Cambridge University Press, 1989).

— *Varieties of Religion Today: William James Revisited* (Cambridge MA, and London: Harvard University Press, 2002).

Tcherkézoff, S., *Dual Classification Reconsidered: Nyamwezi Sacred Kingship and Other Examples* (Cambridge: Cambridge University Press; Paris: La Maison des Sciences de l'Homme, 1987 [French edn 1983]).

Thomas, K., *Religion and the Decline of Magic* (Harmondsworth: Penguin, 1973).

Thomas, T., '"The Sacred" as a Viable Concept in the Contemporary Study of Religions', *British Association for the Study of Religions Occasional Papers* 13 (British Association for the Study of Religions) (1994), pp. 15-37.

Tilley, C., *The Phenomenology of Landscape* (London: Berg, 1994).

Tobler, J., '"Home is Where the Heart Is?": Gendered Sacred Space in South Africa', *Journal for the Study of Religion* 13.1/2 (2000), pp. 69-98.

Towler, R., *The Need for Certainty: A Sociological Study of Conventional Religion* (London and Boston: Routledge and Kegan Paul, 1984).

Townsend, R.F., 'Geography', in Eliade (ed.), *Encyclopedia of Religion*, V, pp. 509-13.

Treggiari, S., *Roman Marriage: Iusti Coniuges from the Time of Cicero to the Time of Ulpian* (Oxford: Clarendon Press, 1991).

Tuan, Y.-F., *Space and Place: The Perspective of Experience* (Minneapolis: University of Minnesota Press, 1977).

Turner, B.S., *The Body and Society: Explorations in Social Theory* (London, Thousand Oaks, New Delhi: Sage, 2nd edn, 1996).

— *Religion and Social Theory* (London: Heinemann Educational Books, 1983).

Turner, H.W., *From Temple to Meeting House: The Phenomenology and Theology of Places of Worship* (The Hague: Mouton, 1979).

Turner, K., *Beautiful Necessity: The Art and Meaning of Women's Altars* (London: Thames & Hudson, 1999).

Turner, V., and E. Turner, *Image and Pilgrimage in Christian Culture* (Oxford: Basil Blackwell, 1978).

Unwin, T., 'A Waste of Space? Towards a Critique of the Social Production of Space', *Transactions of the Institute of British Geographers* 25.10 (2000), pp. 11-29.

Urban, H.B., 'The Cult of Ecstasy: Tantrism, the New Age, and the Spiritual Logic of Late Capitalism', *History of Religions* 39.3 (2000), pp. 268-304.

— 'The Extreme "Orient": The Construction of "Tantrism" as a Category in the Orientalist Imagination', *Religion* 29.2 (1999), pp. 123-46.

— 'The Power of the Impure: Transgression, Violence and Secrecy in Bengali śākta tantra and Modern Western Magic', *Numen* 50.3 (2003), pp. 269-308.

Valentine, G., *Social Geographies: Space and Society* (Harlow: Prentice–Hall [Pearson Education], 2001).

Valins, O., 'Stubborn Identities and the Construction of Socio-Spatial Boundaries: Ultra-Orthodox Jews Living in Contemporary Britain', *Transactions of the Institute of British Geographers* NS 28 (2003), pp. 158-75.

Vertovec, S., 'Religion and Diaspora', in P. Antes, A.W. Geertz and R. Warne (eds.), *New Approaches to the Study of Religion* (Berlin and New York: W. de Gruyter, 2004) (an electronic version of this paper is available as a Transnational Communities Programme working paper on <http://www.transcomm.ox.ac.uk/working%20papers/Vertovec01. pdf>).

Walton-Roberts, M., 'Three Readings of the Turban: Sikh Identity in Greater Vancouver', *Urban Geography* 19.4 (1998), pp. 311-31.

Waterhouse, H., *Buddhism in Bath: Authority and Adaptation* (Leeds: Community Religions Project, University of Leeds, 1997).

Waters, M., *Globalization* (London: Routledge, 1995).

Wayman, A., *The Buddhist Tantras: Light and Indo-Tibetan Esotericism* (New York: Samuel Weiser, 1973).

Webster, R., *A Brief History of Blasphemy: Liberalism, Censorship and 'The Satanic Verses'* (Southwold: Orwell Press, 1990).

Weller, P., A. Feldman and K. Purdam, *Religious Discrimination in England and Wales* (London: Home Office Research Study 220, 2001).

Werbner, P., 'The Place which is Diaspora: Citizenship, Religion and Gender in the Making of Chaordic Transnationalism', *Journal of Ethnic and Migration Studies* 28.1 (2002), pp. 119-33.

— 'Public Spaces, Political Voices: Gender, Feminism and Aspects of British Muslim Participation in the Public Sphere', in W.A.R. Shadid and P.S. van Koningsveld (eds.), *Political Participation and Identities of Muslims in Non-Muslim States* (Kampen: Kok Pharos, 1996), pp. 53-70.

—'Stamping the Earth with the Name of Allah: Zikr and the Sacralizing of Space among British Muslims', in Daly Metcalf (ed.), *Making Muslim Space*, pp. 167-85.

West, Rosemary, *Rosemary West's Left Handed World*, http://www.rosemarywest.com/left/ (accessed 7 April 2003).

Wheatley, P., *The Pivot of the Four Quarters* (Chicago: Aldine, 1971).

White, D.G., *The Alchemical Body: Siddha Traditions in Medieval India* (Chicago and London: Chicago University Press, 1996).

—'Introduction', in *idem* (ed.), *Tantra in Practice*, pp. 7-9.

White, D.G. (ed.), *Tantra in Practice* (Princeton and Oxford: Princeton University Press, 2000).

Whitehead, N.E., 'Is There a Link Between Left-Handedness and Homosexuality?', <http://www.narth.com/docs/lefthand.html> (accessed 18 October 2002).

Williams, R.B., *An Introduction to Swaminarayan Hinduism* (Cambridge: Cambridge University Press, 2001).

Wilson, B., *Contemporary Transformations in Religion* (London: Oxford University Press, 1976).

—*Religion in Sociological Perspective* (London: Oxford University Press, 1982).

—'Secularization: The Inherited Model', in Hammond (ed.), *The Sacred in a Secular Age*, pp. 9-20.

Wolffe, J., 'Evangelicals and Pentecostals: Indigenizing a Global Gospel', in *idem* (ed.), *Global Religious Movements in Regional Context* (Aldershot and Burlington, VT: Ashgate, in association with the Open University, 2002), pp. 13-108.

Yeğenoğlu, M., 'Sartorial Fabric-ations: Enlightenment and Western Feminism', in Donaldson and Kwok (eds.), *Postcolonialism, Feminism, and Religious Discourse*, pp. 82-99.

Yengoyan, A.A., 'Language and Conceptual Dualism: Sacred and Secular Concepts in Australian Aboriginal Cosmology and Myth', in Maybury-Lewis and Almagor (eds.), *The Attraction of Opposites*, pp. 171-90.

Index of Authors

Index of Subjects